Cambridge English

SECOND EDITION

Advanced TRAINER

SIX PRACTICE TESTS WITH ANSWERS

Felicity O'Dell and Michael Black

Cambridge University Press
www.cambridge.org/elt

Cambridge Assessment English
www.cambridgeenglish.org

Information on this title: www.cambridge.org/9781107470279

First published 2012
Second edition 2015

20 19

Printed in Great Britain by CPI Group (UK) Ltd, Croydon CR0 4YY

A catalogue record for this publication is available from the British Library

ISBN 978-1-107-47027-9 Six Practice Tests with answers with Audio
ISBN 978-1-107-47026-2 Six Practice Tests without answers with Audio
ISBN 978-1-107-47030-9 Audio CDs (3)

Additional resources for this publication at www.cambridge.org/advancedtrainer

Contents

Acknowledgements		4
Introduction		5
Training and Exam practice		
Test 1	Reading and Use of English	10
	Writing	42
	Listening	51
	Speaking	61
Test 2	Reading and Use of English	69
	Writing	86
	Listening	92
	Speaking	100
Practice tests		
Test 3	Reading and Use of English	108
	Writing	120
	Listening	122
	Speaking	127
Test 4	Reading and Use of English	130
	Writing	142
	Listening	144
	Speaking	149
Test 5	Reading and Use of English	152
	Writing	164
	Listening	166
	Speaking	171
Test 6	Reading and Use of English	174
	Writing	186
	Listening	188
	Speaking	193
Answer key and transcripts		196
Sample answer sheets		252
Speaking appendix	*(colour section pages S1–S21)*	

Acknowledgements

The authors would like to thank Alison Silver and Catriona Watson-Brown for their painstaking editing and helpful feedback. Thanks also go to Kay George, Sharon McCann and Lorraine Poulter and the rest of the production team at Cambridge University Press for their support and hard work.

Development of this publication has made use of the Cambridge English Corpus (CEC). The CEC is a computer database of contemporary spoken and written English, which currently stands at over one billion words. It includes British English, American English and other varieties of English. It also includes the Cambridge Learner Corpus, developed in collaboration with Cambridge English Language Assessment. Cambridge University Press has built up the CEC to provide evidence about language use that helps to produce better language teaching materials.

This product is informed by the English Vocabulary Profile, built as part of English Profile, a collaborative programme designed to enhance the learning, teaching and assessment of English worldwide. Its main funding partners are Cambridge University Press and Cambridge English Language Assessment, and its aim is to create a 'profile' for English linked to the Common European Framework of Reference for Languages (CEF). English Profile outcomes, such as the English Vocabulary Profile, will provide detailed information about the language that learners can be expected to demonstrate at each CEF level, offering a clear benchmark for learners' proficiency. For more information, please visit www.englishprofile.org.

Cambridge dictionaries are the world's most widely used dictionaries for learners of English. The *Cambridge Advanced Learner's Dictionary* is available in print and online at dictionary.cambridge.org. Copyright © Cambridge University Press, fourth edition 2013, reproduced with permission.

The authors and publishers acknowledge the following sources of copyright material and are grateful for the permissions granted. While every effort has been made, it has not always been possible to identify the sources of all the material used, or to trace all copyright holders. If any omissions are brought to our notice, we will be happy to include the appropriate acknowledgements on reprinting.

National Geographic for the text on pp. 31–32 adapted from 'Europe's Largest Glacier Comes to New York' by Rena Silverman, *National Geographic*, 29.06.13. Reproduced with permission; New Statesman for the text on pp. 33–34 adapted from 'Good Idea: Urban Jungles' by Alyssa McDonald, *New Statesman*, 16.07.10. Reproduced with permission; Tribune Content Agency for the text on pp. 36–37 adapted from 'Stuff symphony: Beautiful music makes better materials' by Markus J. Buehler, *New Scientist*, 05.02.14. Copyright © 2014 Reed Business Information – UK. All rights reserved. Distributed by Tribune Content Agency. Reproduced with permission; News Syndication for the text on p. 39 from 'Science thrillers have a rich history' by Erica Wagner, *Eureka/Times Science Magazine*, August 2010. Copyright © Eureka/NI Syndication 2010. Reproduced with permission; The Random House Group Ltd for the text on p. 41 from Everest: *Reflections from the top* by Margaret Gee, published by Rider. Reproduced with permission of The Random House Group Limited; The Jean V. Naggar Literary Agency, Inc. for the listening exercise on pp. 57–58 and the audio recording and audio script on p. 208, adapted from an interview with Torre DeRoche by permission of Torre DeRoche in care of the Jean V. Naggar Literary Agency, Inc. (permissions@jvnla.com) Copyright © 2013 by Torre DeRoche; The Telegraph for the text on p. 70 adapted from 'Wearable book allows reader to feel emotions of characters' by Lucy Kinder, *The Telegraph*, 28.01.14. Copyright © Telegraph Media Group Limited 2014. Reproduced with permission; The Telegraph for the text on p. 72 adapted from 'SME Masterclass: How to take on an intern' by Rachel Bridge, *The Telegraph*, 08.01.14. Copyright © Telegraph Media Group Limited 2014. Reproduced with permission; New Statesman for the text on pp. 77–78 from Ray Mears: 'What I believe defines us as human is our mastery of fire' by Ray Mears, *New Statesman*, 20.03.14. Reproduced with permission; Janine Utell for text C on p. 81 from 'Talking about the Humanities: Value v. Meaning' by Janine Utell, www.insidehighered.com, 08.12.13. Reproduced with permission; National Geographic for the text on pp. 82–83 adapted from 'Yukon: Gold Fever' by Tom Clynes, *National Geographic*, February 2014. Reproduced with permission; Healthy magazine for the text on p. 85 adapted from 'The Healthy 2014 fitness challenge: I want to become a runner' by Charlotte Haigh MacNeil, *Healthy*, March 2014. Reproduced with permission; Peter Lawrey for the listening exercise on p. 97 and the audio recording and audio script on p. 222 adapted from 'Interview: Starting out as an IT Consultant' from http://vanillajava.blogspot.co.uk/2014/01/interview-starting-out-as-it-consultant.html. Reproduced with permission; Guardian News and Media Ltd for the text on p. 114 adapted from 'Why painting still matters' by Nicholas Wroe and Simon Grant, *The Guardian*, 08.11.13. Copyright Guardian News & Media Ltd 2013. Reproduced with permission; Management Today for the text on pp. 116–117 adapted from 'The way we work now' by Jeremy Hazlehurst, *Management Today*, June 2013. Reproduced with permission; Royal Holloway for the text on p. 130 adapted from 'Royal Holloway awarded £1.3m for television technology research' by the Royal Holloway, University of London, Press Office, *Higher*, Issue 19, Winter 2013. Reproduced with permission; Guardian News and Media Ltd for the text on p. 131 adapted from 'Prehistory: not just Denis', *The Guardian*, 05.12.13. Copyright Guardian News & Media Ltd 2013. Reproduced with permission; ict4dc (Information and Communication Technologies for Development) for the text on p. 132 from 'About us' www.ict4dc.org. Reproduced with permission; Cambridge University Press and David Crystal for the text on pp. 134–135 from *The Cambridge Encyclopedia of Language* by David Crystal, published by Cambridge University Press 1987, 3rd Edition 2010. Reproduced with permission; Geographical for the text on pp. 138–139 adapted from 'Ice-cold exploration' by Robbie Shone, *Geographical*, December 2013. Reproduced with permission; Rita Carter for the text on pp. 156–157 adapted from 'I've been here before ...', http://www.ritacarter.co.uk/articles.html. Rita Carter's *Mapping the Mind* is published by Orion (9780753827956, 2010) and *The Brain Book* is published by Dorling Kindersley (9781405341295, 2009). Reproduced with permission; Guardian News and Media Ltd for the text on pp. 160–161 adapted from 'The Forgotten Story of ... Russell Mockridge' by Greg Langley, Guardian.com, 13.11.13. Copyright Guardian News & Media Ltd 2013. Reproduced with permission; The Independent for the text on p. 174 adapted from 'Racing pulse, glowing cheeks and a heavy heart: "Body atlas" heatmaps reveal where we feel different emotions' by Adam Withnall, *The Independent*, www.independent.co.uk, 31.12.13. Reproduced with permission; Sir Alistair MacFarlane for the text on pp. 182–183 adapted from 'Ada Lovelace (1815–1852)' by Alistair MacFarlane, https://philosophynow.org Copyright © Sir Alistair MacFarlane 2013. Reproduced with permission; Text on p. 185 adapted from 'Good employees make a good business', Keys to Operating a Successful Business, http://www.hdkeys.com/The_Importance_of_Good_Customer_Service. Copyright © Keys to Operating a Successful Business.

Photo acknowledgements
The authors and publishers acknowledge the following sources of copyright material and are grateful for the permissions granted. While every effort has been made, it has not always been possible to identify the sources of all the material used, or to trace all copyright holders. If any omissions are brought to our notice, we will be happy to include the appropriate acknowledgements on reprinting.

Key: T = top, B = bottom, TR = top right, TL = top left, C = centre
S1 (T): Getty Images/Stockbyte/© Stephen Simpson; S1 (B): Alamy/© IMAGEMORE Co., Ltd; S2 (T): Alamy/© Thomas Imo; S2 (B): Corbis/© Troy House; S3 (TL): Alamy/© David Grossman; S3 (TR): Alamy/© Andres Rodriguez; S3 (B): Corbis/© Wavebreak Media Ltd; S4 (TL): Thinkstock/iStock/© Nathan Allred; S4 (TR): Corbis/© Eric Cahan; S4 (B): Alamy/© Pat Tuson; S6 (TL): SuperStock/© Blend Images; S6 (TR): Getty Images/Iconica/© Barry Austin Photography; S6 (B): Getty Images/AFP/© Antonin Thuillier; S7 (TL): Alamy/© David J. Green – lifestyle 2; S7 (TR): Getty Images/Photodisc/© Alexa Miller; S7 (B): Shutterstock/© Syda Productions; S8 (TL): Rex Features/© Nils Jorgensen; S8 (TR): Corbis/© jf/cultura; S8 (B): Alamy/© Caro; S10 (TL): Corbis/Blend Images/© John Lund; S10 (TR): Thinkstock/iStock/© LuckyBusiness; S10 (B): Shutterstock/LuckyImages; S11 (TL): Alamy/© Anthony Thorogood; S11 (TR): Getty Images/Stockbyte/© Martin Siepmann; S11 (B): Corbis/© Monty Rakusen; S13 (TL): Alamy/© Patrick Ward; S13 (TR): Getty Images/The Image Bank/© Dirk Anschutz; S13 (B): Corbis/Reuters/© China Photos; S14 (TL): Alamy/© Rami Aapasuo; S14 (TR): Alamy/© Jochen Tack; S14 (B): Alamy/© Janine Wiedel Photolibrary; S16 (TL): Getty Images/© DAJ; S16 (TR): Alamy/© blickwinkel; S16 (B): Shutterstock/auremar; S17 (T): Alamy/© David Bagnall; S17 (BL): Alamy/© Chris Cooper-Smith; S17 (BR): Getty Images/© Chung Sung-Jun; S19 (T): Alamy/© MIXA; S19 (C): Alamy/© Paul Doyle; S19 (B): Getty Images/FB Archive/© Peter Bischoff; S20 (TL): Shutterstock/© Monkey Business Images; S20 (TR): Alamy/© PBPA Paul Beard Photo Agency; S20 (B): Alamy/© Caro.

Illustrations: David Benham (Graham-Cameron Illustration)

Picture research: Louise Edgeworth
Text permissions: Rebecca Pratt-Smith
Designed and typeset by Wild Apple Design
Audio produced by Leon Chambers and recorded at dSound, London

Introduction

Who is *Advanced Trainer* for?

This book is suitable for anyone who is preparing to take *Cambridge English: Advanced*, also known as *Certificate in Advanced English (CAE)*. You can use *Advanced Trainer* in class with your teacher or – if you have the 'with answers' edition of the book – on your own at home.

What is *Advanced Trainer*?

Advanced Trainer contains six practice tests for *Cambridge English: Advanced*, each covering the Reading and Use of English, Writing, Listening and Speaking papers. The first two tests are 'guided tests', which means that they contain extra training and support to help you with each of the tasks in the exam. Tests 3 to 6 are purely practice tests. All six tests are at *Cambridge English: Advanced* level and match the exam in format and standard.

In Test 1, each part of each paper consists of a Training section and an Exam practice section. The Training sections give information about each part of the exam and have advice and practice to help you prepare for it. They focus on grammar, vocabulary and functional language directly relevant to particular task types. This is supported by work based on correcting common grammar and vocabulary mistakes made in the exam by *Cambridge English: Advanced* candidates, as shown by the Cambridge Learner Corpus. (For more information on the **Cambridge Learner Corpus**, see page 7.) The Exam practice sections consist of the test itself accompanied by an Action plan, giving step-by-step guidance for each task, with tips on general strategy and advice linked to the specific questions. A Follow-up task at the end of the Exam practice section invites you to reflect on the task and consider how you could improve your performance.

Test 2 also consists of a Training section and an Exam practice section for each part of the exam. The Training sections are shorter than those in Test 1. They review the information provided in Test 1 and also include further practice for that part of the test. The Exam practice sections provide additional tips and advice.

Tests 3 to 6 are complete practice tests without advice or training. They give you the opportunity to practise the advice and skills you have acquired while working through Tests 1 and 2.

There is an Explanatory answer key (see below) for each test.

Features of *Advanced Trainer*

- Full-colour **visual material** for the Speaking paper of all six tests.
- **Explanatory answer keys** in the 'with answers' edition of the book, not only giving information about which answers are right, but also, where appropriate, explaining *why* certain answers are correct and other options are not.
- **Notes on all writing tasks** to explain what is required, with, in addition, **model answers** for each task type in the 'with answers' edition.
- In the 'with answers' edition, a **Listening transcript** with underlining to indicate the sections that provide the answers to the exam questions.
- **Photocopiable answer sheets** for the Reading and Use of English and Listening papers. Before you take the exam, you should study these so that you know how to mark or write your answer correctly. In Writing, the question paper has plenty of lined paper for you to write your answers.
- **Downloadable audio** (also available separately as three CDs) consists of the recordings for the six Listening tests plus some Listening and Speaking practice materials relating to Tests 1 and 2. The audio can be downloaded from www.cambridge.org/advancedtrainer.

How to use *Advanced Trainer*

Test 1 Training

- For each part of each paper, you should begin by studying the **Task information**, which tells you the facts you need to know, such as what the task type tests and the kinds of question it uses.
- Throughout Test 1, you will see information marked **Tip!** These tips give you practical advice on how to tackle each task type.
- In all papers, training exercises help you develop the skills you need, e.g. working out meaning from context, by working through example items.
- Answers to all the training exercises are in the **Explanatory answer key** in the 'with answers' edition.

- Throughout Test 1, there are **Useful language** sections, which present and practise grammatical structures, vocabulary or functional expressions that are often tested by particular task types.
- Many exercises involve focusing on and correcting common language mistakes made by actual *Cambridge English: Advanced* candidates, as shown by the **Cambridge Learner Corpus** (see page 7).
- In **Listening**, you are prompted to use the downloadable audio or one of the numbered CDs: 1 02 If you are using the downloadable mp3 files, please note that the track numbers are the same as on the CDs. If you are using the CDs, you will need a CD player (or a computer that plays CDs). In both cases, you will also need a watch or clock to make sure that you keep to the time allowed for each part of the test.
- In **Writing**, the **Explanatory answer key** contains model answers for the tasks. Although there are many different ways of answering each question, it is worth studying these and thinking about the structure and language of each of the answers provided.
- In **Speaking**, you are sometimes prompted to use the audio recordings and do tasks as you listen. You can practise speaking on your own or with a partner, using what you have learnt in **Useful language** and in **Tips!**.

Test 1 Exam practice

- Look first at the **Action plan**, which gives you clear step-by-step guidance on how to approach each task type.
- Read any further **Tips!** for that part of the exam.
- Work through an exam-style task, following the **Action plan** and making use of the **Advice** boxes, which suggest ways of dealing with specific items.
- Answers to all items are in the **Explanatory answer key**, which explains why the correct answers are right and others are wrong. For **Listening**, the parts of the **Transcripts** which give the correct answers are underlined.
- After doing the exam task, look at the **Follow-up** task and consider how you can do better in this part of the exam in future.

Test 2 Training

- Answer the questions in the **Review** section, as these will remind you about this part of the exam. If you need to, use the cross-reference to Test 1 to check your answers.
- Look at the **Tips!** and work through the exercises which focus on other useful exam techniques and language to help with this part of the exam.
- There is further work based on mistakes frequently made by *Cambridge English: Advanced* candidates, as shown by the **Cambridge Learner Corpus**.
- There is also an emphasis on revision, with cross-references for each task type to the relevant **Task information** and **Action plan** in Test 1. You can refer back to these before you begin working through each section.

Test 2 Exam practice

- Think about the **Action plan** for this part of the exam. Use the cross-reference if you need to.
- Use any **Tips!** on strategy and **Advice** relating to specific questions to help you work through the exam task.
- Do the task under exam conditions if possible, i.e. not using a dictionary and spending an appropriate amount of time on the task.
- Check your answers in the **Explanatory answer key**.

Tests 3–6 Exam practice

- In Tests 3, 4, 5 and 6, you should apply the skills, techniques and language you have learnt in Tests 1 and 2.
- You can do these tests and the four papers within them in any order, but you should always try to keep to the time recommended for each paper. For the Listening paper, you must listen to each recording **twice only**.
- It will be easier to keep to the exam instructions if you can find somewhere quiet to work, and ensure there are no interruptions.
- For the Speaking paper, it is better if you can work with a partner, but, if not, you can follow the instructions, and do all four parts on your own.
- If you have the 'with answers' edition of the book, you can check the answers and explanations for them, and also study the Listening transcripts, after you have completed the tasks.

Audio

In the *Cambridge English: Advanced* Listening Test, the recordings are always played a second time in all four parts. However, the *Advanced Trainer* recordings are repeated for only Part 1 of the Listening Test. For Parts 2, 3 and 4 listen to the recording twice. You will need to replay the track after a first listen.

The Cambridge Learner Corpus (CLC)

The CLC is a large collection of over 200,000 exam scripts written by candidates taking Cambridge ESOL exams around the world. It is growing all the time. It forms part of the Cambridge International Corpus (CIC) and it has been built up by Cambridge University Press and Cambridge English Language Assessment. The CLC currently contains scripts from over:

- 150 different first languages
- 200 different countries.

Exercises in *Advanced Trainer* which are based on the CLC are indicated by this icon: Find out more about the Cambridge Learner Corpus at www.cambridge.org/corpus.

Level of *Cambridge English: Advanced*

- *Cambridge English: Advanced* is at level C1 on the Common European Framework of Reference for Languages (CEFR). Achieving this level means that your English is good enough for you to study or work in most situations where English is the main language used.
- A pass mark at *Cambridge English: Advanced* is given a grade: A, B or C.
- Achieving a grade A means that your English is considered to be at level C2 on the CEFR.
- If you do not get enough marks for a grade C in the examination, you may get a certificate stating that your English is at level B2, provided you have demonstrated that is the case.

Grading

- The overall Cambridge English Scale score that you receive for the exam is the average of the separate scale scores you receive for each of the four skills and Use of English.
- The overall score determines your grade and CEFR level.
- There is no minimum score for each paper, so you don't have to pass all four papers to pass the exam.
- Candidates whose performance is below Level C1, but falls within Level B2 receive a Cambridge English certificate stating that they have demonstrated ability at Level B2.
- Whatever your grade, you will receive a Statement of Results. This includes your overall scale score, your scale score in each of the four skills and Use of English, your CEFR level and your grade. Any Cambridge English Scale scores below 142 are not reported for Advanced.
- For more information on grading and results, go to the Cambridge English Language Assessment website (see Further information on page 9).

Content of *Cambridge English: Advanced*

Cambridge English: Advanced has four papers, each with several parts in it. For details of each part, see the page reference under the *Task information* heading in the tables on the following pages.

Reading and Use of English 1 hour 30 minutes

There are eight parts to this paper and they are always in the same order. Parts 1–4 contain texts with accompanying grammar and vocabulary tasks. Parts 5–8 contain a range of texts and accompanying reading-comprehension tasks. The texts used are from newspapers, magazines, journals, books, leaflets, brochures, etc.

Part	Task type	No. of questions	Format	Task information
1	Multiple-choice cloze	8	A text with eight gaps, each with four options. This mainly tests vocabulary: idioms, collocations, fixed phrases, etc.	page 10
2	Open cloze	8	A text with eight gaps which must be filled with one word each.	page 14
3	Word formation	8	A text with eight gaps. Each gap corresponds to a word. The stems of the missing words are given and must be changed to form the missing word.	page 17
4	Key word transformation	6	Six questions, each with a gapped sentence which must be completed in three to six words, including a given key word.	page 21
5	Multiple choice	6	A reading text followed by multiple-choice questions.	page 24
6	Cross-text multiple matching	4	Four short texts, followed by multiple-matching questions. You must read across texts to match a prompt to elements in the texts.	page 29
7	Gapped text	6	A text with missing paragraphs. You must use the missing extracts to complete the text.	page 33
8	Multiple matching	10	A text (or several short texts) with multiple-matching questions.	page 38

Writing 1 hour 30 minutes

You have to do Part 1 (Question 1) plus any **one** of the Part 2 tasks. In Part 2, you can choose one of questions 2 to 4. The possible marks for Part 1 and Part 2 are the same. In all tasks, you are told what kind of text you must write, who you are writing to, and why you are writing.

Part	Task type	No. of words	Format	Task information
1	essay	220–260	You have to write an essay based on two points in given information. You need to decide which of the two points is more important, and to explain why.	page 42
2	report review letter/email proposal	220–260	You are given a choice of tasks which specify the type of text you have to write, your purpose for writing, and the person or people you have to write for.	page 46

Listening approximately 40 minutes

You will both hear and see the instructions for each task, and you will hear each of the four parts twice. You will hear pauses announced and you can use this time to read the questions. There is one mark for each question in this paper. At the end of the test, you will have five minutes to copy your answers onto the answer sheet.

If one person is speaking, you may hear announcements, radio broadcasts, speeches, talks, lectures or anecdotes, for example. If there are two speakers, you might hear a radio interview, discussion or conversation, for example.

Part	Task type	No. of questions	Format	Task information
1	Multiple choice	6	You hear three short extracts and have to answer two multiple-choice questions on each. Each question has three options: A, B and C.	page 51
2	Sentence completion	8	You hear a recording and have to write a word or short phrase to complete sentences.	page 54
3	Multiple choice	6	You hear a recording and have to answer multiple-choice questions, each with four options: A, B, C and D.	page 56
4	Multiple matching	10	You hear five short extracts. There are two matching tasks focusing on the gist and the main points of what is said, the attitude of the speakers and the context in which they are speaking, etc.	page 59

Speaking 15 minutes

You will probably do the Speaking test with one other candidate, although sometimes it is necessary to form groups of three. There will be two examiners, but one of them does not take part in the conversation. The examiner will indicate who you should talk to in each part of the test.

Part	Task type	Format	Task information
1	Three-way conversation between two students and one of the examiners	The examiner asks you both some questions about yourself and your interests and experiences.	page 61
2	Individual 'long turn' with brief response from partner	You are each given some visual and written prompts; the examiner will ask you to talk about these for about a minute. You are asked to give a short response after your partner has finished their 'long turn'.	page 63
3	Collaborative task	You are given some spoken instructions and written stimuli for a discussion or decision-making task and you discuss these prompts with your partner.	page 65
4	Three-way interaction between students and one of the examiners	The examiner asks you and your partner questions relating to topics arising from Part 3.	page 67

Further information

The information about *Cambridge English: Advanced* contained in *Advanced Trainer* is designed to be an overview of the exam. For a full description, including information about task types, testing focus and preparation for the exam, please use the *Cambridge English: Advanced* Handbook, which can be obtained from Cambridge English Language Assessment at the address below or from the website at www.cambridgeenglish.org.

Cambridge English Language Assessment
1 Hills Road
Cambridge
CB1 2EU
United Kingdom

Test 1 Training Reading and Use of English (1 hour 30 minutes) Part 1

Task information

- In this task, there is a text with eight gaps (plus one example).
- For each gap, there is a choice of four words or phrases: A, B, C and D. You have to choose the correct one to fill the gap.
- You need to read the text carefully and think about its meaning in order to fill the gaps correctly.
- The gaps focus on vocabulary items rather than grammar words.
- To fill some of the gaps correctly, you will need to know how words often combine in collocations and set phrases.

Useful language: putting words in context

Explain why the underlined words do not fit in these sentences. Then suggest a word which could replace it without making any other changes to the sentence.

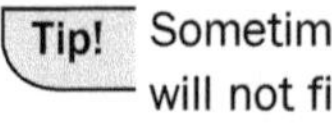
Tip! Sometimes a word will not fit because of something in the grammar around it.

1 Jackie has got a good work as PA to a successful novelist.
2 You can count George to be willing to help you out if you encounter any problems.
3 Don't worry to ask if you need any help with your project.
4 The hotel receptionist will explain you how to get to the conference centre.
5 The train travel from Moscow to Beijing takes several days.
6 A police is questioning the person who they suspect of stealing my bike.

Useful language: identifying collocations

1 **Three of the words in each set collocate with the given verb. One does not. Which are the three correct collocations?**

Tip! Sometimes choosing the right word is a matter of identifying the right collocation.

1 give permission / someone a favour / a presentation / someone a hand
2 lay claim to / the blame on / the table / an excuse
3 make a mistake / plans / a noise / your best
4 pay attention / a ticket / tribute to / a compliment
5 run an exercise / a business / a race / a campaign
6 shoot a film / past someone / an arrow / a camera
7 stand a possibility / a chance / trial / for parliament
8 take care / measurements / a promise / the train

2 **Now choose one of the collocations from Exercise 1 to complete each sentence.**

1 It isn't fair that they .... you for other people's mistakes.
2 It says in the papers that four men are to .... next month for that robbery at our local bank.
3 Paul crept in at about 2 am trying his best not to .... and wake his parents.
4 I've got to .... about my research at a seminar next week.
5 The engineer .... very careful .... before he cut the metal panel.
6 We've chosen a new advertising agency to .... for our latest range of products.
7 The Minister made a speech to .... the soldiers who had fought for their country.
8 I was winning the race until the very end when Jo .... me.

3 Choose the correct option to complete each sentence. In each case, the answer will depend on a collocation.

1 The sales team .... a very successful time at the exhibition.
A spent **B** passed **C** had **D** made

2 When she was transferred to the New York office, Sarah joined an evening class in order to .... friends.
A have **B** find **C** meet **D** make

3 The proud father was very excited when his son .... his first steps.
A made **B** took **C** gave **D** did

4 The lecturer .... the class's attention to an error in the calculations.
A drew **B** attracted **C** put **D** showed

5 My parents contributed a .... amount of money to the fund.
A big **B** large **C** grand **D** high

6 There was a time when the .... person could not afford a mobile phone.
A usual **B** normal **C** regular **D** ordinary

7 The CEO will .... a meeting with her management team this morning.
A visit **B** join **C** attend **D** follow

8 All the students on the course are required to .... sport every afternoon.
A go **B** do **C** train **D** practise

Thinking about meaning

Choose the correct option to complete each gap.

Tip! To find the correct option, you need to think carefully about the meaning of all the different options.

1 The graduation ball promises to be the social .... of the year.
A event **B** activity **C** programme **D** festival

2 People often find it difficult when someone in their own family tries to .... them how to drive.
A learn **B** practise **C** teach **D** qualify

3 Computer programming is certainly not my .... of expertise.
A part **B** section **C** system **D** area

4 The college offers a .... range of evening courses.
A wide **B** distinct **C** changeable **D** various

5 At the moment, the country has a number of .... economic problems.
A tricky **B** serious **C** difficult **D** hard

6 The students would find the flat more .... if it were closer to the university.
A reasonable **B** adequate **C** convenient **D** helpful

Test 1 Exam practice Reading and Use of English Part 1

Action plan

1 Read the title and, if there is one, look at the picture – these tell you the topic of the text.
2 Read the whole text before you start answering the questions.
3 When you answer each question, look at both what comes before and what comes after the gap.
4 Think of a word you might expect to fill the gap before looking at the options.
5 Consider each of the options, eliminating those you know are incorrect.
6 Check that the word you choose for each gap makes sense.
7 Check that the answer you choose fits the sentence grammatically.
8 When you have finished, read through the whole text to make sure it makes sense.

Follow the exam instructions, using the advice to help you.

For questions **1–8**, read the text below and decide which answer (**A, B, C** or **D**) best fits each gap. There is an example at the beginning (**0**).

Mark your answers **on the separate answer sheet.**

Example:

0 **A** chief **B** vital **C** principal **D** focal

0	A	B	C	D
	▭	▬	▭	▭

Three theories about sleep

People spend about one-third of their lives asleep. It seems certain, therefore, that sleep has a **(0)** .... function. However, what that function might be is still in **(1)** .... Scientists are far from being in agreement about **(2)** .... why so much of our precious time is given over to sleep.

There seem to be three main theories. The most popular states that the functions and **(3)** .... of sleep are primarily physiological. It claims that we sleep in order to **(4)** .... the health of our body. In other words, biological processes work hard as we sleep to repair any damage done during the day and to restore ourselves to **(5)** .... efficiency. However, a second theory places more emphasis on the learning benefits of sleep. This theory holds that sleep allows us to process the information that we **(6)** .... during the day, and asserts that, without sleep, learning would not take place. A third popular theory is **(7)** .... on ideas about energy, saying that we need **(8)** .... of sleep in order to, in a sense, recharge our batteries and so have an adequate supply of energy for the coming day.

1	**A** discussion	**B** dispute	**C** argument	**D** debate
2	**A** correctly	**B** absolutely	**C** actually	**D** precisely
3	**A** purposes	**B** targets	**C** intentions	**D** points
4	**A** take	**B** maintain	**C** stay	**D** keep
5	**A** strong	**B** utter	**C** full	**D** entire
6	**A** achieve	**B** complete	**C** reach	**D** acquire
7	**A** rooted	**B** supported	**C** based	**D** developed
8	**A** periods	**B** eras	**C** moments	**D** episodes

Advice

1 *Only one of these collocates with 'is still in …' and fits in terms of meaning.*

2 *One of these adverbs collocates strongly with 'why'.*

3 *Only one of these words is appropriate when discussing a physical function of the body rather than conscious behaviour.*

4 *You need to think about both meaning and collocation here to get the correct answer.*

5 *Only one of the options collocates with 'efficiency' to give the idea of 'total'.*

6 *Only one of these verbs collocates with 'information'.*

7 *Only one of these words fits with the preposition 'on'.*

8 *All these words fit the grammar of the sentence and collocate reasonably well, so think about the meaning here.*

Follow-up

What procedure did you follow when you did this task?

Test 1 Training Reading and Use of English Part 2

Task information

- In this task, there is a text with eight gaps (plus one example).
- You have to suggest an appropriate word to fill each gap.
- You need to read the text carefully and think about its meaning in order to fill the gaps correctly.
- The missing words are grammar words rather than vocabulary items.
- The answer will always be a single word. Remember that contractions (*I'll*, *don't*, etc.) count as two words.
- Sometimes there may be more than one possible answer and, if this is the case, the mark scheme allows for it.
- You must spell each word correctly – US and UK spellings are both accepted.

Tip! The words that you will need to write in Part 2 are usually one of these types: prepositions; connectors; auxiliary, modal or other basic verbs; determiners or articles; pronouns, basic adverbs such as *too*, *enough*, *more* or *not*.

Useful language: using prepositions

1 **Correct the errors made by exam candidates with prepositions.**

1 A number of customers complained for the after-sales service.
2 All the work will be done from volunteers.
3 Delegates experienced a number of problems related at the broadband connection at the conference centre.
4 Alexandra was able to make good use of her knowledge in foreign languages.
5 Many people took part to the anniversary festivities.
6 I must congratulate you for your excellent work.
7 I hope my letter will be taken in consideration.
8 The inspector drew the management's attention in some problems in the workshop.
9 There is an urgent need of fresh water supplies in the region.
10 Have you seen the new advertisement of Lotus shampoo?

2 **Sometimes the preposition that is missing is part of a phrasal verb. Find the correct preposition to fill the gap in these sentences.**

1 The company always takes .... new staff for the summer period.
2 Negotiations broke .... because of a disagreement about trading arrangements.
3 The lecturer talks so fast – I just can't keep .... with her train of thought.
4 It was so noisy in the room that I couldn't make .... what Jill was saying.
5 The new management team plans to bring .... a number of changes in the company.
6 No one expected that the new fashion would catch .... as quickly as it has.
7 The robbers made .... with a large amount of money.
8 Wanda asked the bank for a loan in order to set .... a consultancy business.
9 However hard things may seem, it is important not to give .... and stop trying.
10 Mark thinks there are problems in the contract and he is dead set .... our signing it.
11 The noise in the library immediately put me .... the idea of studying there.
12 Many people don't have much money, just enough to get ....

Tip! Whenever you note down a phrasal verb in your vocabulary notebook, write it down in its full context, as this will help you remember what it means and how it is used.

Useful language: using connectors

1 Choose a word from the box to complete each sentence in a logical way.

Tip! Thinking about the meaning of the surrounding text will help you to choose the right connector.

although	because	provided	unless
until	whatever	whenever	whereas

1 Nina is good at maths, ... her twin brother is better at languages.
2 Dan will go to university next year .... he passes all his exams.
3 I'll do .... you want me to do.
4 You'll never be able to afford a car like that – .... you win the lottery.
5 Sally enjoys her work, ... she doesn't get very much free time.
6 It was not .... I got on the train that I realised I'd left my laptop at home.
7 I'm really lucky – I can take a coffee break .... I want one.
8 I like my desk .... I have a very good view of the sea while I'm working.

2 Some connectors are made up of more than one word. Choose the correct phrase from the box to complete each sentence.

as if	as long as	as soon as	despite the fact that	even though
in accordance with	in case	in order to	no sooner	so as not to

1 You must fill in the form .... the instructions on the opposite page.
2 Ursula has taken on extra work .... earn enough money for a holiday.
3 My father said I could go to the party .... I'm home by midnight.
4 I managed to complete the essay on time .... I was suffering from a heavy cold.
5 We closed the door very quietly .... wake the baby.
6 You'd better take a notebook with you .... you want to write something down.
7 Simon looks .... he didn't sleep a wink last night.
8 Please call me .... you get this message.
9 I feel I know him quite well .... we've only met a few times.
10 .... had we left the house than the rain started.

Useful language: using pronouns

Fill each gap with the necessary pronoun.

Tip! Make a note of any grammar errors that your teacher corrects in your homework and do some extra practice using this language correctly.

1 I met a footballer from our national team, ... I found very exciting as I'd never met anyone famous before.
2 Final-year students told the freshers about everything .... would help them settle into life at the college.
3 .... the psychologist focuses on in his book is the way people from different countries behave in trains.
4 Do you know .... mobile phone this is?
5 .... being an unexpectedly pleasant day, the students decided to read their books outdoors.
6 The professor was satisfied with the way in .... the students had decided to deal with their project.
7 That's the car .... owner I was just telling you about.
8 .... was suggested that the problem could be tackled in a number of different ways.

Test 1 Exam practice Reading and Use of English Part 2

Action plan

1. Read the title and, if there is one, look at the picture – these tell you the topic of the text.
2. Read through the text and think about what it means before answering the questions.
3. Look at the words before and after each gap.
4. Think about what part of speech is needed (e.g. a preposition or pronoun) to complete the gap.
5. Do the questions you can answer easily first.
6. Write your answers in capital letters. The answer will always be a single word. Remember that contractions (*I'll*, *don't*, etc.) count as two words.
7. Go back to the more difficult gaps at the end.
8. Always write something, even if you are not totally sure that it is the correct answer.
9. Check you have spelt all the words correctly. Remember that US and UK spellings are both accepted.
10. Read through the whole text to check it makes sense before transferring your answers to the answer sheet.

Follow the exam instructions, using the advice to help you.

Tip! Even if you are sure two answers are possible, only write one of them.

For questions **9–16**, read the text below and think of the word which best fits each gap. Use only **one** word in each gap. There is an example at the beginning (**0**).

Write your answers **IN CAPITAL LETTERS on the separate answer sheet**.

Example: | 0 | B Y |

Hedgehogs

A hedgehog is a small mammal characterised **(0)** .... the sharp spines which cover its body. **(9)** .... hedgehogs are found in many different parts of the world, none is native to either America or Australia.

All species of hedgehog share the ability **(10)** .... roll into a tight ball when attacked, **(11)** .... that their spines point outwards. The effectiveness of this as a defence mechanism, depends, of course, **(12)** .... the number of spines the hedgehog has. Some desert hedgehogs have evolved to carry **(13)** .... weight, and consequently, they have fewer spines and are thus more likely to attempt to run into their attacker, using their ball rolling ability **(14)** .... a last resort.

Hedgehogs are primarily nocturnal and sleep for much of the day, either under cover of bushes **(15)** .... in a hole in the ground. Despite the **(16)** .... that all hedgehogs can hibernate, not all choose to do so; in suitable conditions, some will stay awake all year round.

Advice

9 Read the whole sentence before deciding what is needed to fill this gap.

10 Which word is most likely to follow 'have the ability ...'?

11 The word you need combines with 'that' to explain the purpose for an action.

12 If you ignore the phrase in parenthesis ('of course'), you may find it easier to fill this gap.

13 This gap could be filled with either 'less' or 'more', but which matches the meaning in this context?

14 This is part of a fixed expression.

15 The word you need here often follows on from a phrase beginning with 'either'.

16 The word you need is part of a fixed phrase.

Follow-up

Did you remember to read through the text at the end to make sure it all made sense?

Reading and Use of English Part 3

Task information

- In this task, there is a text with eight gaps (plus one example).
- At the end of each line with a gap, you will see a word in capital letters, e.g. *USE*.
- You have to form a new word based on the word in capitals to fill the gap. So from *USE*, you might form *useful*, *usefully*, *usefulness*, *useless*, *user*, *usage*, etc.
- You need to decide what kind of word goes in the gap – an adjective (e.g. *strong*), a verb (e.g. *strengthen*), a noun (e.g. *strength*) or an adverb (e.g. *strongly*).
- You must spell each word correctly to get the mark – US and UK spellings are both accepted.
- You need to know how prefixes and suffixes are used in forming words – you might add the prefix *im-* to *PERFECT* to make *imperfect*, for example, or the suffix *-ion*, to make *perfection*, or even both, to make *imperfection*.
- You need to know about compound words in English – *kind-hearted*, *cold-hearted* and *hard-hearted*, for example, are compound adjectives (formed by combining two words).
- You also need to think about the meaning of the text – if the gap needs an adjective, should it be positive (e.g. *comfortable*, *useful*) or negative (e.g. *uncomfortable*, *useless*), for example?

Useful language: identifying parts of speech

1 **What part of speech is needed to complete each gap – an adjective, an adverb, a verb or a noun? How do you know? Suggest a word that could fill each gap.**

Camco is one of the most **(1)** .... companies in the country. A few years ago, it hit the **(2)** .... because of its controversial research programme. Since then, scarcely a month has gone by when it has not **(3)** .... in the news for some **(4)** .... or another. But if you visit company headquarters, there is every likelihood that you will be **(5)** .... impressed by what you see.

2 **Complete this table. The first row has been completed as an example.**

noun	verb	adjective	adverb
comparison	compare	comparative (in)comparable	comparatively (in)comparably
(in)stability stabiliser			
		high	
power			
	observe		
	develop		
doubt doubter			

Tip! When you learn a new word, use a good dictionary to find out what other words are in the same word family (e.g. *broad*, *broaden*, *breadth*, *broadly*, *broadminded*, etc. = a word family).

Tip! Learning about prefixes and suffixes will also sometimes help you work out the meanings of words you do not know, which can be useful for the Reading and Use of English and Listening papers.

Useful language: understanding suffixes

1 **Here are just a few of the suffixes used in English. Complete the table with some examples.**

suffix	effect	meaning	examples
-er, -or	makes a noun from a verb	• person who does something • object that does something	computer, hairdryer, fighter, commuter sailor, infiltrator, processor, compressor
-dom	makes a noun from another noun or an adjective	• state or condition • realm or territory	
-ee	makes a person noun from a verb	person affected by the verb	
-en	makes a verb from an adjective	cause to have a quality	
-hood	makes an abstract noun from a person noun	the state of being a particular type of person	
-less	makes an adjective from a noun	being without something	
-ment	makes a noun from a verb	process or result of making or doing something	
-proof	combines with a noun to form an adjective	cannot be harmed by	

2 **Make new words from the words in CAPITALS at the end of each line to complete the sentences. The words all use a suffix from Exercise 1.**

1 The writer spent his .... in a quiet seaside village. **BOY**

2 We were so busy at work that there was no time to suffer from .... **BORE**

3 Can you lend me your penknife? I just need to .... my pencil. **SHARP**

4 We had four good applicants for the job, so it was hard to decide who would make the best .... **APPOINT**

5 It was very .... of you not to give Sue a call on her birthday. **THINK**

6 The presidential car will, of course, be completely .... **BULLET**

7 The morning trains to the city are always packed with .... **COMMUTE**

8 We are looking for staff who will offer total .... to the company. **COMMIT**

Useful language: understanding prefixes

1 **Match the underlined prefixes in these sentences to the meanings of the prefixes in the box. Then explain the meanings of the words with the underlined prefixes.**

again not against not below not enough not too much

1 Luke's very late – I guess he must have overslept again.
2 The teacher asked us to rewrite the exercise correcting all our mistakes.
3 We underestimated the amount of money we would spend on holiday.
4 There have been a number of anti-government demonstrations in the last year.
5 The little boy excitedly unwrapped the parcel.
6 It's very irresponsible to go climbing without telling anyone your plans.
7 Unfortunately, this work is sub-standard.
8 Fletcher thought he had scored, but the goal was disallowed by the referee.

2 **Suggest three more examples of words for each of the prefixes in Exercise 1.**

3 **Make new words from the words in CAPITALS at the end of each line to complete the sentences. The words all use a prefix from Exercise 1. You may need to add a suffix as well.**

1 We had an unusually cold winter, with .... temperatures for two months. **ZERO**
2 Everyone .... his story – it just didn't seem at all plausible. **BELIEVE**
3 Teachers sometimes complain of being .... and overworked. **PAY**
4 Students often tend to be a bit ...., but they usually become less radical with age. **ESTABLISH**
5 I'm sorry to be so .... – I'd like to think things over for another day or two. **DECIDE**
6 George means well, but his contributions to our meetings are often rather .... **HELP**

Test 1 Exam practice Reading and Use of English Part 3

Action plan

1 Read the title and, if there is one, look at the picture – these tell you the topic of the text.
2 Read the whole text through before filling any of the gaps.
3 For each gap, think about what part of speech is needed – a noun, verb, adjective or adverb.
4 When you have completed the task, read through the text to make sure it makes sense.
5 Check you have spelt the words you write correctly. Remember that US and UK spellings are both accepted.
6 At the end of the test, carefully transfer your answers (using CAPITAL LETTERS) to the answer sheet.

Follow the exam instructions, using the advice to help you.

For questions **17–24**, read the text below. Use the word given in capitals at the end of some of the lines to form a word that fits in the gap **in the same line**. There is an example at the beginning (**0**).

Tip! There are often clues both **before** and **after** the gap.

Tip! If an adjective or adverb is needed, remember to think about whether it has a positive or a negative meaning.

Write your answers **IN CAPITAL LETTERS on the separate answer sheet.**

Example: **0** E X P L O R A T I O N

Exploring the world by sea

People have been carrying out **(0)** .... by sea for thousands of years. **EXPLORE**
Our distant ancestors set out on **(17)** .... voyages on primitive rafts **PERIL**
and ships with no guarantee of ever seeing land again. **(18)** .... though **BELIEVE**
it may seem, there is evidence to suggest that sailors from Polynesia began to
undertake long and **(19)** .... journeys, as far back as 1200 BC. They **RISK**
may even have travelled as far as South America. **(20)** .... of fossilised **ANALYSE**
chicken bones found in Chile suggests that Polynesian sailors had made
their way to South America long before the **(21)** .... of the Spanish. **ARRIVE**
While Polynesians were exploring the Pacific, Vikings were sailing the Atlantic.
Viking explorers reached North America but did not establish a permanent
(22) .... there. They returned home with tales of a land where grapes **SETTLE**
grew in profusion and fish were **(23)** .... too. It is impossible not to feel **PLENTY**
great respect for the **(24)** .... of these intrepid early explorers. **BRAVE**

Advice

17 What part of speech do you need here?

18 Is a positive or a negative word likely to be needed here?

19 Which suffix is required to form the adjective here?

20 Is a singular or a plural word needed here?

21 Which suffix is needed to make the part of speech you need here?

22 Do you need a singular or a plural word here?

23 Do you need an adjective or an adverb here?

24 Here you need a relatively unusual suffix for forming abstract nouns.

Reading and Use of English Part 4

Task information

- Part 4 consists of six questions (plus one example).
- Each question consists of an example sentence, a key word and a second sentence with a gap in the middle of it.
- You have to complete the second sentence using the key word, so that it has the same meaning as the example sentence.
- You must not change the form of the key word.
- You will need to write between three and six words to complete each gap.
- Part 4 tests the ability to express an idea in different ways, as well as knowledge of vocabulary and grammar. The mark scheme divides the answer into two parts and you get a mark for each part that you write correctly.
- You need to spell the words correctly to get the marks. US and UK spellings are both accepted.

Useful language: correcting some common mistakes

1 **Choose the correct alternative in these examples where exam candidates made mistakes.**

1 I'm sure you won't have any difficulties *finding / to find* the solution to the problem.
2 Did you have the chance *of getting / to get* to know any Native Americans when you were living in the States?
3 Everybody who *work / works* here *get / gets* a good salary.
4 I suggest you *buy / to buy* a telephone card as soon as you arrive in the country.
5 You *either can / can either* finish reading this book or choose another one.
6 Not only *was the food / the food was* bad, but the sports facilities were not as you stated in the brochure.
7 The hotel offers *French traditional / traditional French* cuisine.
8 Some of the lessons that we attended in the last course *could be / could have been* better prepared.

2 **Complete the second sentence so that it has a similar meaning to the first sentence. You must use between three and six words, including the word in capitals, without changing it.**

1 I like all the people working as managers in this company.
WHO
I like everyone .... position in this company.

2 The service was first-class and the rooms were excellent too.
ONLY
Not .... the service was first-class too.

3 You have two possibilities – driving there or going by train.
EITHER
You .... there by train.

4 At the concert I didn't play as well as I expected.
SHOULD
I .... at the concert.

5 You'll easily manage to finish the work by Friday.
DIFFICULTY
You .... the work by Friday.

6 The food at this restaurant is delicious, and the prices are very reasonable.
MEALS
This restaurant .... very reasonable prices.

7 I think this type of mobile phone would be the best choice for you.
SUGGEST
I .... this type of mobile phone.

8 I hope to be able to see the Bolshoi Ballet when I'm in Moscow.
CHANCE
I hope I .... to the Bolshoi Ballet when I'm in Moscow.

3 The key word for all the following transformation sentences is EYE. Choose one of the expressions from the box to complete each sentence, making all the necessary changes.

Tip! Often the answers depend on knowledge of typical English collocations or idioms.

catch someone's eye	turn a blind eye to	
see eye to eye	keep an eye on	in the public eye

1 Although I love my sister, I don't always agree with her.
I love my sister despite .... with her.

2 The teacher pretended not to see what the children were doing.
The teacher .... the children's behaviour.

3 It must be hard for celebrities never to have any privacy, mustn't it?
It must be hard for celebrities always .... , mustn't it?

4 We'll pay the bill and leave as soon as the waiter notices we're waiting.
As soon as .... , we'll pay the bill and leave.

5 Sarah watched the children while they were playing in the garden.
Sarah .... children while they were playing in the garden.

Test 1 Exam practice Reading and Use of English Part 4

Action plan

1. Read the first sentence carefully.
2. Make sure the second sentence conveys exactly the same meaning as the first one and that you have not added any new ideas or left anything out.
3. Write your answer in CAPITAL LETTERS.
4. Use the key word exactly as it is written – do not change it in any way.
5. Check that what you write fits with both what goes before and what comes after the gap.
6. Count the number of words to make sure you have not written more than six or less than three.
7. Remember that contractions (*I'll*, *don't*, etc.) count as two words.
8. Check your spelling.
9. At the end of the test, carefully transfer your answers to the answer sheet.

Follow the exam instructions, using the advice to help you.

For questions **25–30**, complete the second sentence so that it has a similar meaning to the first sentence, using the word given. **Do not change the word given.** You must use between **three** and **six** words, including the word given. Here is an example (**0**).

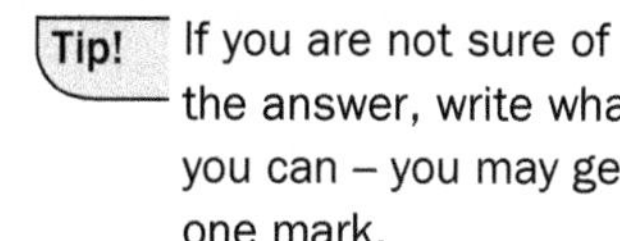

Tip! If you are not sure of the answer, write what you can – you may get one mark.

Example:

0 Mark told Patti he thought her dress was beautiful.

ON

Mark .... dress.

The gap can be filled with the words 'complimented Patti on her beautiful', so you write:

Example: | **0** | COMPLIMENTED PATTI ON HER BEAUTIFUL

Write **only** the missing words **IN CAPITAL LETTERS on the separate answer sheet**.

Tip! Check that (a) you have not used too many or too few words, (b) your spelling is correct, and (c) what you have written fits grammatically.

---

25 Could you watch my suitcases while I go and buy my ticket?

EYE

Would you mind .... my suitcases while I go and buy my ticket?

26 The rainfall in the west of the country usually exceeds that in the east.

HIGHER

The rainfall in the west of the country tends .... is in the east.

27 It's hard to be sure, but I think unemployment rates are beginning to fall.

TELL

As .... , unemployment rates are beginning to fall.

28 It would be wonderful to sit down and relax for a few minutes.

FEET

I wish that I .... for a few minutes.

29 We were very grateful that Kate thought of suggesting we ask Max for help.

CAME

We were very grateful that Kate .... asking Max for help.

30 Don't forget to take gloves, as it may well be cold in the mountains.

CASE

You should .... cold in the mountains.

Advice

25 Which expression with 'eye' means 'watch' in the sense of 'look after'?

26 What form of a verb follows 'tends'?

27 Here you need an expression with 'tell' meaning 'from what I have noticed or understood'.

28 Which idiom based on 'feet' means 'relax'?

29 Which phrasal verb is often used with words like 'suggestion' or 'idea' to mean 'think of'?

30 Which tense is used after 'in case' when you're thinking about the future?

Follow-up

How could you help yourself to improve your performance in this part of the test?

Test 1 Training Reading and Use of English Part 5

Task information

- In Part 5, you will read a text followed by six four-option multiple-choice questions.
- The text may come from a range of sources such as a newspaper, a magazine or journal, or a book of fiction or non-fiction.
- The questions will focus on things such as the main idea and details of the content of the text, the writer's opinion and attitude, the purpose and implications of the text, and features of text organisation, e.g. the use of examples, comparisons or reference words.

Choose the best option (A, B or C) to complete the tips for Reading and Use of English Part 5.

1 You will find the answer to each question
- **A** in your own knowledge of the topic.
- **B** only in the text itself.
- **C** in a combination of A and B.

2 Titles, sub-headings and, occasionally, visuals should all
- **A** be ignored as they are only there to make the page look better.
- **B** be looked at after reading the main body of the text.
- **C** give you useful information about the content of the text.

3 The context will often help you to work out the
- **A** origin of a word.
- **B** meaning of a word.
- **C** pronunciation of a word.

Using the title

Titles are important as they give readers an idea of what the text is likely to be about. What do you think articles with the following titles will be about?

Example: *Blizzards bring country to standstill* – about snowstorms causing serious transport problems

1 Getting air traffic under control
2 Worlds collide at the National Gallery's new exhibition
3 Diary of a teenage millionaire
4 Fashion to cheer you up
5 Secrets of stunning photography
6 How to eat well: it's all in the presentation

Working out meaning from context

You almost certainly will not know every word in the text. However, often it is possible to understand roughly what it means from the context. What helps you guess what the underlined words in these sentences mean? Note that you need to think about the whole context, not just the sentence in which the word appears.

Example: *Many of us share elements of a globalised culture, at least, perhaps watching Japanese movies, listening to K-pop, or eating Indian food.* – It is clear that K-pop is something that people listen to and is going to be some kind of popular music. The context suggests that the 'K' is likely to refer to some area of the world (South Korea, in fact).

1 Why is it, then, that so many of us tussle with the basics of global communication?
2 As an artificial language, it is appreciated as being devoid of ideological or political connotations.

3 Esperanto may well be the answer that second-language learners have been seeking.
4 The main criticism of Esperanto is that, despite its lofty ideals, the language never really caught on.
5 It may even be considered as maintaining a primarily Western point of view, something the creator of Esperanto initially set out to mitigate.
6 However, advocates of Esperanto would counter this criticism by maintaining that all languages can be considered as artificial.
7 Proponents of the language assert that it has succeeded in areas where English might have failed.
8 The global uptake of Esperanto may not eventually topple English from its perch, consigning it to a status similar to that of modern-day Latin.

Useful language: paraphrasing

Texts often use different words to refer to the same thing rather than repeating the same word. In a text, a dance might also be referred to, more generally, as a party or a social event or, more specifically, depending on the context, as a ball or a disco. Similarly, options in Reading and Use of English Part 5 will usually use different words to convey the ideas in the text.

1 **Put the words in the box into pairs of synonyms.**

~~advocates~~	at first	be aware	connections	consequence	fascinating	
for certain	have in common	initially	intend	interesting	key	main
realise	result	share	~~supporters~~	ties	undeniable	wish

Example: *advocates* – supporters

2 **Rewrite these sentences so they do not use any of the underlined words.**

Example: *Why is it, then, that so many of us tussle with the basics of global communication?*
Why is it, then, that so many of us struggle with even simple aspects of global communication?

1 What is interesting is that, over a hundred years ago, a Dr Ludwig Zamenhof published a book about a new language that he had developed.
2 It is claimed to be easy to master.
3 It is appreciated as being devoid of the ideological or political connotations that accompany languages of former colonial powers.
4 The language never really caught on among the global population in the way its creator intended.
5 What Esperanto lacks in culture it makes up for in efficiency.
6 Esperanto has built up a history of its own, one shared by the thousands who speak it and use it as an international means of communication.

Action plan

1 Read the title. This will give you some idea of the topic of the text.
2 Read the text first, then read each question very carefully in turn. Underline key words in the question.
3 Remember that questions follow the order of the text. Find the part of the text the question refers to. Check the text carefully before answering.
4 Are you confident about the answer? If so, note it down and move on.
5 If the answer is not obvious, eliminate the options you are sure are wrong.
6 If you find one question difficult, move on to the next one.
7 When you have finished, go back to any questions that you left out and look at them again. They may seem easier now. If they do not, just choose one of the options you have not eliminated. Do not leave any questions blank.

Follow the exam instructions, using the advice to help you.

You are going to read an article about Esperanto. For questions **31–36**, choose the answer (**A, B, C** or **D**) which you think fits best according to the text.

Mark your answers **on the separate answer sheet**.

Breaking down the language barrier?

A look at Esperanto

We are supposed to live in a 'globalised' world, or so we are increasingly taught in school. Many of us share elements of a globalised culture, at least, perhaps watching Japanese movies, listening to K-pop, or eating Indian food. Why is it, then, that so many of us tussle with the basics of global communication in this age of instant messaging, email and video conferencing? English may certainly be the (self-appointed) lingua franca of the globalised world, with millions of students struggling daily to learn its phrasal verbs and idioms. But English is the mother tongue of only a relatively small percentage of the global population, so wouldn't it be easier if we all spoke a simpler language? Perhaps what is needed is an international language.

What is interesting is that, over a hundred years ago, a Dr Ludwig Zamenhof published a book about a new language that he had developed, with the intention of providing an appropriate international means of communication. He called this language 'Esperanto', and it is said that hundreds of thousands of people have learned to speak it, with about one thousand today even using it as their first language. It is claimed to be easy to master and, more significantly, as an artificial language, it is appreciated as being devoid of any of the ideological or political connotations that accompany languages of former colonial

Tip! You may find it useful to read the questions, but not the options, before you read the text – this may help you focus on the most appropriate bits of the text.

Tip! Do not expect to understand every word or phrase in the text. The general context may help you to understand roughly what unfamiliar words or expressions mean.

Tip! The answer must say the same as what is in the text – do not choose an option just because it states something true, if that truth is not in the text. And do not choose an option just because it uses some words from the text.

powers, such as English. It is said to be learnt much faster than English, with a one-symbol-one-sound writing system (making spelling easier) and a grammar with a limited number of rules. Vocabulary even borrows a number of words that are already shared internationally, such as *telefono* (telephone) and *matematiko* (mathematics). In short, Esperanto may well be the answer that second-language learners have been seeking.

The problem is that it is likely that, before reading this article, you might never have heard of Esperanto, and you would almost certainly not be alone on that point. The main criticism of Esperanto is that, despite its lofty ideals, the language never really caught on among the global population in the way its creator intended. Whether there was a vested interest in preventing the language from spreading is hard to say. The key factor is that the language does, in fact, look rather similar to Romance languages such as French, Spanish or Italian, at the expense of other popular languages such as Arabic or Mandarin. As such, the 'international' language is perhaps not international enough, and may even be considered as maintaining a primarily Western point of view, something the creator of Esperanto initially set out to mitigate.

As mentioned, Esperanto is what is known as an 'artificial language'. Those involved with the development of its vocabulary and structures were well aware that the language they were creating had few ties with languages of the past, and so one of the basic features of any other language – that of a cultural heritage – can be considered missing for speakers of Esperanto. However, advocates of Esperanto would counter this criticism by claiming that all languages can be considered as artificial, in the sense that the creators of any language were human. What Esperanto lacks in culture, it makes up for in efficiency, and as language learners in the busy modern world are constantly under pressure of time, it is possible that, for some, it is worth developing communicative efficiency at the expense of a certain prestige. In addition, as Esperanto itself is now a over a century old, one might argue that this language, too, has built up a history of its own, one shared by the thousands who speak it and use it as an international means of communication.

Whether we consider the Esperanto experiment a success or failure, one thing is for certain: an international language should reflect all aspects of global society, while at the same time be easy to learn, free from ambiguity, and neutral in terms of ideology. Critics of Esperanto claim its failure in each of these aspects, while proponents of the language assert that it has succeeded in areas where English might have failed. While there may not be enough global uptake of Esperanto to eventually topple English from its perch, there is no doubt that it has provoked increased interest in the debate on language in the shadow of globalisation, and this debate is far from over.

31 What is the main point the writer is making in the first paragraph?

A English has difficult features, but can still be an effective global language.
B Schools tend to exaggerate the extent of globalisation in the world today.
C Global communication is less straightforward than it should be.
D World culture continues to become increasingly globalised.

32 What does the writer suggest is the main reason why Esperanto appeals to learners?

A Its spelling accurately reflects its pronunciation.
B Its grammar and vocabulary are relatively simple.
C It is becoming increasingly widely spoken.
D It lacks associations with a specific culture.

33 How does the writer explain the fact that Esperanto has been less successful than initially hoped?

A Esperanto is too closely associated with European languages.
B Many learners find English more interesting than Esperanto.
C Speakers of Arabic and Chinese find Esperanto difficult.
D Esperanto has not been promoted widely enough.

34 How does the writer suggest that Esperanto is now changing?

A It can no longer be considered artificial.
B It is developing its own culture.
C Its vocabulary is rapidly expanding.
D Its prestige is beginning to increase.

35 The writer concludes that

A Esperanto is in some ways superior to English.
B Esperanto meets all the criteria for an international language.
C it is hard to predict what the future fate of Esperanto will be.
D Esperanto has prompted useful discussions about language.

36 What does 'it' in line 56 refer to?

A Esperanto
B uptake
C perch
D English

Advice

Title *What does the title tell you about the text?*

31 *Read the whole of the first paragraph before answering this question.*

32 *Look for a phrase that suggests something is the main reason, rather than being just one of several reasons.*

33 *The final sentence of the third paragraph should help you find the answer.*

34 *Read the whole of the fourth paragraph before choosing your answer to this question.*

35 *Remember that the question is asking about the writer's conclusion, rather than just a point made by the writer.*

36 *Try replacing 'it' with each of the options to see which one makes the sentence make sense.*

Follow-up

Did you follow all the steps in the Action plan?

Test 1 Training Reading and Use of English Part 6

Task information

- In Part 6, you have to read four short texts on the same topic, and answer four multiple-matching questions about the texts.
- The questions require you to read across the texts in order to find the answers.
- The questions will require you to find opinions in the texts.
- The questions will ask you to say which expert shares an opinion with or has a different opinion from another of the text(s).
- It is unlikely that there will be one answer for each of the texts – one of the texts will probably have two answers while another has none.

Approaching the task

Read the rubric carefully, as it will introduce you to the subject of the texts. The best way to approach the task is to make a note beside each question of the letters that could provide the answers to that question. For example, if the question asks *Which expert shares C's opinion about the quality of the main actor's performance in the film?,* then you would note down A, B, D, as clearly C cannot be the answer here. Then, as you read the texts, you can put a line through any of the letters that you are certain do not provide the required answer.

1 **Read these questions and note down the letters for possible answers after each question.**

Which expert

1 shares expert B's interest in the historical aspects of the issue?
2 shares expert A's opinion on the impact that the type of course that is chosen has?
3 holds a different view from expert B on the value of making more degree places available?
4 shares expert D's doubts about the financial benefits of taking a degree?

2 **When you first read the texts, it can be useful to think about how you would summarise each of the expert's opinions. Read each of the four texts dealing with the question of the value of doing a university degree course (see page 30). Make notes on each text.**

Tip! Getting a sense of the main points the expert is making will help you find the answers more quickly.

3 **Now look at the texts again and choose your answers to the questions in Exercise 1.**

Tip! As will often be the case in the exam, one of the texts is the answer to two of the questions.

4 **Check the answers to the task by answering these questions.**

1 Which phrases in the text that answers question 1 suggest a historical approach?
2 How does the writer of the text that answers question 2 make it clear that he or she believes that the choice of course is crucially important?
3 Which sentences give B's opinion on the value of degree courses, even in less vocational subjects?
4 Which sentences in the text that answers question 4 express a degree of scepticism about whether taking a degree is financially worthwhile?

A

There is increasing divergence of views these days over the value, for the individual, of doing a degree course as opposed to going straight into work. In the past, the consensus was that attending university was always worthwhile for anyone who had the ability to gain a place. But this attitude has shifted in recent years, no doubt in part because of the steadily increasing cost of spending three or four years in higher education. However, it must be stressed that the potential advantage of university depends in large part on what any particular course offers in terms of providing practical experience, a sound theoretical understanding or specific transferable skills. The nature of the chosen discipline and the quality of the selected course are the key factors to be taken into account when a school leaver is considering whether a degree course will be worth the investment.

B

Since the 1980s, there has been an enormous increase in the number of institutions in the UK providing degree courses, as well as a steadily growing diversity in the range of courses available to students. As a result, a far higher proportion of young people are now graduates. Some have claimed that this has led to a decline in both the quality and the economic value of a degree. However, it remains a fact that graduates earn considerably more than non-graduates. Although a degree is no guarantee of wealth and success, figures show that it is significantly more likely to lead to a higher salary and a more prestigious job. This general tendency holds true even for graduates in subjects that have no obvious links with traditionally well-paid professions.

C

Many university students have reported that they believe that an increase in confidence and maturity was their main gain from the years they spent in higher education. Those who select a vocational degree, such as veterinary science or aeronautical engineering, invariably and unsurprisingly focus more on the importance of the knowledge and skills they acquired. The social side of university life tends to be appreciated by students in all disciplines, although medical, engineering and law students claim to have had insufficient leisure to enjoy this aspect of the experience. While the most advanced professional skills probably need to be learnt in a higher education institute, improved confidence can be achieved equally effectively and probably more rapidly while in salaried employment, and an exciting social life is similarly not the exclusive prerogative of university students.

D

The problem with providing university education to an increasingly large contingent of students is that it is unrealistic in the way that it raises young people's expectations of the kinds of career opportunities that will open up for them. There simply are not enough graduate posts available for those who believe – usually rightly – that they are qualified to take on such a role. The size of the competition they face is disheartening, as is the inevitable disappointment experienced by young graduates who either remain unemployed or take on a job that could be done equally well by someone who has only just left school. Were they to have gone straight into employment at the age of 16, they would have been earning rather than spending money on fees, and they would probably be better able to tolerate the humdrum aspects of a routine job.

Test 1 Exam practice Reading and Use of English Part 6

Action plan

1 Read the introduction to the texts, noticing the topic.
2 Read the questions to get an idea of what you are looking out for.
3 Read each of the texts, thinking about the writer's opinions as you do so.
4 Read each question carefully and underline any key words or phrases in it.
5 Write the letters of the texts that might provide the answer next to the question.
6 Go back to each of the relevant texts and think about whether it is the answer or not. If not, put a line through that letter next to the question. If you are not sure, put a question mark next to that letter.
7 Before finally choosing your answer, check that you have been focusing on the correct attitude, for example a shared opinion rather than a differing opinion.

Follow the exam instructions, using the advice to help you.

You are going to read four reviews of a work of art on show at the Museum of Modern Art PS1 (MoMA PS1) in New York. For questions **37–40**, choose from the reviews **A–D**. The reviews may be chosen more than once.

Mark your answers **on the separate answer sheet**.

Review of a work of art

A

Olafur Eliasson's installation at the Museum of Modern Art PS1 in New York, *Your Waste of Time*, consists of broken chunks of Iceland's Vatnajökull, Europe's largest glacier. The museum had to turn one of their main galleries into a walk-in freezer to be able to display them, a costly exercise but one that is justifiable in terms of its powerful impact. According to the museum, the pieces of ice chosen for the project are about 800 years old. That sounds about right to Ted Scambos, lead scientist at the National Snow and Ice Data Center. Scambos speculates that the ice came from the 'Little Ice Age', the period between the 16th and 19th centuries during which glaciers grew larger than they ever have since – and advanced quickly. 'These glaciers bear testimony to our history – being suspended and frozen for thousands of years – and now they are melting away, as if our whole history is fading,' said Eliasson. Stunning to look at, sad message.

B

Deep in the basement of MoMA PS1, there's a freezing cold room. This contains a number of large chunks of bluish-white ice brought together by the controversial artist Olafur Eliasson. The installation is called *Your Waste of Time* and its lesson would appear to be that global warming is having a devastating impact on our world. But that's hardly news. Ironically, the piece is itself contributing not inconsiderably to the problem, as an extraordinary amount of electricity is required to stop the installation from melting over the floor of the basement gallery. It's a curious piece with a carbon footprint that seems hard to justify on artistic grounds. It lacks beauty, and the skills involved in the installation's creation would seem to be less those of the artist whose name is on the gallery wall than of the technical staff who transported the ice blocks from the Arctic to New York. Are they in fact the people who have been wasting their time?

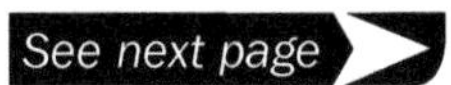
See next page

C

More and more artists are beginning to tackle the causes and consequences of global warming, particularly the rapidly retreating polar ice caps. Thus, when the artist Olafur Eliasson produced his latest installation, *Your Waste of Time*, his Icelandic background (notable, of course, for having numerous glaciers) may have contributed to the sense of irony conveyed by this thought-provoking, infuriating, but at the same time elegantly crafted exposé on the dangers of glacial extinction. He even brought some of that background with him for the installation itself, constructed using Icelandic glacial ice which must be kept below freezing for the duration of the exhibition, at a cost of, arguably, a little of that Icelandic background in years to come in terms of the power needed to maintain such an icy temperature for four weeks. Despite Eliasson's positive environmental message, the irony of the manner of this installation's construction is not lost on the observer.

D

The very notion of a glacier is one of an unmoving edifice against the sands of time, a frozen state standing firm against the fluidity and pace of the modern world. Yet, through our best (or worst) efforts, the reality of the impact of global warming on these last remnants of the ancient world is now regularly beginning to feature in the art of those who live in the shadow of such edifices, a shadow that Eliasson is surely aware is getting smaller by the day. While his portfolio contains a variety of photographs and other works focused on this appealing icy subject, when regarding his new installation, *Your Waste of Time*, it then begs the question that if preserving the ice used in this installation at temperatures below freezing for four weeks is not of the utmost irony, then how does he reconcile the power needed to preserve his installation at the cost of preserving his own cultural and environmental heritage? Whose time has been wasted here?

Which reviewer

shares reviewer A's view that *Your Waste of Time* is visually attractive? **37** [ ]

shares reviewer D's interest in reflecting on the title of the installation? **38** [ ]

has the same opinion as reviewer D about the attraction that glaciers possess for artists? **39** [ ]

has a different opinion from the other reviewers on the environmental contradictions of the installation? **40** [ ]

Advice

37 Which words could be synonyms for 'visually attractive'?

38 What is the installation called?

39 First check exactly what reviewer D says about the appeal of glaciers as subject matter for the artist.

40 What exactly is the environmental contradiction of the installation?

Follow-up

Is there anything you would now like to add to or modify in the Action plan?

Test 1 Training — Reading and Use of English Part 7

Task information

- Part 7 consists of one long text with six gaps numbered 41–46.
- Six paragraphs have been removed from the text and placed after it in random order. There is also a seventh paragraph that does not fit in the text at all. These paragraphs are labelled A–G.
- You have to decide which of the paragraphs A–G fits in each of the six gaps in the text.
- The text has a title, and there is often also some general information about the content of the text under the title.
- The task checks your understanding of the overall structure of the text and the way in which it develops its ideas.

Useful language: working with reference clues

1 **Look at this text, which has some missing paragraphs. Underline any words both before and after the gap that might help you find what is missing.**

Trees and the urban environment

Who doesn't like trees? Nobody. Everybody likes trees. But some people really, really like trees. The staff of an organisation in the UK called The Woodland Trust, for example.

1	

How can this possibly be? Well, unexpected heatwaves can cause serious health problems, the argument goes, and cities get hotter than rural areas, because buildings retain warmth. But trees have the opposite effect: while shade from their branches cools people under them, evaporation from their leaves cools the air around them. Researchers at the UK's Manchester University estimate that increasing the city's green spaces by ten per cent could bring the city's temperature down by several degrees. Which might not have the residents of Manchester cheering now, but once global warming kicks in, they might be a bit more grateful.

2	

For example, The Woodland Trust goes on to argue, albeit in a tone more hopeful than forceful, 'there is strong evidence' that green spaces 'promote inward investment by creating a more attractive environment for businesses and their staff'. True or not, greenery is certainly good for city birds and animals.

3	

Given such striking benefits, the trust's report concludes that 'it is vital that the government sets targets for new woodland'. Really, though? It seems unlikely to become a government priority in these straitened times, whatever the long-term financial benefits.

4	

All the same, just reading about sitting in the cool shade under a leafy tree seems to be having a positive effect on my mental health. Stature and beauty alone can be enough to do it.

2 **Think about each of the gaps in Exercise 1. What is likely to be the topic of the text that fills the gap?**

3 **Now look at options A–D which fill the gaps in Exercise 1. Underline the phrases in each of these options which connect it to other parts of the text. Then decide which option fits where and why. How accurate were your predictions in Exercise 2?**

Tip! Connecting words or phrases like *moreover* and *in contrast* will help you work out how the paragraphs fit together.

Tip! Words like *they*, *so*, *there*, *those*, etc. that refer to other parts of the text will also provide useful clues.

A Before that happens, however, they might be pleased to know that the city's rainfall is being quietly managed by its plant life, which reduces water run-off: research indicates that tree cover in cities reduces the cost of drainage and other water management issues. And there are other economic advantages, too.

B Besides, some of the report's claims are a bit shaky. All but 284 of those who died in the most recent heatwave were over 75; trees would not have saved most of them for long. And, with press accounts of aggressive foxes venturing into cities, maybe being kind to urban wildlife isn't as valued as it might be.

C Business covered, the report turns back to health issues. Poor air quality shortens 24,000 lives a year; trees absorb the filth. Without green spaces to walk in, city people get fat, lazy and stressed; trees help with that, too. There are reports that link greenery with reducing blood pressure, raising self-esteem and even controlling behavioural problems in children.

D 'We need more native trees and woods in urban areas,' insists the Trust's report *Greening the Concrete Jungle*. Stature and beauty aside, trees have a positive effect on physical and mental health, they bring financial benefits to the cities where they grow and they are good for urban wildlife. They can even save lives, possibly.

Test 1 Exam practice Reading and Use of English Part 7

Action plan

1 Read the title and, if there is one, the introduction to the text – it will give you an overview of the topic.

2 Read through the text without trying to work out which paragraph goes where.

3 Read through the options A–G, noticing the differences between them.

4 Look carefully at the words before and after the missing paragraph and make sure your choice of paragraph fits 'at both ends'.

5 If you are sure you know the answer to any of the gaps, fill those in first.

6 Do not leave any answers blank – make an intelligent guess if you are not sure of the answer.

7 When you have finished, read through the text with your answers in place to check that it all makes sense.

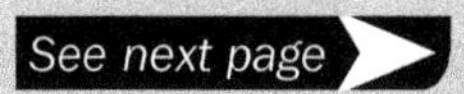

Follow the exam instructions, using the advice to help you.

You are going to read an extract from a magazine article. Six paragraphs have been removed from the extract. Choose from the paragraphs **A–G** the one which fits each gap (**41–46**). There is one extra paragraph which you do not need to use.

Mark your answers **on the separate answer sheet**.

Beautiful music makes better materials

The hidden structures of music are universal patterns of nature – and they can help us create new materials like artificial silk.

Our world consists of only about 100 different chemical elements. It is the arrangement of these elements, or building blocks, into molecules that gives rise to the rich set of materials around us – from the sugar molecules in the food we eat to the oxides in the Earth's crust.

41 ____________

The properties of a piece of matter, however, are defined not by these basic building blocks themselves but by the way they are arranged. For instance, spider silk is one of the most remarkable examples of nature's materials, created from a simple protein but spun into fibres stronger than steel.

42 ____________

A composer uses a limited set of tones as the starting point for melodies, which in turn are arranged into complex structures to create symphonies. Think of an orchestra, where each instrument plays a relatively simple series of tones. Only when combined do these tones become the complex sound we call classical music.

43 ____________

Composers have made use of the idea of interconnecting patterns for thousands of years, but only recently have these systems been understood mathematically. This maths shows that the principles of musical composition are shared by many seemingly quite different systems in the natural world.

44 ____________

The problem lies in our ignorance of the ways in which these are arranged. But in fact it is not the building block itself that is limiting our ability to create better materials, but rather our ignorance of the way in which these building blocks are arranged. To try to understand this better, scientists are copying the structure of silk fibres and turning it into musical compositions. This will help them create artificial materials for medical and engineering applications.

45 ____________

Listening to the music that was produced in this way improved their understanding of the mechanism by which the patterns of amino acids work together during the silk-spinning process. The patterns of amino acids that formed silk fibres of poor quality, for example, translated into music that was aggressive and harsh, while the ones that formed better fibres sounded softer and more fluid. In future work it is hoped that the design of the silk can be improved by enhancing those musical qualities that reflect better properties.

46 ____________

Using music as a tool to create better materials and to improve urban living may seem like an unusual proposal, but when we appreciate that the underlying mathematics of the structure of music are shared across many fields of study, it begins to make sense. Nature does not distinguish between what is art and what is material, as all are merely patterns of structure in space and time.

Advice

41 *The phrase 'these basic building blocks themselves' gives a clue as to what fits in gap 41.*

42 *Given the sentence after the gap, what topic must be introduced in the missing paragraph?*

43 *Looking at the paragraphs before and after the text should suggest what the basic topic of the missing paragraph must be.*

44 *What does the use of 'But' immediately following the gap tell you about what must go in 44?*

45 *Look at the sentence before and the one after this gap. What do these sentences tell you about the content of the intervening paragraph?*

46 *What does the use of 'to improve urban living' after the gap suggest about what might go in 46, given that this is not a topic that has been focused on elsewhere in the text?*

Tip! Look at the connecting words in options A–G for clues about what must go before or after them.

A In essence, a musician's piece is just one example of a system where smaller patterns are found inside larger ones – similar to the way characters form words, which form sentences, then chapters and eventually a novel.

B Using this theory, we can discover universal patterns that form the blueprints of our world. We may be able to make everything we know – molecules, living tissues, music, the universe – by applying universal patterns in different physical contexts. For example, a pattern of building blocks might be represented as music, to create a certain melody, or might be represented as DNA to create a certain protein.

C This approach has implications far beyond the design of new materials. In future, it might be possible to translate melodies to design better sequences of DNA, or even to reinvent transportation systems for cities.

D Similarly, in the living world, a limited set of building blocks of DNA and amino acids creates some of the most remarkable materials we know of, the stuff that builds our bones and skin, and complex organs such as the brain.

E In this translation from silk to music, they replaced the protein's building blocks with corresponding musical building blocks (tones and melody). As the music was played, they could 'hear' the different series of organic compounds they had used, and could then work out how certain qualities of the material, such as its mechanical strength, appear in musical terms.

F As we begin to appreciate the importance of such patterns, engineers are applying this knowledge to the design of synthetic materials. Doing so, they can gain inspiration from a surprising source: music.

G Even though nature uses this approach, people have failed to exploit the concept themselves when it comes to developing new materials. We have created thousands of different materials, originating from very different sources, such as plastics, metals or ceramics. But it seems we could benefit considerably from learning more about how nature uses its building blocks.

Follow-up

Did you find the clues before or those after the gap more useful in each case?

Reading and Use of English Part 8

Task information

- In Part 8, there are ten questions.
- You have to read either one long text divided into (usually) four sections labelled A–D or four shorter texts labelled A–D.
- You have to find the text, or section of text, which answers each of the ten questions and write down the appropriate letter.
- Part 8 tests your ability to locate specific information relating to detail, opinion and attitude.

Reading the questions

1 Look at this extract from an exam question. Which words would you underline in it?

Tip! It is important to read the questions carefully. It can help to underline or highlight key words so that you know what to focus on.

In which book review are the following mentioned?

1 a character with a resemblance to a real-life celebrity
2 a story that is partially based on the author's own childhood
3 a book which has not been adapted very successfully to another medium
4 a story that has an unexpected twist at the end
5 a gripping book with an eccentric main character
6 a detective story which holds the reader's attention until the very last page
7 an over-complicated and not totally convincing plot
8 a story which is set in the past but has a modern feel to it

2 The texts are unlikely to use the same words as the questions. Answer these questions about the task in Exercise 1.

Tip! Try to think of synonyms or paraphrases for key words as you read the questions.

1 What phrase might convey the idea of *having a resemblance to*?
2 What adjective might be used to say that a text is based on the author's life?
3 What is the most likely other medium for a book to be adapted to?
4 Which of these phrases might be used to replace *unexpected twist*: *unusual turn of events or surprising location*?
5 Which of these words might a reviewer use to convey a similar idea to *gripping*: *thrilling, amusing, spellbinding, puzzling, engrossing, inspiring*?
6 How might the reviewer convey the idea of an eccentric main character?
7 What phrase could be used instead of *detective story*?
8 What phrase might be used instead of *until the very last page*?
9 What would be another way of saying *over-complicated*?
10 How might the reviewer express the idea that he or she did not find the plot totally convincing?
11 How might a reviewer express the idea of a story being set in the past?
12 How might a reviewer express the idea that a story has a modern feel to it?

Scanning

1 **Take ten seconds to scan this text. What is it about?**

Tip! In this part of the test, you should scan the text rather than read it in detail.

Science in Fiction

Science-fiction thrillers have a rich history. Erica Wagner picks her favourites.

By the time of his death in 2008, Michael Crichton had become the giant of the science-thriller genre. He was perhaps best known for his novel *Jurassic Park* – published in 1990 – and the film spin-offs of his books. (I say 'best known' but let's not forget that he was also the man behind the famous story of the little alien ET, who befriends a small boy.)

For my money, however, his finest and most frightening novel was one of the earliest: *The Andromeda Strain,* published in 1969. The novel builds on the premise that if we are ever to encounter aliens from another galaxy, they are much less likely to be little green men than microscopic life forms.

On a slightly jollier note, sticking to alien life, there's Carl Sagan's *Contact*, published in 1985, the tale of a radio astronomer who encounters a signal that could have been sent only by an intelligent life form. On one visit to the Jodrell Bank Observatory in Cheshire, I was heartened to discover that this book (and the 1997 film starring Jodie Foster) was a favourite of the astronomers there.

But back to putting a shiver down your spine. How about Mary Shelley's *Frankenstein*? First published, anonymously, in 1818, it shows that even in what the writer and academic Richard Holmes so memorably termed 'The Age of Wonder', the dark side of scientific research was never far from imaginative minds.

2 **Now take one minute and find the answers to these questions about names and numbers. The questions do not follow the order of the text.**

1 Who is the author of this article?
2 Which is the oldest book she mentions?
3 Which is the most modern?
4 What can be found in Cheshire?
5 Which creations bearing Michael Crichton's name are mentioned in the article?
6 Which of these does the reviewer say she likes most?
7 Which of Jodie Foster's films is mentioned in this article?
8 Whose name was on the title page of the first edition of *Frankenstein*?
9 When was the book that the Jodrell Bank astronomers like published?
10 Who coined the phrase 'The Age of Wonder'?
11 Which age does 'The Age of Wonder' refer to?
12 When did Michael Crichton die?

Test 1 Exam practice Reading and Use of English Part 8

Action plan

1. Read the introduction to the text(s) to get a general idea of what you are going to read about.
2. Remember that the questions come before the text(s), as you are supposed to focus on these first.
3. In this task, the questions do not match the order in which the answers appear in the text(s).
4. Skim the text(s) to get a quick impression of the content. Do not read it/them in detail.
5. Read each question and scan the text(s) to find the information or opinion that you need.
6. Remember to check your answers. Check the questions against the text(s).
7. The questions usually use different words to communicate the ideas in the text(s), so if you find identical words in the question and the text(s), it does not mean you have found the right answer.

Follow the exam instructions, using the advice to help you.

You are going to read four short articles by people who have climbed Mount Everest. For questions **47–56**, choose from the articles (**A–D**). The articles may be chosen more than once.

Mark your answers **on the separate answer sheet**.

In which article is the following mentioned?

a remarkable coincidence	47
a suggestion that other climbers sometimes take risks	48
a determination to continue climbing despite a problem	49
an awareness of the dangers of the descent	50
an obsession the climber briefly experienced	51
the temporary nature of the sense of achievement	52
the fact that the writer made the climb without some support that could have been used	53
the appeal of climbing to one of the senses other than sight	54
something that failed to live up to expectations	55
a claim that the writer rejects	56

Advice

47 *This answer should stand out, as it is based on a surprising anecdote.*

48 *It should be straightforward to pick up the references to other people, as most of the texts are focusing on the writer's own intense feelings.*

49 *Several of the texts refer to a problem, but only one does so in a way that matches the whole phrase.*

50 *The reference to going back down the mountain may be indirect as long as it is unarguably in the text.*

51 *You will see the word 'obsessed' in one of the texts but, in fact, this makes it the least likely text to contain the answer to this question.*

52 *What verb is often used to describe the gradual disappearance of a feeling (or a colour)? If you see this word in a text, it will take you to the answer.*

53 *The support that most climbers use might refer to sherpas, oxygen or types of equipment – which text refers to managing without one of these?*

54 *The other four senses are hearing, smell, touch and taste – which of these is commented on specifically in one of the texts?*

55 *How do you feel if something 'failed to live up to expectations'? You are likely to find that word, or something very similar, in the text.*

56 *What is another word for 'rejecting' another person's claim or belief? Bearing in mind other possible ways of expressing this idea may help you to locate the answer.*

How I felt on conquering Everest

Four climbers who succeeded in climbing the world's highest mountain write about how they felt when they reached the summit.

A Roddy Mackenzie

It has occasionally been claimed that people climb for the smell of it. Air at very high altitude smells completely different. When I reached the South Summit, I was suffering from a lack of Spanish olives. I was preoccupied with thoughts of a tin of them sitting in my tent at base camp. This was the result of a very intense dream about olives that was interrupted by the alarm summoning me to our summit attempt. At the South Summit, the view of the main summit fascinated me from a mountaineering point of view and all dreaming of olives evaporated. On the summit, I felt a mixture of apprehension and curiosity. It seemed to me that the curvature of the Earth was apparent, and I spent some time trying to think of a means to test if this was a real observation or an illusion. Many people on the Indian subcontinent believe that the ascent of Everest confers on the climber a greater wisdom in manifold subjects. That is something I do not agree with but never dispute.

B Anna Czerwinska

When I reached the South Summit, I looked back at the mists rising from the valleys and I could feel their damp touch on my face. They prevented me from looking down on the long painful way up, but it was not only that. The curtain of mist had closed over my past. My oxygen was running out, and common sense demanded that I return, but before long I was climbing on an exposed ridge to the foot of the Hillary Step. A crampon had come undone and I painfully put it on again. Everest was doing everything to discourage me. I registered that dreamily and, as if dreaming, conquered the final metres of the snowy slope. Suddenly the clouds above me lifted in one blue moment and, very low down, I saw a rugged precipitous ridge. The wind was growing stronger and it was snowing lightly. I did not get the beautiful view as a reward and I felt fleetingly disappointed. However, those few minutes on the highest spot on Earth were worth every effort and have given me joy ever since.

C Andy Politz

On the summit, I set out to get some sponsor photos, which at 8,850 metres without oxygen gives a unique insight into hypoxia. At one point, I looked down at Nepal and the South East Ridge only to be surprised by another climber coming up through the clouds. He was startled to see someone looking down at him. He was also climbing without oxygen and was tiring. The other thought I had, remembering six years of attempting to climb Everest, was 'He could take my picture'. Through scudding cloud, I saw that the colour and design of his clothing were unmistakably French. I do not speak French. As this Frenchman was taking his last steps to the summit, I made the international hand sign for 'Stop and I'll take your picture'. While I was struggling to focus the camera, he looked hard at me and exclaimed 'Andy!' To my amazement, it was my close friend Ed Viestours on his second ascent of the mountain.

D Frits Vrijlandt

I approached Everest with respect and was well aware of being just a small human being. An excellent preparation is very important but far from a guarantee that you'll reach the summit. You have to be mentally ready to go for it, sufficiently experienced and a brave and careful climber. Before our summit bid, our team agreed that returning without injuries was our main objective. Some people can be blindly obsessed by Everest. I reached the top after eight hours of climbing. After I contacted base camp and they had congratulated me, I replied, 'Thank you, but first I have to get back down safely.' After my return to Kathmandu, I felt like a super-being because I had stood on the top of the world. I still had this feeling when I came back home but it soon faded away. The world or your life doesn't change because you climbed a mountain, even if it is the highest. But climbing Everest was a spiritual experience for me. It puts your feet back on the surface of mother Earth.

Follow-up

How could you improve your performance in this kind of task in future?

Test 1 Training Writing (1 hour 30 minutes) Part 1

Task information

- Part 1 is a compulsory task.
- In Part 1, you have to write 220–260 words.
- You have to write an essay.
- The question consists of a statement of the topic, three bullet points relating to the topic and three opinions, referring back to each of the bullet points in turn.
- You must only write about two of the bullet points in the question.
- You may use the opinions presented in the question, but you can deal with the bullet points in a different way if you wish.
- You must explain which of your two bullet points you consider to be more important/ effective/useful ... giving reasons for your opinion.

Understanding how writing is assessed

1 The people who mark your writing – for both Parts 1 and 2 – ask themselves a number of questions about your work. Match each of their questions (1–6) with the aspect of language that it is focusing on (A–F).

1 Does the answer cover all the necessary points?
2 Does the answer contain a lot of language errors?
3 Does the answer use a variety of words and structures?
4 Is the answer written in clear, well-connected paragraphs?
5 Is the answer in an appropriately formal or informal style?
6 Would the answer have the right effect on the reader?

A Organisation
B Language – range
C Register
D Content (dealing with the necessary points)
E Communicative achievement
F Language – accuracy

2 This piece of writing got a poor mark for accuracy. Correct the ten language errors in it.

I am writting this letter to discuss about the advantages and disadvantages of building a new theatre at the college. At first, I would like to draw your attention on the fact that our college has a drama department for the last ten years and yet it still doesn't have an own theatre. This means that drama students must to put on there productions in a theatre in the city, what is expensive and, of course, not very convenient too.

3 This piece of writing got a poor mark for range. Change the underlined words to more interesting words, adding to or expanding on them, in order to gain better marks.

I would recommend that you choose Brown's Hotel for your holiday. We had a <u>great</u> time there last year. The rooms were <u>beautiful</u>, the food was <u>good</u> and the staff were very <u>nice</u> too. It's central so <u>you can walk to lots of interesting places</u>.

4 Do these sentences that candidates wrote use an appropriate register? If not, say why not and write an improved version of the sentence.

1 (*Letter to a friend*) Would you do me the honour of accompanying me to the theatre next Saturday?
2 (*Proposal to a town council*) It'd be great if you can see your way to putting my ideas into practice. Am sure you won't regret it!
3 (*Opening sentence in a review for an international magazine*) Its main disadvantage is the fact that its public transport system is so poor, although I suppose some people would say that it's not a bad idea to walk everywhere anyway, given that it's a relatively small town without many hills and so it's pretty easy to make your way around its picturesque little streets on foot.
4 (*Report for a college principal*) I'd love to write more about this topic and must apologise for simply not having adequate time to do so.

5 Here is an example of a Part 1 Writing task. Read the task below and answer these questions.

1 What are the main content points that the examiners will be looking for?
2 What are the conventions of essay writing in English which you should follow?
3 What register will you need to use?
4 How many paragraphs will you need, and what will the topic of each one be?
5 What effect will you want to have on the target reader?

You **must** answer this question. Write your answer in **220–260** words in an appropriate style.

---

1 Your class has listened to a radio discussion about the advantages and disadvantages of receiving different types of presents. You have made the notes below:

Types of present

- luxuries
- homemade items
- experiences

Some opinions expressed in the discussion:

"The best presents are things you couldn't afford to buy for yourself."

"If someone's spent time making a present for me, it shows how much they care."

"I don't need more things – I'd rather be taken to the theatre or a football match."

Write an essay discussing **two** of the types of present in your notes. You should **explain which of these types of present is best to receive, giving reasons** in support of your answer.

You may, if you wish, make use of the opinions expressed in the discussion, but you should use your own words as far as possible.

Test 1 Exam practice Writing Part 1

Action plan

1 Read the question very carefully, highlighting all the significant points you must include in your answer.
2 Allow plenty of time to plan your answer carefully.
3 Decide which **two** of the three listed points you are going to write about.
4 Think about how you are going to expand each of these two points – the quotes from the discussion may help to give you ideas, but you may prefer to use other ideas of your own.
5 Think about how you are going to compare these points and which you will say is more important (or effective or useful, etc.) and why.
6 Remember that you are writing an essay, so your style of writing should be neutral or formal rather than informal.
7 Organise your writing in clear paragraphs.
8 Write 220–260 words. If you write less, you probably will not deal with all the aspects of the question or show an adequate range of language.
9 When you want to make a correction, do so as neatly as possible.
10 Spend time checking your work.

1 First answer these questions about the task on page 45.

1 What are the main content points that the examiners will be looking for?
2 What kind of text do you have to write?
3 What are the conventions of this text type in English which you should follow in your answer?
4 What register will you need to use?
5 How many paragraphs will you use, and what will the topic of each one be?
6 What effect will you want to have on the target reader?

2 How could you express these points from the input text in other (if possible more formal) words?

1 people with work experience
2 give wise advice
3 manage your money
4 living independently

3 What example could you give to illustrate each of these points?

1 work
2 relationships
3 finance

4 Which two of these points do you think it will be best for you to deal with in your answer?

5 Now write your answer to the task.

Follow the exam instructions, using the advice to help you.

You **must** answer this question. Write your answer in **220–260** words in an appropriate style.

---

1 Your class has watched a round-table discussion about what young people can learn from older generations. You have made the notes below:

<u>Areas where young people could learn from older generations</u>

- work
- relationships
- money

Some opinions expressed in the discussion:

"People with work experience can tell you what the job you're considering is really like."

"Older people can give wise advice when you have a problem with a friend."

"It's hard to manage your money when you start living independently."

Write an essay discussing **two** of the areas in your notes. You should **explain in which area young people could gain most from older generations, giving reasons** in support of your answer.

You may, if you wish, make use of the opinions expressed in the discussion, but you should use your own words as far as possible.

Follow-up

Did you read the question carefully and do exactly what it asked you to do?

Tip! Keep to the word limit suggested. If you write too much, you are likely to make more mistakes and to make your points less effectively.

Advice

Look at the exam question. Which of the three areas would you find it hardest to write about? Do not attempt it and focus your plans on the other two instead.

Can you think of specific examples that would illustrate how an older person's advice could help a younger person deal with each of the remaining two areas?

You may find it hard to select an area of a younger person's life which is more likely to benefit from an older person's advice, but remember that the most important thing is to write well – so choose either of your two areas and make an argument to support your choice.

You should aim to spend about 45 minutes on your answer, including planning and checking time.

Tip! Make it clear where one paragraph ends and the next begins (either by indenting or by leaving an extra line between the paragraphs).

Test 1 Training Writing Part 2

Task information

- In Part 2, you have to write 220–260 words.
- You have to choose one task from a choice of three.
- You may be asked to write a letter or email, a review, a report or a proposal.
- The instructions will state clearly *what* you have to write and *why* you are writing it, as well as *who* you are writing for.

Identifying types of writing

1 The following statements are true about one or more of the types of text you may have to write in Part 2. Choose A, B, C and/or D. Some questions have more than one answer.

Text types	
A	Review
B	Letter/ Email
C	Proposal
D	Report

1 It is good to give this type of writing a title.
2 Headings within the text are appropriate.
3 This kind of text will begin *Dear* … .
4 This kind of text has to be clearly organised into distinct paragraphs.
5 This kind of text aims to persuade the reader.
6 The writer usually knows exactly who will read the text.
7 This kind of text usually tries to evaluate something that has happened or that the writer has experienced.
8 This kind of writing is more likely to be in a formal or neutral style than an informal one.
9 The writer usually begins with an overview of his or her reasons for writing the text.
10 The writer will try to begin this text in a way that will catch and hold the reader's interest.

2 Complete these sentences – taken from either a review, a letter/email, a proposal or a report – with the appropriate preposition. Then identify the text type that the sentence is most likely to have come from.

1 I look forward ……to…… hearing from you again soon. Letter/Email
2 ………… conclusion, the campaign can be considered as having been a total success.
3 I've been terribly busy this month, but ………… last I've managed to find enough time to sit down and write to you properly.
4 *Casablanca* has to be one ………… the most romantic films ever made.
5 I recommend the first of the two options outlined above ………… a number of different reasons.
6 Do you prefer listening to music ………… your own or ………… the company of other people?
7 I am writing to congratulate you ………… the service which my wife and I received ………… your restaurant last night.
8 ………… the few slight problems which the group experienced this year, I have no hesitation ………… recommending the course for other students ………… the future.
9 The following recommendations are based ………… generally accepted estimates ………… regard to the city's probable future needs for leisure facilities.
10 According ………… the results of our survey, female students make more use ………… the college's libraries than male students do.

Identifying what, why and who

1 What you have to write affects how you write your answer. Complete the table below with the appropriate text type from the box.

Review	Report	Letter/Email	Proposal

Text type	Layout features	Language features
1	Title Sub-headings	Early statement of reason for writing Absolute clarity of language describing something precisely Ends with a conclusion – often a recommendation
2	Title Sub-headings	Early statement of reason for writing Absolute clarity of language Persuasive language Argument backed up by clear reasons
3	Title	Early statement of the subject Some factual information about the subject More of the content of the text should be devoted to the writer's opinion than to facts about the subject Writer's opinion backed up by examples relating to the subject
4	Opening and closing formulae (e.g. *Dear* ..., and *Best wishes* or *Yours sincerely/faithfully*)	Clear opening paragraph giving reason for writing Style will vary considerably depending on the intended reader

2 What you have to write usually includes two or three specific points that you have to deal with in your answers. Note down the three points of the topic in each of these exam tasks. The first one is done for you.

1 A student website has asked readers to write a review of a website that they have found useful in their studies. The review should outline the content of the website, explaining why the reader has found it useful. It should also state how the reader would like to see the website develop in future.

Write your **review**.

The specific points here are:

- *naming a website and outlining its contents*
- *explaining how you have found it useful*
- *suggesting how the website might usefully be developed in future*

2 You have received a letter from an English friend:

> *... As you know, I'm planning to study medicine at university. However, three friends are taking a year out and are setting off around the world when we leave school in June. I want to join them, but my parents say I'm too young and that it won't benefit my studies in any way. How can I persuade them to let me go? And why don't you come too?*

Write your **letter** in reply. You do not need to include postal addresses.

3 The college where you study English wants to encourage students who are new to the local area to get involved in community life. You feel it would be particularly beneficial for students to do some voluntary work in their free time. Write a proposal for the college principal, outlining what kinds of voluntary work students could do. You should also explain how voluntary work benefits both the volunteers and the community.

Write your **proposal**.

3 **When we write something, our aims can be described in functional terms: we may be writing, for example, in order to explain, to give our opinion, to recommend, to suggest, to apologise, to complain, to persuade, etc. Look at the questions in Exercise 2 and note which functions are involved in each question. (There is more than one function in each question.)**

4 **Who we are writing for affects how we write. Look again at the questions in Exercise 2. Who are you writing for in each case? How does this affect what you write and how you write it?**

Useful language: expressing functions

1 **Match the sentences below with the main function they are used to express from the box. One sentence is expressing a function that is not in the box. Which sentence is that? What function is it expressing?**

apologising	complaining	congratulating	recommending	suggesting

1. One possibility would be to organise a meeting to find out how other students feel about the proposed new timetable.
2. It is disgraceful that members of your staff should have such a careless attitude towards their work.
3. I should not have borrowed your bicycle without asking your permission.
4. One of the options would be more expensive to implement than the others.
5. The third option seems to me to be the preferable choice because it would benefit the largest number of people.
6. Your success is a magnificent achievement and one that you should take great pride in.

2 **In the *Cambridge English: Advanced* exam, you need to show that you can express functions in more than one way. Here are example sentences using some of the functions that you often need to express in the exam. In each case, one word is missing. Complete the sentences with appropriate words.**

Complaining

1. I am writing to complain .... the service I received in your hotel last weekend.
2. If I do not receive a satisfactory response, then I shall have no .... but to send a full account of the way I was treated to your Head Office.
3. It was very upsetting to be spoken .... so impolitely .... your reception staff.

Persuading

4. I feel sure you would .... it if you did not .... advantage of this exceptional opportunity.
5. There's no denying the .... that this is a very generous offer.
6. Surely you must .... that opportunities like this do not arise very frequently.

Recommending

7. If I were in your .... , I wouldn't hesitate to seize the opportunity on offer.
8. .... my opinion, the best .... of action would be to carry out a survey to discover how local residents feel about the proposal.
9. .... no circumstances should you .... a hasty decision.

Giving reasons

10. There are a number of reasons .... I am of this opinion.
11. I should like to .... forward the case for a rather different approach from the one that has been taken in the past.
12. The project has been temporarily suspended owing .... a lack of funding.

Test 1 Exam practice Writing Part 2

Action plan

1 Choose the task that you think you can write the best answer to.
2 Read the question very carefully, underlining the key points. Think about *what kind of text* (e.g. letter, report, proposal, etc.) you have to write and follow the English conventions for that text type.
3 Think about *who* you are writing for – should your language be formal, informal or neutral?
4 Think about *why* you are writing (for example, to inform, to entertain, to persuade, to complain, etc.) and how this will affect your response.
5 Make a plan before you start writing.
6 Organise your answer in clear paragraphs.
7 Use a variety of structures and vocabulary – make a quick list of possible structures and vocabulary before you start.
8 Allow time to check your writing.
9 Aim to spend about 45 minutes on your answer, including planning and checking time.

Follow the exam instructions, using the advice to help you.

Write an answer to **one** of the questions **2–4** in this part. Write your answer in **220–260** words in an appropriate style.

You can write in either British or American English, but keep to one or the other. Do not write, for example: *The theater is in the centre of the town*.

---

2 Your company would like to offer work-experience placements to students in an international college. Write a letter for publication in the student newspaper at the college.

Your letter should explain what your company does, what kind of work-experience placements are available, and how students would benefit from the experience.

Write your **letter**.

3 A website has asked readers for reviews of new software applications. Write a review of an application that you have used. Your review should comment on what is special about the software. It should also explain who might find the software most useful or appealing and why. Your review should also suggest one way in which the software could be improved.

Write your **review**.

Advice

2 *A letter like this wants to encourage the right kind of students to apply, so it needs to provide clear information about the nature of the work on offer.*

3 *Even if you are describing software that you feel is perfect, you need to make at least one suggestion for its improvement. Do not forget that it is not essential to tell the truth – you could, for example, always say that the Help notes are not comprehensive enough, even if you have found them very thorough and clear.*

See next page

4 Your local city council is investigating whether the city centre meets the needs of the city's inhabitants. You have been asked to write a report for the council.

Your report should discuss the entertainment and restaurant facilities in the city centre from the point of view of people of your age group. It should also describe at least one way in which the city centre could be improved to meet your age group's needs more effectively.

Write your **report**.

Follow-up

Did you check your work for your most frequent errors?

Advice

4 Remember that your report must focus on one particular age group – do not forget to say which at the start of your report – and not on the needs of the city's inhabitants in general!

Choose the question for which you feel you have the language to write the best answer, even if that is not the question that interests you most.

Only answer a work-related question if you have some experience of a workplace, as that is essential to give the answer an authentic flavour.

Listening (approximately 40 minutes) Part 1

Task information

- Part 1 consists of three short recordings, each with two three-option multiple-choice questions.
- Each recording lasts about one minute and is played twice.
- The recordings are about unrelated topics.
- The recordings are taken from a wide range of contexts and cover a range of topics, styles of delivery and voices.
- Each recording involves more than one speaker.
- The questions may focus on a variety of aspects of the recordings (for example, detail, gist, speakers' opinions, feeling, attitude, purpose, function, agreement and listener course of action).

Understanding different aspects of the recording

1 1 02 **Listen to the recording and answer these questions about it.**

1 **Context:** Where are the speakers?
   A in a restaurant
   B at a hotel
   C on a motorway

2 **Relationships:** What is the most likely relationship between the speakers?
   A driver and client
   B husband and wife
   C receptionist and customer

3 **Opinion:** What do the speakers agree about?
   A how tired they are
   B how hungry they are
   C how attractive the place looks

4 **Detail:** What does the man remind the woman to find out about?
   A relevant charges
   B what to do with their luggage
   C parking places

5 **Function:** What are the speakers trying to do?
   A settle an argument
   B come to a decision
   C express dissatisfaction

Tip! Questions can have different focuses. Being aware of some of these different focuses can give you a better understanding of spoken language.

2 **Why are the other options incorrect?**

Tip! There will usually be something in the recording that might distract you into choosing the wrong option, so make sure you listen carefully.

Test 1 Exam practice Listening Part 1

Action plan

1 Use the listening preparation time to read the questions and think about possible answers.
2 Underline key words in the question or statement.
3 Choose all the correct answers you can the first time you listen to the recording.
4 Do not worry about missing a question; leave it and listen for the answer to the next question.
5 Check your answers when you listen to the recording for the second time and answer any questions you have missed.
6 Do not leave any answers blank. Make a guess if you are not sure.
7 At the end of the test, carefully transfer your answers to the answer sheet.

1 03 **Follow the exam instructions, using the advice to help you.**

You will hear three different extracts. For questions **1–6**, choose the answer (**A**, **B** or **C**) which fits best according to what you hear. There are two questions for each extract.

Extract One

You hear two students discussing a lecture.

1 What surprised the woman about the lecture?

A the topic of the lecture
B the lecturer's approach to his subject
C the other students' reactions

2 What do the speakers agree?

A They would like to do some follow-up work.
B They should have prepared better for the lecture.
C The handouts they received will be very useful.

Advice

1 Listen to the whole recording before you answer either of the questions relating to it.

2 The word 'agree' is important in Question 2 – both speakers must share this opinion.

Extract Two

You hear two business people discussing a meeting they attended.

3 Why did they go to the meeting?

A to gain some information
B to influence a decision
C to offer some advice

4 How does the man feel about the meeting?

A satisfied with his contribution
B pleased with its outcome
C doubtful about its value

Advice

3 You get information from both speakers that will help you to answer Question 3.

4 Question 4 focuses on detail here. What do each of the other five Part 1 questions focus on – gist, relationship, opinion, function, etc.? Before you listen, think carefully about what each of the adjectives in the options means in this question.

Extract Three

You hear a scientist being interviewed about her career.

5 What is the woman's attitude to her career?

- **A** She regrets not achieving more than she has.
- **B** It has been the most important aspect of her life.
- **C** It turned out unexpectedly well for her.

6 What does the woman say is the most important quality she looks for in young scientists hoping to work in her lab?

- **A** curiosity about the world around them
- **B** ability to deal with setbacks in a positive way
- **C** appreciation of the need for accuracy

Advice

5 Before listening, think about what kind of language the speaker might use to express the ideas in Question 5.

6 Look carefully at the meaning of the three options. How might the woman use different words to express these ideas?

Follow-up

Did you follow all the steps in the Action plan?

Test 1 Training Listening Part 2

Task information

- Part 2 consists of a monologue (for example, a talk, a lecture or a broadcast) providing factual information and opinion.
- The recording will last approximately three minutes and is played twice.
- On the question paper, there are eight sentences about the recording, each with a gap.
- The sentences focus on specific information and stated opinions in the recording.
- You must complete the gap with an appropriate word or short phrase from the recording.
- Questions follow the order of information in the recording.
- You must spell the words correctly, although some minor variations are allowed in Part 2. UK and US spellings are both accepted.

Choosing the right answer

1 Look at this question from a Listening task.

The speaker's interest in playing music was first awakened by his ....

Write down six words that could complete the sentence.

Tip! Often you will hear several words that could fit the gap, but only one matches the meaning of the sentence.

2 Now look at the first part of the recording script. Which four words from the script *could* fill the gap in Exercise 1? Which of these words is actually the correct one? Why are the others not correct?

> I wanted to learn about music from a very young age. I think it all started when my father took me to stay with my grandmother one magical summer at the age of about six. My cousin was also there and she spent every evening practising the piano. I was spellbound by her playing and as soon as I got back home I pestered my parents to let me have lessons too. So they asked around and found me a teacher.

3 1 04 Look at the next two questions. Listen to the next part of the recording and note down the answers.

1 When he was eight years old, the speaker played a piece called .... in a school concert.

2 His piano teacher said that his performance at the concert was ....

4 1 04 Listen again and answer these questions.

1 Which words could be mistaken for the answer in each case?

2 Why are those words incorrect?

Test 1 Exam practice Listening Part 2

Action plan

1 Read the introduction and the title to help you understand the context and topic.
2 Use the preparation time to read the questions carefully before you listen.
3 Try to predict what sort of word is needed in each gap. For example, is it a noun? If so, is it singular or plural?
4 Remember that the answers will come in the order of the questions.
5 You will hear a word or phrase in the recording that matches something on the question paper. This will give you a clue that the answer is coming soon.
6 Remember that the answers are short – usually one to three words – and are often nouns.
7 You do not need to make any grammatical changes to what you hear.
8 Never leave a blank. Make a logical guess – you may be lucky.
9 At the end of the test, carefully transfer your answers to the answer sheet. As you transfer your answers, check your spelling and grammar and that what you have written makes sense.

1 05 **Follow the exam instructions, using the advice to help you.**

You will hear a musician called Anita Kumar talking to a group of students about her life.
For questions **7–14**, complete the sentences with a word or short phrase.

ANITA KUMAR

Anita plays the **(7)** .... in an orchestra.

Anita studied **(8)** .... at university.

Anita had a job as a **(9)** .... when she joined her first orchestra.

Anita's orchestra has just returned from a tour in **(10)** ....

Anita is particularly proud of the person who is the **(11)** .... in her orchestra.

What Anita enjoys most about playing in an orchestra is **(12)** ....

Her orchestra has recently appeared in a film called **(13)** ....

Anita says that the word **(14)** .... sums up her work best.

Advice

7 Anita names two instruments. Which is the correct one?

8 Two possible subjects are mentioned, but which is the one that Anita studied?

9 Do you need to write a word for a job or a place here?

10 Several countries are named. Make sure you listen carefully for the correct one.

11 The question makes it clear that you are listening for a person who has a specific role in an orchestra.

12 Two possible aspects of working for the orchestra are mentioned – remember that the question is asking about what Anita enjoys most.

13 Two films are named, but which is the one that has already been made?

14 Anita uses a number of adjectives, but which one fits the question?

Follow-up

Did you remember to check that the word(s) you wrote fitted grammatically and was/were spelt correctly?

Test 1 Training Listening Part 3

Task information

- Part 3 consists of a recording with two or more speakers (e.g. an interview or a discussion).
- The recording lasts approximately four minutes and is played twice.
- You have to answer six four-option multiple-choice questions about the recording.
- The questions focus mainly on the speakers' feelings, attitudes and opinions.
- Some questions will also focus on detailed or gist understanding of the recording.
- The questions follow the order of the recording.

Understanding distraction

1 Study the multiple-choice question and the extract from the recording script, and answer the two questions which follow.

1 What does Rose sometimes do nowadays instead of writing?

A She looks after her young children.
B She does a variety of paid jobs.
C She helps a family member in their business.
D She goes for walks.

Interviewer: Thanks for being my guest today, Rose! Tell us, when did you start writing for children?

Rose: I've been writing children's books since I was a child myself! Seriously, I was one of those kids always writing and illustrating stories, and this has been my passion for as long as I can remember. I was an English undergraduate at Middleton University – where my youngest started last term – and took the two children's literature courses offered at the time. I had a patchwork quilt of jobs after graduating and getting married, including working in a college office, writing for newspapers and magazines, helping out in an art gallery and selling a few watercolours of my own, working for a horse-riding for the disabled project, and teaching English part-time. With the publication of my first book in 2010, I began walking this path full-time, apart, that is, from the occasional day in my cousin's restaurant when she needs extra staff for some reason. And I hope that's the way I'll be able to continue.

1 What is the correct answer?
2 Why might you be distracted by the other options?

Tip! In multiple-choice questions, there will always be something in the recording that suggests each of the distracting options, but only one option will exactly match what the recording says.

Tip! Listen carefully to everything that the speaker says before choosing your answer. Aspects from each option may be mentioned, but only one will reflect exactly what is said and answer the question.

2 1 06 **Look at the next question and listen to the next part of the recording. Which is the correct option?**

What encouraged Rose to start working at the wildlife reserve?

A her lifelong interest in deer
B a friend's involvement in the project
C the need to research a writing project about deer
D a desire to work in the open air

3 1 06 **Listen again. Why might you be distracted by each of the other options?**

Test 1 Exam practice Listening Part 3

Action plan

1 Use the preparation time to read the questions carefully and think about possible answers.
2 Underline key words in the question or statement introducing the options to help you focus on what you have to listen for.
3 Choose all the correct answers you can the first time you listen to the recording.
4 Do not worry about missing a question: leave it and listen for the answer to the next question.
5 Check your answers when you listen to the recording the second time. Answer any questions you have missed.
6 Do not leave any answers blank. Make a guess if you are not sure.
7 At the end of the test, carefully transfer your answers to the answer sheet.

1 07 **Follow the exam instructions, using the advice to help you.**

You will hear part of a radio interview with a travel writer called Marina Vardy. For questions **15–20**, choose the answer (**A**, **B**, **C** or **D**) which fits best according to what you hear.

---

15 What made Marina start travelling?

A a sudden desire to overcome her fear of the sea
B a difficult problem in the life she had at the time
C an unexpected opportunity to escape a boring routine
D a friend's wish for a travelling companion

16 What is Marina's main reason for being happy about her decision to go on that first journey?

A It led to a successful career as an author.
B It gave her a more positive outlook on life.
C It offered her some exciting adventures.
D It taught her to cope with difficulties.

17 How did Marina first get into writing?

A She wanted to describe the different exotic places she visited.
B She found it satisfying to write her private feelings in a teenage diary.
C She enjoyed the reaction of others to something she wrote as a young girl.
D She was keen to be like her father, who was an enthusiastic writer.

18 What does Marina say is her greatest challenge?

A feeling uncertain about the quality of her work
B coping with some lack of support from her family
C having to face danger for the sake of a story
D finding things to write about that will interest her readers

Advice

15 *Listen to everything Marina says about why she started travelling and pick the option which exactly matches what she says.*

16 *All these ideas are suggested in the recording, but which does Marina actually say is the main reason why she feels no regrets?*

17 *Try reading the question and then listening to the recording before reading options A to D. Does this help you to find the right answer without being distracted?*

18 *Listen to everything Marina says about the challenges she faces and do not jump too quickly to conclusions.*

Tip! Remember that the questions follow the order of the recording.

See next page

19 Marina says that aspiring travel writers must ensure that they

A work hard to make their writing style as good as they can.
B try to make their readers experience strong emotions.
C offer much more than an account of their own adventures.
D keep their own grandmother in mind as they write.

20 What does Marina say she finds particularly rewarding about being a travel writer?

A It has developed her powers of observation.
B It offers her the chance to take revenge on unkind people.
C It provides her with an adventurous lifestyle.
D It gives her a satisfying psychological detachment.

Advice

19 *You may feel that Marina is implying several of the options, but you must go for the one that she actually says.*

20 *Think about the gist of what Marina is saying – which of these options conveys that idea?*

Follow-up

Did you find any of the distracting options particularly tempting?

Test 1 Training Listening Part 4

Task information

- Part 4 consists of a series of five short monologues, each lasting about 30 seconds.
- You will hear the recording twice.
- The monologues are all on a related topic.
- There are two parallel matching tasks relating to the monologues.
- Each task consists of five questions and you have to select the correct option from a set of eight.
- You have to choose the correct options to match with each monologue.
- The tasks focus on two different aspects of the monologues (for example, identifying what happened to the speaker and understanding why the speaker chose a particular course of action).
- You have to complete both tasks while you listen.
- The answers in each monologue can be in any order, for example, you might hear the answer to Task 2 before the answer to Task 1.

Finding the perfect match

Study the exam task. Then read the first part of the recording script below. Which are the two correct answers for Speaker 1? Which of the other options might some people be distracted by? Why are these options incorrect?

You will hear five short extracts in which people are talking about changing their jobs.

Tip! With each speaker, there will be one or two options that distract but are not the right answer. You must read the options very carefully to find the perfect match.

TASK ONE

Choose from the list (**A–G**) the job that each speaker used to do.

A teacher
B nurse
C photographer
D lawyer
E electrician
F journalist
G shop assistant

TASK TWO

Choose from the list (**A–G**) each speaker's reason for changing jobs.

A They were keen for more challenge.
B They disliked a colleague.
C They were offered more pay.
D They wanted to be with a spouse who had to move.
E They had the chance for an easier journey to work.
F They were keen to work part-time.
G They wanted more variety.

Speaker 1

Well, I stack shelves in a supermarket now, but until a few months ago I was a reporter on a local paper. It was a pretty good job. I spent most of my time going out with the paper's photographer interviewing an amazing variety of local people who'd done something special. My colleagues were interesting characters on the whole – I didn't care for one or two of them, but that's inevitable in any job. I worked long hours and the pay wasn't brilliant but I'd never have left if it hadn't been for my husband. He'd been teaching in the same primary school for years and he was keen to take on a more challenging post, so he went for a deputy headship. Much to his surprise, he got it, but it was in a town 200 miles away – too far for me to commute. Oh well, this isn't too bad a job really. The pay's better than you might imagine. I'm considering going part-time because I find it a bit difficult to be doing the same thing all day every day, but haven't come to a definite decision yet.

TASK ONE ....
TASK TWO ....

Test 1 Exam practice Listening Part 4

Action plan

1. Use the preparation time to read the instructions and options for both tasks very carefully.
2. Before you listen, think about words and phrases a speaker might use to express the ideas in the options in a different way.
3. As you listen to each speaker, try to answer the questions in both tasks.
4. If you cannot answer one of the questions on your first listening, do not worry. When you listen again, the answer may come more easily (as some answers will already be eliminated).
5. Remember that the answers to the tasks may come at the beginning, middle or end of what each speaker says.
6. The speaker is unlikely to use exactly the same words as the options, so listen for paraphrases.
7. At the end of the test, carefully transfer your answers to the answer sheet.

Follow the exam instructions, using the advice to help you.

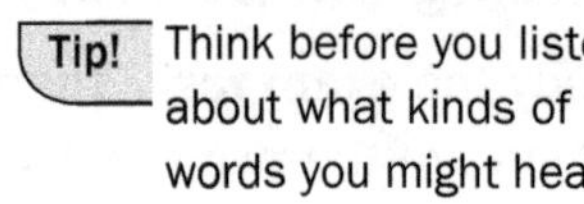

Think before you listen about what kinds of words you might hear in TASK ONE.

You will hear five short extracts in which people are talking about their jobs.

TASK ONE

For questions **21–25**, choose from the list (**A–H**) what made each speaker choose their career.

TASK TWO

For questions **26–30**, choose from the list (**A–H**) the difficulty each speaker has had to overcome.

While you listen you must complete both tasks.

A a wish to help others
B the influence of a family member
C a chance encounter
D a teacher's advice
E an inspirational book
F a desire to travel
G a gift for a specific academic skill
H an unusual skill

Speaker 1		21
Speaker 2		22
Speaker 3		23
Speaker 4		24
Speaker 5		25

A having to meet tight deadlines
B mastering some complex technology
C living far from work
D fierce competition
E combining work and study
F rapid turnover of staff
G obtaining finance
H a difficult working relationship

Speaker 1		26
Speaker 2		27
Speaker 3		28
Speaker 4		29
Speaker 5		30

Advice

21 The speaker mentions several different influences from the first list of options, but which one answers the question?

27 Remember that the answer to TASK TWO may sometimes come before the answer to TASK ONE.

30 The speaker here mentions several things that he has not had difficulty with in his current job. But which one ***is*** *a difficulty for him?*

Follow-up

How did you approach this question? Did you do TASK ONE on the first listening and TASK TWO on the second listening? Or did you do them both on both listenings? Some people prefer to do it one way and some the other – both approaches are acceptable.

Test 1 Training Speaking (15 minutes) Part 1

Task information

- Part 1 lasts about two minutes.
- You are with a partner for all parts of the Speaking test. Occasionally, candidates are in a group of three.
- There are two examiners. One is the interlocutor and he or she will ask you questions. The assessor completes the mark sheet while he or she listens to what you say.
- First, the interlocutor tells you the names of the examiners and takes your mark sheet.
- In Part 1, the interlocutor talks to you and your partner individually.
- You have to answer general questions about yourself (your life, your interests, your past experiences, your plans for the future, etc.).
- One aim of Part 1 is to help you to relax by asking you about topics that you are familiar with.

Understanding how your speaking is assessed

1 **The examiners who assess your speaking consider five criteria. Match the criteria (1–5) with their definitions (A–E).**

1 Grammatical resource
2 Vocabulary resource
3 Discourse management
4 Pronunciation
5 Interactive communication

A how easy it is to understand what you say, including how well you use stress and intonation
B how well you initiate and respond in conversations with the interlocutor and with your partner
C how accurately you use English structures and how wide a range of structures you use
D how coherently you speak by linking what you say and by not hesitating too much
E how appropriately you choose words to express your ideas and how wide a range of words you use

2 1 09 **Listen to these speakers. The first time you listen, decide which speaker in each pair is better, A or B. Put a tick (✓) in the table. The second time you listen, decide which of the criteria listed in Exercise 1 each pair illustrates. Write 1, 2, 3, 4 or 5. The first question has been done as an example.**

	Question 1	Question 2	Question 3	Question 4	Question 5
Speaker A	✓				
Speaker B					
Criterion	4				

3 **Here are some answers. What do you think the questions were? How could you improve the answers?**

1 Detective stories. I think they're very exciting.
2 I went to the cinema. Then I went home and went to bed at about 10.30.
3 I try not to eat too much and I do plenty of exercise.
4 I think I'll probably need to speak it both at work and when I'm travelling.

Tip! Where appropriate, try to include examples and reasons in your answers.

4 1 10 **Work with a partner if possible. Practise responding to the questions you hear on the recording. If you have a partner, comment on their answers using the five criteria in Exercise 1.**

Test 1 Exam practice Speaking Part 1

Action plan

1 Be polite and friendly to the examiners.
2 Try to relax – imagine you are talking to someone you know.
3 Listen carefully to the interlocutor and answer the questions that he or she asks you.
4 Look at the interlocutor when you are answering his or her questions.
5 If you do not understand something, politely ask for repetition, e.g. *I'm sorry, could you repeat that, please?*
6 Do not answer just *Yes* or *No*.
7 Remember, where possible, to give reasons and examples in your answers.
8 Do not learn prepared answers by heart – they will not make your English sound natural or fluent.
9 Listen to what your partner says and react if you wish to – but make sure you keep what you say brief until it is your turn to answer the interlocutor's questions.

Do the exam task, following the instructions below.

Part 1 2 minutes (3 minutes for groups of three)

It is not essential to be truthful in the exam if you do not know the vocabulary for a totally honest answer.

The interlocutor will ask you some questions about yourself, your home, work or studies and familiar topics.

Good morning/afternoon/evening. My name is ..... and this is my colleague ..... .
And your names are?
Can I have your mark sheets, please?
Thank you.

First of all, we'd like to know something about you.

- Where are you from?
- What do you do here/there?
- How long have you been studying English?
- What do you enjoy most about learning English?

Tip! Speak loudly and clearly so that both examiners can hear you.

The interlocutor will then ask you some questions about one or two other topics, for example:

- Do you think you have the right balance between work and relaxation in your life?
- If you could change one thing about the place where you live, what would it be?
- How important is it to have friends who share the same interests as you?
- What would you do if you suddenly won a lot of money?

Follow-up

How do you think you did in your practice of this part of the test?
How could you improve your performance in future?

Test 1 Training Speaking Part 2

Task information

- In Part 2, which lasts about four minutes, you have the opportunity to speak for a minute without interruption.
- The interlocutor will give you a set of three pictures and will ask you to comment on two of them.
- The interlocutor will ask you two questions relating to the pictures and these will also be written above the pictures.
- The questions will require you to speculate about the content of the pictures, rather than simply describe them.
- Your partner should not interrupt, but will be asked a question related to the pictures requiring a brief answer (for about 30 seconds) after you have finished speaking.
- Your partner will have to speak for a minute about a different set of pictures.
- You must listen to what your partner says and be ready to answer a question when the interlocutor asks you to do so.

Useful language: hypothesising

1 1 11 **Listen to a student talking about the first picture on page S1. Note down some of the language that he uses when he is hypothesising about how the people are feeling.**

2 **Look at the second picture on page S1, read the question and complete each sentence responding to the question. You can use the same ideas in your sentences if you wish.**

- What do you think the people in this picture are talking about?

1 I think they might be …
2 I wonder if they could be …
3 I think the man might have …
4 Perhaps the woman has …
5 I don't think that they can … because …
6 It's most likely that they …
7 But it could also be that …
8 I think it's quite possible that they …
9 They look as if they …
10 I imagine they must be …

Useful language: comparing and contrasting

1 **In Part 2, you have to compare two pictures on a related theme. Look at how some students do this. There is a mistake in what each student says. Correct the mistakes.**

1 In the first picture, everyone looks as if they're enjoying themselves. On contrast, in the other one, the people seem rather miserable.
2 The girls in this picture are working hard, whereby the girls in the other picture are simply having fun.
3 By or large, the people in the second picture seem more interested in what they're doing than the people in the first picture.
4 All for all, I think the people in the first picture are feeling more relaxed than those in the second picture.
5 In the whole, the children in this picture seem to be having a good time, but there is one little boy who is clearly not enjoying himself.
6 The people in this picture might be going on holiday. On another hand, they could simply be on their way to work.

2 **Now look at the two pictures on page S2. Talk about them for one minute using some of the expressions practised above. Talk about the different aspects of college life that they show and compare how the students might benefit from learning in the ways shown in each picture.**

Tip! It is useful to practise speaking for a minute. It is not as long as it seems at first!

Action plan

1 Listen carefully to the interlocutor's instructions.
2 Remember to answer the questions above the pictures, as well as comparing two of the pictures.
3 Answer the questions, giving examples and reasons where appropriate.
4 Remember that you must only talk about two of the pictures – not all three of them.
5 Do not waste time saying which pictures you are going to talk about – it will be obvious from what you say about them.
6 Speculate about what might be happening in the pictures (for example, how people might be feeling). This is much more important than describing the pictures in great detail.
7 Speak clearly and keep going until the interlocutor says 'thank you'.
8 Be ready to respond when the interlocutor asks you a question after your partner's turn.
9 Do not interrupt when your partner is speaking.

Do the exam task, following the instructions below.

Part 2 4 minutes (6 minutes for groups of three)

Work in groups of three if possible. One of you is the interlocutor and the other two are the candidates. The interlocutor should lead the task using the script below. Refer to the pictures on pages S3 and S4.

The interlocutor will give you three pictures and ask you to talk about two of them on your own for about a minute. You will then be asked a question about your partner's pictures which you will need to answer in no more than 30 seconds.

Interlocutor In this part of the test, I'm going to give each of you three pictures. I'd like you to talk about **two** of them on your own for about a minute, and also to answer a question briefly about your partner's pictures.

(*Candidate A*), it's your turn first. Here are your pictures. They show **people reading in different situations**.

I'd like you to compare **two** of the pictures and say **what you think the people are reading about and how important reading might be to the people in these situations**.

All right?

After 1 minute Thank you.

(*Candidate B*), **who do you think is most interested in what they're reading? (Why?)**

After approximately 30 seconds Thank you.

Now, (*Candidate B*), here are your pictures. They show **people travelling in different ways**.

I'd like you to compare **two** of the pictures and say **why the people might be making these journeys and what difficulties they might face in making their journeys**.

All right?

After 1 minute Thank you.

(*Candidate A*), **which type of journey do you think is most comfortable? (Why?)**

After approximately 30 seconds Thank you.

Follow-up

How easy did you find it to speak for a minute? What else could you have said about the topic?

Test 1 Training Speaking Part 3

Task information

- In Part 3, which lasts about four minutes, you and your partner have to discuss a task together.
- The interlocutor will give you a set of prompts and a question about them.
- The prompts will be either single words or phrases.
- The interlocutor will explain the task to you, for example, *First talk to each other about …* .
- You and your partner will be expected to discuss each of the prompts in relation to the question.
- The interlocutor will not take part in your discussion but, after a few minutes, will stop you and ask you another question where you have to make a decision related to the prompts. You will have one minute for this.
- There is no right or wrong answer to this task.
- You will be marked on your ability to use the language of negotiation and collaboration.
- You won't lose any marks if you do not come to a conclusion.

Useful language: negotiating

1 **The phrases below can be useful when negotiating with your partner in Part 3. In each case, a word is missing. What is it? You are given the first letter and a gap for each missing letter to help you.**

1 I can't *h* …… …… …… thinking that …
2 I e …… …… …… …… …… …… …… agree.
3 I take your *p* …… …… …… ……, but …
4 Isn't it more a *m* …… …… …… …… …… of …?
5 It's interesting you *s* …… …… …… …… …… say that because …
6 What you say reminds me *o* …… …
7 That's all very *w* …… …… ……, but …
8 *W* …… …… …… …… …… '…… you say so?
9 Yes, but we shouldn't *f* …… …… …… …… …… about …
10 You wouldn't disagree *w* …… …… …… that, would you?

2 **Look at the expressions in Exercise 1. Which of them are:**

a expressing agreement?
b expressing partial or complete disagreement?
c asking for someone's opinion?
d developing an idea someone has mentioned?

Giving yourself time to think

1 1 12 **It is useful to have some natural English phrases for when you need to give yourself time to think about what you want to say. Listen to two speakers talking about electric cars. Note down the expressions that they use to give themselves a bit of extra thinking time.**

2 **Work with a partner if possible and take it in turns to ask each other these difficult questions. Use some of the phrases from Exercise 1 as you work out how you want to answer the question.**

1 What would you say is the best film you've ever seen?
2 What would you do if you were the President of your country?
3 What do you think the international community should do about the problem of pollution?
4 What is the most important subject for children to study at school, in your opinion?

Test 1 Exam practice Speaking Part 3

Action plan

1 Listen to the instructions carefully.
2 Check the task question at the centre of the prompt phrases.
3 Look at your partner rather than the examiners when you are talking.
4 Speak clearly so the examiners can hear what you are saying.
5 Discuss one prompt fully with your partner – agreeing or disagreeing about it – before moving on to the next one.
6 Listen and respond to each other – do not just give your own opinion.
7 Use fillers like *Well, let me think* to give yourself a bit of thinking time.
8 Do not hurry to reach an agreement.
9 If appropriate, try to comment on the positive and negative aspects of each of the options.
10 Give reasons for your opinions.

Do the exam task, following the instructions below.

Part 3 4 minutes (6 minutes for groups of three)

Work in groups of three if possible. One of you is the interlocutor and the other two are the candidates. The interlocutor should lead the task using the script below. Refer to the task sheet on page S5.

The interlocutor will give you a task sheet to discuss together.

Interlocutor Now, I'd like you to talk about something together for about two minutes.

Here are some purposes for which a knowledge of foreign languages might be useful and a question for you to discuss. First you have some time to look at the task. (*About 15 seconds*)

Now, talk to each other about **how knowing a foreign language might be useful for each purpose**.

After 2 minutes Thank you. Now you have about a minute to decide **which purpose it is most important to know a language for**.

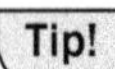
After 1 minute Thank you.

Tip! When you disagree with your partner, do so politely, e.g. *Yes, but I think there might be another way of looking at it* or *I know what you mean, but isn't it also true that …?*

Follow-up

If you worked with a partner, did you remember to really discuss the topic with each other – listening and responding to your partner rather than just stating individual opinions?

Test 1 Training Speaking Part 4

Task information

- Part 4 will continue the theme of Part 3 and lasts about five minutes.
- The interlocutor will ask you and your partner questions which broaden the topic of Part 3.
- Part 4 gives you the opportunity to give and justify your opinions, as well as to express agreement or disagreement with your partner.
- You might want to invite your partner's opinion or to comment on what your partner says.
- At the end of Part 4, the interlocutor will thank you and say the test has ended.

Useful language: giving your opinion

1 **Here are some useful phrases for giving an opinion. Fill in the missing words. In Questions 7–10, you are given letters at the beginning of the words.**

1 .... my opinion, schooldays are not always the happy time that adults often say they are.
2 .... I see it, society should look after its old people better.
3 .... my point of view, the government interferes too much in education.
4 As .... as I'm concerned, men aren't always better drivers than women.
5 The .... I see it, the first five years of a child's life have a huge impact on their adult life.
6 From .... I stand, the government should spend more on healthcare and less on defence.
7 To be *p*................................ honest, I don't think that current recycling measures are having much effect.
8 I'd *ar*................................ that everyone should be taught at least two foreign languages at school.
9 It's not something I have very *s*................................ views about, but I do rather feel that celebrities shouldn't complain so much about being followed by paparazzi.
10 I *t*................................ to agree with people who say students shouldn't have to pay fees.

2 **Work with a partner if possible. Take it in turns to read out the statements in Exercise 1. After each one, the other student should respond, saying either:**
- I agree. / I quite agree. / I agree 100 per cent, because …
- I don't agree. / I can't agree with you on that, because …
- I agree with you up to a point, but …

3 **Work with a partner if possible. Discuss the following topics using some of the expressions from the previous exercises.**
Childhood: In what ways do you think that people's characters are influenced by being an only child or the oldest, the middle or the youngest child in a family?
Do you think it's better for children to grow up in a town or in the countryside? Why?
Careers: What kinds of job do you think deserve the highest salaries and why?
In what ways do you think the current generation's working lives are likely to be different from those of their parents or grandparents?
Celebrity: Why do you think celebrity magazines and TV programmes about celebrities are so popular? What do you think would be the disadvantages of a celebrity lifestyle?

4 **Write down a possible discussion question relating to each of the following topics: Education; Leisure; Work; Relationships. If possible, work with two or three other students. Discuss the questions you have each thought of.**

Tip! If you have a partner, bring them into the discussion. After making a point, say *Do you agree?* or *What do you think?*

Test 1 Exam practice Speaking Part 4

Action plan

1 Listen carefully to the interlocutor's questions – they are not written down for you, unlike Parts 2 and 3.
2 You are marked on your English rather than your ideas, so do not feel you have to give original or particularly clever opinions.
3 If you do not have a particular opinion about the subject, remember that it is important – in the test – to say something (rather than nothing), so do not worry about expressing an opinion that is not exactly what you really think.
4 Listen carefully to what your partner says and, if possible, comment on or develop something he or she says.
5 If you disagree with your partner, do so politely.
6 At the end of the Speaking test, do not ask the examiners how you did – they are not allowed to tell you.
7 Say goodbye in a polite and friendly way as you leave the room.

Do the exam task, following the instructions below.

Part 4 5 minutes (8 minutes for groups of three)

Work in groups of three if possible. One of you is the interlocutor and the other two are the candidates. The interlocutor should lead the task using the script below.

The interlocutor will ask some general questions which follow on from the topic in Part 3.

Interlocutor

- Do you think it's better to know one foreign language really well or three or four less well? (Why?)
- Would the world be a better place if everyone spoke English? (Why? / Why not?)
- What do you find the most interesting aspect of learning another language? (Why?)
- What advice would you give to an English speaker who wanted to learn your first language? (Why?)
- How important do you think it is to study grammar when you're learning a language? (Why?)

Thank you. That is the end of the test.

Follow-up

How could you improve your performance in this part of the test?

Tip! Try to use some of the language practised on the previous page.

Reading and Use of English (1 hour 30 minutes) Part 1

Page 10 *Task information*

Review

Answer the questions about Reading and Use of English Part 1.

1 Before attempting any of the questions, what should you do first?
2 How can an awareness of collocations help you do well in Part 1?
3 How can a knowledge of prepositions help you do well in Part 1?
4 If you are not certain about any of the answers, is it worth guessing?

Useful language: checking for correct collocations

Tip! Sometimes it is useful to think about what word might go in a gap before you look at the alternatives offered.

1 **Exam candidates often make mistakes with certain words. Choose the correct alternative in *italics*.**

At the beginning of term, the attention of all students at this university is always **1** *called / drawn* to the fact that they must **2** *attend / join* at least three-quarters of the lectures for any course that they are **3** *following / taking* to be allowed to do the exam at the end of the course. And students already **4** *learn / know*, of course, that if they don't **5** *stand / sit* the exam, then this will affect their chances of **6** *achieving / reaching* their aim of **7** *having / getting* a good job. And this may in turn **8** *get / have* an enormous impact on the rest of their lives.

2 **Use your knowledge of collocations to fill these gaps with one word. The collocations in this exercise are ones that exam candidates often make errors with. In some cases, there is more than one possible answer.**

1 It sometimes takes time to .... friends when you go and live in a different country.
2 My cousins .... sailing most weekends.
3 Would you like to .... a fancy–dress party here at home for your birthday?
4 We must .... steps to avoid the problem occurring again in the future.
5 Unfortunately, the course Jim took last winter didn't really .... his needs.
6 I'm planning to .... some improvements to my coursework essay this weekend.
7 The village has a small cinema which .... a different film every week.
8 Look at the college map to .... out where the law library is.
9 The college offers a wide .... of language courses.
10 Thermodynamics is not my .... of expertise.

Useful language: thinking about prepositions

1 **Look at the preposition after the alternatives and choose the word in *italics* which fits best.**

1 I don't have much *knowledge / information* of local history.
2 My *stay / visit* to my grandparents' was a great success.
3 The new student didn't *participate / contribute* in the discussion.
4 When does your plane *get / arrive* to Rio?
5 Polly wrote to *congratulate / thank* the professor for his inspiring lecture.
6 My grandfather never *talks / discusses* about his life as a coal miner.
7 The article considers the *consequences / reasons* for the workers' strike.
8 I saw an *advertisement / article* for a language course in the paper.

2 **Now rewrite the sentences in Exercise 1 using the other word and changing the preposition, as required.**

Page 12 Action plan

Follow the exam instructions, using the advice to help you.

For questions **1–8**, read the text below and decide which answer (**A**, **B**, **C** or **D**) best fits each gap. There is an example at the beginning (**0**).

Mark your answers **on the separate answer sheet.**

Example:

0 **A** allows **B** lets **C** makes **D** gives

0	A	B	C	D
	▬	▭	▭	▭

A wearable book

Researchers at Massachusetts Institute of Technology have created a 'wearable' book which **(0)** .... the reader to experience the main character's emotions.

Using a combination of sensors, the book senses which page the reader is on and **(1)** .... vibration patterns through a special vest. The vest **(2)** .... a personal heating device to change skin temperature and a compression system to **(3)** .... tightness or loosening through airbags. The book itself has 150 LEDs to create ambient light which changes depending on the **(4)** .... and mood of different sections of the book.

The researchers used a science-fiction novella, *The Girl Who Was Plugged In* by James Tiptree Jr, as their prototype story for **(5)** .... the wearable book. They **(6)** .... it because it 'showcases' an incredible **(7)** .... of locations and emotions. The main protagonist experiences both deep love and ultimate despair, the freedom of Barcelona sunshine and the captivity of a dark, damp cellar. Volunteers who have tried the vest have **(8)** .... the experience as 'remarkable'.

1	**A** provokes	**B** impels	**C** originates	**D** triggers
2	**A** contains	**B** involves	**C** consists	**D** occupies
3	**A** realise	**B** convey	**C** pass	**D** construct
4	**A** setting	**B** position	**C** environment	**D** part
5	**A** enabling	**B** developing	**C** affecting	**D** imagining
6	**A** took	**B** kept	**C** picked	**D** got
7	**A** scale	**B** size	**C** amount	**D** range
8	**A** commented	**B** described	**C** called	**D** explained

Advice

1 The word you need is generally used either about the reaction of a mechanism or about the starting of something bad, e.g. violent behaviour.

2 Imagine what the vest looks like and it may become easier to choose the right word here.

3 Think about what the relationship is between the compression system, the airbags and the reader and it may become clearer which word you should choose.

4 One of these words has a much stronger association with books and films than the others.

5 Only one of these words can be associated with clothing – which one?

6 The word you need can be used as a synonym for 'chose'.

7 The sentence which follows helps to give the sense of the word you need here.

8 Only one of these words fits the grammar of the sentence.

Test 2 Training Reading and Use of English Part 2

Page 14 *Task information*

Review

Answer the questions about Reading and Use of English Part 2.

1 Is it a waste of time to read the whole text through before you start answering the questions?
2 Is it important to fill all the gaps in order?
3 What is the maximum number of words you may write in any one gap?
4 What kinds of word will you need to fill the gaps?
5 If you can think of two different ways of filling one gap, should you write both possibilities down?

Considering meaning and grammar

Tip! Consider both meaning and grammar when deciding which word to choose to fill a gap.

1 **Which of the words suggested fits the gap? Why is the other word not appropriate?**

1 When I got to the lecture theatre, it was already .... full. *much* or *very*?
2 The .... refurbished building is very attractive. *new* or *newly*?
3 It is important for students to eat .... *healthy* or *healthily*?
4 The weather was .... hot we could eat outside every evening. *so* or *too*?
5 The lecture programme was .... disappointing. *very* or *absolutely*?
6 I would like to suggest some changes .... the schedule. *in* or *to*?
7 Our room was on the fifth floor, but there was .... lift available. *no* or *not*?
8 We had to wait for three hours without .... for the children to do. *anything* or *nothing*?

2 **Think about meaning and grammar to decide what word should fill each gap.**

1 When I was a teenager, I .... always write my diary before I went to bed.
2 You may have to queue for tickets for .... couple of hours.
3 We got up early because we were afraid of .... our flight.
4 All the articles in the magazine were written .... talented young journalists.
5 I've only seen a photo of Joanna, ... may mean I don't recognise her when I go to meet her.
6 The noise from the wedding reception did not cause any problems .... the other hotel guests.
7 I can't understand .... Grace changed her mind so suddenly.
8 I hope that everyone who .... to go to the gig will be able to get a ticket.

Useful language: focusing on phrasal verbs

Choose the correct form of *do*, *make*, *go*, *get*, *put*, *take* or *bring* to fill the gaps in these sentences.

1 Chris didn't .... up golf until he retired.
2 My favourite group are .... out a new album next month.
3 Hannah has always .... on well with her colleagues.
4 We can easily .... you up if you'd rather not stay in a hotel.
5 Alan brought me some lovely flowers to .... up for missing my birthday.
6 I like both these dresses – I just can't decide which one to .... for.
7 I could .... with a new bike – this one's getting very old and rusty.
8 The robbers .... off with money and jewellery.
9 I'm so tired. Do you think I could .... out of going to Diana's this evening?
10 Are there any issues you would like to .... up at tomorrow's meeting?

Tip! When you listen to or read anything in English, try to notice phrasal verbs and how they are used. Being able to use them naturally will make your English sound much better.

Page 16 Action plan

Follow the exam instructions, using the advice to help you.

For questions **9–16**, read the text below and think of the word which best fits each gap. Use only **one** word in each gap. There is an example at the beginning (**0**).

Write your answers **IN CAPITAL LETTERS on the separate answer sheet.**

Example: | 0 | O R D E R |

Employing an intern

Interns are typically graduates who come to work in a business for a short time in **(0)** .... to gain experience. **(9)** .... done right, the arrangement can work well for both the intern and the business. So here's **(10)** .... to do it right.

Above all, you need to think carefully about what you want to gain from employing an intern. Your priority might be to create stronger ties **(11)** .... your local community, for example, or to provide a way of getting young ideas into the business – **(12)** .... it is, you need to have a clear vision from the outset.

Then you need to give careful thought **(13)** .... the recruitment process. **(14)** .... the fact that an intern may only be with you for a short time, they will still be privy to the innermost workings **(15)** .... your business, so you should take the time to choose carefully. You need to find someone **(16)** .... qualities match those you would look for in a permanent employee.

Advice

9 You need a conjunction here. There are two possibilities, but you must only write one of these.

10 You need a connector that conveys the idea of 'the way in which'.

11 The preposition you need here is often used with synonyms of 'ties' like 'connections', 'links' and 'associations'.

12 This is one word that means 'no matter what'.

13 Read the whole phrase, not just the previous word, before deciding which preposition you need here.

14 The word you need is part of a connecting phrase that has the same meaning as 'although'.

15 You are looking for the right preposition here.

16 Which relative pronoun would make this sentence hang together?

Test 2 Training Reading and Use of English Part 3

 *Task information*

Review

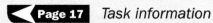

Answer the questions about Reading and Use of English Part 3.

1 Why is it better to read the whole text before you start trying to fill the gaps?
2 Is spelling important in this part of the exam?
3 What sorts of change do you usually have to make?
4 If you know that a noun is needed, what other things do you need to think about?

Useful language: spelling correctly

Tip! You need to spell the words you write correctly to gain the marks, so it is worth spending time learning the spellings of words that students typically find difficult.

1 **Find a word that matches the definition. You are given the first letter(s). The words are all ones that students frequently misspell.**

1 a place where you live *ac*............................
2 a group of people who take decisions *c*............................
3 try to reach a business or political agreement *n*............................
4 start (*noun*) *b*............................
5 relating to work that needs special education or training *p*............................
6 suitable *a*............................
7 the opposite of boring *i*............................
8 the way words are said *p*............................
9 essential *n*............................
10 get *r*............................

2 **Use the word in capitals to make a word which fits the gap. The words are all frequently misspelt.**

1 This kind of food is .... of the region. CHARACTER
2 Students .... write a dissertation in their final year. NORM
3 Helen was .... that she didn't get the job. APPOINT
4 The weather can be very .... at this time of year. CHANGE
5 I think Erica's sculptures are .... original. MARVEL
6 Sarah has done a course in .... administration. BUSY
7 It's .... that Patsy should behave so rudely. SHAME
8 The students' antics caused their college some .... EMBARRASS

Useful language: noting words from the same root

Fill the gap in each sentence with a word based on the word in capitals for that set.

Tip! Write down words formed from the same root in one place to help you remember them.

DEVELOP
1 There have been some interesting .... at work recently.
2 Paul has decided he would like to become a property ....
3 Although the north of the country is industrial, the south is relatively ....

INTERPRET
4 The argument was simply because Matilda totally .... something I said.
5 The rules are vague and open to .... in different ways.
6 Simultaneous .... earn a good salary, but their work can be stressful.

APPLY
7 The regulations are .... to anyone entering the country by sea.
8 Dave didn't get a university place in 2013, but he .... in 2014 and was accepted then.
9 How many job .... did you fill out before you eventually found work?

Page 20 Action plan

Follow the exam instructions, using the advice to help you.

For questions **17–24**, read the text below. Use the word given in capitals at the end of some of the lines to form a word that fits in the gap **in the same line**. There is an example at the beginning (**0**).

Mark your answers **on the separate answer sheet**.

Example: | **0** | I N C I D E N C E |

Exercise and happiness

There is evidence to show that regular exercise and sport are associated not only with physical fitness but also with a lower **(0)** .... of depression. Scientists have been conducting research to discover why people who exercise on a regular **(17)** .... frequently report that physical activity improves their mood, making them feel calmer and less **(18)** .... Explanations as to precisely why it is mood-enhancing differ, with some researchers arguing that exercise may be acting as a **(19)** .... from negative thoughts, while others claim that it is developing a **(20)** .... of a new skill that is the most **(21)** .... factor.

INCIDENT (0)
BASE (17)
APPREHEND (18)
DIVERT (19)
MASTER (20)
SIGNIFY (21)

In addition, it is **(22)** .... true that the social contact which participation in sporting activities often involves also plays its part in mood enhancement. **DENY**

Whatever the reasons may be why **(23)** .... activity should have such a powerful effect on how people feel, it has been shown that exercise is as potent as any medication against **(24)** ....

VIGOUR (23)
DEPRESS (24)

Advice

17 *What part of speech is required here?*

18 *If you are not sure what the adjective form of 'apprehend' is, perhaps you know the adjective form of 'comprehend' and this may help you.*

19 *Remember that the final consonant of a word sometimes changes when the word becomes another part of speech.*

20 *There are two possible abstract nouns with this root – 'masterfulness' and 'mastery' – but which fits the meaning here?*

21 *Do you need a positive or a negative word here?*

22 *Do you need a prefix here or not?*

23 *Remember also the spelling change that occurs in the middle of this word when you add the adjective suffix.*

24 *Thinking about the noun forms of other words ending in '-press' (e.g. 'impress', 'suppress', 'compress') may help you to find the right form here.*

Page 21 Task information

Review

Answer the questions about Reading and Use of English Part 4.

1 What is the maximum number of words you can write in Part 4?
2 How many words do contractions like *don't* or *wasn't* count as?
3 Can you change the form of the word in capitals?
4 How many marks are there for each sentence?

Useful language: choosing the right expression

1 **Choose the correct expression in italics from these sentences written by exam candidates.**

1 The linguistics lecture last night *resulted in / turned out* to be disappointing.
2 I would like you to publish *an apology letter / a letter of apology* in the next issue of your magazine.
3 They offered Margot *the opportunity / the possibility* to work in Rome.
4 I hope you had no difficulty *to find / finding* your way here.
5 I'll *leave / let* you details of my trip when I set off.
6 I wouldn't recommend *going / to go* to that conference.
7 She took pride in *cleaning and decorate / cleaning and decorating* her new flat.
8 No one knows for sure *where he found / where did he find* the information.

Tip! This exercise requires accurate use of grammar and vocabulary. It can be useful to focus on errors that students at this level often make so that you avoid similar mistakes.

2 **Complete the second sentence so that it has a similar meaning to the first sentence, using the word given. Do not change the word given. You must use between three and six words, including the word given.**

1 Please don't forget to take your projects home after school today.
LEAVE
I must remind you .... school today.

2 Betsy was more likeable than expected.
TURNED
Betsy .... likeable.

3 It was easy to find the information I needed.
DIFFICULTY
I .... hold of the information I needed.

4 Where did Lisa go today, I wonder?
KNOW
I'd love .... today.

5 I thought it was an excellent restaurant for a meal.
RECOMMEND
I .... at that restaurant.

6 It was such a noisy party that Sven apologised to his neighbours in writing.
APOLOGY
Sven wrote his neighbours .... such a noise at the party.

7 University was not an option for women in the eighteenth century.
OPPORTUNITY
Women did .... to university in the eighteenth century.

Tip! Improve your accuracy by paying careful attention to corrections your teacher makes to your written work and try to use the same language correctly in your next piece of writing.

Page 22 Action plan

Follow the exam instructions, using the advice to help you.

For questions **25–30**, complete the second sentence so that it has a similar meaning to the first sentence, using the word given. **Do not change the word given**. You must use between **three** and **six** words, including the word given. Here is an example (**0**).

Example:

0 Milly burst out laughing when she saw herself in the mirror.

SIGHT

Milly burst into .... herself in the mirror.

The gap can be filled with the words 'laughter when she caught sight of', so you write:

Example: | **0** | LAUGHTER WHEN SHE CAUGHT SIGHT OF |

Write **only** the missing words **IN CAPITAL LETTERS on the separate answer sheet**.

---

25 They all assume that James will be willing to work late.

GRANTED

Everyone .... that James will be willing to work late.

26 As far as I'm concerned, this is the best college to study at.

RATHER

There .... study at than this one.

27 You need to make up your mind about the topic for your dissertation soon.

COME

You must .... about the topic for your dissertation soon.

28 Given that Sarah hasn't contacted us, I think she probably caught her flight.

MISSED

If Sarah .... have been in touch with us.

29 My boss said I should do some work on my French so I could take part in meetings.

BRUSH

My boss encouraged .... so I could take part in meetings.

30 Tina said she was pleased I had let her know what was going on.

PICTURE

Tina thanked me .... about what was going on.

Advice

__25__ Does 'everyone' need a singular or a plural verb?

__26__ Which auxiliary or modal verb is used with 'rather' to mean 'prefer'?

__27__ Which verb + preposition collocates with 'a decision' and means 'decide'?

__28__ Think about the meaning of both sentences – do you need to talk about Sarah catching or missing the plane in the second sentence?

__29__ 'Encourage' takes the same structure as several other verbs relating to how people affect what others do, e.g. 'want', 'tell', 'ask', 'persuade'.

__30__ Which idiom with 'picture' has the meaning of 'keep someone informed'?

Page 24 Task information

Page 26 Action plan

Review

Tick (✓) the pieces of advice which you think are good tips for Reading and Use of English Part 5.

1 Read the text carefully before looking at the questions.
2 Read the questions carefully and make sure you choose the answer that matches the question.
3 When answering a question, find the relevant bit of text and read it again very carefully.
4 Do not expect to understand every word in the text.
5 You can often work out the meaning of unfamiliar words and expressions from the context.
6 Do all the questions you can first, then go back and look again at the harder ones.
7 Do not leave any questions out – if you are not sure of the answer, pick the one that seems most likely.

Follow the exam instructions, using the advice to help you.

You are going to read an article from a magazine written by a man who teaches survival skills. For questions **31–36**, choose the answer (**A**, **B**, **C** or **D**) which you think fits best according to the text.

Mark your answers **on the separate answer sheet**.

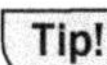

Help yourself prepare for the Reading and Use of English paper by reading a variety of types of text in English.

Remember that many words in English have a number of different meanings. If something does not seem to make sense in its context, consider whether it might have a different meaning.

The importance of fire

We share our lives on this incredible planet with many other creatures, each of which has its own special trait or survival skill, a characteristic attribute by which it can be defined. Our special trick gives us the impression that we are in some way elevated above other animals, but of course we are not; it is important to remember that we are mammals, upright walking creatures, descended from an ancient line of apes believed to have originated in Africa. With a free thumb, we have the ability to fashion tools easily. It is believed that we have been making tools for more than 2.5 million years. Yet that does not define us. Other animals can make tools, too: sea otters use stones to break open oyster shells, and other primates even fashion weaponry for hunting.

What I believe defines us as human is our mastery of fire. Before we assume that we are the only *users* of fire in nature, we should think again. Just last year I watched hawks in Australia pick up burning sticks from a bushfire and drop them to spread the fire, flushing out or scorching potential prey. But no other creature has been found who can make fire at will.

In the world of archaeology, the earliest sign of human control of fire is a hotly debated topic, with few definite remains surviving from such antiquity. However, evidence appears to show fire hearths dating from one million years ago. It is reasonable to assume that fire was originally obtained from natural sources such as bushfires, which could then be kept burning.

Fire altered humankind's potential for ever. Now, we wielded a tool powerful enough to keep even the most ferocious early Palaeolithic predators at bay; the fear of nocturnal dangers was dispelled; and the fire became a focus for life, around which our forebears could gather in good cheer. (That sight is still played out nightly in the villages of the San Bushmen of the Kalahari.) In the flames and coals of their fires, our ancestors learned to alter their food, to improve its flavour, to neutralise plant toxins and destroy harmful bacteria. Consequently, our dietary range grew and diversified. It has been argued that our 'fire-improved' diet may well have been a catalyst for the development of our large brain.

Until fire was harnessed, the length of the day was determined by sunlight; firelight extended the working day, made time available to communicate, to share ideas and be creative. In the sign language of Native Americans, the concept of meeting for a talk is defined by coming to a fire and sharing ideas, and even today the footlights of our theatres mimic the flickering light of a fire on the face of an ancestral storyteller. We don't have to have been there to realise that the question of how to make fire from scratch would have occupied the minds gathered at the campfire. If I could travel back in time, I would hope to witness the first of our ancestors achieving this remarkable skill. The consequences of that first ember were astonishing. No modern invention comes close in importance to the creation of the first fire. For more than 30 years, I have been teaching students how to make fire, by every primitive means known. Although we will never know which was the first method of fire-lighting, some things never change. Each time a student succeeds in friction fire-lighting, their face lights up with a huge sense of achievement. Like an ancient ritual, the drama of the first fire is relived.

Being able to make fire at will brings confidence. Our ancestors were able to spread out, exploring their landscape in smaller foraging parties with fire for safety and with smoke to locate each other again. (I have witnessed Aboriginals in Australia's Arnhem Land watching for smoke across flooded swamps to track the movements of family members.) Now, even colder landscapes posed little obstacle as our ancestors migrated across the planet, perhaps clinging to the unexplored coastline or following seasonal migrations of game inland. The fireside became our most important laboratory. Here, as we stared into the flames, we observed the way fire could transform materials. We learnt to harden the points of wooden spears, to soften thermoplastic tree resins and use them as adhesives. Here, too, we would discover that clay could be hardened into pottery. The process of scientific investigation was reinforced along the way through observation, hypothesis and experimentation. Inevitably, we discovered metal and the rest is history. Everything flows from here, from the clothes we wear to the incredible devices contained in our pockets and the means by which my words reach you now. All this derives from our mastery of fire.

31 What is the main point the writer is making about the human ability to make tools?

A It is only possible because of the way the human hand is structured.
B It is important but not the unique talent that it is sometimes considered to be.
C It is one of the characteristics that sets people apart from most other creatures.
D It has allowed human beings to develop the way of life that they have.

32 What impressed the writer about the hawks he observed in Australia?

A They were not afraid of fire.
B They seemed to be cooking their prey.
C They were able to start a fire.
D They took advantage of a bushfire.

33 The writer says that archaeologists investigating people's relationship with fire

A have proved that humans have sat round fires for at least a million years.
B disagree about exactly when and how people began to master fire.
C have found evidence to show people first took fire from fires occurring in nature.
D are still searching for remains to support their theories about the control of fire.

34 According to the text, the San Bushmen of the Kalahari

A continue to gather around a fire every evening.
B still cook their food on an open fire in their villages.
C live in the same way as many generations of their ancestors.
D use fire to destroy harmful elements in their food.

35 What does the writer say he would like to have experienced?

A the very first stories that were told around a fire
B the discussions that led to people being able to make fire
C the original creation of fire by human hand
D the way the discovery of fire transformed life for ancient peoples

36 The writer says that being able to light a fire whenever you wished brought confidence because

A it stopped people fearing the cold.
B it led to the discovery of metal.
C it started a scientific revolution.
D it enabled safer travel.

Advice

31 *If a question asks about the main point or the main reason, then the text is likely to mention several points or reasons, but one will be identifiably more significant than the others.*

32 *Think carefully about not only what the writer saw but also about what impressed him.*

33 *Notice the extent of the evidence and proof that archaeologists have uncovered.*

34 *The information in parenthesis about the Bushmen is referring back in the paragraph rather than forward.*

35 *The expression 'from scratch' in the relevant section of text means 'from the very beginning', i.e. without making use of naturally starting bushfires.*

36 *The sentence that follows the one about confidence expands on the idea, explaining why increased confidence was a result of the discovery of how to start a fire whenever one was needed.*

Test 2 Exam practice Reading and Use of English Part 6

Page 29 *Task information*

Page 31 *Action plan*

Review

Answer the questions about Reading and Use of English Part 6.

1 What is the connection between the four texts?
2 There are four questions. Does that mean that there will always be one A, one B, one C and one D answer?
3 Will you find the answer to each question by looking at just one of the texts?
4 Is it better to read the questions or the texts first?

Follow the exam instructions, using the advice to help you.

You are going to read extracts from articles in which four writers give their opinions on the relationship between the study of literature and job prospects. For questions **37–40**, choose from the extracts **A–D**. The extracts may be chosen more than once.

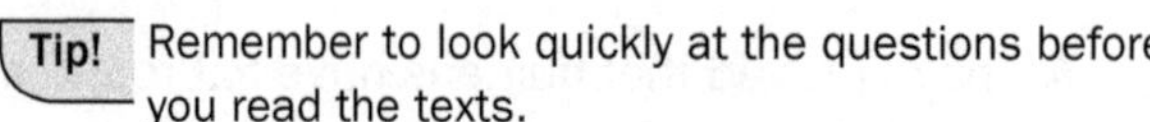
Tip! Remember to look quickly at the questions before you read the texts.

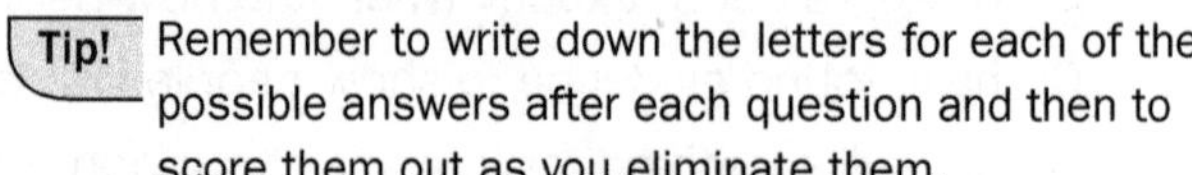
Tip! Remember to write down the letters for each of the possible answers after each question and then to score them out as you eliminate them.

Mark your answers **on the separate answer sheet.**

The relationship between the study of literature and job prospects

A

Most of the lecturers from university literature departments interviewed in our survey said their aim is to provide an education for its own sake rather than to focus on any skill likely to be required in the workplace. However, they also believed that what they were teaching would stand students in good stead in their future employment. Their main argument was that appreciation of writing style makes students more effective employees when they join the workforce. Yet, curiously, none of the lecturers reported actually stressing that point in their classes. As a result, few students ever considered mentioning this skill when it came to applying for work. Had they done so, provided that their claims were reinforced by a well-written application, they might have found it more straightforward to acquire a position.

B

Literature students are often concerned about the utilitarian value of what they are doing. This is understandable, but it is misguided. It is undoubtedly true that few jobs will require an employee to discuss a poem's rhyme scheme or to consider the influence of one 19th-century novelist on another. But life is about more than simply one's employment prospects. Literature teaches us about ourselves and other people and why we behave as we do. It encourages us not just to read, but to reflect on what we have read, and this makes us much more rounded people. It achieves this by helping us to examine our assumptions and the ways in which we relate to the world. The lessons of literature have a profound impact on our minds and souls, and surely this is as significant as any of the practical skills whose importance no one questions.

C

When students are worried about the job market, when they perceive an urgent need for job skills and training, how do I argue for the value of the study of literature and the humanities more broadly? Well, I do what any judicious participant in the neoliberal university does: I tell them that the study of literature will make them entrepreneurial. It will make them attractive to employers because they will be adaptable and flexible. They will have good critical-thinking skills and be better writers than most of the people competing for those same positions. They will be able to manipulate and manage a wide range of information. They will become comfortable with ambiguity. They will learn empathy, which will help them deal with people from a wide range of backgrounds. They will become creative problem-solvers, which is so crucial in the 21st-century knowledge economy.

D

The pragmatic English literature student will consider doing a combined degree course. Studying English with another subject, such as psychology or Spanish, will bring enormous benefits in terms of employability. Such graduates will develop a wider range of skills, and far more employers will be prepared to consider their applications. It is also the case that an unusual proportion of joint honours graduates end up in managerial positions. This may be because such students have shown themselves capable of multi-tasking and of coping with an exceptionally heavy workload. The choice of which subject to combine with English is, of course, not unimportant. One with a more transparently practical element is advisable; thus, a foreign language or psychology may prove more sensible choice than, say, history.

Tip! If you find one question difficult, leave it and do the other ones – as you do those, you may notice clues that help you with the harder question.

Which expert

shares expert B's opinion on the relationship between studying literature and understanding human psychology?	**37**	
has a different opinion from the other experts on whether a literature degree will help with employment prospects?	**38**	
shares expert A's view on the need for students to be aware of the skills they are gaining?	**39**	
shares expert C's view on the way in which literature develops thinking skills?	**40**	

Advice

37 *Underline what expert B says on this topic and then look for a parallel idea in one of the other texts.*

38 *The first sentence of A may make you want to jump to the conclusion that this expert does not see the value of literature studies from an employer's point of view, but read to the end of the text to check that this is really the case.*

39 *Mark the part of the text in which expert A comments on student awareness and what the general point that he is making is.*

40 *All the other texts refer to 'skill' or 'skills', but which does so in relation to the development of thinking skills?*

Follow-up

Which of the tips did you follow when you did this task?

Test 2 Exam practice Reading and Use of English Part 7

Page 33 *Task information*

Page 35 *Action plan*

Review

1 Put these stages for dealing with Reading and Use of English Part 7 in order (1–6).

A Look before and after the gaps for clues as to what must fill the gap.
B Work through the remaining gaps in turn, checking which of the remaining options fits each one.
C Look at the title to see what the text is going to be about.
D Read through the whole text with the paragraphs you have chosen in place – does it all make sense?
E Read through the text (but not the options) to get an idea of the structure of the text.
F Read through the options. Are there any paragraphs that you can immediately place?

2 What goes before and after?

Go through the exam practice text below and on the following page and underline any words or phrases in both the text and the options (A–G) that seem to refer to something outside that paragraph.

Follow the exam instructions, using the advice to help you.

You are going to read an extract from a magazine article. Six paragraphs have been removed from the extract. Choose from the paragraphs **A–G** the one which fits each gap (**41–46**). There is one extra paragraph which you do not need to use.

Looking immediately before and after the gap will help you to work out what you need to find in the missing text.

Mark your answers **on the separate answer sheet.**

Yukon: Canada's Wild West

A modern-day minerals rush threatens one of North America's last great wildernesses

Shawn Ryan recalls the hungry years, before his first big strike. The prospector and his family were living in the Yukon, in a metal shack on the outskirts of Dawson, the Klondike boomtown that had declined to a ghostly remnant of its glory days. They had less than $300 and no running water or electricity. One night, as wind sneaked through gaps in the walls, Ryan's wife, Cathy Wood, worried aloud that they and their two children might even freeze to death.

41 ______

The minerals rush has reanimated Dawson's bars and hostels, whose facades glow in pastel hues during midsummer's late-night sunset. The scene could be from more than a century ago, with bearded men bustling along wooden sidewalks and muddy streets, stopping to chat and trade rumors of the latest strikes and price spikes.

42 ______

It's well worth that investment in technology and people. The claim-staking boom may have cooled since the price of gold has stabilized, but an ongoing high demand for minerals and the Yukon's industry-friendly regulations continue to attract mining companies from as far away as China. Shawn Ryan's business is as successful as any of them.

43 ______

In his small office, radios and bear-spray canisters surround a trio of computer screens atop a plywood table. A self-taught geologist, Ryan uses the left-hand screen to

Advice

41 What is the situation in the first paragraph of the text? Which paragraph takes that situation a little further?

42 What does the sentence that follows this gap suggest about what has just preceded it?

43 Look at the sentence just before and the sentence just after this gap – what do they tell you about what might be in the missing paragraph here?

display the colored maps he generates from his ever-growing database of soil samples, looking for anomalies that might betray a hidden body of precious ore. On the center screen, a blue grid overlays a map of the Yukon, showing the claims he currently owns; since 1996, he and his crews have staked more than 55,000 claims, enough to cover a landmass larger than Jamaica. Ryan uses the right-side screen to track his gold-related holdings, which notch up in value whenever an economic jolt sends investors fleeing to precious metals.

44	

Trish Hume, for example, has expressed concern. Though she is involved in mapping work that's mining related, she worries that the Yukon is reaching a tipping point where the environmental and cultural costs of mining outweigh the benefits. "The people coming up and taking out minerals aren't asking what happens to the animals we hunt, the fish we eat, the topsoil that holds it all together. And when the boom is over, how does our tiny population afford to clean up the toxic mess?" The population is small, but the area of the Yukon is enormous.

45	

Walled off by some of the country's highest peaks and largest glaciers, the territory is almost completely unsettled, its sparse population scattered over a few small communities and the capital, Whitehorse. It is also rich in wildlife, an Arctic safari park whose extreme seasonal shifts beckon vast herds of caribou and other animals into motion.

46	

It is crucial that such a remarkable environment, as this clearly is, is not lost for ever, destroyed by the businesses anxious to exploit its mineral wealth for their own ends.

Advice

***44** What does 'for example' suggest about what the writer has just mentioned?*

***45** Can you find anything in any of paragraphs A–G which connects with the tiny population and the enormous area referred to at the end of the paragraph preceding gap 45?*

***46** What does the phrase 'as this clearly is' tell you about what must have been in the previous paragraph?*

A It is even larger than the state of California, but with only 37,000 inhabitants, it drives an immense wedge between Alaska and the bulk of Canada. From its north coast, the Yukon stretches to the south and south-east, taking in tremendous expanses of lake-dotted tundra, forests, mountains, wetlands, and river systems.

B At his expanding compound at the edge of town, helicopters thump overhead, fetching GPS-equipped prospectors to and from remote mountain ridges. Ryan is 50 years old, but he radiates the eagerness and intensity of a much younger man. "This is the biggest geochemical exploration project on the planet right now," he says, his grin revealing a couple of missing upper teeth, "and maybe in history."

C Today, the couple could buy—and heat—just about any house on Earth. Ryan's discovery of what would eventually amount to billions of dollars' worth of buried treasure has helped reinfect the Yukon with gold fever, and fortune seekers have stormed the Canadian territory in numbers not seen since the 1890s.

D In contrast, the Yukon's early inhabitants hunted bison, elk, caribou, woolly mammoths, waterfowl, and fish, and they competed for resources with carnivores such as wolves and Beringian lions. Due to climate warming and other factors, some of these animals died off. But others, such as the barren-ground caribou, thrived in such numbers that native peoples adapted their own movements and lifestyles to the animals' migrations.

E Such creatures are especially to be found in the Peel watershed, an immense wilderness which drains an area larger than Scotland. "The Peel watershed is one of the few places left where you still have large, intact predator-prey ecosystems," says a representative of the Yukon Conservation Society. "From wolves and grizzlies and eagles on down, it's a wildlife habitat of global importance."

F As the material needs of the world's seven billion people continue to grow, the rush to exploit the Yukon's exceptionally rich resources—gold, zinc, copper, and more—has brought prosperity to a once forsaken corner of the continent. But the boom has brought to the fore a growing tension between those who would keep one of North America's last great wildernesses unbroken and those whose success depends on digging it up.

G But in other ways, things are different now. During the first Klondike stampede, prospectors plied nearby creeks with picks and pans and shovels, and a bartender could sweep up a small fortune in spilled gold dust at the end of a big night. Nowadays, mining's heavy lifting is done by a mechanized army of bulldozers, drilling rigs, and flown-in workers.

Page 38 Task information

Page 40 Action plan

Review

Which of these pieces of advice are good ones for Reading and Use of English Part 8?

1 Read the questions before you read the texts.
2 Read the texts before you read the questions.
3 Read one text and find all the questions associated with that text before moving on to the next text.
4 As you read the questions, think about other words that might be used to express the same idea.
5 Skim the texts first when trying to find an answer, then check you have found the right answer by reading the text in more detail.

Follow the exam instructions, using the advice to help you.

You are going to read an article about taking up running. For questions **47–56**, choose from the sections of the article (**A–D**). The sections may be chosen more than once.

Mark your answers **on the separate answer sheet**.

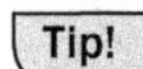

Tip! Read the questions first so you know what to look out for as you read the texts.

In which section does the writer

explain why a friend's idea not to do something alone turned out to be a good one?	47	
comment on how she helped herself to overcome a psychological barrier?	48	
describe what she did to prepare herself physically immediately prior to an event?	49	
explain why running is an appropriate activity for her?	50	
mention how she solved a physical problem?	51	
suggest that something was less daunting than she had anticipated?	52	
mention receiving some useful pieces of advice?	53	
say why running is good for your physical wellbeing?	54	
comment on how an unexpected situation had a negative effect on her?	55	
reflect on when she realised her initial attitude to running had changed?	56	

Advice

47 What was the friend's idea and where do we learn about how it turned out in practice?

48 What is often a psychological barrier that prevents people from keeping up a sport?

49 What is another way of saying 'immediately prior to'?

50 In which part of the text does the writer refer to her own circumstances, and in which part does she also talk about the benefits of running?

51 What part of the body are runners particularly likely to have a problem with?

52 If you find something 'daunting', how do you feel?

53 What other words might be used instead of 'useful pieces of advice'?

54 Which part of the body is running said to be particularly good for?

55 If something has a negative effect on you, how might it make you feel?

56 What does the writer say about her attitude towards running at the beginning of the text – and which later part of the article refers back to this?

I want to become a runner

A

Last year, it began to hit me that I needed to start taking my fitness more seriously. I'd been doing yoga, but it wasn't giving me a cardiovascular workout, and as a sports journalist, I know how important aerobic activity is for heart health.

I'm self-employed with unpredictable working hours, so running seemed a good option. It's free and easy to fit into your life, as you can do it any time, and pretty much anywhere. Unfortunately, I've always found it very dull. A friend suggested I get past this by running with a club, so I signed up for a beginners' course with a club near my home. I strapped on some old trainers and turned up for my first session feeling apprehensive that I wouldn't be able to keep up. But we took it slowly, jogging or walking until we were able to build up to running for 15 minutes. In between the weekly classes, I tried to do one or two runs on my own.

B

I knew I'd begun to overcome my boredom barrier when I spent 20 minutes jogging in the park on a beautiful summer evening without thinking about when I could stop. The club definitely helped. It's more fun and it isn't as easy to give up. I also picked up some useful tips. The group leader stressed the importance of pacing to maintain energy for the end of a run, and I learnt to focus on pushing out my breath when I felt tired, to help me run more efficiently and in a more relaxed way.

After the first few weeks, I noticed my knees were aching a little, so I went to a specialist running shop and got fitted for shoes to suit my gait – I over-pronate, meaning my foot rolls inwards. The other must-have for me was a running jacket to keep out the wind and chill – essential, as I feel the cold and could easily be deterred by bad weather.

C

The final session of the running course was a 5km, race, and suddenly I turned competitive. To my surprise, I had become one of the faster runners in the group, so I was nurturing an ambition to win. I made sure I ate well that day, avoiding anything too heavy and drinking plenty of water, with a flapjack two hours beforehand to keep me going. Sadly, two other women streaked ahead of me, but I came in third with a pretty respectable time of 30 minutes 53 seconds. The end of the course coincided with a change in my working circumstances, which meant I could no longer go to the club. I tried to continue on my own, but found it hard to motivate myself.

D

My solution to this problem was to set myself a goal. I signed up for a 10km event and told friends and family about it, which put pressure on me, in a good way, to train. I began to fit running into my life, for example, running part of the way home from work, about 6km, every week. On race day, I began to feel nervous as, to my alarm, it turned out to be a proper event, with lots of people from running clubs coming with the intention of getting good times. However, I hadn't really allowed enough time to train, so was worried about getting round the course. The first part was uphill, so I struggled at around the 4km mark and had to slow down to a walk for a few minutes. But other than that, I kept going and even enjoyed some of it. I finished in one hour and 13 minutes, not too embarrassing, but my next goal is to run 10km in around an hour.

Writing (1 hour 30 minutes) Part 1

Page 42 *Task information*

Review

Correct these statements about Writing Part 1.

1 In Part 1, you have a choice of task.
2 You usually have to write a letter.
3 You have to write 250 words.
4 You can choose which information you use from the text on the question paper.
5 It is important to copy phrases carefully from the text on the question paper.

Reading the question

Read the task below, then answer these questions about it.

1 What is the aim of the essay?
2 Which two points will you choose to focus on?
3 What examples could you include for each point?
4 Which of your two chosen points will you say is more effective, and what reason will you give for this?

1 Your class has listened to a panel discussion about how schools can best prepare young people for their future working lives. You have made the notes below:

<u>Strategies aimed at preparing young people for their future working lives</u>

- teaching practical skills
- providing information about jobs
- establishing links with local community

Some opinions expressed in the discussion:

"Schools should spend more time teaching practical things like car mechanics, cooking, computer programming, etc."

"Young people need to know about a wide range of possible jobs."

"Kids should have the opportunity to get work experience in local workplaces."

Write an essay discussing **two** of the strategies in your notes. You should **explain which strategy is most likely to be effective, giving reasons** in support of your answer.

You may, if you wish, make use of the opinions expressed in the discussion, but you should use your own words as far as possible.

Useful language: showing a range of vocabulary

1 Read and answer the questions.

1 What other examples of practical skills could you use – to avoid just lifting language from the task?
2 Can you think of at least three other ways of saying 'provide information about jobs'?
3 What examples could you give to illustrate what 'get work experience' might mean in practice?
4 What other words could you use to avoid saying 'young people' all the time?
5 What other words could you use to avoid saying 'work' all the time?

Tip! The Part 1 task is likely to involve four paragraphs:

1 Introduction
2 Expansion of one bullet point
3 Expansion of a second bullet point
4 Explanation of which of these two points is more important

2 Below is a sample answer for the task. Read it and answer the questions.

1 Is the answer in the typical essay format?
2 Would the writing be likely to have a positive impact on the teacher as target reader?
3 Does it deal with two of the three bullet points in the task?
4 Does it expand each of these points in a coherent way?
5 Has the writer put any opinions presented in the task into their own words?
6 Does the writer say which of the two selected points is more important, giving at least one reason to support their opinion?
7 Can you find any examples of language that demonstrate a good range of vocabulary or structures?
8 Is the organisation of the answer clear?
9 What mark out of five do you think this answer got?

Tip! You will not get marks for copying phrases from the information provided, so try to reword language from the input text (what is written on the question paper) as long as it is possible to do this in a natural way.

One of the essential goals of school education is to ensure that pupils are well prepared for their future lives in the workplace. This is arguably as important a task as teaching such academic subjects as history or chemistry.

There are many different ways in which schools can work towards achieving this aim. Firstly, they can make sure pupils learn basic practical skills. In the past, girls used to be taught how to knit and sew while boys learnt metalwork and carpentry. However, these days other skills such as working with spreadsheets or using computer-aided design software may be of more use to young people, both boys and girls, as they are skills that are frequently required in the modern workplace.

Another way in which schools can prepare youngsters for their working lives is by providing them with information about a wide variety of different careers. This is essential, as otherwise students would be likely to restrict their job choices to careers already familiar to them, often because of family members' involvement in those fields. It is clearly preferable for young people to be made aware of the enormous range of types of work that is available for them to choose from.

Of the two ways outlined above, informing pupils about career opportunities is the more important. This is because, while it is certainly not impossible to learn practical skills later in life, selecting which career path you wish to follow is a decision that cannot be delayed but has to be taken as soon as you leave school.

Test 2 Exam practice **Writing Part 1**

Page 44 *Action plan*

Review

Look at the exam task below, then answer these questions.

1 What is the issue that you have to discuss?
2 How could each of the three points relate to the topic?
3 Which two of the three points are you going to focus on?
4 To what extent will you use the opinions expressed in the task in your answer?
5 Which of the two points you've selected will you say is more effective?
6 What reasons will you give in arguing that this point is more effective than the other one?

Follow the exam instructions, using the advice to help you.

You **must** answer this question. Write your answer in **220–260** words in an appropriate style.

---

1 Your class has listened to a radio discussion about how to help people live healthier lives. You have made the notes below:

Measures to help people to live healthier lives

- education
- legislation
- facilities

Some opinions expressed in the discussion:

"People need to know about the benefits of exercise and a healthy diet."

"There should be laws that totally ban unhealthy habits like smoking."

"The government needs to sponsor facilities to make them affordable for everyone."

Write an essay discussing **two** of the measures in your notes. You should **explain which measure is most likely to be effective, giving reasons** in support of your answer.

You may, if you wish, make use of the opinions expressed in the discussion, but you should use your own words as far as possible.

Tip! Good candidates sometimes lose marks simply because they do not read the question carefully enough. Make sure you do exactly what you are asked to do.

Advice

Remember that 'education' can refer not just to education in schools but also, for example, to educating the public through media campaigns.

What other unhealthy habits, apart from smoking, might a government consider banning?

What legislation could encourage healthy habits (as opposed to just banning unhealthy ones)?

What sorts of facilities could help people to lead healthier lives?

Page 46 Task information

Review

Answer these questions about Writing Part 2.

1 How many words do you have to write in this part?
2 How many paragraphs are you likely to write in an answer of that length?
3 Which are the only four types of text you might have to write?

Organising your writing

1 **Look at the task below and the sample answer to it. Then answer these questions.**

1 What is the topic of each paragraph in the sample answer?
2 A sentence which introduces or summarises the theme of the paragraph can be called the *topic sentence*. Underline the topic sentence of each paragraph.
3 What do you notice about where the topic sentence occurs?

You see this announcement on a website.

> We are looking for reviews of the best and the worst music video you have ever seen. Write us a review briefly describing these two videos, explaining why you think they are particularly good or particularly bad and commenting on how important you think music videos are for fans.

Write your **review**.

Sample answer

1 *The best and worst music videos I have ever seen were curiously by the same band. They were both for songs by The Reds, one of my favourite bands of all time. The best one was for their song 'Dream Song', which was one of their first-ever releases. The worst was for 'Night Rider', a hit they had last year.*

2 *The video for 'Dream Song' looked as good as the song sounded. It opened with a young girl lying asleep in a hammock. You were shown what she was dreaming about and it was very beautiful and romantic. It matched the song's lyrics perfectly.*

3 *The video for 'Night Rider' began effectively but soon deteriorated. The dramatic opening sequence of a horseman riding through a dark forest was followed by a rapid sequence of different shots which were not obviously connected and didn't make sense to me. I couldn't understand what relation the pictures had to the music.*

4 *Music videos are popular with fans because they help them to understand the meaning of the songs they accompany. They also enjoy seeing the stars performing. The videos make the music an experience for the eyes as well as the ears. In short, there are a number of reasons why music videos appeal.*

5 *Although music videos like 'Dream Song' can be dramatic and original films, I generally prefer to listen to my music without an accompanying video. That way I can focus more on how the music sounds. I'd much rather use my own imagination to picture what the track relates to.*

2 Now look at these tasks. Write a plan for a four- or five-paragraph answer to each one.

A This is part of an email you receive from an English-speaking friend:

> … In class, we've been discussing the relationships between teenagers and adults. Can you write and tell me about the situation in your country? How do teenagers and adults see each other? What sorts of things do teenagers and adults tend to disagree about? What do you think could be done to improve the relationship between these generations?

Write your **email**.

B An international sporting organisation has asked your college for information about its students' involvement in sport. As you are class representative, Dr Anna Jones, the College Principal, has asked you to write a report summarising your class's attitude to sport. You should provide information about the class's interest in sport both as participants and as spectators and should suggest at least one way in which the college could do more to encourage students' involvement in sport.

Write your **report**.

3 Write a topic sentence for each paragraph of the two tasks you planned in Exercise 2.

Useful language: good beginnings

Which do you think is the better beginning for each of the three tasks from Exercises 1 and 2? Why is the other beginning not so good?

1a *Music videos are sometimes very good and sometimes very bad.*

1b *Music videos differ enormously in terms of originality, production values and appeal.*

2a *Thanks for your email. I've found it very interesting to give some thought to your questions about how teenagers and adults get on in this country.*

2b *Thanks for your email. I don't have too much news for you at the moment – I've been so busy preparing for my exam that I haven't had time for anything else.*

3a *It's hard to believe, but only two-thirds of the students in my class actually bother to participate in any kind of sport.*

3b *This report is based on a survey administered to 30 students in the Advanced English class at Shakespeare College in Quebec.*

In real life, emails are sometimes written in extremely informal English using abbreviations and occasionally including unconventional spelling and punctuation. However, in the exam, you must take as much care with writing an email as with writing any other type of text – it may be appropriate to use informal language, but do all you can to avoid language errors.

Test 2 Exam practice Writing Part 2

Page 49 *Action plan*

Look at each of the tasks below 2–4 and answer the questions.

1 Which task do you think would be the best one for you to choose?
2 What factors do you need to consider when choosing a task?

Follow the exam instructions, using the advice to help you.

Write an answer to **one** of the questions **2–4** in this part. Write your answer in **220–260** words in an appropriate style.

---

2 You have received a letter from an English friend:

> ... Before I come to visit you this summer, I'd like to learn some of your language. What advice could you give me about how best to learn a language? What do you think I'll find most difficult about learning your language? What do you think are the most important things for me to focus on?

Write your **email**.

3 The college where you study has funds available for an online subscription to newspapers and magazines. You decide to write a proposal to the College Principal recommending two publications the college should subscribe to. Your proposal should describe each publication, saying why a subscription would benefit students at the college. Your proposal should also explain which of the publications is the most useful, assuming there isn't enough money for both.

Write your **proposal**.

4 An international arts magazine has asked readers to send in reviews of live theatre performances **they** have attended. Write a review of a play or other performance you have recently seen at the theatre. Your review should briefly describe the performance and should comment on its strengths and weaknesses. You should also give your opinion on how good a venue the particular theatre where you saw the performance is.

Write your **review**.

Advice

2 Think about the style you need for an email to a friend. What sort of words would be appropriate? Would you use contractions?

3 In a proposal, it is important to be persuasive, but in a way that is as clear, rational and objective as possible. Headings may help you do this effectively.

4 A review has to interest readers from the start, so it is important to begin effectively – with a question, perhaps.

Test 2 Training Listening (approximately 40 minutes) Part 1

Task information

Review

Answer these questions about Listening Part 1.

1 You are given time before the recording starts. What can you usefully do with this time? Why is it useful?
2 You are given some time between the first and second time you hear the recording. How can you best use this time?

Reading the questions

1 Prepare for the exam practice task on page 93 by reading the questions and options. Answer the following questions about them.

Tip! Reading the questions before you hear the recording will help you follow what the recording is about.

Extract One

1 Whose opinion does the first question focus on?
2 Does the second question focus on fact or opinion?
3 Whose intention does the second question focus on?

Extract Two

1 What are the two speakers discussing?
2 How do the three possible reactions offered in Question 3 differ?
3 Is Question 4 asking about something the man has already done?

Extract Three

1 From the wording of Question 5, who is more likely to be the boss – the man or the woman?
2 Whose feelings must you focus on in answering Question 6?
3 What do the options for Question 6 suggest about what they are discussing?

2 Look at the options suggested for Questions 1 to 6. Do any of them stand out as being more or less likely than the others?

Test 2 Exam practice Listening Part 1

Page 52 *Action plan*

13 Follow the exam instructions, using the advice to help you.

You will hear three different extracts. For questions **1–6**, choose the answer (**A**, **B** or **C**) which fits best according to what you hear. There are two questions for each extract.

Tip! Often the questions in Part 1 check understanding of chunks of recording rather than of specific details, so listen carefully to get a general understanding of what is said.

Extract One

You hear two business people discussing a workshop they have just attended.

1 What do they agree about?

A The presenter had some original ideas.
B The topic of the workshop was very useful.
C The participants made some sensible suggestions.

2 What is the woman planning to do next?

A make a change to her habits
B read about a related issue
C ask someone for advice

Advice

1 In a question that asks about agreement, it often happens that the opinions in the distracting options are stated by one of the speakers only. Listen carefully for the statement that they both agree is true.

2 People often talk about plans using 'going to'. If you hear this form, it may signal that you are about to hear the answer.

Extract Two

You hear two students talking about a project they are working on.

3 How does the woman feel about the comments they have received from their tutor?

A She is disappointed that he did not notice an improvement in their work.
B She is frustrated that he failed to offer some guidance at an earlier stage.
C She is annoyed that he is questioning the accuracy of their work.

4 What does the man promise to do?

A provide some visual material
B carry out a small experiment
C check some information

Advice

3 Focus on the gist of what the woman says. She will probably not use the specific words 'disappointed', 'frustrated' or 'annoyed'.

4 The dialogue is likely to mention all three of the actions in the options, but perhaps the distracting actions have already been done or will be done by someone else.

Extract Three

You hear two colleagues discussing an issue at work.

5 The man would like the woman to

A take part in a meeting with him.
B redo a recently completed task.
C change another colleague's point of view.

6 What has surprised the woman?

A some fluctuations in the company's sales
B the interest in the company from other countries
C a decrease in the company's production costs

Advice

5 With a question like 5, the answer might come from a number of different clues throughout the recording, so keep both questions in mind as you listen, rather than waiting to hear the answer for 5 and then listening out for 6.

6 Each of these options has two elements – you must make sure you find an answer where both of these elements match.

Test 2 Training Listening Part 2

Task information

Review

Answer these questions about Listening Part 2.

1 When you read the questions before you listen to the recording, what should you think about?
2 Is it necessary to spell the words correctly?
3 Will you need to make changes to the words you hear so they fit the grammar of the gapped sentence?
4 How many words will you need to write in each gap?

Answering accurately

1 14 **Spelling is important in this part of the exam. Listen and write down the ten phrases you hear. They all use words that are frequently misspelt.**

2 **You must make sure that what you write both fits grammatically and makes sense. Replace the words in italics below so that the sentences are both grammatically correct and make sense.**

1 Claire Davis was working as a *mechanical engineering* before she lost her job.
2 On returning to work after suffering from *broke a leg*, Claire learnt she had lost her job.
3 Claire almost immediately decided to visit *American*.
4 Claire decided to spend time improving her *swim* when she returned from her trip.
5 Claire loved seeing *the France* when she was working as a holiday representative.
6 Claire now realises that her life in the past was very *unsatisfactorily*.
7 Claire would advise other people who lose their jobs not to *worrying*.
8 Claire has no feelings of *angry* towards the people who made her redundant.

Tip! You will not be expected to write something in a different form from what you hear on the recording, so listening carefully will help you to avoid mistakes of the kind focused on in Exercise 2.

Tip! Another aspect of writing accurately is recognising and avoiding distraction. With many questions in Listening Part 2, you will hear two things that would be a logical answer to the question. For example, if the question says 'Laura worked as a ___', the recording will mention at least two jobs.

3 15 **Listen to the recording and answer these questions about each item (1–4).**

- **Which words do you hear that could fill the gaps in these sentences?**
- **Which is the correct word?**
- **Why is the other word incorrect?**

George was born in **(1)** .... in the 1950s.

George describes his childhood as **(2)** ....

George decided to study **(3)** .... at university.

George's first job was as a **(4)** .... in New York.

Test 2 Exam practice Listening Part 2

Page 55 Action plan

16 **Follow the exam instructions, using the advice to help you.**

You will hear a woman called Sally Batting talking about her experiences in the Antarctic. For questions **7–14**, complete the sentences with a word or short phrase.

Tip! As you read the questions before listening, think about what words might be used to indicate that you are about to hear the answer. Remember that the recording will usually use synonyms rather than the exact words in the questions.

SALLY BATTING: CYCLING IN THE ANTARCTIC

Sally's favourite **(7)** .... inspired her to go to the Antarctic.

Sally travelled mainly on **(8)** .... on her first visit to the Antarctic.

It was the **(9)** .... that first struck Sally about the Antarctic.

After two years working as a **(10)** .... , Sally decided to return to the Antarctic.

Sally's favourite part of her cycle ride across Antarctica was the **(11)** .... stage.

Sally found the **(12)** .... the hardest thing to deal with in the Antarctic.

While cycling across the Antarctic, Sally kept in touch with her family through a **(13)** ....

A **(14)** .... was what Sally missed most on her long cycle trip.

Advice

7 How might the recording express 'favourite' differently?

8 What kind of word would you expect to fill gap 8?

9 What are you going to be listening for here?

10 What kind of word is going to fit here?

11 'Stage' does not mean part of a theatre here – what is it likely to be referring to?

12 How might the speaker express the idea of 'hardest thing to deal with'?

13 What answer would you predict here? You may not predict the right word, but predicting may help you to catch the correct answer.

14 What might you predict as the answer here? Try to think of three or four possibilities.

Test 2 Training Listening Part 3

 *Task information*

Review

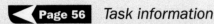

Answer these questions about Listening Part 3.

1 Why is it a good idea to read the questions before listening to the task?
2 Why is it useful to think about other ways of saying the points made in the questions and the options?
3 Do the questions come in the order that you hear the answers?
4 If you are not sure of the answer, should you guess or leave a blank?

Useful language: topic vocabulary

Match the words in the box with their definitions. Use a dictionary to help you.

start-up	external	in-house	entrepreneur
erratic	recruitment	challenging	diversify
undercharge	mentor	take on	skill

1 employ
2 person who starts their own business
3 sell for too low a price
4 start making new products or offering new services
5 technical ability
6 experienced person who gives advice to new employees
7 not regular
8 from outside an organisation
9 process of finding people to work for a company
10 business in its early stages
11 testing your abilities or determination
12 done within an organisation rather than by people from outside

Using the preparation time

1 **Look at the exam instructions and questions (15–20) on the next page, without reading the options (A–D). In one sentence, what do they tell you about what you are going to hear?**

2 **Now look at questions 15 to 20 in more detail. What do they tell you about what you are going to hear? Tick (✓) the points that you think you will hear about.**

1 Paul's work experience before he set up his own business
2 Paul's motivation in setting up his own business
3 the different sorts of people Paul has as clients
4 Paul's life outside the workplace
5 what Paul finds challenging about his work life
6 Paul's approach to using a mentor
7 Paul's explanation for his own success
8 how Paul feels he has changed
9 Paul's plans for the future

Test 2 Exam practice Listening Part 3

Page 57 *Action plan*

17 **Follow the exam instructions, using the advice to help you.**

You will hear an interview with an IT consultant called Paul about how he started his own business. For questions **15–20**, choose the answer (**A**, **B**, **C** or **D**) which fits best according to what you hear.

---

15 What does Paul say about the first years of his working life?

- **A** He got a teaching post in the university where he had studied.
- **B** His first job began to feel rather monotonous as time went by.
- **C** The kind of tasks he was instructed to do gradually changed.
- **D** The work became less enjoyable when some colleagues moved away.

16 What does Paul say made him decide to start his own consultancy business?

- **A** He was persuaded to do so by some friends.
- **B** He read a book which inspired him to take action.
- **C** He thought he could take advantage of a growing trend.
- **D** He realised he had the skills to make a success of his own company.

17 What does Paul suggest is his favourite type of client?

- **A** people he knew when he was a student
- **B** people recommended by agents
- **C** people he has met at conferences
- **D** people he has worked with previously

18 What does Paul find the most difficult aspect of running his business?

- **A** gaining a quick understanding of an unfamiliar situation
- **B** setting fees that match the effort involved
- **C** making a good impression on a new team of people
- **D** getting reliable advice from financial experts

19 What does Paul say about the way he uses a business mentor?

- **A** He uses his mentor differently from the way others use theirs.
- **B** He finds his mentor often comes up with fresh ideas for his business.
- **C** He gets information about the latest business theories from his mentor.
- **D** He likes to gets his mentor's reactions to plans that he is considering.

20 Paul explains that in the coming year he is going to

- **A** employ some new consultants.
- **B** have more variety in his work.
- **C** move to a more convenient office.
- **D** learn some additional skills.

Advice

__15__ Can you think of a synonym for 'working life'?

__16__ What phrasal verb is often used meaning 'start (a business)'?

__17__ Paul is likely to mention all these types of clients. How might he convey the idea of one of these types being his favourite?

__18__ How might Paul express the idea of something as the 'most difficult aspect'?

__19__ How could each of the four options here be expressed differently?

__20__ What is another way of saying 'in the coming year'?

Test 2 Training Listening Part 4

Page 59 *Task information*

Review

Answer these questions about Listening Part 4.

1 How many speakers do you have to listen to?
2 What is the connection between the speakers?
3 How many questions do you answer for each speaker?
4 With each speaker, do the answers to the questions come in the order they are written on the page?
5 What must you do before you listen to the speakers?
6 How many options do you have to choose from?
7 How might the speakers distract listeners into choosing the wrong answer?
8 Is it better to do the first set of questions the first time you hear the recording and then do the second set of questions the second time you hear it?

Reading the questions

1 Look at TASK ONE on the next page. If the speaker says these things, what is the answer?

Tip! Use the preparation time well. Think about the meaning of the options and how the speakers might give the answers using different words from those on the question paper.

1 'It's not very big, but I like being on the edge of town – it's quick and easy either to get to the centre or to go out into the countryside.'
2 'I didn't think I'd enjoy being so high up, but I love being able to see right over the city.'
3 'There's a grocer's underneath, which is really handy when I need to buy bread or milk.'
4 'I love waking up to the gentle sound of the water lapping outside the window.'
5 'My room looks out over the fields, and in spring I wake up to the sound of lambs baaing under my window.'
6 'My kitchen is what used to be the ticket office and my sitting room was once a waiting room.'
7 'I often babysit my nephews in exchange for being charged much lower rent than I'd normally have to pay for a bedsit.'
8 'I love the picturesque thatched roof and the uneven floors, and everyone says how pretty it is.'

2 Note down one or two other phrases that might be used to describe each type of accommodation (A–H).

3 Look at TASK TWO. Answer these questions about the options.

Tip! 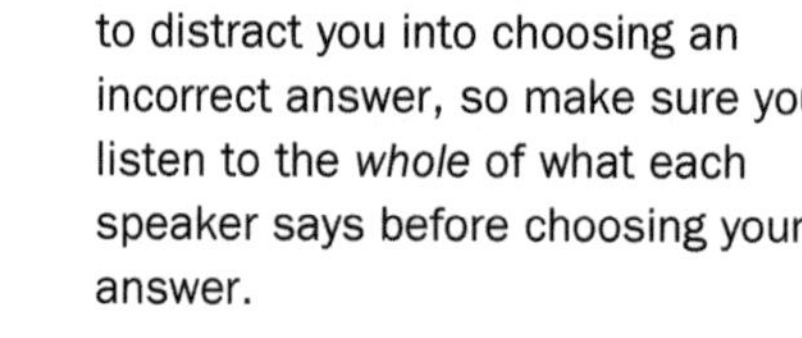
Remember, of course, that some of these phrases may also be used to distract you into choosing an incorrect answer, so make sure you listen to the *whole* of what each speaker says before choosing your answer.

1 How might someone explain that a place *can be noisy*?
2 What is another way of saying that *parking is difficult*?
3 What are some synonyms for *expensive*?
4 How else can you say that you have *a long journey to work*?
5 How else can you say that a place *lacks storage space*?
6 What words and phrases might be used to talk about the *reputation* of a neighbourhood?
7 How might the point that a place *doesn't have interesting views* be expressed?
8 What are some phrases that could be used to suggest that a *building is in need of repair*?

Test 2 Exam practice Listening Part 4

Page 60 *Action plan*

1 18 **Follow the exam instructions, using the advice to help you.**

You will hear five short extracts in which people are talking about where they live.

TASK ONE

For questions **21–25**, choose from the list (**A–H**) where each speaker currently lives.

TASK TWO

For questions **26–30**, choose from the list (**A–H**) what each speaker finds difficult about the place where they live.

While you listen you must complete both tasks.

A in a cottage in a village
B above a shop in a town
C in a converted railway station
D in a top-floor city flat
E in a room in a relative's house
F in a house in the suburbs
G on a farm
H in a houseboat

Speaker 1		**21**
Speaker 2		**22**
Speaker 3		**23**
Speaker 4		**24**
Speaker 5		**25**

A It can be noisy.
B Parking is difficult.
C The rent is expensive.
D It's a long journey to work.
E It lacks storage space.
F The area has a reputation for being boring.
G It doesn't have interesting views from the windows.
H The building is in poor repair.

Speaker 1		**26**
Speaker 2		**27**
Speaker 3		**28**
Speaker 4		**29**
Speaker 5		**30**

Test 2 Training **Speaking** (15 minutes) **Part 1**

Page 61 *Task information*

Review

Which of these are the two main aims of Speaking Part 1?

1 To relax candidates by asking some simple questions
2 To see how well candidates can answer complex questions
3 To check the accuracy of candidates' pronunciation
4 To notice how well candidates interact with each other
5 To test candidates' ability to give personal information fluently

Useful language: talking about yourself

1 Work with a partner if possible to ask and answer these questions.

- Where do you come from?
- Where exactly do you live?
- What do you think of it as a place to live?
- Who do you live with?
- What is your first language?
- How does that language compare with English?
- How have you learnt English?
- What have you found the most effective and enjoyable ways of improving your English?
- Which English-speaking countries have you visited, if any?
- What do you enjoy doing in your spare time?

2 Write five more questions that might be asked in this part of the test, one for each of the topics suggested. Then take turns with a partner, asking and answering each other's questions.

1 People: ....
2 Work and study: ....
3 Leisure: ....
4 Travel: ....
5 Where you live: ....
6 Learning English: ....

3 Look at these examples of candidates' responses to the same question from the interlocutor. Then answer these questions:

- What is the problem with each response?
- How could the response be improved?

Interlocutor: What do you see yourself doing in the future?

Tip! Remember: you can invent information about yourself if you wish.

Tip! It is not a good idea to prepare answers which you learn and use word-for-word, as this will sound unnatural and inappropriate. However, practising talking about yourself with a partner will help you speak confidently and fluently in this part of the test.

a *'I don't know. I'm not sure yet.'*

b *'It depends of my exam results. I am interesting for a lot of things. I hope I am going to get a work the next year after I will finish my career at the university. I am studying the informatics so I think I get easily a good work.'*

c *'Who knows? It is hard to know what life will bring us. Sometimes happiness, sometimes sadness. If the right party wins the next election, then the future will be much better for everyone in this country.'*

Test 2 Exam practice Speaking Part 1

Page 62 *Action plan*

Do the exam task, following the instructions below.

Part 1 2 minutes (3 minutes for groups of three)

The interlocutor will ask you some questions about yourself, your home, work or studies and familiar topics.

Good morning/afternoon/evening. My name is ..... and this is my colleague ..... .
And your names are?
Can I have your mark sheets, please?
Thank you.

First of all, we'd like to know something about you.

- Where are you from?
- How long have you lived here/there?
- What do you do?
- What do you enjoy most about your job/course?

The interlocutor will then ask you some questions about one or two other topics, for example:

- What kind of TV programmes do you most enjoy?
- Tell me about a special meal that you recently had.
- How do you feel about extreme sports?
- What would be your ideal job?

Tip! Do not give very brief answers. For example, in answer to *What would be your ideal job?* Do not just say: *Journalism.*

Say instead:

Well, what I'd really like to do is be a journalist and I'd love to work on a big national newspaper. I enjoy writing and I'm really interested in current affairs, so it seems like the ideal job for me. I'd particularly like to be a foreign correspondent ...

Tip! If you cannot think of an answer immediately, give yourself a little more time to think by using phrases like: *I'm not sure ..., It's hard to say ..., I'm never sure what to say when people ask me that.*

Test 2 Training Speaking Part 2

Page 63 *Task information*

Review

Work with a partner if possible and discuss whether these statements about Speaking Part 2 are true or false. If the statement is false, correct it.

1 In Part 2, you have to speak for two minutes.
2 You have to comment on three pictures.
3 The interlocutor will ask you a question relating to the pictures and another question will be written above the pictures.
4 You have to describe the pictures in as much detail as possible.
5 Your partner will have to speak for a minute on the same set of pictures as yours.
6 You may help your partner if they are finding it hard to think of enough to say.
7 After your partner has spoken for a minute, the interlocutor will ask you a question and will give you a minute to reply.

Useful language: a sample response

1 **This is the beginning of what one candidate said about the pictures on page S6. Fill each gap with one appropriate word.**

> The first picture I'd like to discuss **(1)** .... two people **(2)** .... married. This is obviously a very important ceremony for **(3)** .... of them. It would **(4)** .... involved a lot of preparations **(5)** .... the part of the bride and the groom and their families as **(6)** .... They'd have had **(7)** .... do all sorts of things like **(8)** .... decisions about venues, choosing **(9)** .... to wear, getting **(10)** .... hair done and so **(11)** .... They **(12)** .... well have had to organise a honeymoon too …

2 1 19 **Listen to the recording and check your answers.**

3 **Work with a partner if possible. You should each talk about one of the other pictures on page S6, answering both the questions.**

4 **What would you say if you were the listening candidate and the interlocutor then asked you:**

- Which of these ceremonies do you think would be most significant for the people?

5 1 20 **Listen to the recording of a possible answer by the listening candidate.**

Test 2 Exam practice Speaking Part 2

Page 64 *Action plan*

Do the exam task, following the instructions below.

Part 2 4 minutes (6 minutes for groups of three)

Work in groups of three if possible. One of you is the interlocutor and the other two are the candidates. The interlocutor should lead the task using the script below. Refer to the pictures on pages S7 and S8.

The interlocutor will give you three pictures and ask you to talk about two of them on your own for about a minute. You will then be asked a question about your partner's pictures which you will need to answer in no more than 30 seconds.

Interlocutor In this part of the test, I'm going to give each of you three pictures. I'd like you to talk about **two** of them on your own for about a minute, and also to answer a question briefly about your partner's pictures.

(Candidate A), it's your turn first. Here are your pictures. They **show people who need some help**.

I'd like you to compare **two** of the pictures and say **what you think has happened in each case and how the people might be feeling**.

All right?

After 1 minute Thank you.

(Candidate B), **which person do you think needs the most help? (Why?)**

After approximately 30 seconds Thank you.

Now, *(Candidate B)*, here are your pictures. They show **people listening to music**.

I'd like you to compare **two** of the pictures and say **what kind of music the people are listening to and how the music might affect the way they feel**.

All right?

After 1 minute Thank you.

(Candidate A), **which people do you think are enjoying listening to music the most? (Why?)**

After approximately 30 seconds Thank you.

Tip! Try to use modals to express what you think *might* or *could* be happening in the pictures, e.g. *From the expressions on the children's faces, I think they might be feeling excited* or *The man at the front looks as if he could be getting a little bit anxious or impatient.*

Speaking Parts 3 and 4

Task information

Part 3

Review

Choose the correct way to complete these statements about Speaking Part 3.

1 The prompts in Part 3 *are / are not* on the same theme as the pictures in Part 2.
2 Part 3 *is / is not* more like a conversation than Part 2.
3 It *is / is not* important that you come to a decision in Part 3.
4 You *should / should not* invite the interlocutor to give their opinion in Part 3.
5 It *is / is not* important that you and your partner should agree in Part 3.
6 It *is / is not* essential to discuss all the prompts you are given in Part 3.

Part 4

Review

Choose words from the box to complete the paragraph about Speaking Part 4.

develop	discussion	interlocutor	explain	opinion	topic	way

In Part 4, you will continue your **(1)** .... of the **(2)** .... that was the focus of Part 3. The **(3)** .... will ask you some further questions to **(4)** .... this theme further. You are likely to be asked to give your **(5)** .... and to **(6)** .... why you think that **(7)** ....

Useful language: choosing the right words

1 Look at the exam task below. Think about what you would say in answer to the question.

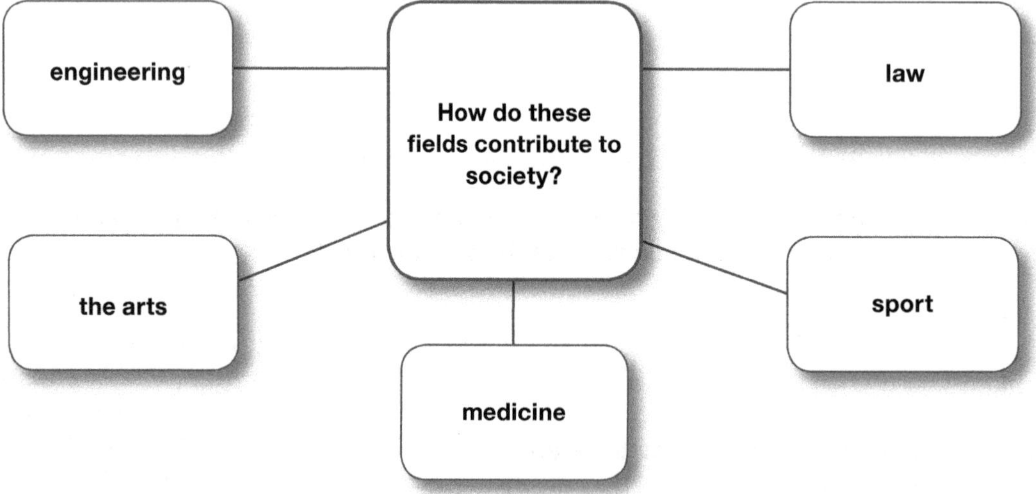

2 🎧1 21 **Look at how some students dealt with the first part of the task. Choose the correct alternative in italics. Then listen to the recording and check your answers.**

A: Shall I start? I think they all contribute to society *but / and* in very different *manners / ways*. For example, medicine is probably the most important, because it makes it possible for people to live longer and healthier lives and so contribute more to society. *Do you / Are you* agree?

B: Well, up to a *bit / point*. I agree that medicine is very important, but *so / also* are other fields like sport.

A: Well, yes, that *does / goes* without saying, but surely it's the *case / matter* that you can't fully enjoy sport unless you're in good health.

B: OK, *fair / good* enough. So what do you *believe / think* about the arts? I can't help *wondering / thinking* whether they really contribute all that *many / much* to society.

A: But *surely / certainly* they make a huge contribution. They enrich people's lives enormously, for a *start / beginning*.

3 **Work with a partner if possible. Choose two of the fields in the prompts and discuss them with your partner, considering how valuable a contribution each makes to society. Try to use some of the correct expressions from the previous exercise.**

4 **Work with a partner if possible. Discuss with your partner what questions the interlocutor might ask in Part 4 to extend and develop the topic. Note down three possible questions.**

1 ....
2 ....
3 ....

5 🎧1 22 **Now listen to the recording. Write down the three questions the interlocutor actually asked.**

1 ....
2 ....
3 ....

6 **Work with a partner if possible and discuss your questions and those from the recording.**

Test 2 Exam practice Speaking Parts 3 and 4

 Pages 66 and 68 *Action plan*

Do the exam task, following the instructions below.

Tip! Remember that this is not a monologue. Make sure you listen to your partner and respond to what he or she says.

Part 3 4 minutes (6 minutes for groups of three)

Work in groups of three if possible. One of you is the interlocutor and the other two are the candidates. The interlocutor should lead the task using the script below. Refer to the task sheet on page S9.

The interlocutor will give you a task sheet to discuss together.

Interlocutor Now, I'd like you to talk about something together for about two minutes.

Here are some things people consider when choosing to live in a rural area and a question for you to discuss. First you have some time to look at the task. (*About 15 seconds*)

Now, talk to each other about **how important these considerations are when choosing to move to a rural area**.

After 2 minutes Thank you. Now you have about a minute to decide **which of these things can affect life in a rural area the most**.

After 1 minute Thank you.

Advice

Try to think of a way in which each aspect of life is better in a rural community and a way in which each aspect of life is not as good there as in a city.

Part 4

5 minutes (8 minutes for groups of three)

Work in groups of three if possible. One of you is the interlocutor and the other two are the candidates. The interlocutor should lead the task using the script below.

The interlocutor will ask some general questions which follow on from the topic in Part 3.

Interlocutor

- How would life in a modern megacity differ from life in an ordinary city or large town? (Why?)
- How different are holidays in the countryside from those in a city? (Why?)
- What impact does people commuting to work from a village to a city have on life in the village? (Why?)
- What advice would you give to someone from a rural area who was planning to go and live in a megacity? (Why?)
- What do you think governments and city councils should do to improve life in big cities? (Why?)

Thank you. That is the end of the test.

Tip! If you are asked to discuss a question together, do that. If the question is addressed to one of you, answer it alone.

Tip! Always try not just to give your opinion, but also to give a reason for it or an example.

Advice

- *If you find it hard to think of an answer to this immediately, start describing the characteristics of a megacity – and then move from there towards thinking about how these characteristics affect people's lives.*
- *Thinking about specific aspects of holidays may help you think of things to say, e.g. travel, accommodation, food, sporting activities, entertainment, meeting people, etc.*
- *If you are asked a question that you have never thought about before, do not be afraid to start with what might seem like an obvious answer to the question and see where this leads you – you could say, for example: 'That's an interesting question. I've never actually thought about it before, but I suppose it must mean that there are relatively few people in the village during the day. I guess that would have a considerable impact on things like the village shop, …'*
- *Again, thinking about specific aspects of the quality of everyday life may help you to come up with ideas, e.g. getting to work, choosing living accommodation, sustaining relationships, enjoying leisure time, staying healthy, etc.*
- *Do not think too long about what might be the most important measure that governments could take – go for the first idea that comes to you and develop that.*

Test 3 Reading and Use of English (1 hour 30 minutes) Part 1

For questions **1–8**, read the text below and decide which answer (**A**, **B**, **C** or **D**) best fits each gap. There is an example at the beginning (**0**).

Mark your answers **on the separate answer sheet**.

Example:

0 **A** occurrence **B** presence **C** life **D** existence

0	A	B	C	D
	▭	▭	▭	▬

The lightest materials in the world

Aerogels are the lightest solid materials in **(0)** .... Invented in 1931, they are gels (like hair gel) in which gas has been **(1)** .... for the liquid. They have unique **(2)** .... that have still to be exploited to the **(3)** ....

Aerogels can be rigid – making them suitable for windows – or flexible; the latter type could be used for blankets and outdoor clothes. As well as being extremely lightweight – air can **(4)** .... as much as 99.8% of the material – aerogels are remarkably effective as insulators: a flower placed on a piece of aerogel held over the flame of a Bunsen burner will be **(5)** .... by the heat.

This means that aerogels have considerable **(6)** .... for use in the building and construction **(7)** .... , instead of conventional insulation. However, production costs are very high, so even though it is the best insulator we have, its use is currently limited, mostly to drilling operations and other **(8)** .... environments.

1	**A** substituted	**B** replaced	**C** changed	**D** relieved
2	**A** possessions	**B** belongings	**C** contents	**D** properties
3	**A** total	**B** full	**C** extent	**D** entirety
4	**A** put in	**B** make up	**C** fill in	**D** build up
5	**A** unaffected	**B** unconcerned	**C** uninfluenced	**D** unimpressed
6	**A** possibility	**B** ability	**C** potential	**D** capacity
7	**A** category	**B** division	**C** sector	**D** region
8	**A** extreme	**B** intense	**C** excessive	**D** immoderate

Test 3 Reading and Use of English Part 2

For questions **9–16**, read the text below and think of the word which best fits each gap. Use only **one** word in each gap. There is an example at the beginning (**0**).

Write your answers **IN CAPITAL LETTERS on the separate answer sheet.**

Example: | **0** | T | O | O |

Applying for your first job?

Getting a job is **(0)** .... important to leave to chance; **(9)** .... all, work is likely to play a significant role in your life for many years. So before sending in any applications, think hard about **(10)** .... would really suit you. Concentrate on jobs for **(11)** .... you have an aptitude – **(12)** .... can be very demoralising to have your application turned down. Ideally, your job should be not only one you can do well, **(13)** .... also one that makes you look forward to going to work every morning.

It's important to consider the culture of the organisations you're applying **(14)** .... Some companies are **(15)** .... obsessed with results and profits that employees are under stress all the time. You need to be clear in your own mind **(16)** .... or not you could work in an environment like that.

Making an effort in the early stages of applying for a job will almost certainly pay off in the long run.

For questions **17–24**, read the text below. Use the word given in capitals at the end of some of the lines to form a word that fits in the gap **in the same line**. There is an example at the beginning (**0**).

Write your answers **IN CAPITAL LETTERS on the separate answer sheet.**

Example: | 0 | F A S C I N A T I N G |

Introduction to Mexico's long history

Mexico has a long and **(0)** .... history. For some people, Mexico is	**FASCINATE**
synonymous with the Aztecs, who dominated the country from the fourteenth	
century until they declined in the sixteenth, as a result of **(17)** .... by	**CONQUER**
the Spanish, and disease. But before the arrival of Europeans, a number of	
(18) .... existed in different parts of Mexico, going back at least to the	**CIVILISE**
Olmecs. The Olmecs are virtually **(19)** .... now, but they flourished for	**KNOW**
over a millennium, from around 1500 BC.	
Mexico from the Olmecs to the Aztecs, by Michael D. Coe and Rex Koontz,	
is an excellent introduction to the period, and a very **(20)** .... guide	**INSTRUCT**
to these early **(21)** .... The authors draw on numerous recent	**INHABIT**
(22) .... , and discuss topics ranging from the beginnings of agriculture	**DISCOVER**
and writing to **(23)** .... against the ruling elite.	**RISE**
Of particular interest is the authors' discussion of recent developments in	
radiocarbon dating. The **(24)** .... of these are likely to transform	**IMPLY**
our understanding of the timescale of the region.	

Test 3 Reading and Use of English Part 4

For questions **25–30**, complete the second sentence so that it has a similar meaning to the first sentence, using the word given. **Do not change the word given**. You must use between **three** and **six** words, including the word given. Here is an example (**0**).

Example:

0 People think the first email was sent in 1971.

THOUGHT

The first email .... in 1971.

The gap can be filled with the words 'is thought to have been sent', so you write:

Example: | **0** | IS THOUGHT TO HAVE BEEN SENT |

Write **only** the missing words **IN CAPITAL LETTERS on the separate answer sheet**.

---

25 I'm sure Ben wasn't pleased when Myra arrived, because he's never liked her.

CAN'T

Ben has never liked Myra, so he .... see her arrive.

26 Jenny very rarely follows other people's advice.

EVER

Jenny .... other people advise her to do.

27 I eventually realised that the woman waving at me was an old friend.

TURNED

I couldn't at first see who was waving at me, but she .... an old friend.

28 It was the most dangerous situation I had ever been in.

A

Never before .... dangerous situation.

29 When the managing director resigned unexpectedly, the company struggled to replace him.

FILL

The company struggled .... by the unexpected resignation of the managing director.

30 The millionaire had made it clear how he wished his donation to be allocated, and that was how it was done.

ACCORDANCE

The millionaire's donation was allocated .... wishes.

Test 3 Reading and Use of English Part 5

You are going to read a review of a book about birds. For questions **31–36**, choose the answer (**A**, **B**, **C** or **D**) which you think fits best according to the text.

Mark your answers **on the separate answer sheet.**

Birdlife, by Glenda Hurst, reviewed by Carl Truman

Birds are present in our lives in so many ways – as pets, as part of many people's diet, even as a source of inspiration – that Glenda Hurst's *Birdlife* is, in some respects, a welcome miscellany of fact and fiction. Her previous book, *Gold*, was a best-seller, and Hurst has, understandably, chosen to repeat a winning formula. In that book, each chapter focused on a different aspect of the metal, from its financial use to edible gold leaf, but the apparently random order of chapters meant *Gold* lacked continuity: there was no sense of the author presenting a case and leading us through the steps of her argument. While each chapter was interesting enough in itself, overall the book seemed lightweight, a series of magazine articles. Nevertheless, *Gold* sold in large numbers, and I see no reason why *Birdlife* should not repeat that success.

Birds have played a role in myths for millennia, from ancient China to Egypt to Central America, and birds are often used as symbols: the dove to represent peace, the eagle for power and so on. In her chapter on mythology, Hurst takes the reader on a world tour at breakneck speed, but the lack of comparison and cross-referencing means that readers are often left to their own devices if they wish to interpret the information or identify similarities between cultures. Furthermore, this approach means that a fair amount of potentially tedious repetition is unavoidable. There is a great deal of detail and not enough synthesis, leaving the reader wondering what point, if any, is being made.

I enjoyed the chapter on birds working with human beings. It gives the familiar example of taking canaries into mines so that if methane or carbon dioxide is present, its effect on the bird gives the miners early warning of danger. However, I suspect I am not alone in being unfamiliar with the East African honeyguide, a wild bird which leads people to bee colonies. The men searching for honeycomb make specific noises, and when the honeyguide hears them, it replies, with a particular call that it restricts to that one situation. The people smoke out the bees and take the honeycomb, leaving a little as a reward for the bird – which in this way avoids having to tackle the bees itself. This is thought to be the only instance of birds in the wild deliberately communicating with human beings to the advantage of both parties.

An area that has seen a great deal of research in recent years is bird migration, a phenomenon that used to be totally misunderstood: a couple of centuries ago, it was thought that birds that disappeared for the winter were hiding in mud. We now know a great deal about migration. The Arctic tern, for instance, breeds in the Arctic, flies south to the Antarctic in August or September, arriving back in May or June – a round trip of over 70,000 kilometres. And the bird appears to be determined to reach its destination: even if fish are being caught below it, and birds that are not migrating dive down to steal some, the Arctic tern cannot be deflected from its journey. Although the Arctic tern holds the record, feats on this scale are far from rare.

Birdlife ends with a short epilogue in which Hurst lays out her vision of an ideal future: restoring habitats that have been transformed by drainage or by grubbing up hedges, in both cases to improve agriculture; from the birds' point of view, their habitat is damaged or even destroyed. It is here that Hurst reveals her true colours, as food production comes a poor second to protecting an environment in which birds can thrive. Reverting to the farming methods of the past is a forlorn hope, however: she can hardly expect us to sacrifice the enormous increase in agricultural output that we have achieved, when even that is not enough to feed the world's population.

While *Birdlife* has little to say to serious ornithologists, professional or amateur, if picked up in an airport bookshop or given as a present, it might well broaden the horizons of others.

31 The reviewer mentions *Gold* in order to

A emphasise the wide range of topics that Hurst covers in each book.
B explain what he sees as a weakness in Hurst's approach.
C support his opinion that *Birdlife* deserves to be very popular.
D express his disappointment with *Birdlife* in comparison with *Gold*.

32 The reviewer suggests that in the chapter on birds in mythology, Hurst

A misses opportunities to draw conclusions from the information she presents.
B misunderstands the significance of some of the myths that she mentions.
C uses repetition rather than discussion to support her interpretations.
D tries to cover too wide a range of cultures.

33 The reviewer refers to the honeyguide to suggest that birds

A and human beings can co-operate to their mutual benefit.
B can be trained to assist human beings.
C could be exploited by human beings to a greater extent.
D are not as useful to human beings as is sometimes claimed.

34 The phrase 'feats on this scale' (line 27) refers to the ability of some birds to

A avoid getting distracted.
B survive without eating.
C live in cold climates.
D fly long distances.

35 What does the reviewer say about the epilogue?

A It overestimates the damage done to birds by changes in agriculture.
B It reveals Hurst's lack of understanding of certain subjects.
C It is unlikely to have the effect that Hurst would like.
D It convinced him that Hurst's concern for birds is justified.

36 In the text as a whole, the reviewer gives the impression of thinking that *Birdlife*

A reveals how much more there is to discover about its subject.
B is readable without providing new insights into the subject.
C provides a clear overview of a subject with many facets.
D is unusual in bringing together diverse aspects of the subject.

Test 3 Reading and Use of English Part 6

You are going to read extracts from an article in which four artists give their views on the creative process. For questions **37–40**, choose from the artists **A–D**. The artists may be chosen more than once.

Mark your answers **on the separate answer sheet**.

The artist at work

Four artists give their views on how they create their work.

A

When you convert something from the real world into a painting, it has to function within the painting. And when it comes down to it, everything is a form of geometry on a flat surface, so when I look at something and consider using it in a painting, I spend ages trying to make sure that the geometry will work. With one object, I might see pretty quickly how to compose the painting, but I might reject another one because it just doesn't seem right. Then I work out how to get from that starting point to the finished painting. At the back of my mind, there's always the nagging thought that really, I want people to look at the finished painting and make some sense of it, regardless of what that is. All in all, I'm under so much self-imposed pressure while I'm working that it's a great relief when a painting is finished.

B

What my drawings depict doesn't concern me as much as drawing them. I'm just not interested in knowing about, say, what images tell us. That cat, those stairs, this or that tree is really just a support for the drawing itself. They're all chosen pretty arbitrarily, as a means to a drawing's own end. People have the habit of reading an image, but my activity is different from that of a reader. This really works for me when the drawing itself is allowed to appear slowly on behalf of the things it depicts. I really let the painting evolve in its own way, until I realise that it's complete. I'm always surprised how tense I feel while I'm painting, though – it's a bit like giving birth. And when I finish, it generally takes me days to recover.

C

People often describe my paintings as abstract. I don't consider them abstract because I'm working from a somewhat indistinct and hazy place towards a very specific and concrete image. I'm constructing an image from an object or shape that has to mean something to me, though it may be nothing to other people, and I try to define it very clearly, so it becomes legible. But if in the end people can't see it as I do, so be it. After making that initial choice, I let the painting itself take over – it's a very spontaneous process. I usually feel as though I'm in the hands of the painting, almost its slave, having to do whatever it requires, however unreasonable it seems at the time. When the painting's complete, I have a strong emotional reaction, a kind of euphoria at having survived.

D

I'm usually surprised by how my paintings turn out, because I don't feel I exert control over what happens. The subject slips away if you try to grab it. When I paint a real place, it's less a celebration of the ordinary than a demonstration of the idea that by painting something that is apparently nothing, it has the opportunity to become everything in the eyes of anyone who sees it. I suppose that's one of my motives for painting – to make people observe. Why I happened to paint this place rather than that has no significance – it could simply be finding somewhere to sketch without being run over (I usually sketch in the street). It's what I do with it then that matters. I know artistic creation is often seen as a struggle with something inside; well, for me it's almost the reverse, almost a relaxation – painting is an escape from the demands of everyday life.

Which artist

shares artist C's opinion on whether other people should share the artist's interpretation of their paintings? | 37 | |

expresses the same opinion as artist D regarding the choice of subject matter? | 38 | |

has a different opinion from artist C on how they experience the act of painting? | 39 | |

expresses a different view from the others on whether the painting process should be consciously planned? | 40 | |

Test 3 Reading and Use of English Part 7

You are going to read an extract from a magazine article. Six paragraphs have been removed from the extract. Choose from the paragraphs **A–G** the one which fits each gap (**41–46**). There is one extra paragraph which you do not need to use.

Mark your answers **on the separate answer sheet.**

Is work changing?

Cromford Mill, in the north of England, is now a museum, but when it was constructed in 1771, it was the site of one of the most influential workplace experiments ever seen. This was where textile entrepreneur Richard Arkwright set up shop. Cotton-spinning had been a cottage industry, but at Cromford Mill, spinners from all around came together to use machines provided by Arkwright. It was the world's first factory, and it was soon followed by many more.

41 ______

There are good reasons why the model has flourished. Centralising production allowed for dramatically greater efficiency. And bosses – then as now suspicious that workers were not always working hard – could keep an eye on them.

42 ______

Two of the biggest forces changing work and the nature of the company are technology and demographic shifts. Unskilled work still exists, as does highly skilled work, but the jobs in the middle have to a large extent been automated or outsourced away. Furthermore, technology has made the move to an economy based on knowledge, not skills, possible.

43 ______

As a result of such changes, many of the old certainties are breaking down. You often hear it said that people used to work for money – very much a hangover from the Industrial Revolution, when work was viewed as a straight trade of time for money – but now it's claimed that we are more interested in having rewarding work.

44 ______

In other words, what we mean by the workplace is changing – it's no longer always a grand (or otherwise) building with the company's name on top. Increasingly, we can work anywhere – in a coffee shop or at the kitchen table. The demand that employees work in more flexible ways is encouraging this trend, with workers (especially younger generations) no longer expecting to be chained to a desk from nine to five every day.

45 ______

In a world of decentralised, non-hierarchical organisations, permanent full-time employment could become the exception. So will the firm of the future be made up of loose groupings of self-employed people, forming and re-forming on a project by project basis? Will workers effectively be their own chief executives, using technology to sell their skills to the highest bidder and with little attachment to a place of work, each other or the firms that employ them? It's tempting to think so, but reality is starting to interfere with this picture.

46 ______

There is one particular reason why tomorrow might turn out to be not so different from today: human nature. We are social creatures and tend to be at our best in groups rather than operating alone. Work is where we bond, gossip, fight, love and hate – in short, it's where we live.

So the prospects for at least some of the familiar aspects of the old Arkwrightian corporate model may not be quite so bleak as painted. Yes, things are changing, but the advocates of the brave new, networked world should remember that work is not the only – or, arguably, even the most important – thing we do when we are at work.

A In addition, we are all living longer and working for longer. In fact, in some countries there are now reckoned to be four or even five distinct generations making up the workforce.

B For firms, this can seem a no-brainer – they save money on expensive office space while giving their employees a valuable and appreciated perk. It can be tough to implement, though video conferencing and private networks have improved things greatly.

C But times are changing, and the pace and uncertainty of the modern world demand more flexibility and responsiveness than hierarchies like this can provide. Organisational structures need to be based on serving the customer rather than preserving the rank and status of managers.

D This is true up to a point, but perhaps more significant is the erosion of the boundary between work and other parts of life – education, leisure, play; between me-in-work and me-in-my-own-time.

E Above all, this format is popular because it works. Or rather, it worked, as, after over 200 years, some observers reckon that the end of employment as we have known it may be near. Are they right?

F Of course, we are living in a time of disruption, change and novelty, but the fact is that there are also strong continuities with the past. As a result, that unstructured form of work may remain a dream.

G This groundbreaking idea has become the norm for millions of us to this day, whether we are architects or economists, agronomists or oculists, because modern offices are based on exactly the same principles. They are places where you go in order to work for specific hours, using facilities and equipment provided by your employer to do a job, for a wage.

Reading and Use of English Part 8

You are going to read a magazine article in which five careers advisers write about going to university. For questions **47–56**, choose from the extracts (**A–E**). The extracts may be chosen more than once.

Mark your answers **on the separate answer sheet.**

Which careers adviser

recommends being prepared for any job applications young people might make?	47
claims that the public perception of students applies only to a minority?	48
suggests doing what is necessary for students to feel at ease in their room?	49
mentions some potential drawbacks of working during term time?	50
warns of the danger of borrowing money?	51
recommends formulating a financial plan to cover a period of time?	52
suggests being adventurous with regard to non-academic interests?	53
contrasts university studies with studying at school?	54
recommends caution concerning socialising?	55
points out that students are not the only ones affected by being away from their loved ones?	56

Going away to a UK university

A

Going away to university is likely to be a major turning point in your life. After all, it's probably your first time away from your home and family, perhaps living in a room that is far less comfortable than you are accustomed to, and having to take responsibility for yourself, for everything from getting up in the morning to making sure you can afford whatever textbooks you need. Your experience until now has probably been that homework was pretty much regulated, with repercussions if you didn't do it; a degree course requires far more independent work. A few people go to university determined to prioritise their social life. Although that tends to be the stereotype that everyone knows, most students are level-headed, and don't merit the bad reputation that they suffer from as a group.

B

Unless you have an income of your own, or your parents provide you with one, being a student can make you wonder where your next meal is coming from. It's useful to draw up a budget, listing your likely outgoings during the term – not forgetting the rent for your room, if you pay in instalments – and how much you'll have available. If the figures don't balance, the only way to survive may be to find part-time work, such as serving in a restaurant two or three evenings a week. At least you'll meet members of the general public, which is preferable to spending your entire time with other students. However, there's the danger of falling behind with your studies, or not having enough time to sleep. And let's face it, if your friends are planning a fun evening and you have to go to work instead of joining in, it could be very frustrating!

C

As soon as you arrive, you'll start meeting new people. It may be that nobody you know from school has gone to the same university, so you're surrounded by strangers. Certainly get to know as many people as possible, but remember that initial enthusiasms can soon fade, so if a friendship doesn't endure more than a week or two, it's no reflection on you. On the same subject, don't let yourself get caught up in a group that is more affluent than you are: unless you can withstand pressure easily, you might try to keep up with them, and find yourself heavily in debt. Many students look for part-time jobs to supplement their income, but this may not always be advisable.

D

Many universities hold a 'freshers' week' for new students, which is a chance to meet people, make new friends and join university clubs. It's all too easy to just carry on with what you did while you were at home – tennis, singing, or whatever. Instead, you should see this as a good chance to try something new, or something you'd never imagined doing before. Universities often cater for minority interests, for instance providing facilities for sports that are uncommon elsewhere. If you need to earn some money, this may also be a good time to find out from the university about internal work opportunities, perhaps in the library or the registrar's department. Ensure your CV is up-to-date and accessible on your computer, because you'll need to produce it every time you go after a position.

E

Whether you're living in a university hall of residence or sharing a flat, you should make your space truly yours; paradoxically, this is particularly important if getting a job means you spend very little time there. Ideally, it will have an area for studying: as you probably found when you were at school, a comfortable chair is a good aid to reading and writing. You shouldn't need to spend any money – some photos or favourite posters brought from home are enough to make a big difference. Even if you're only going to be there for a matter of months, living and studying will be much less challenging if you have a comfortable base. Remember, too, that your going to university may be a big change for your family, so don't live so much in the present, exciting though it is, that you forget to keep in touch with them.

Test 3 Writing (1 hour 30 minutes) Part 1

You **must** answer this question. Write your answer in **220–260** words in an appropriate style on the separate answer sheet.

---

1 Your class has listened to a panel discussion about the benefits to a country of people gaining experience of life abroad. You have made the notes below:

Benefits to a country of people spending time abroad

- business
- culture
- understanding

Some opinions expressed in the discussion:

"People who've spent time abroad are then well equipped to conduct business with different countries."

"It teaches people about different traditions in local cultures."

"People become aware that there are other ways of looking at the world."

Write an essay discussing **two** of the benefits in your notes. You should **explain which benefit you think is most important, giving reasons** in support of your answer.

You may, if you wish, make use of the opinions expressed in the discussion, but you should use your own words as far as possible.

Test 3 Writing Part 2

Write an answer to **one** of the questions **2–4** in this part. Write your answer in **220–260** words in an appropriate style on the separate answer sheet. Put the question number in the box at the top of the page.

---

2 The firm that you work for would like to use an external IT company to maintain equipment and train employees. Write an email to an IT company that has been recommended to you.

Your email should explain

what your firm does, what kind of maintenance work you require, and why your training needs are urgent.

Write your **email**.

3 You recently completed a new course at an international college. The College Principal has asked you to write a report on the course highlighting its strengths and weaknesses. You should also make recommendations about how the course could be improved.

Write your **report**.

4 Your local town council would like to improve the appearance of the town by creating more green spaces and by introducing more street art such as sculptures or wall paintings. Write a proposal for the council in which you make specific suggestions about both green spaces and street art. Your proposal should also explain how you think your suggestions will improve the quality of life in your town.

Write your **proposal**.

Test 3 Listening (approximately 40 minutes) Part 1

2 01 You will hear three different extracts. For questions **1–6**, choose the answer (**A**, **B** or **C**) which fits best according to what you hear. There are two questions for each extract.

Extract One

You hear two friends discussing the woman's new job.

1 What is the woman doing during the conversation?

- **A** admitting that she has made a mistake
- **B** justifying a decision she has made
- **C** complaining about too much work

2 With regard to her working hours, the woman is pleased that

- **A** she now starts work later than she used to.
- **B** she doesn't need to work on Friday afternoons.
- **C** she can sometimes work when nobody else is present.

Extract Two

You hear two friends discussing a play they have both seen.

3 What did the woman think of the play they saw?

- **A** She was disappointed with the production.
- **B** She found it an entertaining production.
- **C** She had her eyes opened by the production.

4 What do they agree was an effective aspect of the production?

- **A** the lighting
- **B** the sound
- **C** the scenery

Extract Three

You hear a man telling a friend about a phone call he has just had.

5 How does the man feel about Isabel not helping him?

- **A** He is surprised that she has changed her mind about it.
- **B** He is annoyed that she won't do what she had agreed to do.
- **C** He is disappointed that she is unexpectedly prevented from doing it.

6 How will the man solve his problem?

- **A** He'll ask somebody else for a lift to the conference.
- **B** He'll cancel his booking for the conference.
- **C** He'll arrive late at the conference.

Test 3 Listening Part 2

02 You will hear a woman called Susan Foster talking about holidays organised by the company that she works for. For questions **7–14**, complete the sentences with a word or short phrase.

BENNETT'S HOLIDAYS

The company originally organised inclusive one-day trips by **(7)** .... from Manchester to the English Lake District.

The company now specialises in holidays in **(8)** .... and South America.

Susan uses the word **(9)** '..' to sum up her opinion of Buenos Aires.

One option in Buenos Aires is to go up in a **(10)** .... at sunset for an aerial view of the city.

Susan is particularly impressed by the **(11)** .... of Montevideo.

One tour includes a three-day visit to see mountains and **(12)** ....

Susan mentions the penguins and two species of **(13)** .... that can be seen off the Valdes Peninsula at certain times of the year.

A holiday in Argentina can include a one-day round trip by train to a **(14)** ....

Test 3 Listening Part 3

2 03 You will hear a conversation on a local radio station between a presenter and Angela Staveley, the director of an arts festival in the town of Marston. For questions **15–20**, choose the answer (**A**, **B**, **C** or **D**) which fits best according to what you hear.

15 What was the town council's main reason for holding a festival?

A to celebrate an important landmark in the town's history
B to encourage different groups of people to mix
C to collect money for local charities
D to raise the town's profile

16 Angela was appointed as festival director because of her

A experience of running festivals.
B skill at managing large-scale events.
C useful contacts with artists and performers.
D familiarity with a wide range of arts.

17 What difficulty has Angela had organising the festival?

A making sure everything is done in time for the festival
B raising enough funding to cover the full cost of the festival
C making use of all the offers of help she has received
D finding people with the areas of expertise she needs

18 How does Angela feel that organising the festival is affecting her?

A It is teaching her a great deal about working with people.
B It is making her aware that her reactions are sometimes inappropriate.
C It is proving to her than she can cope with stress better than she thought.
D It is making her realise that she should change the way she works.

19 Angela and the interviewer agree it is a good idea for the programme

A to present the widest possible variety of art forms.
B to form connections that make one event lead into the next.
C to make links between the events and aspects of the town.
D to give local clubs and organisations an active role in the festival.

20 How does Angela feel about organising another festival in the future?

A She would want to take part in the early decision making.
B She would be interested in organising one that is not for the arts.
C She would like to have a different role in a festival.
D She would need to have more assistants.

2 04 You will hear five short extracts in which people are talking about speaking to the store manager in a shop.

TASK ONE

For questions **21–25**, choose from the list (**A–H**) the reason each speaker gives for speaking to the store manager.

While you listen you must complete both tasks.

A to exchange a faulty purchase
B to cancel a delivery
C to get the price of a purchase reduced
D to place a special order
E to get information about some products
F to complain about poor service
G to return an unwanted item
H to praise a shop assistant

Speaker 1 [ ] 21
Speaker 2 [ ] 22
Speaker 3 [ ] 23
Speaker 4 [ ] 24
Speaker 5 [ ] 25

TASK TWO

For questions **26–30**, choose from the list (**A–H**) how each speaker felt after speaking to the store manager.

A shocked that the manager didn't believe them
B disappointed that their loyalty to the store was undervalued
C relieved that the manager seemed sympathetic
D confused by the manager's attitude
E embarrassed at having made a mistake
F determined never to go to the store again
G reluctant to accept the manager's offer
H irritated by the manager's behaviour

Speaker 1 [ ] 26
Speaker 2 [ ] 27
Speaker 3 [ ] 28
Speaker 4 [ ] 29
Speaker 5 [ ] 30

Test 3 Speaking (15 minutes) Part 1

Part 1 2 minutes (3 minutes for groups of three)

The interlocutor will ask you some questions about yourself, your home, work or studies and familiar topics.

Good morning/afternoon/evening. My name is ….. and this is my colleague ….. .

And your names are?

Can I have your mark sheets, please?

Thank you.

First of all, we'd like to know something about you.

- Where are you from?
- What do you enjoy about learning English?
- What do you do?
- How long do you plan to continue doing that?

The interlocutor will then ask you some questions about one or two other topics, for example:

- How important do you think it is to get on well with your neighbours?
- Tell me about a special journey you have made.
- What kind of music do you enjoy most?
- What famous person would you most like to have dinner with?

Test 3 Speaking Part 2

Part 2 4 minutes (6 minutes for groups of three)

Work in groups of three if possible. One of you is the interlocutor and the other two are the candidates. The interlocutor should lead the task using the script below. Refer to the pictures on pages S10 and S11.

The interlocutor will give you three pictures and ask you to talk about two of them on your own for about a minute. You will then be asked a question about your partner's pictures which you will need to answer in no more than 30 seconds.

Interlocutor In this part of the test, I'm going to give each of you three pictures. I'd like you to talk about **two** of them on your own for about a minute, and also to answer a question briefly about your partner's pictures.

(*Candidate A*), it's your turn first. Here are your pictures. They show **people who are laughing**.

I'd like you to compare **two** of the pictures and say **what you think the relationships between the people are, and why they are laughing**.

All right?

After 1 minute Thank you.

(*Candidate B*), **which people do you think will laugh for the longest time? (Why?)**

After approximately 30 seconds Thank you.

Now, (*Candidate B*), here are your pictures. They show **people learning a new skill**.

I'd like you to compare two of the pictures and say **why people want to learn skills like these, and how difficult these skills might be to learn**.

All right?

After 1 minute Thank you.

(*Candidate A*), **who do you think will have most difficulty learning this new skill? (Why?)**

After approximately 30 seconds Thank you.

Test 3 Speaking Parts 3 and 4

Part 3 4 minutes (6 minutes for groups of three)

Work in groups of three if possible. One of you is the interlocutor and the other two are the candidates. The interlocutor should lead the task using the script below. Refer to the task sheet on page S12.

The interlocutor will give you a task sheet to discuss together.

Interlocutor Now, I'd like you to talk about something together for about two minutes.

Here are some factors that might influence people's job choices and a question for you to discuss. First you have some time to look at the task. (*About 15 seconds*)

Now, talk to each other about **how these factors might influence a person's job choices.**

After 2 minutes Thank you. Now you have about a minute to decide **which of these factors you think is the most important to consider**.

After 1 minute Thank you.

Part 4 5 minutes (8 minutes for groups of three)

Work in groups of three if possible. One of you is the interlocutor and the other two are the candidates. The interlocutor should lead the task using the script below.

The interlocutor will ask some general questions which follow on from the topic in Part 3.

Interlocutor

- Do you think it's better to work in one place for life or to change jobs frequently? (Why? / Why not?)
- What are the advantages of working for a small company rather than a large one? (Why?)
- Do you consider ambition to be a positive or a negative quality? (Why?)
- What kinds of jobs deserve the highest salaries? (Why?)
- What should employers do to help employees enjoy their work? (Why?)

Thank you. That is the end of the test.

Test 4 Reading and Use of English (1 hour 30 minutes) Part 1

For questions **1–8**, read the text below and decide which answer (**A**, **B**, **C** or **D**) best fits each gap. There is an example at the beginning (**0**).

Mark your answers **on the separate answer sheet.**

Example:

0 **A** turned **B** made **C** allowed **D** enabled

0	A	B	C	D
	▭	▬	▭	▭

Research into television technology

Why do old television programmes look so strange and formal? And how has technology **(0)** .... modern shows possible? Researchers will **(1)** .... these questions in a study into the history of television technology since 1960, the first of its **(2)** .... in the country. From the over-rehearsed **(3)** .... of early black-and-white news interviews to the filming of reality television, a team **(4)** .... by Professor John Ellis, of Royal Holloway, University of London, will research the technological **(5)** .... and developments that have given programmes their unique appearance. 'With a huge amount of archive programming now being shown by satellite and cable channels, there has never been a more important time to tell the story of how it was filmed,' Professor Ellis said.

Researchers will work with **(6)** .... television technicians to discover how the technology available over the years, and what it could and couldn't do, **(7)** .... changes within the industry. They will film **(8)** .... of old programmes and interview technicians about the difficulties they had adapting to technological changes.

1	**A** search	**B** explore	**C** seek	**D** enquire
2	**A** brand	**B** class	**C** category	**D** kind
3	**A** feel	**B** touch	**C** sight	**D** taste
4	**A** ruled	**B** governed	**C** headed	**D** controlled
5	**A** limitations	**B** bans	**C** handicaps	**D** borders
6	**A** archaic	**B** bygone	**C** former	**D** outgoing
7	**A** hurried	**B** drove	**C** exerted	**D** pressed
8	**A** duplicates	**B** reconstructions	**C** likenesses	**D** replicas

Test 4 Reading and Use of English Part 2

For questions **9–16**, read the text below and think of the word which best fits each gap. Use only **one** word in each gap. There is an example at the beginning (**0**).

Write your answers **IN CAPITAL LETTERS on the separate answer sheet**.

Example: | **0** | I N T O |

The early human race

Scientists traditionally believed that a species which ranged over parts of Africa, Europe and Asia, eventually developed **(0)** .... both Homo sapiens (the species modern human beings belong to) and Neanderthals. **(9)** .... Neanderthals, who evolved in Europe and Asia, Homo sapiens emerged in Africa, later spreading into Europe and replacing Neanderthals.

Not **(10)** .... ago, some remains of what appeared to be a distinct species of early human beings were found in Siberia, but it was far **(11)** .... clear where this group – given the name 'Denisovans' – fitted into the picture. They were assumed to have hardly **(12)** .... connection with Homo sapiens.

However, tests on fossils in Spain have uncovered DNA that includes Denisovan material. This suggests that they, or at **(13)** .... their DNA, might have spread much further than was previously thought, interbreeding **(14)** .... Homo sapiens, and possibly also Neanderthals. **(15)** .... the precise connection may have been, the population dynamics are potentially very complex.

We would know nothing about the relationship were **(16)** .... not for recent advances in DNA retrieval and sequencing.

Reading and Use of English Part 3

For questions **17–24**, read the text below. Use the word given in capitals at the end of some of the lines to form a word that fits in the gap **in the same line**. There is an example at the beginning (**0**).

Write your answers **IN CAPITAL LETTERS on the separate answer sheet.**

Example: **0** | C | O | M | M | I | T | M | E | N | T |

The ICT4D (Information and Communication Technologies for Development) Collective

The ICT4D Collective was initiated in 2004 and is a group of people with a	
(0) .... to undertaking the highest possible quality of research in the field	**COMMIT**
of ICT4D, and making the results of this available freely to the **(17)**	**GLOBE**
community. We do this **(18)** .... in the interests of poor people and	**PRIME**
(19) .... communities, wherever they may be found. Membership of the	**MARGIN**
Collective implies strict **(20)** .... with its basic principles of membership	**COMPLY**
and partnership.	
Based at Royal Holloway, University of London, the Collective carries out research	
and undertakes teaching at undergraduate and postgraduate levels. The Collective	
also operates as a **(21)**	**CONSULT**
The Collective draws on the **(22)** .... of staff, postgraduates	**EXPERT**
and undergraduates in a range of academic departments. We welcome	
(23) .... work with colleagues across the world who share our core	**COLLABORATE**
objectives, and wish to establish partnerships with us to deliver practical ICT4D	
activities that will **(24)** .... poor people.	**POWER**

Test 4 Reading and Use of English Part 4

For questions **25–30**, complete the second sentence so that it has a similar meaning to the first sentence, using the word given. **Do not change the word given**. You must use between **three** and **six** words, including the word given. Here is an example (**0**).

Example:

0 'Marilyn didn't crash the car, John did,' Keith said.

IT

According to .... who crashed the car, not Marilyn.

The gap can be filled with the words 'Keith it was John', so you write:

Example:	**0**	KEITH IT WAS JOHN

Write **only** the missing words **IN CAPITAL LETTERS on the separate answer sheet**.

---

25 The film was so confusing, I couldn't follow what was happening.

SUCH

It was .... no idea what was happening.

26 The finance director disagreed with the company's change of policy, so she resigned.

RESULTED

The finance .... her disagreement with the company's change of policy.

27 I have yet to meet anyone as considerate as my cousin.

EVER

My cousin is the .... met.

28 It can take time to get used to a major change in your life.

TERMS

It can take time to .... a major change in your life.

29 Without Miranda, I would never have managed to find a house that suited me.

STILL

If it hadn't .... be looking for a suitable house.

30 It was difficult to work out what had happened, because of the conflicting witness statements.

PIECE

The conflicting witness statements .... what had happened.

Reading and Use of English Part 5

You are going to read part of a book about the study of languages. For questions **31–36**, choose the answer (**A**, **B**, **C** or **D**) which you think fits best according to the text.

Mark your answers **on the separate answer sheet**.

Language change

The phenomenon of language change probably attracts more public notice and criticism than any other linguistic issue. There is a widely held belief that change must mean deterioration and decay. Older people observe the casual speech of the young, and conclude that standards have fallen markedly. They place the blame in various quarters – most often in the schools, where patterns of language education have changed a great deal in recent decades, but also in state public broadcasting institutions, where any deviations from traditional norms provide an immediate focus of attack by conservative, linguistically sensitive listeners.

It is understandable that many people dislike change, but most of the criticism of linguistic change is misconceived. It is widely felt that the contemporary language illustrates the problem at its worst, but this belief is shared by every generation. Moreover, many of the usage issues recur across generations: several of the English controversies which are the focus of current attention can be found in the books and magazines of the 18th and 19th centuries – the debate over *it's me* and *very unique*, for example. In 1863, Henry Alford listed a large number of usage issues which worried his contemporaries and gave them cause to think that the language was rapidly decaying. Most are still with us, with the language not obviously affected.

There are indeed cases where linguistic change can lead to problems of unintelligibility, ambiguity, and social division. If change is too rapid, there can be major communication problems, as in contemporary Papua New Guinea, where by some counts over 800 languages have evolved, most spoken by fewer than 3,000 people. But as a rule, the parts of language which are changing at any given time are tiny in comparison to the vast, unchanging areas of language. Indeed, it is because change is so infrequent that it is so distinctive and noticeable. Some degree of caution and concern is therefore always desirable, in the interests of maintaining precise and efficient communication; but there are no grounds for the extreme pessimism and conservatism which is so often encountered.

For the most part, language changes because society changes. To stop or control the one requires that we stop or control the other – a task which can succeed to only a very limited extent. Language change is inevitable and rarely predictable, and those who try to plan a language's future waste their time if they think otherwise – time which would be better spent in devising fresh ways of enabling society to cope with the new linguistic forms that accompany each generation. These days, there is in fact a growing recognition of the need to develop a greater linguistic awareness and tolerance of change, especially in a multi-ethnic society. This requires, among other things, that schools have the knowledge and resources to teach a common standard, while recognizing the existence and value of linguistic diversity. Such policies provide a constructive alternative to the emotional attacks which are so commonly made against the development of new words, meanings, pronunciations, and grammatical constructions. But before these policies can be implemented, it is necessary to develop a proper understanding of the inevitability and consequences of linguistic change.

Some people go a stage further, and see change in language as a progression from a simple to a complex state – a view which was common as a consequence of 19th-century evolutionary thinking. But there is no evidence for this view. Languages do not develop, progress, decay, evolve, or act according to any of the metaphors which imply a specific endpoint and level of excellence. They simply change, as society changes. If a language dies out, it does so because its status alters in society, as other cultures and languages take over its role: it does not die because it has 'got too old', or 'become too complicated', as is sometimes maintained. Nor, when languages change, do they move in a predetermined direction. Some are losing inflections (endings, like 's' to indicate plurality); some are gaining them. Some are moving to an order where the verb precedes the object; others to an order where the object precedes the verb. Some languages are losing vowels and gaining consonants; others are doing the opposite. If metaphors must be used to talk about language change, one of the best is that of the tide, which always and inevitably changes, but never progresses, while it ebbs and flows.

31 In the first paragraph, what point does the writer make about languages?

A Young people tend to be unaware of the differences between their language and that of older people.
B The way that schools teach language is raising awareness of language change.
C Many people believe that any change in a language is undesirable.
D Public understanding of how languages develop is increasing.

32 The writer mentions *it's me* and *very unique* in the second paragraph to show that

A recent controversies may be nothing new.
B the speed of linguistic change is greater than in the past.
C every generation has its own list of unacceptable changes.
D a linguistic change may take place over a long period.

33 What is the writer's intention in referring to Papua New Guinea?

A to challenge a prevailing view concerning linguistic change
B to give an example of linguistic change that is unusual
C to show the danger of making generalisations about linguistic change
D to illustrate conflicting views about the potential effects of linguistic change

34 In the third paragraph, the writer claims that

A the public are inconsistent in the value they place on accurate communication.
B changes that take place in a language can be difficult to reverse.
C caution is necessary when attempting to measure language change.
D public attention to linguistic change reflects the essential stability of languages.

35 What point does the writer make in the fourth paragraph?

A Trying to prevent change should have a lower priority than dealing with its effects.
B Multi-ethnic societies need a shared language to make communication possible.
C Language change tends to be tolerated in multi-ethnic societies.
D The emergence of new linguistic forms often leads to communication difficulties.

36 In the fifth paragraph, the writer argues against the notion that languages

A change in apparently random ways.
B improve by becoming increasingly complex.
C should in some circumstances be allowed to die out.
D can be categorised according to stages in their evolution.

Reading and Use of English Part 6

You are going to read four reviews of a book about documentary films. For questions **37–40**, choose from the reviews **A–D**. The reviews may be chosen more than once.

Mark your answers **on the separate answer sheet**.

Documentaries – do they have a future?

Four reviewers comment on journalist Sharon Miller's book

A

The documentary has recently become a field of serious study, the latest entrant to which being Sharon Miller's new book. As a journalist, her credentials might be regarded as somewhat suspect, but in fact not being a filmmaker herself enables her to take a more objective approach than is often the case. For example, she criticises the TV companies for not satisfying the public's appetite for quality documentaries, but without the anger that a documentary maker might feel. It is hard to fault her analysis of this situation. The same applies to Miller's final chapter, in which she explains why documentaries shown on the big screen will eventually evolve into full-length films commanding as much attention as the standard cinema material. She may prove wrong on detail, but her conclusions are convincing. Miller rarely makes claims she cannot substantiate, and her thorough reading of much of the existing literature clearly informs her argument.

B

It is a relief to read that Miller believes the documentary has a glorious future, even if I would reach the same destination by a different route. However, that is one of few assertions that I can concur with; for instance, she blames television companies for their caution with regard to documentaries, without taking into account the numerous constraints that they suffer. Miller is, no doubt, a skilled journalist, and can put together a plausible article whenever one is required. But while that may suit a newspaper which is read and then forgotten, a book stakes a claim to be long-lasting; and Miller is clearly unaware of many aspects of the world in which documentary makers operate. To her credit, though, she has included an extensive bibliography, but to be brutally frank, the book is no more than a just-about-adequate summary of earlier studies.

C

Sharon Miller, while primarily a journalist, has also written an excellent introduction to the sociology of social media, and her new book, *Documentaries*, is further evidence that she is a writer to be reckoned with. Her reading on the subject is extensive, and forms a firm foundation for her argument, that the documentary film is far from being the endangered species it seemed not long ago. With a few minor reservations, I was carried along by her optimism about its future. It is only when Miller turns her attention to documentaries on television that I feel the need to take issue with her. Although many of the television companies are certainly as guilty of ignoring the documentary as she claims, there are also many, admittedly smaller, companies that have done sterling service in stretching the boundaries of the genre.

D

As a former television programme controller myself, I can back up Sharon Miller's opinion of the TV companies' attitude towards documentaries. The little that some companies have done to advance the genre is easily outweighed by the harm done by the majority. I was also taken by her overview of earlier studies of the documentary. It is thorough, and she is careful to ensure that both her facts and her opinions are consistent with what her predecessors have established. The only time she comes to grief, in my view, is in the rosy future she promises for the documentary: the evidence underpinning her assertion simply doesn't stand up to close scrutiny. What it comes down to is that Miller's work is rather too hit-and-miss: she picks a topic – the documentary – apparently at random, and does a fair amount of research into it, but it takes the inside knowledge she lacks to turn that into the definitive account she was aiming to write.

Which reviewer

has a different opinion from reviewer B regarding Miller's view of the future of documentaries? **37** ☐

shares an opinion with reviewer C on the subject of Miller's qualifications for writing the book? **38** ☐

takes a different view from the others on Miller's use of earlier studies? **39** ☐

holds the same opinion as reviewer A concerning Miller's position on television documentaries? **40** ☐

Test 4 Reading and Use of English Part 7

You are going to read an article about exploration of a glacier in the Alps. Six paragraphs have been removed from the extract. Choose from the paragraphs **A–G** the one which fits each gap (**41–46**). There is one extra paragraph which you do not need to use.

Mark your answers **on the separate answer sheet**.

Exploring the Gorner Glacier

Towering above the Alpine villages of Switzerland, Italy and France, the imposing peaks of the Matterhorn and its neighbours have long been a desirable destination for mountaineers and explorers alike. Today, while cable cars and a mountain railway transport hordes of tourists to the more accessible areas, pioneering exploration continues, not on the surface, but far out of sight in the icy depths of the second-largest glacier system in the Alps, on the eastern side of the tourist town of Zermatt.

41 ____________

At the end of October last year, I joined a seven-person British team that was returning to the Gorner Glacier for its second expedition exploring, mapping and photographing the sub-glacial world of moulins – well-like shafts through which meltwater drains from the surface of the glacier – and the ice caves that they help to create.

42 ____________

The weather seemed calm and benign, but overnight, considerably more snow fell than had been forecast and the next day, the Gornergrat mountain railway – the first stage in our journey up to the glacier – was closed. The advance party, they later told us, was completely snowed in.

43 ____________

Thankfully, the weather eventually cleared, and the following day we began digging out a path from our camp towards the glacier. Meanwhile, the advance team was heading back towards us. Eventually both teams met up, shared a few jokes and plodded back up to our temporary camp for a meal and a good night's sleep before we started the work we had come to do.

44 ____________

I flitted between both parties, desperately trying to capture as many images of this wonderful environment as possible. The dramatically sculpted ice walls reminded me of shapes I'd seen before in cylindrical caves formed in limestone. Looking up, I noticed rocks and pebbles of varying sizes emerging from the roof of the ice caves.

45 ____________

Typically moving at about 15 metres a year, the Gorner Glacier picks up speed due to meltwater falling through these moulins and acting as a lubricant along its base. Although the glacier has a total area of more than 50 square kilometres, making it the second largest glacial system in the Alps, it has receded every year since 1892 – since then it has shrunk by almost 2.5 kilometres, including a staggering 290 metres over the summer of 2007.

46 ____________

Seeing how vast and extensive the glacier's moulins and ice-cave systems can be gives an indication of just how much water flows through them during the summer. Sadly, this is also an indicator of the rate at which the Alps' majestic rivers of ice are shrinking. One member of the team, Sam Doyle, a glaciologist from the University of Aberystwyth, spends most of his time in Greenland, studying the rate at which the ice sheet is moving. He was concerned to see many similarities between the moulins on the Gorner Glacier and the movement of the ice sheet.

A So, a day later than planned, we travelled up the mountain to the station, the starting point for our hike to the glacier. When we alighted, however, we discovered an expanse of knee-deep snow. It was too late to cover the three kilometres we still needed to travel, so we set up camp close to the station.

B We arrived in Zermatt late in the evening, heavily laden with equipment and enough food for a week. By now, the three members of the group who had already left to set up camp on the edge of the glacier were probably tucked up in their sleeping bags, awaiting our arrival the next morning.

C All these fascinating sights kept me engrossed in my photography. Meanwhile, members of the two teams set about surveying the caves, while others rigged ropes around large areas of meltwater and moulins that led to other levels of the system.

D Here, two big glaciers fall into the deep on either side of Monte Rosa, the highest mountain in Switzerland. To the left is the Findelen Glacier and to the right is the 14-kilometre-long Gorner Glacier.

E We set off to follow the advance party as best we could, given the difficult weather conditions, while they waited in the shelter of their tents. There was great relief all round when we finally reached them.

F We had two great days exploring the spectacular world beneath the glacier's surface. More moulins had opened up since last year's expedition, and the team split into two and began abseiling down into those that looked the most encouraging.

G This was one reason why it was so important to identify what exactly was happening. We discovered, surveyed and photographed three enormous ice caves. Descending through one moulin, we followed an eight-metre-deep trench where the water had carved its way through the ice.

Test 4 Reading and Use of English Part 8

You are going to read a magazine article in which four fashion designers write about their careers. For questions **47–56**, choose from the extracts (**A–D**). The extracts may be chosen more than once.

Mark your answers **on the separate answer sheet**.

Which designer

set up a business despite feeling unqualified?	**47**
found a job through a personal contact?	**48**
has broadened the range of products they manufacture?	**49**
found that their early success did not continue?	**50**
regrets accepting a job they were offered?	**51**
mentions impressing other people with their enthusiasm?	**52**
was surprised by the help they received from more experienced designers?	**53**
has found that working in fashion is different from what they expected?	**54**
realised the need to develop skills that were in demand?	**55**
learnt how to run a company before starting their own?	**56**

A career in fashion

Four fashion designers write about their careers.

Fashion designer A

Fashion wasn't my first choice of career: I only thought of it when I threw in a disastrous job in advertising, and sat wondering what to do next. A friend pointed out that I'd always been keen on fashion, and that made me realise that was what I wanted to do. I managed to get a place on a fashion course, and the tutors were very positive about my designs. I even won a couple of awards. Of course that made me think that when I left college I'd just walk into a job, but I soon found out my mistake! Eventually, though, I managed to talk my way into an interview with a fashion business, and they took me on – they told me afterwards that I seemed over-confident, but my saving grace was that I was so eager to learn more about clothes design. It wasn't a very good job, really, but at least it gave me good experience for the next one I got.

Fashion designer B

As a child, I loved the glamour of the world of fashion and daydreamed about being the person whose designs the models were wearing. I took a fashion course, then begged for a job with a small fashion business. I think they took me on as a favour, really, because to be honest I had very little to offer them. Still, it was invaluable for me. It was a great introduction to the manufacturing process, and the boss seemed happy to teach me all about the business side of things. That really stood me in good stead when I eventually left to start my own fashion design business. Since then, we've branched out into household goods like tablecloths and bedding. It's still early days, so we'll wait and see how that goes. But don't let anyone tell you it's an easy life. There may be a touch of glamour occasionally, but nine-tenths of the time it's sheer hard work, long hours and a lot of stress.

Fashion designer C

In my first job interview after leaving college, they wanted someone with strong skills in computer-aided design – CAD – and my college hadn't offered that as an option, so I didn't have a chance. That made me realise I needed to learn CAD, and I enrolled on a course, and got a job in a supermarket to finance it. When I finished, a tutor on the course put me in touch with a fashion business she knew, even though they weren't advertising for designers. Her recommendation must have swung them in my favour, because they took me on. It wasn't ideal, though, as it was a very inward-looking firm, and I didn't get the chance to go to fashion shows or network with other designers, which you need to do if you want to start your own business. In retrospect, I think I'd have been better off setting up on my own as soon as I got the CAD qualification, even though it would have been very hard work.

Fashion designer D

There are lots of people chasing very few jobs in fashion, so it's hard even to get as far as an interview – and a lot of firms don't even advertise: they can find staff more cheaply through contacts or unsolicited applications that people have sent in. After college, I applied to dozens of firms, but got nowhere. It was very demoralising. So I took a chance and started a firm with a couple of friends who were in the same boat. What we knew about running a company you could write on the back of an envelope – we all saw ourselves as designers, not business people – but somehow we muddled through. To a great extent, that was down to contacts we met at networking events: a couple of established designers gave us some invaluable advice on how to market our designs. Without that, we'd probably have gone under in the first six months. And given that we were trying to compete with them, it was remarkably generous of them.

Test 4 Writing (1 hour 30 minutes) Part 1

You **must** answer this question. Write your answer in **220–260** words in an appropriate style on the separate answer sheet.

---

1 Your class has listened to a radio discussion about how important it is to keep up-to-date with aspects of culture and current affairs. You have made the notes below:

<u>Aspects of culture and current affairs where people like to keep up-to-date</u>

- news
- fashion
- the arts

Some opinions expressed in the discussion:

"Being well-informed about what's going on in the world may help us to avoid problems in future."

"Fashionable clothes make people look more interesting – and they don't need to be expensive."

"Knowing about the latest books and films gives you lots of interesting things to talk about."

Write an essay discussing **two** of the aspects in your notes. You should **explain which aspect is most important to keep up-to-date with**, **giving reasons** in support of your answer.

You may, if you wish, make use of the opinions expressed in the discussion, but you should use your own words as far as possible.

Test 4 Writing Part 2

Write an answer to **one** of the questions **2–4** in this part. Write your answer in **220–260** words in an appropriate style on the separate answer sheet. Put the question number in the box at the top of the page.

---

2 A website has asked readers to write reviews of videos that ordinary people have posted online. You decide to write a review comparing two videos, one that you enjoyed and one that you didn't.

Your review should briefly describe each of the videos and should explain why one was good and the other was not.

Write your **review**.

3 You work for an international company. Someone from the Australian branch of your company is coming to work in your branch for three months. Write a letter to your Australian colleague, explaining what you think is distinctive about your branch and the people who work there. You should also give some advice about how the visitor can make the most of their free time while they are in your country.

Write your **letter**.

4 An international organisation is investigating transport issues in different towns. You have been asked to write a report in which you give information about the traffic situation in your town.

Your report should briefly describe the public transport system, discussing whether it meets the needs of the local population. It should also explain what the most serious traffic problem in the town currently is.

Write your **report**.

Test 4 Listening (approximately 40 minutes) Part 1

2 05 You will hear three different extracts. For questions **1–6**, choose the answer (**A**, **B** or **C**) which fits best according to what you hear. There are two questions for each extract.

Extract One

You hear two friends discussing an art exhibition.

1 The woman was disappointed that

A the exhibition did not match its advance publicity.
B her favourite artist was not represented.
C the paintings were poorly displayed.

2 What is the man's attitude towards art exhibitions?

A They make him feel that he doesn't know enough about art.
B He assumes he won't like the people who regularly attend.
C It annoys him that paintings aren't discussed in enough depth.

Extract Two

You hear two friends, Tony and Marion, discussing a problem at Tony's workplace.

3 In Tony's opinion, a colleague is treating him badly because

A he has a different standard of living from her.
B he is the newest member of the department.
C he is much younger than she is.

4 What do they agree that Tony should do?

A look for a new job
B ask his line manager for help
C talk to the person who is treating him badly

Extract Three

You hear a writer called Ross telling a friend called Erica about a problem he has with his publisher.

5 Why is Ross annoyed about what his publisher wants him to do?

- **A** He hasn't been consulted about the changes.
- **B** He will have to cancel his holiday.
- **C** He won't be paid for the extra work.

6 Why does Erica talk about her cousin?

- **A** to suggest to Ross that he should not overreact
- **B** to remind Ross of his motives for writing the book
- **C** to encourage Ross to negotiate with his publisher

Test 4 Listening Part 2

2 06 You will hear Jack Charlesworth, the manager of a UK supermarket, talking to a group of business students about his work. For questions **7–14**, complete the sentences with a word or short phrase.

WORKING IN A SUPERMARKET

Jack's main concern is what he calls the customers' **(7)** ....

Jack believes it is important to treat customers in a friendly way, particularly if they feel **(8)** .... on arrival.

Managers and other staff working as **(9)** .... look for customers who need help.

All staff are encouraged to contribute to a **(10)** ....

The store sometimes organises what Jack calls a **(11)** '..' , for employees to consult him about promotion.

Some of the supermarket staff start work at 6 am to deal with all the **(12)** .... that has been delivered to the store.

The store uses a **(13)** .... system to order goods from the distribution centre.

When placing orders, managers always evaluate the impact of various things, including the **(14)** .... , on sales.

Test 4 Listening Part 3

2 07 You will hear a geology professor asking two students, Cathy and Jason, about a field trip they have just returned from. For questions **15–20**, choose the answer (**A**, **B**, **C** or **D**) which fits best according to what you hear.

---

15 What do Cathy and Jason agree was disappointing?

A the length of the field trip
B the number of people participating
C the type of accommodation they had
D the level of support from the tutors

16 They both think they benefited from the field trip by learning

A not to get distracted.
B to consider other people's opinions.
C to trust his own judgment.
D not always to follow his first idea.

17 How does Cathy feel about her project?

A She is not certain that she chose the topic wisely.
B She thinks she has done as well as she can.
C She wonders if her approach to the topic is mistaken.
D She hopes she has done some original work.

18 What do they agree about the field trip in relation to the rest of their course?

A It brought the subject to life.
B It was enjoyable without contributing significantly to their understanding.
C It was useful but should have been shorter.
D Its timing has negatively affected other aspects of their studies.

19 What does Jason suggest about the impact of the field trip on his feelings about geology?

A It has revived his initial enthusiasm for the subject.
B It has reinforced his reservations about geology as a career.
C It has demonstrated to him that he lacks some skills that geology requires.
D It has raised fresh doubts about his enjoyment of the subject.

20 What type of work does Cathy expect to do when she graduates?

A developing alternative sources of energy
B minimising the environmental impact of fossil-fuel extraction
C encouraging a reduction in energy consumption
D increasing the efficiency of fossil-fuel extraction

2 08 You will hear five short extracts in which people are talking about their leisure activities.

TASK ONE

For questions **21–25**, choose from the list (**A–H**) the original reason each speaker gives for choosing their leisure activity.

TASK TWO

For questions **26–30**, choose from the list (**A–H**) how each speaker feels about their leisure activity now.

While you listen you must complete both tasks.

Task One

- **A** They wanted to get fit.
- **B** They wanted to make new friends.
- **C** They wanted mental stimulation.
- **D** A friend recommended it.
- **E** They were told they weren't suited to doing it.
- **F** It was popular with other students.
- **G** They wanted a career doing that activity.
- **H** One of their parents introduced them to it.

Speaker 1 [ ] 21

Speaker 2 [ ] 22

Speaker 3 [ ] 23

Speaker 4 [ ] 24

Speaker 5 [ ] 25

Task Two

- **A** aware they are less skilled than they thought
- **B** surprised at the standard they have reached
- **C** unsure whether or not to continue
- **D** delighted they have achieved a target
- **E** concerned they made a poor choice
- **F** disappointed that they cannot carry on
- **G** pleased they have become well known
- **H** puzzled by its lack of popularity

Speaker 1 [ ] 26

Speaker 2 [ ] 27

Speaker 3 [ ] 28

Speaker 4 [ ] 29

Speaker 5 [ ] 30

Speaking (15 minutes) Part 1

Part 1 2 minutes (3 minutes for groups of three)

The interlocutor will ask you some questions about yourself, your home, work or studies and familiar topics.

Good morning/afternoon/evening. My name is ..... and this is my colleague ..... .
And your names are?
Can I have your mark sheets, please?
Thank you.

First of all, we'd like to know something about you.

- Where are you from?
- Where do you work/study?
- What do you enjoy most about your work/study?
- When did you start learning English?

The interlocutor will then ask you some questions about one or two other topics, for example:

- How important is sport in your life?
- Tell us about a story that is currently in the news.
- What was your journey here like today?
- Which time of year do you enjoy most?

Test 4 Speaking Part 2

Part 2 4 minutes (6 minutes for groups of three)

Work in groups of three if possible. One of you is the interlocutor and the other two are the candidates. The interlocutor should lead the task using the script below. Refer to the pictures on pages S13 and S14.

The interlocutor will give you three pictures and ask you to talk about two of them on your own for about a minute. You will then be asked a question about your partner's pictures which you will need to answer in no more than 30 seconds.

Interlocutor In this part of the test, I'm going to give each of you three pictures. I'd like you to talk about **two** of them on your own for about a minute, and also to answer a question briefly about your partner's pictures.

(*Candidate A*), it's your turn first. Here are your pictures. They show **people putting on a performance for an audience**.

I'd like you to compare **two** of the pictures and say **what you think the performance is about, and how memorable the performances might be for the audience**.

All right?

After 1 minute Thank you.

(*Candidate B*), **which performance do you think requires the most talent? Why?**

After approximately 30 seconds Thank you.

Now, (*Candidate B*), here are your pictures. They show **people dancing in different situations.**

I'd like you to compare **two** of the pictures and say **why the people are dancing in these situations and what they might be feeling**.

All right?

After 1 minute Thank you.

(*Candidate A*), **which people do you think are enjoying dancing the most? (Why?)**

After approximately 30 seconds Thank you.

Test 4 Speaking Parts 3 and 4

Part 3 4 minutes (6 minutes for groups of three)

Work in groups of three if possible. One of you is the interlocutor and the other two are the candidates. The interlocutor should lead the task using the script below. Refer to the task sheet on page S15.

The interlocutor will give you a task sheet to discuss together.

Interlocutor Now, I'd like you to talk about something together for about two minutes.

Here are some subjects that children usually do at school and a question for you to discuss. First you have some time to look at the task. (*About 15 seconds*)

Now, talk to each other about **how important studying these subjects is for a person's future life**.

After 2 minutes Thank you. Now you have a minute to decide **which of these subjects requires the most study time at school.**

After 1 minute Thank you.

Part 4 5 minutes (8 minutes for groups of three)

Work in groups of three if possible. One of you is the interlocutor and the other two are the candidates. The interlocutor should lead the task using the script below.

The interlocutor will ask some general questions which follow on from the topic in Part 3.

Interlocutor

- To what extent should students be able to choose what they study at school? (Why?)
- Should it be the responsibility of schools to teach moral values to young people? (Why? / Why not?)
- What – if any – are the advantages of single-sex education? (Why?)
- How can young people benefit from school trips and other school activities outside the classroom? (Why?)
- What would you say are the qualities of a good teacher? (Why?)

Thank you. That is the end of the test.

Test 5 Reading and Use of English (1 hour 30 minutes) Part 1

For questions **1–8**, read the text below and decide which answer (**A**, **B**, **C** or **D**) best fits each gap. There is an example at the beginning (**0**).

Mark your answers **on the separate answer sheet**.

Example:

0 **A** thoughts **B** ideas **C** wits **D** emotions

0	A	B	C	D
	▭	▭	▬	▭

Why do we love horror films?

Why will some people pay good money to be scared out of their **(0)** .... ? As someone who has seen just one horror film in their life, this never ceases to **(1)** .... me. You can keep your horror; to be **(2)** .... , I would rather have surgery without anaesthetic. But according to psychologists, the fear we **(3)** .... is safe: we know that when the film ends, we'll be unharmed.

Horror films make our hearts **(4)** .... , and that's part of what **(5)** .... to us: if our lives are uneventful, we seek excitement – in fact, it's good for our nervous system.

A study carried out in 1995 showed that the higher people **(6)** .... on a scale that measures sensation-seeking, the more likely they are to be fans of horror films. People in their teens and twenties tend to seek out **(7)** .... experiences, and this makes them the biggest audience for horror films. That usually **(8)** .... with age: maybe we start to realise that real life is scary enough.

1	**A** daze	**B** baffle	**C** elude	**D** defy
2	**A** direct	**B** clear	**C** distinct	**D** honest
3	**A** crave	**B** wish	**C** yearn	**D** long
4	**A** shake	**B** batter	**C** pound	**D** knock
5	**A** attracts	**B** engages	**C** entices	**D** appeals
6	**A** score	**B** mark	**C** grade	**D** point
7	**A** severe	**B** burning	**C** intense	**D** fierce
8	**A** fades	**B** dissolves	**C** disintegrates	**D** pales

Test 5 Reading and Use of English Part 2

For questions **9–16**, read the text below and think of the word which best fits each gap. Use only **one** word in each gap. There is an example at the beginning (**0**).

Write your answers **IN CAPITAL LETTERS on the separate answer sheet.**

Example: | **0** | O N E |

Attention all teachers!

Donna-May Photography is **(0)** .... of the leading digital photography services in the region. Whatever the event may be – concert, sports day, prize-giving, etc. – your school needs photographs of the pupils, **(9)** .... is where we come in. We pride **(10)** .... on offering top-quality service and memorable photos.

But **(11)** .... of just listening to us (and of course we're biased!), **(12)** .... not read this letter from a happy headteacher?

"A huge thank you for the photos you took of our school concert. We're sure our pupils will regard them **(13)** .... perfect mementos of a very special occasion. **(14)** .... several complications arose before the concert began, Jane, your photographer, stayed calm and unperturbed.

Numerous parents were present, and many have commented to me on **(15)** .... well Jane interacted with the children. In the end, everything went very smoothly, and the children had a wonderful afternoon. Next time we arrange an event like this, we'll **(16)** .... in touch!"

To find out more, please visit our website, www.donna-mayphotography.com.

Test 5 Reading and Use of English Part 3

For questions **17–24**, read the text below. Use the word given in capitals at the end of some of the lines to form a word that fits in the gap **in the same line**. There is an example at the beginning (**0**).

Write your answers **IN CAPITAL LETTERS on the separate answer sheet.**

Example: | 0 | P E R S O N A L |

A history of science and scientists

Science can be a very **(0)** .... activity. Throughout history, scientists,	**PERSON**
with few **(17)** .... , have carried out their investigations, motivated not	**EXCEPT**
by a desire for glory or wealth, but by a need to satisfy their own **(18)**	**CURIOUS**
about the world around them. Some have gained lasting fame, while others	
have kept their **(19)** .... to themselves, not caring about the	**DISCOVER**
(20) .... of others.	**RECOGNISE**
Scientists build on the research of their predecessors, but they usually	
make their own contributions individually. I therefore decided to take a	
(21) .... approach to the history of science, in the hope of learning,	**BIOGRAPHY**
to some degree, what makes scientists tick. There are even, I think, one or two	
somewhat surprising **(22)** .... contained in this book.	**REVEAL**
This approach is out of favour with today's **(23)** .... , who may well	**HISTORY**
dismiss me as being old-fashioned. But I trust that even if they consider my	
approach **(24)** .... , they will still give my comments a fair hearing.	**ACCEPT**

Test 5 Reading and Use of English Part 4

For questions **25–30**, complete the second sentence so that it has a similar meaning to the first sentence, using the word given. **Do not change the word given**. You must use between **three** and **six** words, including the word given. Here is an example (**0**).

Example:

0 I'm sure the college will offer financial assistance to students who can't afford the fees.

BOUND

Students who can't afford the college fees .... financial assistance.

The gap can be filled with the words 'are bound to be offered', so you write:

Example: | **0** | ARE BOUND TO BE OFFERED |

Write **only** the missing words **IN CAPITAL LETTERS on the separate answer sheet**.

---

25 We'll have to cancel the meeting if we can't find a suitable venue.

CALL

We'll have to .... we find a suitable venue.

26 Henry never misses a party if he can help it.

UP

Henry .... opportunity.

27 Many people wrongly believe that all Australians spend their free time on the beach.

POPULAR

Contrary .... all Australians spend their free time on the beach.

28 Karen hasn't got any money, which is why her clothes are quite shabby.

DUE

The shabbiness of Karen's clothes .... of money.

29 Only when Sarah left did it become clear how much she had contributed to the company's success.

EXTENT

It was not .... of her contribution to the company's success became clear.

30 Jeremy struggled to fully understand the sheer scale of the challenge he faced.

HARD

Jeremy found .... grips with the sheer scale of the challenge he faced.

Test 5 Reading and Use of English Part 5

You are going to read the introduction to a book about *déjà vu*. For questions **31–36**, choose the answer (**A**, **B**, **C** or **D**) which you think fits best according to the text.

Mark your answers **on the separate answer sheet**.

'I've been here before': the *déjà vu* feeling

Most people – two out of three, according to surveys – have experienced *déjà vu* (French for 'already seen'). It is that weird sensation of having 'been here before' or having 'lived this moment already'. You may be visiting some entirely unfamiliar town, for instance, and 'realise' that you have already been in that precise spot, even though you know it is impossible. The feeling goes way beyond any vague sense of having seen or done something similar before – it feels identical to a past experience. Yet trying to pin down the memory is like trying to catch a dream – just as you think you are homing in on it, it turns to vapour. The eeriness of this has led to all sorts of spooky theories. A popular one is that it is the memory of a dream in which the person has lived through the current moment in advance. In recent years, however, neuroscientists have discovered enough about perception and memory to piece together a more plausible explanation.

Every conscious experience we have is 'constructed' by our brain out of lots of different components, rather as a car might be made in a factory. We tend to think of an event as a bundle of sensations: sight, sound, etc., but there is actually much more to it. If you (literally) bump into someone in the street, for example, you will be aware of the sight of them, the touch of them as you bump, the sound each of you makes, and so on. But you will also be aware of the meaning, tone and intention of the sound, the pain from the bump, a sense of irritation or embarrassment; a thought, perhaps, that you, or the other person, is clumsy, and so on. There is much more to experience than simple sensations.

One very important 'component' that often gets added is a sense of familiarity. This is generated in the deep part of the brain that creates emotions. The sense of 'Ah yes! I recognise this!' usually only gets attached to experiences which 'match' stored memories. Sometimes, though, the part of the brain which generates the feeling of familiarity attaches it to an experience that is actually quite novel. This is what seems to happen in *déjà vu*. The brain then tries to dig out matching memories, but of course they aren't there – hence the maddening feeling of chasing shadows.

For most people, *déjà vu* is a rare and fleeting phenomenon, intriguing rather than disturbing. And it doesn't seem to be unhealthy – indeed, *déjà vu* is most commonly reported by people who are young, intelligent and well-educated. Given that it is actually a minor brain malfunction, this may seem strange. The explanation may be that young brains are more 'recognition sensitive', so they are more easily triggered into familiarity mode. Similar sensitivity may also be a factor in intelligence – bright people 'see things' more readily than others, and intelligent people tend to go on to higher education. So *déjà vu* may be a side effect of having a brain that is quick to recognise things.

For an unfortunate few, though, *déjà vu* is a constant companion, and a serious blight on their lives. Dr Chris Moulin is a psychologist who is studying this strange disorder. He first came across it when he was working in a memory clinic: 'We had a peculiar referral from a man who said there was no point visiting the clinic because he'd already been there, although this would have been impossible. *Déjà vu* had developed to such an extent that he had stopped watching TV because it seemed to be a repeat. He even believed he could hear the same bird singing the same song in the same tree every time he went out.

Apart from the sheer tedium of chronic *déjà vu*, the condition can also get people into social difficulties. 'Some patients feel that everyone they meet is familiar, and this makes them dangerously trusting of strangers,' says Moulin. 'If they don't constantly remind themselves that the sensation is false, they are at risk of being exploited.' So next time you find yourself 're-living' an experience, don't struggle to recall the previous time. Just sit back and relax. And make sure that you don't sign on the dotted line until the moment has passed.

31 What point does the writer make about *déjà vu* in the first paragraph?

A Scientists tend to disbelieve people who claim to have had the experience.
B The experience is more common than scientists are prepared to admit.
C Many previous attempts to explain it were based on unscientific beliefs.
D Some evidence of a non-scientific cause cannot be disproved.

32 Why does the writer mention manufacturing a car?

A to indicate that our experiences are more complex than we realise
B to suggest that many of the experiences people have are similar
C to show that different experiences tend to consist of the same components
D to emphasise the role of other people in the experiences we have

33 According to the third paragraph, *déjà vu* seems to be caused by

A emotions that are normally linked with different experiences becoming confused.
B an experience arousing an emotion which is linked with similar previous experiences.
C the brain failing to distinguish between different emotional responses.
D a feeling of recognition mistakenly being linked with a new experience.

34 According to the fourth paragraph, *déjà vu* is probably caused by

A a person's lack of patience.
B the level of education that a person achieves.
C a useful attribute of some people's brains.
D the environment in which some people are brought up.

35 Chris Moulin gives the example of a man

A whose experience of *déjà vu* could not be treated.
B who thought that actual and potential experiences duplicated previous ones.
C who blamed television for making his condition worse.
D who found the familiarity of his experiences somewhat comforting.

36 What advice does the writer give to people who frequently experience *déjà vu*?

A to avoid situations where there is a risk of experiencing *déjà vu*
B not to trust others until they have evidence that they will not be exploited
C to check with people they meet whether or not they have met previously
D not to commit themselves to something on the basis of its apparent familiarity

Test 5 Reading and Use of English Part 6

You are going to read four reviews of a production of Shakespeare's play *Hamlet*. For questions **37–40**, choose from the reviews **A–D**. The reviews may be chosen more than once.

Mark your answers **on the separate answer sheet.**

Hamlet, by William Shakespeare, at the Granary Theatre

Directed by Carol Barlow, starring Paul Mason as Hamlet

A

Carol Barlow has come up with a great number of ingenious devices to distinguish her production of *Hamlet* from the thousands that have gone before. I just wasn't sure how they fitted together to make a coherent whole, and would have been happier with fewer notions, better thought through. Perhaps Barlow's intention was to hold up a mirror to the fragmentary nature of today's world, and if so, she could be said to have succeeded. Paul Mason, playing the role of Hamlet for the first time, certainly delivers his lines thrillingly, the range and resonance of his voice contributing in no small measure. Yet it remained a performance: his gestures and mannerisms kept reminding us that we were watching an actor. As the final curtain fell, I realised I knew the character of Hamlet no better than I did at the beginning.

B

Hamlet is a complex character, which gives scope for many different interpretations. However, there needs to be internal consistency: arbitrarily hugging another character one minute and ignoring them the next tells us nothing about Hamlet himself. Paul Mason seems to want to impress us with all the vocal tricks in his repertoire – and there are many – but long before the final curtain, I wished the character had been killed off in Act 1. As director, Carol Barlow seems to have brainstormed ideas for the production, thrown them up in the air, and let them fall at random. The result is a mishmash that for some unfathomable reason is set in the 1920s. Productions of *Hamlet* often reflect the spirit of the age, so a number of modern versions focus on notions of mental disorder, but Barlow's production tells us nothing about Shakespeare's own time, or about today's world.

C

Paul Mason isn't an obvious choice to play Hamlet – he's too old, and his acting is idiosyncratic; yet somehow he pulls it off. His quirks and eccentricities convey the depth of Hamlet's despair, and his need to present a mask to the world. Initially I found his delivery mannered, but it soon drew me in, and immersed me in the character's predicament and his fractured personality. By the end, I could have gone on listening to him for hours. However, Mason was the redeeming feature of the evening. Barlow continually gives the audience new and highly distracting things to think about. For instance, she sets *Hamlet* in the 1920s, and the costumes, gorgeous though they are, hardly lend themselves to carrying a sword, as many of the characters do. It just made the setting neither modern nor of Shakespeare's own time, or even of the time of the historical Hamlet.

D

How can an audience be made to see a play as well-known as *Hamlet* with fresh eyes? Director Carol Barlow has met the challenge with astonishing bravura. By moving it into the 1920s, she shows the universality of the play's themes, despite the distraction provided by the stunning costumes. Similarly, Barlow's sheer inventiveness teeters on the brink of confusing us and overwhelming the play, but just stops short. My jaw dropped as one mind-boggling and exhilarating idea succeeded another. But Paul Mason's Hamlet! Why on earth did Barlow choose him for the part? As a comic character, he might get away with his over-the-top facial expressions, but as Hamlet he made it impossible for the audience to sympathise, let alone identify, with him. His delivery was a parody, with neither intonation nor stress bearing any relation to the meaning of Shakespeare's lines.

Which reviewer

shares reviewer B's opinion regarding the production's relevance to the present day? 37

holds a different opinion from the other reviewers as to whether Mason gives insight into the character of Hamlet? 38

has the same view as reviewer C on the way Mason speaks? 39

has a different view from reviewer A about the director's ideas for the production? 40

Test 5 Reading and Use of English Part 7

You are going to read part of a newspaper article about an Australian cycling champion. Six paragraphs have been removed from the article. Choose from the paragraphs **A–G** the one which fits each gap (**41–46**). There is one extra paragraph which you do not need to use.

Mark your answers **on the separate answer sheet.**

The forgotten story of a phenomenal Australian cyclist

With his glasses taped to his head and a heavy, bone-shaking push bike for a ride, the lanky 18-year-old seemed an unlikely prospect when he turned up for his first club cycling race one day in 1946. Yet, when he died 12 years later, there was a feeling that Russell Mockridge had not yet reached his full potential.

41 ______

Someone who achieved this degree of success throughout his cycling career was likely to be self-confident, and might even be forgiven for arrogance. Yet, with his two feet on the pavement, Mockridge was a retiring and painfully shy man. He couldn't handle the 'roughness' of most other cyclists, who referred to him in his young days as 'The China Doll'. For his part, Mockridge preferred to spend time with English literature.

42 ______

Officials looked at the skinny Mockridge, at his do-it-yourself bike shoes and at his battered roadster with its handlebars turned down, and wondered what they were seeing. The disbelief grew when Mockridge innocently asked if it would be all right if he stayed out in front all the way – he was concerned that his poor eyesight might cause an accident and endanger other cyclists.

43 ______

The official was amazed. 'Well, you certainly won the race and probably have the fastest time, but we don't actually know what your time for the distance is, so we can't give you that one,' he told Mockridge. However impressed he might have been, he could hardly have foreseen that this was just the start of Mockridge's run of victories.

44 ______

At the Australian 200km road championship, Mockridge was the sole member of his team left riding when it came down to the last few hundred metres. The pack was well ahead and beginning their final sprint while Mockridge, whose appetite was astounding, lagged behind finishing off a snack from his food bag.

45 ______

Another of Mockridge's mad final dashes, on the last day of the 1957 Sun Tour, was one of the most memorable rides of his career. Neck and neck with George Goodwin, Mockridge threw himself into the wending steep hillsides. Goodwin then found himself desperately hanging onto Mockridge's back wheel as the champion unleashed a ride that simply destroyed 28 of Australia's best riders.

46 ______

Goodwin crossed the finish line in a final sprint just ahead of Mockridge – a very rare defeat that Mocka suffered in what can only be considered a brilliant and inspirational career. He deserves to be remembered as one of the greatest cyclists of all time.

A How fast were the pair pedalling? About 100km/h or more. In fact, they were travelling so quickly that the two police motorcycle escorts had sparks shooting up from their footrests hitting the bitumen as they negotiated the treacherous curves.

B This impression of weakness that Mockridge gave was reinforced by his weak vision – he couldn't see the other side of the road without glasses. It was a defect that barred him from most sports, particularly his beloved Australian Rules Football. He was 18 when he entered the weekly Geelong Amateur Cycling Club 40km road race because he was suffering from lack of exercise.

C The next week, and the next, Mockridge again won, and a cycling legend was born. In the following few months, he won eight of his 11 starts. Mockridge was hailed as an emerging champion and his rise from club rider to Olympic champion was meteoric.

D Despite his disappointment, it was during this tour that Mockridge set his sights on making the Australian team for the next Olympic Games. In the lead-up to selection, he won all ten Olympic qualifying races in Australia, then left for Europe.

E Any laughter died when Mockridge settled down to his machine-like rhythm and burned off other competitors. Alex McPherson, who was timing the cyclists for the club, waved them past the halfway mark, and hopped into his car to greet the finishers. When he arrived, he found Mockridge waiting and puzzled.

F His coaches and teammates had given up on him, as Mockridge still trailed well in the rear, but once he was ready to get back to the matter in hand, he settled into some serious pedalling. Ken Graves was being acclaimed the winner by announcers just as Mockridge burst through the pack and cut him down, snatching victory out of almost certain defeat.

G By then 'Mocka', a freakish and courageous talent, had won two Olympic and two Empire gold medals and countless world records. In his day, his feats were as acclaimed as those of other Australian sporting icons, such as cricketer Don Bradman.

Reading and Use of English Part 8

You are going to read four descriptions of research being carried out by staff of a music college. For questions **47–56**, choose from the extracts (**A–D**). The extracts may be chosen more than once.

Mark your answers **on the separate answer sheet.**

Which section mentions the following?

some unexpected information concerning a particular musician	47
a description of the methodology used to generate data	48
the researcher's hope that future research will be carried out into the same materials	49
how some of the material in a planned book will be structured	50
a wish to assist performers	51
the use of source material not previously known	52
exploration of the business context in which performances were given in a particular period	53
the influence that artists had on one another	54
how discoveries in the field of music relate to ones in an academic discipline other than music	55
the use of materials that have previously been studied from a different perspective	56

Some current research by staff of the Department of Music

A

Bernice Mitchell is engaged in researching law-court records from London in the first half of the 18th century, for the light they throw on the city's professional music world of the time. While the materials are familiar to legal researchers, this is thought to be the first time that their relevance to the history of music has been recognised. One objective of the research is to provide guidance on access to the materials and on their interpretation, in the expectation that more scholars will be encouraged to investigate this fascinating resource. To date, Mitchell's research has concentrated on the opera houses, and the documents have yielded considerable new insights into numerous issues, including their management, contracts with singers, musicians and composers, their working conditions, and performance fees. Mitchell is about to broaden her research, to include a detailed comparison between the 18th- and 21st-century conditions in which opera houses flourished – or not, as the case may be.

B

James Rowe's project is being carried out in collaboration with London's Science Museum. Visitors are asked to participate in a series of experiments designed to yield information about the effect of music on the perception of time passing, and so far, more than 800 people have taken part. Participants listen to a piece of music, and are then asked about its duration and their responses to it, including enjoyment and familiarity. They are also asked about personal details, including their musical preferences and level of musical training, if any. Preliminary findings indicate that people who enjoy the music think it lasted longer than those who dislike it. In a follow-up experiment, visitors are asked to memorise a list of random words while listening: this appears to have the effect of shortening the perceived duration of the music. Some of the findings are in line with current theories in psychology about the perception of time, while others appear to contradict them. The results of the research will be published next year.

C

The topic that Colin Saunderson has chosen for his current research is the creative milieu of Paris in the early 20th century, when musicians, painters, sculptors, intellectuals and many others contributed to a ferment of creativity that left its mark on all concerned. Although the topic has already been well researched, a recently discovered archive of unpublished letters is proving a mine of information on the response of the common man and woman – the concert audiences – to the immense creativity they observed. It is also adding some surprising detail on the mannerisms of several famous musicians. The research takes into account amateur music-making at that time, and the use of music in plays. Saunderson hopes the volume he is engaged in writing will provide a more nuanced view of that world than many of the existing studies. One section will quote extensively from the letters, with the extracts presented on a month-by-month basis. The intention is that this will give the reader a sense of history unfolding in front of their eyes.

D

Ray Hutchinson has published numerous books and articles on the physical and psychological demands of music-making, and in his latest research, he is focusing on how musicians manage the daily challenge of making ends meet, and the influence of career insecurity on their way of life. Many of those who are not on the payroll of a permanent orchestra or music college live a hand-to-mouth existence, all too often forced to supplement their meagre and sporadic income by working in ways that will allow them to take time off when the musical engagements come in; for example, Hutchinson interviewed a professional flautist whose bread-and-butter job, rather incongruously, is as a butler who can be hired by the day! Hutchinson's aim is not only to discover the survival strategies that musicians employ, but also to share tips and resources, in order to help them to maximise their professional opportunities.

Test 5 Writing (1 hour 30 minutes) Part 1

You **must** answer this question. Write your answer in **220–260** words in an appropriate style on the separate answer sheet.

---

1 Your class has listened to a radio discussion about the advantages of being self-employed rather than working for someone else. You have made the notes below:

Advantages of being self-employed

- time
- decision making
- money

Some opinions expressed in the discussion:

"You don't have to work from nine to five every day."

"You're in charge of the decisions that affect what you do."

"If you work hard, you make money for yourself, not someone else."

Write an essay discussing **two** of the advantages of being self-employed in your notes. You should **explain which advantage you think is most significant**, **giving reasons** in support of your answer.

You may, if you wish, make use of the opinions expressed in the discussion, but you should use your own words as far as possible.

Test 5 Writing Part 2

Write an answer to **one** of the questions **2–4** in this part. Write your answer in **220–260** words in an appropriate style on the separate answer sheet. Put the question number in the box at the top of the page.

---

2 An international organisation is offering travel grants to students to carry out a research project in another country. Applicants should write a proposal in which they describe what type of research project they would like to do abroad. The proposal should also explain how the proposed activity would benefit others as well as the applicant.

Write your **proposal**.

3 You have read a magazine article which argues that big national celebrations are a waste of time and money. Write a letter to the magazine in which you describe a national celebration in your country. You should explain how this celebration is not only enjoyable for citizens but also has a useful social purpose.

Write your **letter**.

4 A travel website has asked readers to submit a review of a tourist destination that they have visited.

The review should discuss both positive and negative aspects of the destination and should also suggest ways in which it could be made more attractive to tourists.

Write your **review**.

Test 5 Listening (approximately 40 minutes) Part 1

3 01 You will hear three different extracts. For questions **1–6**, choose the answer (**A**, **B** or **C**) which fits best according to what you hear. There are two questions for each extract.

Extract One

You hear two members of an amateur choir discussing a forthcoming concert.

1 The woman is worried that

A the choir may not be ready for the concert.
B some choir members are missing too many rehearsals.
C the concert may not attract a large enough audience.

2 What is the man doing when he speaks?

A asking the woman to help him with something he is going to do
B trying to avoid doing something he had agreed to do
C explaining why he will do something late

Extract Two

You hear two people talking about making new friends.

3 The man says that, compared with southerners, people in the north of the country

A are easier to get to know well.
B are more likely to talk to strangers.
C are more open to making long-term friendships.

4 What does the woman say about making friends in her dance class?

A It took longer than she had expected.
B Other people were too busy to spend time with her.
C She was generally ignored by other people.

Extract Three

You hear two friends discussing a television programme about genetics.

5 What is the man's opinion of the programme?

A It was less informative than he had anticipated.
B It make him realise he knew less about the subject than he thought.
C It assumed the audience already had some knowledge of the subject.

6 What aspect of the programme do the two people disagree about?

A the length of the programme
B the value of the demonstrations
C the presenter's speed of delivery

Test 5 Listening Part 2

3 02 You will hear a student called Caroline talking about her research project into rivers that have been made to flow underground. For questions **7–14**, complete the sentences with a word or short phrase.

RESEARCH INTO RIVERS PUT INTO UNDERGROUND PIPES

In the 18th and 19th centuries, many rivers were covered over in order to deal with **(7)** .... that was being caused.

One advantage of covering rivers was that **(8)** .... carried by water were less likely to spread.

Putting rivers into pipes prevented the creation and survival of **(9)** .... for plants and fish.

Fish were unable to move through a pipe if there was a change in **(10)** .... between sections.

A **(11)** .... or a break in a pipe can increase the risk of flood damage.

Caroline mentions a **(12)** .... that was made unsafe by a river underneath the building.

Old maps and other **(13)** .... are useful for locating unknown rivers.

Caroline uses software and old maps to identify **(14)** .... that might be the site of an underground river.

Test 5 Listening Part 3

03 You will hear an interview for a student magazine with Penny and Giles, who have both just returned to Britain after travelling around the world. For questions **15–20**, choose the answer (**A**, **B**, **C** or **D**) which fits best according to what you hear.

---

15 Why did Giles decide to stay abroad for more than one year?

- **A** to decide which country he would eventually settle in
- **B** to gain work experience in a number of countries
- **C** to try and get his articles published in different countries
- **D** to become familiar with the cultures of other countries

16 What did Penny and Giles both find unexpected about their time abroad?

- **A** how little they knew about other countries
- **B** how difficult it was to learn other languages
- **C** how unadventurous they were about food
- **D** how many people were willing to talk to them

17 What aspect of tourism does Penny criticise?

- **A** the motives that some tourists have for travelling
- **B** its effect on traditional crafts
- **C** the physical changes that are made to some places
- **D** its economic impact on an area

18 Giles's reference to an incident that happened in Thailand is probably intended to illustrate

- **A** his wish to avoid commitments.
- **B** his pleasure in making new friends.
- **C** his sense of responsibility.
- **D** his difficulty in learning foreign languages.

19 In relation to what he does in the future, Giles has decided

- **A** to work abroad for a period as a journalist.
- **B** to go ahead with his plan of becoming a travel journalist.
- **C** to maximise his chances of getting work eventually.
- **D** to change to a career in politics.

20 Penny says that when she arrived back home, she felt that

- **A** some parts of her trip had been disappointing.
- **B** in some ways Britain seemed strange to her.
- **C** the best part of her life seemed to be over.
- **D** it was a relief to resume her usual way of life.

04 You will hear five short extracts in which people are talking about their jobs.

TASK ONE

For questions **21–25**, choose from the list (**A–H**) the mistake that each speaker made in their job.

While you listen you must complete both tasks.

A failing to recognise somebody

B entering incorrect data

C breaking a company rule

D being rude to a colleague

E misunderstanding instructions

F failing to report a possible breach of rules

G missing a deadline

H passing responsibility to someone else

Speaker 1 [ ] **21**

Speaker 2 [ ] **22**

Speaker 3 [ ] **23**

Speaker 4 [ ] **24**

Speaker 5 [ ] **25**

TASK TWO

For questions **26–30**, choose from the list (**A–H**) what each speaker particularly likes about their job.

A having flexible working hours

B getting on well with colleagues

C being trusted by their employer

D feeling satisfied with the quality of their work

E having their contribution recognised by their employer

F being paid for overtime

G finishing work early one day a week

H having a friendly relationship with customers

Speaker 1 [ ] **26**

Speaker 2 [ ] **27**

Speaker 3 [ ] **28**

Speaker 4 [ ] **29**

Speaker 5 [ ] **30**

Test 5 Speaking (15 minutes) Part 1

Part 1 2 minutes (3 minutes for groups of three)

The interlocutor will ask you some questions about yourself, your home, work or studies and familiar topics.

Good morning/afternoon/evening. My name is ..... and this is my colleague ..... .

And your names are?

Can I have your mark sheets, please?

Thank you.

First of all, we'd like to know something about you.

- Where are you from?
- How long have you lived here/there?
- Where do you study English?
- How do you plan to use English in the future?

The interlocutor will then ask you some questions about one or two other topics, for example:

- How do you think the place where you live will change over the next few years?
- How important is reading in your life?
- Tell us about a film that you have recently seen.
- Where would you go if you had a month's holiday and a lot of money?

Speaking Part 2

Part 2 4 minutes (6 minutes for groups of three)

Work in groups of three if possible. One of you is the interlocutor and the other two are the candidates. The interlocutor should lead the task using the script below. Refer to the pictures on pages S16 and S17.

The interlocutor will give you three pictures and ask you to talk about two of them on your own for about a minute. You will then be asked a question about your partner's pictures which you will need to answer in no more than 30 seconds.

Interlocutor In this part of the test, I'm going to give each of you three pictures. I'd like you to talk about **two** of them on your own for about a minute, and also to answer a question briefly about your partner's pictures.

(*Candidate A*), it's your turn first. Here are your pictures. They show **people doing different leisure activities**.

I'd like you to compare **two** of the pictures and say **why the people might have chosen to do these activities, and how beneficial doing these activities might be for the people.**

All right?

After 1 minute Thank you.

(*Candidate B*), **which of these leisure activities do you think appeals to most people? (Why?)**

After approximately 30 seconds Thank you.

Now, (*Candidate B*), here are your pictures. They show **people wearing some unusual clothes.**

I'd like you to compare **two** of the pictures, and say **why the people might be dressed in these ways, and how important you think the clothes are to the people**.

All right?

After 1 minute Thank you.

(*Candidate A*), **which people do you think are enjoying dancing the most? (Why?)**

After approximately 30 seconds Thank you.

Test 5 Speaking Parts 3 and 4

Part 3 4 minutes (6 minutes for groups of three)

Work in groups of three if possible. One of you is the interlocutor and the other two are the candidates. The interlocutor should lead the task using the script below. Refer to the task sheet on page S18.

The interlocutor will give you a task sheet to discuss together.

Interlocutor Now, I'd like you to talk about something together for about two minutes.

Here are some aspects of life which are influenced by technology and a question for you to discuss. First you have some time to look at the task. (*About 15 seconds*)

Now, talk to each other about **how technology impacts on these aspects of life.**

After 2 minutes Thank you. Now you have a minute to decide **which aspect of life is influenced by technology in the most significant way**.

After 1 minute Thank you.

Part 4 5 minutes (8 minutes for groups of three)

Work in groups of three if possible. One of you is the interlocutor and the other two are the candidates. The interlocutor should lead the task using the script below.

The interlocutor will ask some general questions which follow on from the topic in Part 3.

Interlocutor

- How do you think technology will develop in the future? (Why?)
- How do the attitudes of older and younger generations towards technology differ? (Why?)
- Which technological development do you think has had the most positive effect on society? (Why?)
- Do you think parents should impose time limits on a child's use of the computer? (Why? / Why not?)
- What effects do you think computer use has had on literacy? (Why?)

Thank you. That is the end of the test.

Reading and Use of English (1 hour 30 minutes) Part 1

For questions **1–8**, read the text below and decide which answer (**A**, **B**, **C** or **D**) best fits each gap. There is an example at the beginning (**0**).

Mark your answers **on the separate answer sheet**.

Example:

0 **A** bridging **B** fastening **C** unifying **D** linking

0	A	B	C	D
	▭	▭	▭	▬

Emotions and the body

Most languages have expressions like 'to get cold feet', **(0)** .... emotions to different parts of the body. It now seems these associations are **(1)** .... , with the same emotions rooted in the same location, regardless of a person's country of **(2)** ....

Scientists from Aalto University, Finland, **(3)** .... an experiment using more than 700 volunteers from Finland, Sweden and Taiwan. Participants were shown emotional videos, pictures of facial expressions and stories intended to **(4)** .... certain feelings. They then used computer-generated human silhouettes to **(5)** .... where on their bodies they had felt any stimulus.

The results showed **(6)** .... patterns of bodily sensations associated with each of the basic emotions. Many emotions provoked changes in the face, while throat and belly sensations only really appeared in participants feeling disgust. In contrast with all the other emotions, happiness was associated with **(7)** .... sensations all over the body.

The authors said their study could in future be applied to the treatment of emotional **(8)** .... such as depression and anxiety.

1	**A** thorough	**B** universal	**C** sweeping	**D** expansive
2	**A** beginning	**B** source	**C** initiation	**D** origin
3	**A** conducted	**B** administered	**C** directed	**D** operated
4	**A** trigger	**B** set	**C** pioneer	**D** touch
5	**A** design	**B** plan	**C** map	**D** programme
6	**A** steady	**B** consistent	**C** proportional	**D** solid
7	**A** uplifted	**B** glorified	**C** maximised	**D** enhanced
8	**A** disruptions	**B** distractions	**C** disorders	**D** displacements

Test 6 Reading and Use of English Part 2

For questions **9–16**, read the text below and think of the word which best fits each gap. Use only **one** word in each gap. There is an example at the beginning (**0**).

Write your answers **IN CAPITAL LETTERS on the separate answer sheet.**

Example: | 0 | | F | O | R |

College news

Professor Tim Scholes has been nominated **(0)** .... a national award, the Taymon Environmental Prize, in recognition of his research into the impact of deforestation **(9)** .... land in the Amazon basin. He is interested in both its potential benefits for agriculture and the risk of desertification, a process by **(10)** .... formerly fertile land becomes desert. Scholes's most recent study was undertaken **(11)** .... part of an international project led by Professor Clara Berminton.

According to Scholes, a lucrative prize **(12)** .... the Taymon would make a significant contribution to funding for the next stage of his research. The awards ceremony will **(13)** .... place in London on 19 March. Scholes jokes that he **(14)** .... well be the first person in the Taymon's history to be nominated six times without winning. **(15)** .... this prove to be the case, though, Scholes won't be too upset. He believes the publicity generated by the event will raise awareness of the problem of deforestation, if **(16)** .... else.

Test 6 Reading and Use of English Part 3

For questions **17–24**, read the text below. Use the word given in capitals at the end of some of the lines to form a word that fits in the gap **in the same line**. There is an example at the beginning (**0**).

Write your answers **IN CAPITAL LETTERS on the separate answer sheet.**

Example: | 0 | R E T A I L E R |

Job opportunity in IT

The company is a major **(0)** .... , with stores throughout the country. **RETAIL**
A vacancy has **(17)** .... arisen to join its information technology (IT) **EXPECT**
department.

The company is planning to open a distribution centre at the beginning of
next year, and requires a computer service **(18)** .... to start work **TECHNICAL**
as soon as possible. He or she will join an existing team responsible for the
(19) .... of a new computer system before the opening of the **INSTALL**
distribution centre. The team's duties will also cover the upgrading, repair
and **(20)** .... of the computer systems currently in operation in the **MAINTAIN**
company's stores, and provide support to users.

Formal IT qualifications are **(21)** .... but not essential, provided you **DESIRE**
have a thorough working knowledge of computer hardware and software,
excellent problem-solving skills and a **(22)** .... to keep up-to-date **WILL**
with IT developments.

The company aims to achieve **(23)** .... in every aspect of its activities, **EXCEL**
and expects all its **(24)** .... to be committed to the same goal. **EMPLOY**

Test 6 Reading and Use of English Part 4

For questions **25–30**, complete the second sentence so that it has a similar meaning to the first sentence, using the word given. **Do not change the word given**. You must use between **three** and **six** words, including the word given. Here is an example (**0**).

Example:

0 I didn't think you should mention Caroline's new job to her parents.

SAY

I thought it would be best if you .... Caroline's new job to her parents.

The gap can be filled with the words 'didn't say anything about', so you write:

Example:	**0**	DIDN'T SAY ANYTHING ABOUT

Write **only** the missing words **IN CAPITAL LETTERS on the separate answer sheet.**

---

25 Kathy's nomination for an award for bravery came as a surprise to her.

ABACK

Kathy .... being nominated for an award for bravery.

26 Nobody was in the building when the fire occurred.

TIME

The building was .... the fire.

27 Even though the company offered him a higher salary, David was still dubious about accepting the job.

DESPITE

David was still dubious about accepting the job, ... him a higher salary.

28 Sheila missed her train because her husband couldn't drive her to the station.

LIFT

If Sheila's husband had been able to .... have caught her train.

29 The children paid little attention to the dogs.

NOTICE

The children didn't .... the dogs.

30 Local residents have been opposed to the proposal since 1996.

DATES

Local residents' .... to 1996.

Test 6 Reading and Use of English Part 5

You are going to read the introduction to a book by Helen Thornton about the history of drama. For questions **31–36**, choose the answer (**A**, **B**, **C** or **D**) which you think fits best according to the text.

Mark your answers **on the separate answer sheet**.

Introduction

Any writer who boldly attempts to write a history of drama, covering every corner of the world in which the genre has flourished, risks ending up with egg on his or her face, and remaindered copies of the book selling for next to nothing. After all, there already exist a number of excellent works on the subject, so I have to ask myself, have I come to the party empty-handed? That would indeed be humiliating.

I am, I hope, realistic enough to accept that yet another history of drama is unlikely to disturb the bestseller lists; all I can do is rely on the casual browser in a bookshop or book-selling website to read a page or two of this work and feel sufficiently intrigued to want to read more – whether or not they are persuaded by my opinions. I hope to convey something of the fascination I have long experienced for drama, in the belief that enthusiasm, like measles, is catching.

The idea of writing this book came to me five years ago, sparked by reading, in a single sitting, James K. Hyde's slim volume that purported to trace the historical development of drama around the world, but in fact played down the value of any plays that have not survived in written form, or are in languages other than Hyde's own. His attitude – and the fact that he simply couldn't see the value of so much work that can, however loosely, be termed 'drama' – infuriated me to such a degree that I couldn't sleep. In the small hours of the morning, I made up my mind to write my own book, to counterbalance his very circumscribed view of 'good drama'. That decision made, I calmed down and fell asleep.

When I woke the following morning, I was aghast at my foolhardiness. I am far from being an expert on world drama: my particular field is the plays of ancient Greece and Rome. In relation to the drama of other times and places, I have a lively interest, but there are serious gaps in my knowledge. Hence the five-year gestation period that the book has undergone, a period that has seen me carry out a great deal of research, both in libraries and in theatres around the world.

Writing a book like this requires ground rules, one of which is a decision as to whether it should be 'academic', 'popular' or something in between – whatever that may be. As an academic myself, teaching university students of drama, I am under some pressure to write for my colleagues in the field, complete with quotations in the original Greek, Chinese or Sanskrit, footnotes on every page, and a long bibliography in an appendix, listing the numerous sources I have drawn on. That may look good on my CV when I apply for promotion at my university, but it would attract a tiny readership – and I'm arrogant enough to want my labours to be recognised and appreciated by many, on the basis that the harder I've worked, the more readers and – I must confess – praise I want. So that was the road I went down.

In this book, I have aimed to consider a representative sample of plays, of whatever length and written in whatever language. Not to mention plays that haven't survived in written form, though we have information about them, and ones that are ceremonies rather than plays as we understand the term today. Working out a principle to bring order out of this chaos was difficult enough in itself. One option was to focus on the playwrights, but so many of them are anonymous. Another possibility, which had a certain appeal, was to take one genre at a time – tragedy, comedy, farce and so on – and trace its development over the centuries. After considerable agonising, I finally opted for looking at particular locations at particular times. What drama was available? Who was allowed to attend? How did plays written for performance at a royal court differ from those for the general public? To what extent did the plays mirror or challenge the values and beliefs of their audiences? I have spent hours burning the midnight oil as I struggled to reach some tenable conclusions regarding these and many more questions.

In the end, all I can do is present the fruits of my labours and hope – like the spoken prologues of many plays – that you, my readers, will be indulgent and excuse the limitations of this book.

31 In the first paragraph, Thornton expresses her concern that

A the task she has taken on is too difficult for her.
B she has relied too heavily on existing books.
C there is little interest in books about drama.
D she has nothing new to say on the subject.

32 According to the second paragraph, Thornton's purpose in this book is to

A make readers feel as she does about drama.
B write a book that might sell in larger quantities than expected.
C convince readers that her interpretations of drama are correct.
D explore different emotional responses to drama.

33 Why did Thornton decide to write this book?

A The author of another book encouraged her to write it.
B She was annoyed by the narrow focus of a book she had read.
C Another book opened her eyes to drama from around the world.
D She felt that a book she had read failed to distinguish between good and bad drama.

34 What does Thornton explain in the fourth paragraph?

A why the book has taken her a long time to write
B the difficulties she faced in researching the book
C why the book concentrates on ancient Greece and Rome
D how she feels now that the book is complete

35 What does *that* (line 25) refer to?

A making the book academic in nature
B providing information about her source material
C trying to make the book appeal to a wide audience
D applying for promotion at the university where she teaches

36 In structuring her book, Thornton has

A organised the material chronologically.
B described the work of one playwright at a time.
C concentrated on different dramatic genres in turn.
D attempted to place plays in their social context.

Reading and Use of English Part 6

You are going to read extracts from articles in which four experts give their views on a proposed new airport for London. For questions **37–40**, choose from the experts **A–D**. The experts may be chosen more than once.

Mark your answers **on the separate answer sheet.**

Proposal to build a new airport for London, possibly on an artificial island in the estuary of the River Thames

A Larry Jones

Air travel is increasing worldwide, and with London's existing airports operating at close to capacity, we face a stark choice: expansion or an additional airport? A significant benefit of a new-build is that the current airports wouldn't then require new runways – which are strenuously opposed by local residents. In addition, new flight paths could avoid contributing to air and noise pollution over London. A new airport is a new opportunity, and should be designed with an eye on current and future developments in aeronautics: it could take planes with a greater capacity even than the biggest used now, which would at least reduce the impact of the expected growth in total passenger numbers. The Thames estuary is home to vast numbers of birds, which would be seriously affected by an airport. However, if it comes to a choice between birds and people, I'm afraid our own species has to come first.

B Karen Macmillan

The more idealistic among us may believe that the world's love affair with air travel is nearing its end, but I'm certainly not one of them. We can't avoid providing for the additional airport capacity likely to be required over the next 30 to 50 years, and for my money, that means a new airport in the Thames estuary. Even if construction goes ahead, however, it will only be a matter of time before expansion of the existing airports will become inevitable. At least an airport in the estuary would save Londoners from the extra pollution resulting from the alternative, as its flight paths could be largely or entirely over water. Admittedly, it is unfortunate that the Thames estuary provides habitats for many species of birds. Ways will have to be found to mitigate the effects, while enabling construction of the airport to go ahead.

C Bernie Dodd

We share this planet with innumerable other species, all of which – including ourselves – are interdependent. Our wanton disregard of our environment is harmful not only to its other inhabitants, but also to ourselves. Constructing an airport in the Thames estuary would be so destructive of wildlife that it shouldn't even be considered. Yes, some argue that it would benefit the existing airports, but better to bite the bullet and expand those we have now than wreak havoc on a hitherto unspoilt part of the country. Besides, the claim that a new airport would reduce noise and improve air quality in London simply doesn't hold water: maybe it wouldn't worsen the current situation, but that's the best we could hope for. At present, there seems to be no prospect of the air travel frenzy dying down, but let's limit the damage to areas that are already damaged.

D Isabel Smith

Is it really the case that London needs an additional airport? Technology is progressing fast, and with wide-bodied aircraft, fewer flights are needed for the same number of passengers. Besides, the advent of quieter planes will mean that runways that are currently closed at night, because of noise, will be able to operate round the clock. The existing airports will be able to handle growth in passenger numbers for years to come, without needing any new runways to be constructed. Perhaps some carriers would transfer their operations to a Thames estuary airport, and that would lead to an improvement in London's air quality, but a new airport would involve destroying the habitats of thousands of wetland birds, with – to my mind – no justification. A new airport should be ruled out.

Which expert

expresses a different view from Jones on whether a new airport would remove the need for additional runways at existing airports? **37** ___

shares Smith's view about wildlife in the Thames estuary? **38** ___

shares Smith's view about the total number of flights required in the future? **39** ___

has a different opinion from the others about the effects a new airport would have on pollution in London? **40** ___

Test 6 Reading and Use of English Part 7

You are going to read an article about a woman who invented the concept of computer software. Six paragraphs have been removed from the extract. Choose from the paragraphs **A–G** the one which fits each gap (**41–46**). There is one extra paragraph which you do not need to use.

Mark your answers **on the separate answer sheet.**

How the concept of software was invented

In 1842, more than a century before the start of the information age, in a brilliant flash of penetrating insight, Ada Lovelace had a glimpse of the future. She saw that with suitable modifications, Charles Babbage's proposed Analytical Engine would be capable of much more than its intended purpose of simple mathematical calculation.

Ada Lovelace was born in London in 1815, the daughter of the poet Byron. She never met her father: her parents separated a month after her birth, he left England four months later and eventually died abroad. Her upbringing was unusual for the period, in that her mother was determined she should have a thorough grounding in logic, mathematics and the sciences. To that end, Ada was provided with a succession of tutors.

41

Among their number was the mathematician, philosopher, inventor and Professor of Mathematics at the University of Cambridge, Charles Babbage, one of several people credited with being 'the father of the computer'. His importance lies in the fact that he invented several devices which paved the way for modern computers. Lovelace was introduced to him while still in her late teens, and soon afterwards visited his workshop to see his 'Difference Engine'.

42

The device was incomplete, weighed over a ton and was not yet working. Despite these limitations, Lovelace grasped its true significance; whereas Babbage saw it purely being used to increase the accuracy of mathematical processes, it was Lovelace who saw its far greater potential.

43

At this event, Babbage described his proposal for a more advanced computing machine, his Analytical Engine. A mathematician who was present subsequently wrote up the ideas in a memoir in French, and Babbage asked Lovelace to translate it. Because she understood the machine so well, at his request she added a comprehensive set of notes to her translation, much longer than the memoir itself. It was these notes that have established her importance in the development of computers.

44

In this insight, she anticipated the development of both modern computing and artificial intelligence by more than a hundred years. Again, she saw that the Analytical Engine could be used to do much more than even Babbage perceived.

45

The memoir, and Lovelace's notes, attracted little attention at the time, but that does not detract from her achievement, the essence of which is that she grasped how to create physical instances of wholly abstract concepts. In any computer, it is the software which gives the hardware the ability to perform its wonders, a totally new, and very strange, idea for the time.

46

Although her insight is astonishing, that is not all that Lovelace should be remembered for. She also demonstrated beyond any possibility of doubt that women could attain the highest levels of scientific understanding and achievement – something that seemed remarkable in her lifetime. She helped to blaze a trail for later generations of women to become scientists.

A Neither this prototype nor his later devices were completed in his lifetime, although working versions have since been built. However, his efforts to construct them aroused widespread interest, particularly when he attended a scientific conference in Italy and presented his work.

B Of course, the same could be said of many scientists: Leonardo da Vinci, for instance, designed flying machines several centuries before they became a reality, but at least he had the advantage of having seen birds flying.

C Unlike him, Lovelace realised that it could be set to execute any logically coherent sequence of instructions. This in effect made her the world's first computer programmer, as she demonstrated in the document.

D In them, as well as describing the revolutionary implications of Babbage's ideas, Lovelace wrote out the first computer program and made the sensational suggestion that such a device should be able to compose music if a suitable set of rules could be devised.

E One of these was Augustus de Morgan, a leading mathematician of the time. De Morgan soon confirmed Ada's outstanding mathematical ability and, importantly, communicated his admiration to his scientific friends. As a result, long before women were eligible to study for degrees, Ada came to more than hold her own with the leading scientists of the day.

F This realisation, that the right instructions could enormously increase the capabilities of the device, is extraordinary for such an early stage in the history of the computer. Lovelace could see beyond the relatively rudimentary nature of Babbage's machines to the immense possibilities opened up by programmable computers.

G This mechanical calculator was Babbage's first invention. He, like others before him, had realised that logarithmic tables – at that time produced by human 'calculators', and notoriously full of errors – could be generated by machinery.

Test 6 Reading and Use of English Part 8

You are going to read four extracts from an article about customer service. For questions **47–56**, choose from the extracts (**A–D**). The extracts may be chosen more than once.

Mark your answers **on the separate answer sheet.**

In which section does the writer

suggest that customers' comments may be more honest if not made to staff? **47**

mention the effect on sales if customers believe staff are not interested in them? **48**

say that presenting alternative courses of action can lead to a win-win situation? **49**

point out that if assistants do more than the minimum, customers are likely to return? **50**

advise staff how to respond if a customer is dissatisfied? **51**

state that poor service stays in customers' minds? **52**

refer to contact with customers through a range of channels? **53**

give an example of customers responding to employees in the same way they are treated? **54**

point out that customers' behaviour may not be explained by what has happened to them in the store? **55**

mention the value of customers recommending a business to other people? **56**

The importance of good customer service

A

"The customer is always right" is a famous business slogan. The underlying truth behind this statement is recognising that customers are the life blood for any business. Understanding the importance of good customer service is essential for a healthy business in creating new customers, keeping loyal customers, and developing an effective referral system for future customers. Excellent customer service begins at the initial greeting, whether that's in person, on the phone, or via email. In all of these situations, using good people skills will increase the chances of creating a positive impression. For example, saying hello with a smile to a customer who has just walked in the door will invite that person in and make them feel welcome. On the other hand, when an employee doesn't acknowledge the client, or implies they are an inconvenience, that customer immediately feels slighted, and that negative feeling doesn't get the customer in a buying mood.

B

If the employee gives good customer service on the phone, the initial greeting will be courteous. This makes the client feel comfortable. In turn, the customer will appreciate the pleasant greeting and usually be more agreeable on the other end of the phone. This is a much better situation for the client than leaving messages on answering machines, never getting any returned phone calls, or trying to extract some product information from an uncaring employee. Of course, good customer service goes beyond the initial contact. Answering customers' questions and helping them choose the right product or service that best fits their needs is a great example of going the extra mile. This kind of service establishes goodwill, and will eventually lead to loyal customers. Even if that person doesn't purchase anything at that time, the good shopping experience will encourage repeat business.

C

Think about how you've been treated whenever you've been the customer. If you've ever had a bad experience with a company, you know that it's not easy to forget the encounter. Perhaps a shop assistant was too busy stocking shelves to help you pay for your items. Maybe there wasn't anyone around to answer your questions or help you with some additional information. You might have had to deal with an employee who won't help you because of some company rule. In any of these instances, the managers or the owner of the store usually aren't made aware of the poor customer service. Instead, the people that do hear about it are many of the customer's family and friends. Word travels very fast when it comes to communicating negative experiences to the world. Especially with any internet business transactions, product reviews are quite common. Whether it's positive or negative feedback about a product or service, people write without inhibition about their shopping experiences.

D

When dealing with clients, sometimes there are situations that need to be resolved. If the customer is upset about a product or service they've received from the company, the first thing an employee should do is to listen. By taking the time to hear the entire complaint through, the customer feels that you care. Occasionally, the issue is actually not related to your company at all, but the initial problem is merely a catalyst for that person's frustration about other things. Either way, attentive listening will break down that barrier and begin to build a bridge to fix the situation. Usually, discussing different options will bring about a positive outcome for both sides. The retail business is extremely competitive, and there are no guarantees of a company's survival. Of course, other factors play a part, such as value for money, convenient opening hours, and so on, but in the long run, treating people fairly and with respect is the best recipe for success in retailing.

Test 6 Writing (1 hour 30 minutes) Part 1

You **must** answer this question. Write your answer in **220–260** words in an appropriate style on the separate answer sheet.

---

1 Your class has watched a television debate about what should be done to ensure that natural resources, such as water and oil, are not wasted. You have made the notes below:

<u>Ways to ensure natural resources are not wasted</u>

- laws
- media
- industry

Some opinions expressed in the discussion:

"The best method would be to make wasting natural resources a criminal offence."

"Newspapers and TV can have a very powerful impact on people's behaviour."

"Companies should take the lead by avoiding unnecessary packaging."

Write an essay discussing **two** of the ways in your notes. You should **explain which way you think is most effective, giving reasons** in support of your answer.

You may, if you wish, make use of the opinions expressed in the discussion, but you should use your own words as far as possible.

Test 6 Writing Part 2

Write an answer to **one** of the questions **2–4** in this part. Write your answer in **220–260** words in an appropriate style on the separate answer sheet. Put the question number in the box at the top of the page.

---

2 A TV company is preparing a series of documentary programmes about different workplaces. You think one of these programmes could feature your workplace. Write a proposal to the TV company in which you describe what people at your workplace do and explain why this would be of interest to viewers. Your proposal should also make some suggestions about the general approach the programme about your workplace could take.

Write your **proposal**.

3 A sports website has asked for reviews of sports facilities in your area. Write a review of some sports facilities you have used.

Your review should explain who the facilities are most suitable for and describe your own experience of using them. You should also recommend at least one way in which these facilities could be improved.

Write your **review**.

4 An electronics company has invited customers to write a report on an electronic gadget. Write a report on an electronic gadget that you regularly use, such as a mobile phone or a games console.

Your report should outline the gadget's capabilities and what you use it for. It should also comment on the extent to which the gadget meets your needs.

Write your **report**.

Test 6 Listening (approximately 40 minutes) Part 1

3 05 You will hear three different extracts. For questions **1–6**, choose the answer (**A**, **B** or **C**) which fits best according to what you hear. There are two questions for each extract.

Extract One

You hear two friends discussing a new job that the man is about to start.

1 What attracted Donald to his new job?

A He will be able to live within easy reach of mountains.
B He will be back in the town where he was brought up.
C He will have more responsibility than he had previously.

2 Donald thinks the problem with selling his house is that

A it is in a locality that is unattractive.
B it lacks some amenities that are generally expected.
C it is too unusual for the people who want a house at that price.

Extract Two

You hear two friends discussing a novel.

3 What does the man think about the book?

A He could identify with the main character.
B He felt it was inconclusive.
C He didn't get used to the style.

4 Why does the woman want to read the novel?

A It has just won an award for fiction.
B It has been chosen by the book club she belongs to.
C It was written by an author whose work she enjoys.

Extract Three

You hear a husband and wife discussing new appliances for their home.

5 Why are they going to contact the shop?

A to ask for the dishwasher to be exchanged for a different model
B to ask for some information for customers to be corrected
C to ask for a refund of the money they paid for delivery

6 What do they agree about the cooker the woman mentions?

A It would be too complicated to operate.
B There is not sufficient room for it in the kitchen.
C They would not use it enough to justify the expense.

Test 6 Listening Part 2

(3 06) You will hear Gavin McFarland, the manager of a football club, talking to some students about his work. For questions **7–14**, complete the sentences with a word or short phrase.

A FOOTBALL MANAGER'S LIFE

Like most football managers, Gavin has got very little **(7)** .... in his job.

Only Gavin's title is printed on the **(8)** .... that identifies his office.

Unlike many football managers, Gavin doesn't live in **(9)** ....

Most clubs have very limited **(10)** .... of all types, compared with some well-known clubs.

Last summer, Gavin painted all the **(11)** .... in the club.

The most important part of Gavin's job is the **(12)** .... of suitable footballers.

Gavin enjoys meetings with **(13)** ....

Yesterday's training focused on developing the players' skills at **(14)** .... , and making it fun.

Test 6 Listening Part 3

3 07 You will hear an interview on local radio with Jane Robinson, the Public Relations Officer of a company developing a former air base. For questions **15–20**, choose the answer (**A**, **B**, **C** or **D**) which fits best according to what you hear.

---

15 What benefit of the Buckworth East development does Jane emphasise?

A It will mean the shops in Buckworth village will have more customers.
B It will remove pressure on other villages in the area.
C It will form a self-supporting community.
D It will fulfil the council's requirement for new housing in Buckworth village.

16 Jane admits that the development is likely to

A provide housing that is too expensive for many people.
B cause a large increase in the use of cars during the rush hour.
C provide too few jobs to meet the needs of new residents.
D create parking problems for residents with cars.

17 The interviewer thinks local people protesting against the plan are right with regard to

A protection of the environment.
B public transport links.
C the amount of housing planned.
D facilities for pre-school children.

18 With regard to objections, Jane makes the point that

A they shouldn't prevent basic requirements from being provided.
B it is necessary to explain why some objections have to be overruled.
C they are rarely based on accurate information.
D it is useful to evaluate the motives of objectors.

19 Concerning the relationship between residents of Buckworth East and of the existing village, Jane says that

A a shared building is planned that will bring the communities together.
B new residents are unlikely to be interested in the existing community.
C part of the responsibility for integration lies with existing residents.
D the focus of village activities is likely to move to the new site.

20 According to the interviewer, what is the overall opinion of villagers?

A They resent the fact that their views have been overruled.
B They believe the development is undesirable but inevitable.
C They welcome the opportunities that the development will create.
D They think the development will seriously damage village life.

Test 6 Listening Part 4

3 08 You will hear five short extracts in which people are talking about living in a foreign country.

TASK ONE

For questions **21–25**, choose from the list (**A–H**) the reason why each speaker moved abroad.

TASK TWO

For questions **26–30**, choose from the list (**A–H**) what each speaker mentions about their experience of living abroad.

While you listen you must complete both tasks.

Task One

A to get a better job afterwards

B because a foreign organisation approached them

C to study at a well-known institution

D to work on an international project

E to accompany their partner

F to have more job opportunities

G because their research could best be done abroad

H because their employer asked them to relocate

Speaker 1		21
Speaker 2		22
Speaker 3		23
Speaker 4		24
Speaker 5		25

Task Two

A reassessing their work–life balance

B realising the benefit of encountering other cultures

C not being able to adapt to the way of life

D re-evaluating their ideas about their own country

E meeting a number of people who became good friends

F their personal relationships being put under strain

G gaining insight into their strengths and weaknesses

H learning to be less materialistic

Speaker 1		26
Speaker 2		27
Speaker 3		28
Speaker 4		29
Speaker 5		30

Test 6 Speaking (15 minutes) Part 1

Part 1 2 minutes (3 minutes for groups of three)

The interlocutor will ask you some questions about yourself, your home, work or studies and familiar topics.

Good morning/afternoon/evening. My name is ..... and this is my colleague ..... .
And your names are?
Can I have your mark sheets, please?
Thank you.

First of all, we'd like to know something about you.

- Where are you from?
- What do you do?
- How did you get here today?
- What is a typical day like for you?

The interlocutor will then ask you some questions about one or two other topics, for example:

- How do you think your life might change over the next five years?
- What kind of films do you enjoy?
- Tell me about something surprising that has happened to you.
- How good is the place where you live for someone of your generation?

Test 6 Speaking Part 2

Part 2 4 minutes (6 minutes for groups of three)

Work in groups of three if possible. One of you is the interlocutor and the other two are the candidates. The interlocutor should lead the task using the script below. Refer to the pictures on pages S19 and S20.

The interlocutor will give you three pictures and ask you to talk about two of them on your own for about a minute. You will then be asked a question about your partner's pictures which you will need to answer in no more than 30 seconds.

Interlocutor In this part of the test, I'm going to give each of you three pictures. I'd like you to talk about **two** of them on your own for about a minute, and also to answer a question briefly about your partner's pictures.

(*Candidate A*), it's your turn first. Here are your pictures. They show **people having a meal together**.

I'd like you to compare **two** of the pictures and say **why the people might have chosen to eat together in these places, and what they might be talking about**.

All right?

After 1 minute Thank you.

(*Candidate B*), **who do you think will remember the situation for the longest time? (Why?)**

After approximately 30 seconds Thank you.

Now, (*Candidate B*), here are your pictures. They show **people in different work situations**.

I'd like you to compare two of the pictures and **what skills the people might need to do their jobs well, and what disadvantages these jobs might have**.

All right?

After 1 minute Thank you.

(*Candidate A*), **which job do you think is the most rewarding? (Why?)**

After approximately 30 seconds Thank you.

Test 6 Speaking Parts 3 and 4

Part 3 4 minutes (6 minutes for groups of three)

Work in groups of three if possible. One of you is the interlocutor and the other two are the candidates. The interlocutor should lead the task using the script below. Refer to the task sheet on page S21.

The interlocutor will give you a task sheet to discuss together.

Interlocutor Now, I'd like you to talk about something together for about two minutes.

Here are some ways in which people often study and a question for you to discuss. First you have some time to look at the task. (*About 15 seconds*)

Now, talk to each other about **how effective these ways of studying are**.

After 2 minutes Thank you. Now you have a minute to decide **which of these ways of studying is the most demanding**.

After 1 minute Thank you.

Part 4 5 minutes (8 minutes for groups of three)

Work in groups of three if possible. One of you is the interlocutor and the other two are the candidates. The interlocutor should lead the task using the script below.

The interlocutor will ask some general questions which follow on from the topic in Part 3.

Interlocutor

- Do you think people learn more on their own or when they study with a friend? (Why? / Why not?)
- To what extent does the best way of studying change according to what subject is being studied? (Why?)
- What study advice should schools give to young people who are about to go on to higher education? (Why?)
- Why are evening classes popular with many people who work during the day?
- What are the advantages and disadvantages of online courses? (Why?)

Thank you. That is the end of the test.

Answer keys and transcripts

Test 1 Key

Reading and Use of English Part 1

Training

Useful language: putting words in context

1 'Work' is uncountable and so cannot be preceded by 'a'. *Jackie has got a good job as …*

2 'Count' must be followed by 'on'. *You can expect George to be willing …*

3 'Worry' would be followed by 'about asking'. *Don't hesitate to ask if you need …*

4 You 'explain' something 'to' someone. *The hotel receptionist will inform/tell you how to get to the conference centre.*

5 'Travel' can't be used with the definite article. *The train journey from Moscow to …*

6 'Police' takes a plural verb, so it would have to be: *A police officer is questioning the person … The police are questioning …*

Useful language: identifying collocations

1 The correct collocations are:

1	give	permission / ~~someone a favour~~ / a presentation / someone a hand [do someone a favour]
2	lay	claim to / the blame on / the table / ~~an excuse~~ [give/make an excuse]
3	make	a mistake / plans / a noise / ~~your best~~ [do your best]
4	pay	attention / ~~a ticket~~ / tribute to / a compliment [pay for a ticket]
5	run	~~an exercise~~ / a business / a race / a campaign [do an exercise]
6	shoot	a film / past someone / an arrow / ~~a camera~~ [use a camera]
7	stand	~~a possibility~~ / a chance / trial / for parliament [there is a possibility]
8	take	care / measurements / ~~a promise~~ / the train [make a promise]

2 **1** lay the blame on **2** stand trial **3** make a noise **4** give a presentation **5** took; measurements **6** run a campaign **7** pay tribute to **8** shot past

3 **1** C **2** D **3** B **4** A **5** B **6** D **7** C **8** B

Thinking about meaning

1 A **2** C **3** D **4** A **5** B **6** C

Exam practice

1 **B** People can be 'in discussion', but a topic is 'under discussion/debate' or 'a source of argument'.

2 **D** 'Precisely' collocates with 'why' in a way that none of the other adverbs does.

3 **A** 'Functions' and 'purposes' are often used together when describing a particular phenomenon in science or society.

4 **B** 'Maintain' collocates with 'health' and other adjectives such as 'warmth' or 'tidiness' with the meaning of preserving in that condition.

5 **C** 'Full' collocates with words like 'efficiency', 'power' or 'impact' to give the idea of 'total' or 'complete'.

6 **D** The other words do not fit the meaning here – you 'acquire information' through reading or talking to other people, you 'achieve' or 'reach' a goal of some sort, and you 'complete' a task of some kind.

7 **C** Only 'based' is followed by 'on'.

8 **A** 'Moments' is too short and 'eras' too long a period of time to fit here, while 'episodes' is used about usually negative events in a series, e.g. 'episodes of madness/fainting/violence'.

Reading and Use of English Part 2

Training

Useful language: using prepositions

1 **1** A number of customers complained about the after-sales service.
2 All the work will be done by volunteers.
3 Delegates experienced a number of problems related to the broadband connection at the conference centre.
4 Alexandra was able to make good use of her knowledge of foreign languages.
5 Many people took part in the anniversary festivities.
6 I must congratulate you on your excellent work.
7 I hope my letter will be taken into consideration.
8 The inspector drew management's attention to some problems in the workshop.
9 There is an urgent need for fresh water supplies in the region.
10 Have you seen the new advertisement for Lotus shampoo?

2 **1** on **2** down **3** up **4** out **5** about/in **6** on **7** off/away **8** up **9** up/in **10** against **11** off **12** by

Useful language: using connectors

1 **1** whereas **2** provided **3** whatever **4** unless **5** although **6** until **7** whenever **8** because

2 **1** in accordance with **2** in order to **3** as long as **4** despite the fact that / even though **5** so as not to **6** in case **7** as if **8** as soon as **9** even though / despite the fact that **10** No sooner

Useful language: using pronouns

1 which **2** that **3** What **4** whose **5** It **6** which **7** whose **8** It

Exam practice

9 **Although:** If you read to the end of the sentence, it becomes clear that a conjunction is needed for the sentence to hang together. It also becomes clear that a conjunction that gives an idea of contrast is what is required.

10 **to:** Just as you are able to do something, so you have an ability to do something.

11 **so:** The conjunction 'so that' introduces the purpose for doing something.

12 **on:** 'Depend' is followed by 'on', even though there may often be, as here, a phrase in parenthesis between the two words.

13 **less:** You have to think carefully about the meaning of this sentence in order to rule out other words that might fill this gap, such as, for example, 'more', 'no' or 'some'.

14 as: 'As a last resort' is a fixed expression.

15 or: If you see the word 'either', you can expect it to be followed at some point by 'or'.

16 fact: 'Fact' is used in a number of connecting expressions, e.g. 'despite the fact that ...', 'in spite of the fact that …', 'regardless of the fact that …'.

Reading and Use of English Part 3

Training

Useful language: identifying parts of speech

1 1 **adjective:** following 'most' and preceding the noun 'companies' (*unusual, well-known,* etc.)

2 **noun:** after the article and preceding the conjunction (*headlines*)

3 **verb:** past participle needed to follow 'has not' and fit before 'in the news' (*featured, appeared, been*)

4 **noun:** following 'some' and preceding 'or another' (*reason*)

5 **adverb:** qualifying 'impressed' (*extremely, rather,* etc.)

2

noun	verb	adjective	adverb
comparison	compare	comparative (in)comparable	comparatively (in)comparably
(in)stability stabiliser	(de)stabilise	(un)stable stabilising stabilised	(un)stably
height	heighten	high	highly
power	empower power	powerful powerless empowered empowering	powerfully powerlessly
observation observer	observe	observant observational	observantly
development developer	develop	developing (un-/under-/ over-) developed developmental	developmentally
doubt doubter	doubt	doubtful undoubted doubtless doubting	doubtfully undoubtedly doubtless

Useful language: understanding suffixes

Suggested answers (alternatives are possible)

1 -dom freedom, wisdom, stardom, boredom, kingdom, dukedom

-ee attendee, appointee, detainee, trainee, employee, interviewee

-en blacken, dampen, cheapen, sharpen

-hood childhood, motherhood, adulthood, manhood, boyhood

-less airless, heartless, nameless, thoughtless

-ment achievement, commitment, retirement, replacement, payment, attainment

-proof waterproof, fireproof, bulletproof, childproof

2 **1** boyhood **2** boredom **3** sharpen **4** appointee/appointment **5** thoughtless **6** bulletproof **7** commuters **8** commitment

Useful language: understanding prefixes

1 1 over = too much; overslept = slept too long

2 re = again; rewrite = write again

3 under = not enough; underestimated = didn't estimate highly enough

4 anti = against; anti-government = against the government

5 un = not; unwrapped = took the wrapping (paper) off the parcel

6 ir = not (a form of 'in', as are 'il' and 'im'); irresponsible = not responsible

7 sub = below; sub-standard = not up to standard, not good enough

8 dis = not; disallowed = not allowed, not considered acceptable

2 *Suggested answers (alternatives are possible)*

1 over-excited, over-eat, overworked

2 redo, rewrite, re-sit, re-examine

3 under-age, under-educated, underpaid

4 anti-war, anti-establishment, anti-authority

5 unzip, untie, unravel

6 irrelevant, irrational, irregular

7 sub-zero, sub-normal, sub-human

8 disprove, discontinue, disbelieve

3 **1** sub-zero **2** disbelieved **3** underpaid **4** anti-establishment **5** indecisive **6** unhelpful

Exam practice

17 perilous: The context shows that an adjective is required before the noun 'voyages'.

18 Unbelievable: Reading the whole sentence makes it clear that you need a word that suggests the information presented is hard, rather than easy, to believe.

19 risky: You need to add the suffix *-y* to make the adjective from 'risk'.

20 Analysis: The verb 'suggests' shows that you need the singular noun rather than the plural 'analyses'.

21 arrival: The definite article shows that a noun is required here.

22 settlement: The context makes it clear that you need a word that is referring to a place rather than a person (which would be 'settler').

23 plentiful: Remember to have only one 'l' at the end of any adjective ending 'ful' (apart from the word 'full', of course).

24 bravery: This is the abstract noun from 'brave'.

Reading and Use of English Part 4

Training

Useful language: correcting some common mistakes

1 **1** finding **2** to get **3** works; gets **4** buy **5** can either **6** was the food **7** traditional French **8** could have been

2 *The vertical line | shows where the answer is split into two parts for marking purposes.*

1 **WHO holds/has / is in | a management/managerial** 'Everyone' needs a singular verb. You hold or have a management/managerial position in a company.

2 **ONLY were the rooms | excellent but** The verb is inverted when various adverbial expressions like 'Not only' occur at the beginning of a sentence.

3 **can EITHER drive (there) | or go** 'Can' conveys the idea of possibility and 'either … or' is used to present the two alternative actions.

4 **SHOULD have played | better** 'Should have' can be used to express regret about something not happening as you expected or hoped.

5 **will/should have / won't/shouldn't have | no DIFFICULTY / any DIFFICULTY (in) finishing** 'Have difficulty' is followed by a gerund or by 'in' + a gerund.

6 **serves/offers/provides delicious MEALS | at** Note that the preposition associated with selling and 'price' is 'at', although you can talk about buying something 'for a good price'.

7 **(would/'d) SUGGEST (that) you | (should) choose/buy/ get** Note that we never say '~~suggest you to do~~'.

8 **(will)/('ll) have the/a CHANCE / get the/a CHANCE | to go** Both 'having the/a chance' and 'having the/an opportunity' are followed by the infinitive.

3 1 I love my sister despite not always seeing eye to eye with her.

2 The teacher turned a blind eye to the children's behaviour.

3 It must be hard for celebrities always to be / being in the public eye, mustn't it?

4 As soon as we/I catch the waiter's eye, we'll pay the bill and leave.

5 Sarah kept an eye on the children while they were playing in the garden.

Exam practice

The vertical line | shows where the answer is split into two parts for marking purposes.

25 **keeping | an EYE on** As was pointed out in the training section, 'keep an eye on' means 'watch' something or someone.

26 **to be HIGHER | than it** 'Tend' is followed by an infinitive and 'exceed' means 'be higher / more than'.

27 **far as | I can TELL** This is a fixed expression used about what you have noticed or understood.

28 **could put | my FEET up** 'To put your feet up' is an idiom meaning 'to relax'.

29 **CAME up with | the suggestion/idea of** The phrasal verb 'come up with' is often used with 'idea' or 'suggestion'.

30 **take gloves in CASE | it is** 'In case' is usually followed by a verb in the present simple tense.

Reading and Use of English Part 5

Training

1 B 2 C 3 B

Using the title

Suggested answers

1 limiting the number of planes taking off and landing

2 an exhibition involving two different cultures or contrasting ways of life in some way

3 the thoughts of a financially successful young person

4 clothes that will make you feel good

5 how to take good photos

6 how the way food is placed on the plate affects enjoyment of a meal

Working out meaning from context

1 1 'Tussle' must mean something like 'struggle', as the context suggests a surprising reaction towards something that is basic.

2 'Devoid of' must mean 'without' or 'lacking', as clearly a language is more likely to be appreciated if it does not have any ideological or political associations.

3 'Seeking' must mean something like 'looking for' or 'hoping to find', as that makes sense with the idea of second-language learners and the answer that Esperanto may provide.

4 'Lofty' must mean something like 'high', as the context makes it clear that it is some kind of positive adjective reinforcing the concept of ideals.

5 'Mitigate' must mean something like 'reduce' or 'minimise', as the context suggests that the creator of Esperanto would not have wished his new language to present an exclusively Western point of view.

6 'Counter' must mean something like 'argue against', as the context makes it clear that supporters of Esperanto would react negatively to criticisms made against it.

7 'Proponents' must means something like 'supporters' or 'people who are in favour of', as the context makes it clear that proponents view Esperanto in a favourable light.

8 Topple … from its perch' must mean 'remove from its position', as that is what has happened to Latin, once also an international language.

Useful language: paraphrasing

1 at first – initially

be aware – realise

connections – ties

consequence – result

fascinating – interesting

for certain – undeniable

have in common – share

intend – wish

key – main

2 *Suggested answers*

1 What is fascinating is that, more than a century ago, a Dr Ludwig Zamenhof published a book about a new language that he had created/designed.

2 It is said to be simple to learn.

3 It is appreciated as being without any of the ideological or political associations that accompany languages of erstwhile/ previous colonial powers.

4 The language never really succeeded among people worldwide in the way its creator hoped.

5 What Esperanto does not have in culture it compensates for in efficiency.

6 Esperanto has created a history of its own, one shared by the thousands who speak it and use it as a lingua franca/global language.

Exam practice

31 C The writer is making the point that communication is increasingly global, but that although English is frequently used as the means of global communication, it is something that causes many difficulties for learners, and he suggests it would be good if there were a simpler way in which people could communicate with one another. A: The writer emphasises the difficulties of learning English, but does not comment on its effectiveness as a global language. B: The writer says that schools teach about the growing globalisation of the world, but does not suggest that they are exaggerating the importance of this. D: Although this is part of the writer's argument, it is not the main point being made.

32 D The question asks about the main reason for the appeal of Esperanto, and the phrase 'more significantly' is used to introduce the importance of the language's freedom from political associations. A and B: These are also reasons why Esperanto appeals, but neither is presented as the main reason. C: This is true, but is not presented as a reason for Esperanto's appeal.

33 A The answer is provided by the last two sentences of the third paragraph, which point out that Esperanto is too similar to certain European languages to be as international as was originally intended. B: The writer does not comment on the extent to which learners find English interesting. The phrase 'vested interests' means 'a personal interest in something that you can gain an advantage from'. C: Although speakers of Arabic or Chinese are likely to find Esperanto harder than speakers of a Romance language would, this is not presented as a reason for Esperanto's lack of success. D: Although the first sentence of the third paragraph suggests that Esperanto may not be that widely known, there is no suggestion that that is because it has received too little publicity.

34 B The answer is given in the sentence beginning 'In addition, as Esperanto itself …'. A: The argument is not that Esperanto is not an artificial language, but that all languages are in a sense artificial. C: The vocabulary of Esperanto is undoubtedly expanding, but this is not a point that the writer is making. D: The point the writer makes relating to Esperanto and prestige is that Esperanto is efficient but is without the prestige of, say, English.

35 D The answer is given in the final sentence of the last paragraph, where the writer makes the point that Esperanto has initiated useful discussions on the subject of language in the modern world. A: This point is made in passing, but it is not the writer's conclusion. B: The writer makes the point that some people would agree with this and others would disagree. C: This point may well be true, but it is not the writer's conclusion.

36 A 'Esperanto' is the only object that makes sense in the sentence. C: Although a pronoun often refers to the most recently mentioned noun, 'perch' (= position) clearly does not make sense here.

Reading and Use of English Part 6

Training

Approaching the task

1 **1** A C D
2 B C D
3 A C D
4 A B C

2 **A** Whether it is worth doing a degree depends on the subject and the specific course in question.

B Whatever the subject, a university degree tends to lead to graduates having higher salaries and more prestigious jobs than non-graduates.

C What students find valuable about the university experience depends on whether they are doing a vocational course or not.

D An increase in the number of degree places available has unrealistically raised the career expectations of many young people.

3 **1** A
2 C
3 D
4 A

4 **1** '[T]his attitude has shifted in recent years …'
2 Through the conclusion he or she draws in the final sentence of the paragraph.
3 The last two sentences in B.
4 The last two sentences in A.

Exam practice

37 C The phrase 'elegantly crafted' shows that reviewer C finds the sculpture visually attractive. Reviewer A uses the phrase 'Stunning to look at' to convey that they find the piece beautiful.

38 B The final question in B, which echoes the title of the piece in a manner similar to reviewer D, shows that reviewer B is interested in why the installation was given its name.

39 C Reviewer D says that the topic (global warming) 'is regularly beginning to feature [in art]', while reviewer C says that 'More and more artists are beginning to tackle [this topic]'.

40 A Reviewers B, C and D are all concerned about the contradiction that the piece is a protest about climate change but it uses so much electricity to keep it on show. They suggest that they feel there is something wrong about this. Reviewer A, on the other hand, points out that it is an expensive exercise but says it is 'justifiable in terms of its powerful impact'.

Reading and Use of English Part 7

Training

Useful language: working with reference clues

1 *You may have underlined more than these phrases – in a well-constructed piece of writing, most of what is written will help in some way to develop the structure of the text.*

1 *Before gap:* some people really, really like trees. The staff of … The Woodland Trust, for example.

After gap: How can this possibly be?

2 *Before gap:* once global warming kicks in … more grateful.

After gap: For example, The Woodland Trust goes on to argue

3 *Before gap:* a more attractive environment for businesses and their staff

After gap: Given such striking benefits

4 *Before gap:* It seems unlikely

After gap: All the same

2 1 Relationship between trees and health of city people

2 Economic benefits of trees in cities

3 More examples of trees' benefits

4 Something to suggest report may be overstated

3 *Suggested words and phrases to underline*:

A Before that happens, however, they; And there are other economic advantages, too.

B Besides, some of the report's claims are a bit shaky … maybe being kind to urban wildlife isn't as valued as it might be.

C Business covered; reducing blood pressure, raising self-esteem … controlling behavioural problems

D 'We need more native trees and woods in urban areas,' insists the Trust's report; even save lives, possibly.

1 D 2 A 3 C 4 B

Exam practice

41 D The sentence after gap 41 makes it clear that the missing paragraph must refer to the 'basic building blocks' of a piece of matter. D fits here, and this can be confirmed by checking whether 'Similarly' at the beginning of D relates back in a sensible way to the paragraph before gap 41. It does, in that D develops the idea of the structure of inorganic matter presented in the first paragraph of the text, making the point that living matter is structured in this way too.

42 F The paragraph before 42 is talking about the properties of scientific matter, while the paragraph after 42 is talking about music. The missing paragraph must make a link between these two themes and that is what F does.

43 A Music is the theme both before and the gap and so must presumably be the primary theme of the missing paragraph. The reference to the idea of patterns after the gap suggests that this idea may be explained in that paragraph, and this is the case in A.

44 G The reference to 'the building block' immediately after gap 44 makes it clear that building blocks must be referred to in the missing paragraph. They are mentioned in B, D and E as well as G, but none of these other paragraphs fits the gap. Only G introduces the idea of creating better materials, which is taken up in the paragraph following gap 44.

45 E Looking before and after the gap, it becomes clear that the missing paragraph must be providing some more information about the way in which the scientists created musical compositions. This information is provided in E.

46 C It is clear from what follows the gap that the missing paragraph must refer to some aspect of improving urban living. This is to be found in the phrase 'to reinvent transportation systems for cities' in C.

Reading and Use of English Part 8

Training

Reading the questions

1 *Suggested answers*

1 a character with a resemblance to a real-life celebrity

2 a story that is partially based on the author's own childhood

3 a book which has not been adapted very successfully to another medium

4 a story that has an unexpected twist at the end

5 a gripping book with an eccentric main character

6 a detective story which holds the reader's attention until the very last page

7 an over-complicated and not totally convincing plot

8 a story which is set in the past but has a modern feel to it

2 *Suggested answers*

1 looks like / be similar to / reminds the reader of / must surely have been based on

2 autobiographical

3 film/cinema (though of course it could be a play, a musical or even an opera)

4 unusual turn of events

5 'Thrilling', 'spellbinding' and 'engrossing' are all synonyms of 'gripping'.

6 probably through a reference to some unusual act or habit of the person

7 crime fiction

8 to the very end

9 too complex/convoluted

10 by saying that the story was not believable or realistic or true to life

11 by mentioning the actual period in which the story takes place, or by referring to it as historical fiction

12 by suggesting that the characters behave in a contemporary or 21st-century way

Scanning

1 It outlines the writer's three favourite science-fiction thrillers.

2 **1** Erica Wagner **2** *Frankenstein* **3** *Jurassic Park* (though we are not given the date for *ET*) **4** Jodrell Bank Observatory **5** *Jurassic Park*, its film spin-offs, *ET*, *The Andromeda Strain* **6** *The Andromeda Strain* **7** *Contact* **8** No one's – it was first published anonymously. **9** 1985 **10** Richard Holmes **11** 1818-ish – the time when Mary Shelley was writing **12** 2008

Exam practice

47 C 'While I was struggling to focus the camera, he looked hard at me and exclaimed "Andy!" To my amazement, it was my close friend Ed Viestours on his second ascent of the mountain.'

48 D 'Before our summit bid, our team agreed that returning without injuries was our main objective. Some people can be blindly obsessed by Everest.'

49 B 'My oxygen was running out, and common sense demanded that I return, but before long I was climbing on an exposed ridge to the foot of the Hillary Step.'

50 D 'After I contacted base camp and they had congratulated me, I replied, "Thank you, but first I have to get back down safely."'

51 A 'When I reached the South Summit, I was suffering from a lack of Spanish olives. I was preoccupied with thoughts of a tin of them sitting in my tent at base camp.'

52 D 'After my return to Kathmandu, I felt like a super-being because I had stood on the top of the world. I still had this feeling when I came back home but it soon faded away.'

53 C 'He was also climbing without oxygen and was tiring.'

54 A 'It has occasionally been claimed that people climb for the smell of it. Air at very high altitude smells completely different.'

55 B 'I did not get the beautiful view as a reward and I felt fleetingly disappointed.'

56 **A** 'Many people on the Indian subcontinent believe that the ascent of Everest confers on the climber a greater wisdom in manifold subjects. That is something I do not agree with but never dispute.'

Writing Part 1

Training

Understanding how writing is assessed

1 **1** D **2** F **3** B **4** A **5** C **6** E

2 I am writing this letter to discuss ~~about~~ the advantages and disadvantages of building a new theatre at the college. Firstly/First, I would like to draw your attention to the fact that our college has had a drama department for the last ten years and yet it still doesn't have its own theatre. This means that drama students must ~~to~~ put on their productions in a theatre in the city, which is expensive and, of course, not very convenient either.

3 *Suggested answer (alternatives are possible)*

I would recommend that you choose Brown's Hotel for your holiday. We had a very enjoyable time there last year. The rooms were spacious and attractively furnished, the food was delicious and the staff were very helpful too. It's central so there are plenty of shops, museums, theatres and other tourist attractions within easy walking distance.

4 *Suggested answers (alternatives are possible)*

1 This is too formal for a letter to a friend (though someone might write it for ironic or humorous effect).

Would you like to come to the theatre with me next Saturday?

2 Too informal – it would be inappropriate to use contractions or to omit subject pronouns in this kind of writing.

I would strongly recommend that you implement the suggestions in this proposal as I feel they would bring considerable benefits to the project.

3 Part of register is thinking about your audience – this is an international magazine, so you need to let the readers know from the very start which city you are writing about. The long and not very 'tight' sentence structure also makes it feel more like spoken rather than written language. Similarly, the use of vague expressions such as 'not a bad idea' and 'pretty easy' also sound more typical of spoken than written English. Such expressions are particularly unlikely to be used in a review where the writer is trying to both interest and inform his or her readers.

Nagold is a picturesque little town in the heart of Germany; its flatness and compactness make it the perfect place to walk around so that – fortunately – its chaotic public transport causes fewer problems than you might expect.

4 This feels like a mix of registers – 'I'd love to' is informal, whereas 'adequate time' is rather formal. Mixing registers in the exam will be penalised unless it is done for deliberate effect, for example, in a review. The suggestion below is written in a rather formal style.

As requested, I have written a brief report of the workshop. However, if you would like me to address any of the points raised above in greater detail, then I should be happy to do so.

5 **1** • Discussion of the advantages and disadvantages of receiving two of these three categories of present – luxuries, homemade items, experiences

• Selection of one of these as the best to receive, with an explanation as to why you feel it is best

2 Clear paragraphing; usually an impersonal, academic style rather than a colloquial or personal style

3 Neutral or formal, i.e. no use of contractions or very conversational language

4 Probably four

The first will introduce the topic. The second will discuss one of the points in the notes. The third will discuss another of the points in the notes. The fourth will explain which of the points discussed is best.

This pattern will be a straightforward one to follow for any Part 1 essay.

5 You will want the reader to have a clear understanding of your point of view and the reasons for it.

Exam practice

1 **1** • Discussion of two of the following three areas of life where young people might be able to learn from an older generation – work, relationships, money

• Selection of one of these as the area where young people can gain most, with an explanation of your point of view

2 An essay

3 Clear paragraphing; usually an impersonal, academic style rather than a colloquial or personal style

4 Neutral or formal, i.e. no use of contractions or very conversational language

5 Probably four

The first will introduce the topic. The second will discuss one of the points in the notes. The third will discuss another of the points in the notes. The fourth will explain which of the points discussed is best.

This pattern will be a straightforward one to follow for any Part 1 essay.

6 You will want the reader to have a clear understanding of your point of view and the reasons for it.

2 *Possible answers*

1 people who have already spent many years in the workplace, people who have already achieved a great deal in their career

2 offer useful guidance, provide helpful tips

3 deal with your own finances, budget successfully

4 making your own way in the world, moving away from your parents' home

3 *Possible answers*

1 Older people could give advice about, e.g. specific companies it would be best to work for and which to avoid, what kind of training will prove most useful, and might be able to recommend people to contact.

2 Older people could give advice on what is important in a relationship, on the importance of keeping up with friendships, on how to look after children, etc.

3 Older people could give advice on saving money, on budgeting sensibly, on living economically.

4 This will be a matter of personal choice. Choose the two points which you think you will be able to discuss well in English, even if you may find the third point more interesting.

5 Model answer

This model has been prepared as an example of a very good answer. However, please note that this is just one example out of several possible approaches.

> It goes without saying that there are many ways in which young people can learn from the older generation. In both their work and their private lives, youngsters can benefit from the experience of their elders.
>
> As far as work is concerned, the older generation can explain how young people can achieve the career they dream of. For example, they can recommend what to focus on in order to acquire the skills that will give them the best chance of success. They may also be able to give invaluable pointers as to which companies they would advise either applying to or, conversely, not applying to. It may even be the case that the older person will be able to use their own contacts to help the younger one to find a position.
>
> Older people may also be able to use the benefit of their own life experience to help young people with relationship advice. It can happen that older people wish they had acted differently in their own relationships and so they may wish to encourage youngsters to avoid similar mistakes. If young people are prepared to listen to this kind of advice, it may well prove useful for them.
>
> Of the two areas of life discussed above, I think young people can learn most from the older generation in the field of work. After all, no relationship is the same and so what might be right in one situation might not in another. Advice relating to careers is more likely to be relevant to a variety of differing contexts.

Notes

- *First paragraph introduces the topic*
- *Second paragraph deals with one of the points*
- *Third paragraph deals with a second point*
- *Final paragraph explains why one of the points is more valuable*
- *Only two of the three points listed are discussed*
- *Variety in structures and sentence length*
- *Neutral in register – an informal style is not appropriate for an essay*
- *Good use of connecting phrases, e.g. 'It goes without saying', 'As far as … is concerned'*
- *Correct length (260 words)*
- *No language errors*

Writing Part 2

Training

Identifying types of writing

1 1 A, C, D
2 C, D
3 B
4 A, B, C, D
5 C (possibly A)
6 B (and sometimes C and D)
7 D
8 C, D
9 C, D
10 A

2 2 In conclusion, the campaign can be considered as having been a total success. Report
3 I've been terribly busy this month, but at last I've managed to find enough time to sit down and write to you properly. Letter/Email
4 *Casablanca* has to be one of the most romantic films ever made. Review
5 I recommend the first of the two options outlined above for a number of different reasons. Report/Proposal
6 Do you prefer listening to music on your own or in the company of other people? Review
7 I am writing to congratulate you on the service which my wife and I received in your restaurant last night. Letter
8 Despite the few slight problems which the group experienced this year, I have no hesitation in recommending the course for other students in the future. Report
9 The following recommendations are based on generally accepted estimates with regard to the city's probable future needs for leisure facilities. Proposal
10 According to the results of our survey, female students make more use of the college's libraries than male students do. Report

Identifying what, why and who

1 1 Report
2 Proposal
3 Review
4 Letter/Email

2 Task 2

- arguments to persuade parents that Sam should take a year out to travel before starting medical degree
- response to suggest that writer should join Sam and his/her friends on their travels

Task 3

- types of voluntary work students could do
- how it would benefit volunteers
- how it would benefit community

3 Task 1

- describing
- explaining
- suggesting

Task 2

- suggesting
- accepting or declining an invitation

Task 3

- describing
- explaining
- persuading

4 Task 1 is to be written for a student website, so it might be more informal than something written for a printed arts magazine aimed at a broader readership.

Task 2 is to be written to a friend, so your language will be friendly and relatively informal – though you still need to be polite if you want to refuse his or her invitation. As friends, you will have plenty of shared knowledge about each other's lives. You may have met Sam's parents, so your advice would be able to take account of that.

Task 3 is to be written to a college principal, so it will be neutral or formal in its style.

Useful language: expressing functions

1 **1** suggesting **2** complaining **3** apologising **4** This is expressing a different function, i.e. *comparing* or *contrasting* **5** recommending **6** congratulating

2 **1** about **2** alternative/option/choice **3** to; by **4** regret; take **5** fact **6** agree/accept/admit/acknowledge/realise **7** position/shoes ('shoes' is a less formal option) **8** In; course **9** In/Under; take/make **10** why **11** put **12** to

Exam practice

2 **Letter**

Model answer

This model has been prepared as an example of a very good answer. However, please note that this is just one example out of several possible approaches.

> Dear Students,
>
> Are you looking for a work placement that will give you plenty of valuable experience and will look good on your CV? If so, then our company may have something to offer you.
>
> We are an international educational exchange organisation which organises links between schools all over the world. We currently have three work-experience placements available for students from your college. The work would involve a range of office tasks, including dealing with correspondence, arranging meetings and keeping our database up-to-date. We are particularly interested in offering these placements to students with some knowledge of two or more languages.
>
> The placements would be of great benefit to the students who are given this opportunity. It would provide experience of working in a small and dedicated team, which would give you the chance to develop a wider range of office skills than would normally be the case in a larger organisation. Our international network means that you would also gain some contacts all over the world, which might be of particular value to any of you considering a career in some aspect of education.
>
> You will find further information about our organisation and the placements we offer on our website and we look forward to hearing from any of you who think that the work might be right for you – and that you might be the right person for one of these placements.
>
> Best wishes to you all,
>
> Katie Fisher

Notes

- *Good use of a question at the beginning to engage the reader's interest*
- *Clear organisation and paragraphing*
- *Points in the task are all directly addressed*
- *Enough information provided about the work for students to know whether it might be likely to be suitable for them*
- *Variety in structures and sentence length*
- *Not too formal or informal in register – too much formality would be inappropriate for a letter to a student paper, but too informal a style would not be appropriate for someone writing from a serious company*
- *Reader is addressed directly – to make the letter feel more personal and engaging*
- *Correct length (243 words)*
- *No language errors*

3 **Review**

Model answer

This model has been prepared as an example of a very good answer. However, please note that this is just one example out of several possible approaches.

> **London Tourist App**
>
> It's easy to get lost in a big city like London. So when I read about the LondonApp just before I had to spend two weeks there, I did not hesitate and immediately downloaded it to my tablet.
>
> The app allows you to see where you are on a map of Greater London. You can type in where you want to go and it will show you how to get there, either on foot, by using public transport or when driving. It offers alternative routes and suggests how long your journey will take.
>
> It is clearly a very useful app for anyone like me who does not know the city and wants to find their way around. Although London is a big city, the centre is relatively compact. Using it showed me how close I was to some of the places I wanted to go to. As a result, I was able to walk to my destination and so see much more of the city. Had I not had the app, I would probably have used the underground and so would have missed a great deal.
>
> Although I found the app simple to use, I think the developers could make it even more attractive to tourists. Imagine you're walking past an interesting building and would love to know what it is. How good it would be if you could just click on that building's location on the app's map and be taken straight to information about it. It would certainly add extra value to an already excellent app.

Notes

- *Statement of what is being reviewed at the beginning*
- *Some basic information is given about the app but, as is appropriate to a review, the writer's opinion has at least as much importance as any facts about the subject of the review*
- *Clear organisation and paragraphing*
- *Good opening sentence to engage the reader's interest*
- *Variety in structures and sentence length*
- *Not too formal in register – formality is not necessary in a website review*
- *Rounding-off sentence summarises the writer's opinion*
- *Correct length (258 words)*
- *No language errors*

4 Report

Model answer

This model has been prepared as an example of a very good answer. However, please note that this is just one example out of several possible approaches.

> **Skilden Town Centre**
>
> This is a report on Skilden town centre from the point of view of a 20-year-old student currently studying for a degree in sociology at Skilden University.
>
> Entertainment
>
> Skilden town centre has two multiplex cinemas and one theatre. These put on a range of mainstream and more unusual productions and are popular with students. The theatre is regularly used for student productions. However, most people my age are surprised by the fact that there is no large venue suitable for concerts or other musical performances. If we want to hear a well-known singer or group, we have to travel 50 miles to the Welford Stadium. Skilden does, however, have a number of smaller venues used by local performers. These are much frequented by students and usually have a very good atmosphere.
>
> Restaurants
>
> Most students do not have the money to spare for eating in restaurants. However, Skilden town centre has a number of excellent restaurants, which we enjoy when our parents come to visit us. There are also one or two less-expensive establishments where we can occasionally treat ourselves to a meal. The main catering facilities which students enjoy are the coffee shops. These are not cheap, but they are welcoming and comfortable.
>
> Suggested improvements
>
> My recommendation would be to use part of the parkland by the river to build a venue for large musical events. This would greatly add to what is otherwise a good town centre from the point of view of young people.

Notes

- *Statement of what is being reported on at the beginning*
- *All the points in the task are addressed*
- *Clear organisation and paragraphing*
- *Range of vocabulary appropriate to the topic of describing facilities in a town*
- *Variety in structures and sentence length*
- *Good use of headings*
- *Appropriately neutral style for a report – anything too informal would not be suitable*
- *Correct length (250 words)*
- *No language errors*

Listening Part 1

Training

Understanding different aspects of the recording

1 1 B 2 B 3 A 4 C 5 B

2 There is something to suggest the distractors in each case, but listening carefully to the text should make it clear which is the correct option.

Exam practice

1 B A: The topic of the lecture didn't surprise the woman because she implies that, unlike the man, she had read something about the period beforehand. C: The students who are referred to are students from a previous year rather than students attending the same lecture as the speakers.

2 A B: The man wishes he had prepared better, but the woman said she was 'OK on that score'. C: They both felt that the handouts were not as useful as they might have been in that they did not contain a bibliography.

3 A B: The man's last turn makes it clear that their aim was simply to gather information rather than influence a decision. C: Advice is referred to in terms of the advice they are now going to offer their own management committee.

4 B A: The man expresses a feeling that his own contribution could have been better. C: Although he says that he was not initially sure of the value of the meeting, he felt satisfied that it had been useful by the end.

5 C A: The woman is pleased with how much she has achieved. B: She says her family has been an equally important part of her life.

6 B A and C: These are both important but not the most important thing for the woman.

Listening Part 2

Training

Choosing the right answer

Suggested answers (alternatives are possible)

1 mother / brother / schoolteacher / friend / neighbour / grandfather, etc.

2 Possible words that could fill the gap: father / grandmother / cousin / parents – (older) cousin is the correct answer.

His father simply took him to the place where his interest was awakened. His grandmother had the house where his interest was awakened. His parents were the people he had to persuade to let him have lessons.

3 **1** *Raindrops* **2** satisfactory

4 **1** Other possible words that could fill the gap in the first question: 'Summer Time'; other possible words that could fill the gap in the second question: 'excellent', 'wonderful'.

2 'Summer Time' is wrong because that is the piece his sister played; 'excellent' is wrong because that is what his class teacher said; and 'wonderful' is wrong because that is what his parents said.

Exam practice

7 **flute:** It's her sister who plays the violin.

8 **maths:** She was tempted by the thought of doing a degree in music but did not do so.

9 **(bank) cashier:** She was considering becoming a teacher but had not finally decided.

10 **Australia:** The tours to Canada and France are in the future.

11 **conductor:** The marketing manager is not the person she expresses pride in.

12 **the companionship:** She mentions travel but makes it clear that this has its downsides.

13 ***Storm*:** The other film she names is to be made in the future.

14 **fulfilling:** 'Best be described as' gives the same idea as 'sums up' in the question prompt.

Listening Part 3

Training

Understanding distraction

1 1 C

2 You might be tempted by the other options because both her children and a range of jobs are mentioned, but you need to listen carefully to the end of the recording to confirm the correct answer.

2 B

3 The topics of the other options are mentioned, but not in a way that matches the wording in the recording.

Exam practice

15 C A: She mentions that she had a fear of the sea but does not express a desire to overcome it. B: Her life was dull but she does not mention a specific problem she was facing. D: She had only just met the woman in the café, so she could not be called a friend.

16 B The other options are all true, but they are not her main reason.

17 C A: She started writing before she began to travel. B: She says she was not the kind of person who liked to keep her thoughts private. D: Although her verse said she wanted to be like her dad, we do not know whether he was a writer or not.

18 A She implies that each of the other options is to some extent an issue but it is not the greatest challenge for her.

19 C A: She does not say anything specifically about writing style. B: She suggests that making readers either laugh or cry may be a good thing for a writer to do but does not say that the main aim is to make readers experience strong emotions. D: She suggests that in fact it might not be better to think about your grandma because she will be interested just because the experiences you are describing are yours.

20 D A: She talks about experiencing life as an observer but, although she almost certainly has developed her powers of observation, she does not mention this. B: She refers to this as a possibility but does not say that she finds it particularly rewarding. C: This might be the answer that you would expect but the speaker does not mention it.

Listening Part 4

Training

Finding the perfect match

TASK ONE F

TASK TWO D

Exam practice

TASK ONE

21 C 'Got talking to' suggests a 'chance encounter'.

22 G Although the speaker mentions that her father is an accountant, she goes on to make it clear that he advised her against taking up accountancy as a career.

23 D 'Master' is a synonym for '(male) teacher'.

24 B Her aunt is the relative who she says 'got me into' (= inspired her interest in) the career.

25 E 'That was it' means 'that was all that was necessary'.

TASK TWO

26 F 'Constantly having to train new helpers' is a paraphrase of 'rapid turnover of staff'.

27 D The speaker makes it clear that she was lucky to get her position given the number of applicants from this country and elsewhere.

28 C The speaker explains how he and his family eventually moved to a place nearer to the airport because of the pressures of commuting.

29 A The date of the show is the deadline, and what the speaker says about these makes it clear that it can be difficult to meet them.

30 H It is clearly not easy to have a straightforward working relationship with someone who is bad-tempered.

Speaking Part 1

Training

Understanding how your speaking is assessed

1 1 C 2 E 3 D 4 A 5 B

2

	Question 1	Question 2	Question 3	Question 4	Question 5
Speaker A	✓	✓			✓
Speaker B			✓	✓	
Criterion	4	1	2	3	5

3 *Suggested answers*

1 What do you enjoy reading most?
The candidate could have given more information about a specific writer or story they had read.

2 What did you do last night?
The candidate could have spoken about what film they saw, who they went with and what they felt about the film, for example.

3 How do you try to keep fit?
The candidate could have described the kind of exercise they take and could have gone into more detail about their diet, saying how they try to eat fruit as a snack rather than sweets.

4 How do you think you'll use your English in the future?
The candidate could have explained what their plans are for work and study.

Speaking Part 2

Training

Useful language: hypothesising

1 they look as if they're waiting … They may have been waiting for quite a while because … so perhaps he's feeling a little anxious. The couple on the right seem to be work colleagues … they could be discussing … But they seem to be feeling quite relaxed … She looks as if … no one seems to be feeling particularly stressed – they're probably all very used to waiting …

2 *Possible answers*

1 I think they might be talking about a situation at their workplace.

2 I wonder if they could be discussing some kind of problem.

3 I think the man might have a problem at work.

4 Perhaps the woman has been giving the man some advice.

5 I don't think that they can be at home because they are both dressed quite formally.

6 It's most likely that they're discussing something related to work.

7 But it could also be that they're talking about a relationship problem.

8 I think it's quite possible that they're good friends as well as colleagues.

9 They look as if they get on well with each other.

10 I imagine they must be office workers of some kind.

Useful language: comparing and contrasting

1 1 In the first picture, everyone looks as if they're enjoying themselves. In contrast, in the other one, the people seem rather miserable.

2 The girls in this picture are working hard, whereas the girls in the other picture are simply having fun.

3 By and large, the people in the second picture seem more interested in what they're doing than the people in the first picture.

4 All in all, I think the people in the first picture are feeling more relaxed than those in the second picture.

5 On the whole, the children in this picture seem to be having a good time, but there is one little boy who is clearly not enjoying himself.

6 The people in this picture might be going on holiday. On the other hand, they could simply be on their way to work.

Speaking Part 3

Training

Useful language: negotiating

1 1 I can't *help* thinking that …

2 I *entirely* agree.

3 I take your *point,* but …

4 Isn't it more a *matter* of …

5 It's interesting you *should* say that because …

6 What you say reminds me *of* …

7 That's all very *well,* but …

8 *Wouldn't* you say so?

9 Yes, but we shouldn't *forget* about …

10 You wouldn't disagree *with* that, would you?

2 a expressing agreement – 2

b expressing partial or complete disagreement – 1, 3, 4, 7, 9

c asking for someone's opinion – 8, 10

d developing an idea someone has mentioned – 5, 6

Giving yourself time to think

1 Well; let me think; that's quite a difficult one; How can I explain what I mean?
Well, I must admit I haven't really thought about it much before; What's it called?; Wait a moment; It's on the tip of my tongue; you know

Speaking Part 4

Training

Useful language: giving your opinion

1 1 In 2 As 3 From 4 far 5 way 6 where 7 perfectly 8 argue 9 strong 10 tend

Test 1 Transcript

Listening Part 1

Training

Exercise 1

Man: I'm not sure I like the look of this place. It's a bit dingy.

Woman: Mm, I don't know. It's a bit quaint perhaps. Anyway, I'm so shattered, I'd settle for anything. And you've been behind the wheel all day, so I dread to think how you're feeling.

Man: Mm. I am pretty exhausted. And at least it's probably not too late to grab a bite here before turning in. I'm starving.

Woman: Well, I'm not sure I fancy anything at the moment myself. Anyway, it certainly doesn't look too expensive. So, shall I see if they've got any vacancies?

Man: Sure. And check about where to leave the car too, if they have anywhere. I'll be sorting out the luggage while you find out.

Exam practice

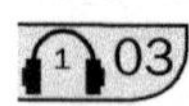

You will hear three different extracts. For questions 1 to 6, choose the answer (A, B or C) which fits best according to what you hear. There are two questions for each extract.

Extract 1

You hear two students discussing a lecture. Now look at questions 1 and 2.

Woman: That was a really interesting lecture, don't you think, Jack?

Man: Not bad at all. I'd heard that the lecturer was brilliant from some students he taught last year, so I was expecting quite a lot.

Woman: Really? I hadn't heard anything about him before. Anyway, I never imagined anyone managing to make a topic that's basically quite tedious into something so fascinating – just by looking at it from a fresh angle.

Man: Mm, I just wished I'd read a bit more about that period in history beforehand. I think I'd have got a bit more out of it if I had.

Woman: I was OK on that score. But I certainly want to go and find out more about it now, even though it's not an essential part of our course.

Man: Me too. Pity he didn't include a bibliography on any of the handouts he gave us.

Woman: Oh well, it won't be too hard to find something relevant, I'm sure.

Extract 2

You hear two business people discussing a meeting they attended. Now look at questions 3 and 4.

Man: Well, I'm glad that meeting's over now. I thought they were never going to bring things to an end!

Woman: I know. I kept thinking they were on the verge of wrapping things up and then someone raised some other issue.

Man: Yes. Still, we achieved what we set out to. I wasn't sure it'd be worth it at first, but I think it was, don't you?

Woman: Certainly. We've got a pretty good picture now of what'd be involved if we do decide to do business with them. And I think you gave them a sense of what we could offer them.

Man: Well, I could have done that better, I think, but never mind. So, do you feel ready to give a full report to our management committee tomorrow?

Woman: Yes, but I'm not sure whether I'd advise them to pursue the partnership or not.

Man: Well, that's up to them. We've done our bit by seeing how the land lies.

Extract 3

You hear a scientist being interviewed about her career.

Now look at questions 5 and 6.

Interviewer: You've had a long and successful career as a biochemist. Would you say that you've achieved everything that you would've wished?

Woman: I don't imagine anyone would ever say that. But I've been very lucky in that I've been able to do far more than I ever dreamt when I started out. It's amazing to have ended up heading the leading research lab in my field.

Interviewer: And that's on top of having four children.

Woman: That's right. My family has always been as important to me as my career. But I've been able to enjoy both. Thanks to a great support network, of course.

Interviewer: What quality do you look for in young scientists who want to work in your lab?

Woman: Well, they should have a natural inquisitiveness about the world. They notice what's going on around them and they want to find out more. I'm looking for people who pay great attention to detail, of course. You have to value precision as a scientist. But I guess the key thing for me is someone who understands that you also learn from experiments that don't work. Of course, it's disheartening to spend six months on something that fails. But a true scientist appreciates that that is also part of working towards the truth.

That is the end of Part 1.

Listening Part 2

Training

Exercises 3 and 4

Man: The first time I performed in public was when I was only eight. My primary school put on a show for our parents, and all the kids had to either play an instrument or sing. My older sister opened the event by playing the violin. She did a piece called *Summer Time*, a pretty melody that I still love. Then my best friend, Sam, sang *Raindrops*, a very appropriate little song, as it was pouring that day! I accompanied him on the piano. I don't remember much about the rest of the concert – I guess I was too overwhelmed by my own performance. My class teacher said I was excellent, and my parents called it wonderful. My piano teacher was a bit less enthusiastic, but she did say it was satisfactory. That was, for her, actually quite high praise!

Exam practice

You will hear a musician called Anita Kumar talking to a group of students about her life. For questions 7 to 14, complete the sentences with a word or short phrase.

You now have 45 seconds to look at Part 2. You will need to play the recording twice.

Anita: I'm here today to tell you about my life as a musician in an orchestra, as I understand some of you may be considering this as a career. If you play the flute, like me, then I'd certainly recommend it as a great way to become a professional musician. I used to wish I played the violin as my sister does, as that'd offer more opportunities for work as a soloist, but now I don't think I'd exchange orchestra work for a solo career – even if I had the opportunity and the talent.

Some of you are studying for a degree in music at the university here. I was very tempted by that option, but in the end my parents persuaded me to do maths instead. They thought it was more likely to lead to a steady job.

After graduating, I was considering becoming a teacher but decided to take a job in a bank first while I made up my mind. Being a cashier during the day left me with plenty of time and energy in the evenings, and I began to play in my local orchestra. I loved it, and when someone suggested I try for one of the bigger national orchestras, I jumped at the chance.

It's extremely enjoyable and I love the path I've chosen, but it's certainly not an easy life. I spend a lot of my time living out of a suitcase. We spent last month playing a series of concerts in Australia, for example. We got back last week and are off again next Monday. To Canada. Then later in the year, we're off to France.

The orchestra I play for is one of the best known in the country. And that's not just because we've got a pretty good marketing manager. The thing is we have a brilliant conductor. He's still quite young and he has an amazing future ahead of him, I'm sure. We all feel very fortunate to have the chance to be working with him.

Although I love travel, I wouldn't say that's the best part of my job. It's often fun, but it can be exhausting. But what I do love is the companionship. It's great to spend one's life with a group of people who share the same passion for music.

Although we spend most of our time giving concerts in this country and abroad, we did have one rather unusual experience last year when we featured in a movie. You may have seen it – it was called *Storm* – and it was about a touring orchestra that got stuck on a Caribbean island during a hurricane. The same director says he's going to use us in his adaptation of a novel called *Piano*, which he's planning to start shooting next year.

I hope this has given you some idea of what life in an orchestra is like. I'd say it can best be described as being fulfilling. I feel incredibly lucky to be paid for doing something I love so much. At times, of course, it's exhausting and difficult, but it's never boring and I have no hesitation in recommending it as a career. So, I'd be happy to answer any questions …

That is the end of Part 2.

Listening Part 3
Training

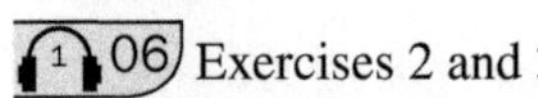
Exercises 2 and 3

Interviewer: I understand you also occasionally volunteer at a wildlife reserve, working with deer. How did that come about, and how has it inspired your writing?

Rose: Well, my children have been fascinated by deer ever since they were tiny, though I must admit that wasn't an enthusiasm I initially shared. However, Alison Greaves, an old classmate of mine, opened a reserve for them and invited me along to have a look – before I knew where I was, I was working there two days a week and really enjoying being outside. Alison was desperate for extra help at the start. But working with the deer has been an amazing blessing and has enriched my life in many ways. A couple of creative projects inspired by them have taken shape but haven't yet found a publishing home.

Listening Part 3
Exam practice

You will hear part of a radio interview with a travel writer called Marina Vardy. For questions 15 to 20, choose the answer (A, B, C or D) which fits best according to what you hear.

You now have 70 seconds to look at Part 3. You will need to play the recording twice.

Interviewer: With me in the studio today I have travel writer Marina Vardy. Marina, how did you get started travelling?

Marina: People often think that those who travel are running away from something. They're right. Aged 24, I decided to run away from a dull job, and a life that had grown stagnant. I set out to find something more, though I had no idea what 'something more' looked like. Thanks to a chance encounter, I met a woman in a café who had a humble sailboat and a dream of exploring the world. Against my better judgement, I decided on the spur of the moment to accept her spontaneous suggestion to join her, despite the fact that I've always had a morbid fear of deep water.

Interviewer: And you didn't regret it?

Marina: At times I did, especially at the beginning, but, rather to my own amazement, I got used to putting up with all sorts of physically difficult situations. That voyage changed the course of my life. It turned me into a travel writer and an adventurer, but above all it made me an optimist. I couldn't have asked for more.

Interviewer: Mm. What made you get started in writing?

Marina: Oh, that happened a good while before I set off travelling and I was inspired to write by what I saw. At about 12, I wrote a little verse that included the line: '*People say I take after my dad. He went bald and grey in his twenties. Great!*' My mother stuck it on the fridge, people laughed, and so began my passion for entertaining people with words. I've never been one for keeping my thoughts private, I'm afraid.

Interviewer: As a travel writer, what's your biggest challenge?

Marina: My greatest passion in life is a midday sleep in a hammock, but people don't want to read about that! So in order to get a good story, I end up doing things that most people avoid due to their ridiculously high risk. But, to be honest, the worst thing's the fact that I constantly battle self-doubt over whether or not my work is any good. You really don't know till you get it done and others read it and pass their verdict. When you're penning your life story, it can seem like you're being very self-indulgent. 'She's supposedly writing a masterpiece, but she hasn't bothered to brush her hair in weeks!' my family say in hushed whispers behind my back. Or they do in my imagination, at least.

Interviewer: What advice would you give to someone who is considering going into travel writing?

Marina: Always assume that your travel experiences are only going to be interesting to your grandma. Attention spans are slim, and there has to be more than a description of what you saw. Nowadays, with all the other calls on people's attention, you have to work harder than ever to keep your readers engaged. How can you give universal appeal to your story? How can you make it a page turner? Can you make your readers laugh? Cry? Think of your travels like the backdrop to a greater story that grips the reader, not the story itself. After all, you're trying to grab the attention of an internet-obsessed generation, which means you've got a big job on your hands.

Interviewer: Mm. What's the biggest reward of life as a travel writer?

Marina: Writing teaches you to experience life as an observer. No matter what situation you're in, there's always that tiny author sitting in the back of your head, narrating the events around you. Bad encounters make good stories, and they're cathartic to write about. Did some horrible person treat you badly? Not to worry – put him in your next story. And I'm nice about kind people too, of course. Channelling your experiences into art is deeply enriching, I find.

Interviewer: Thank you very much, Marina.

That is the end of Part 3.

Listening Part 4
Exam practice

Part 4 consists of two tasks. You will hear five short extracts in which people are talking about their jobs. Look at Task 1. For questions 21 to 25, choose from the list (A–H) what made each speaker choose their career. Now look at Task 2. For questions 26 to 30, choose from the list (A–H) the difficulty each speaker has had to overcome. While you listen you must complete both tasks.

You now have 45 seconds to look at Part 4. You will need to play the recording twice.

Speaker 1

When I was at school, I had a talent for chemistry, and my teachers advised me to become a research scientist. But in the summer holidays after I finished school, some friends and I went travelling round Europe by train. In Greece, we got talking to a group of archaeologists and they suggested we join them on a dig. I was hooked from the first moment. Luckily, I was then able to get a place on a university course and I've never looked back. It hasn't all been plain sailing, but I've been fortunate enough to get funding for the projects I've wanted to work on, which can often be a major issue for archaeologists. I suppose the main problem is constantly having to train new helpers – most of the people who come and work on digs are only doing it for a few months at a time.

Speaker 2

I was very fortunate indeed to get this job. It's a first-rate accountancy firm, and lots of highly-qualified people both from this country and from abroad compete to work here, though few get taken on. My dad's an accountant, but that's not what got me into this field – in fact, if anything, he advised me against it. He remembered how hard he'd found it as a young man spending years studying in the evenings after working all day. But that wasn't too much of a problem for me. I've just always had a flair for working with figures and I find it very satisfying to immerse myself in a client's accounts. Some of my friends find that a bit weird, I think. But I think numbers can be much more straightforward to work with than people – and there's plenty of good software to help you with most of the more tedious operations these days.

Speaker 3

I work as an airline pilot. It's not quite as glamorous as people often think it sounds, as you don't really get to see much of the places you travel to. Fortunately, I was aware of that before I decided to go for this as a career. I fly out of an airport that's over 40 miles from the town where I used to live with my family. I commuted for about ten years, but then we decided it was all too much, especially when I was either leaving early or getting back late, so we uprooted, and things are much easier for me now. It was my old geography master who suggested I might enjoy flying, actually. He'd have loved to have been a pilot himself, but said he couldn't afford the training. My granddad actually financed mine, which was amazingly kind of him.

Speaker 4

It's quite hard working in the fashion business. But it's fun, of course, too. I love being creative and helping other women look their best. But you wouldn't believe how tense it can be in those last few days before a major show. You just have to get everything ready on time, and that can often mean a few all-nighters. I enjoy working with the models – even the top ones are nothing like as temperamental as the press often makes out. My aunt used to be one, and I guess it was her stories that got me into the business in the first place. People have often told me I'm very talented, but I don't think I am – it's just a matter of being prepared to put in the hard graft. And that's never been an issue for me. I guess I'm a bit of a workaholic really.

Speaker 5

Other young boys usually go through a stage of wanting to be astronauts or circus clowns, but I've only ever wanted to be a civil engineer ever since I was a small kid. I think I was enthused when I came across a biography of the man who built some of the first ever iron bridges – that was it, as far as I was concerned. I certainly don't have any regrets. It's a rewarding job and I even quite enjoy the buzz of working to deadlines. Fortunately, these days most of the design is done using computer programs – I'm sure I'd have found it very difficult doing precise drawings by hand as they used to have to. My boss can be a bit bad-tempered at times. I don't like it, but I've learnt not to let it bother me too much. If it got too bad, I'd try to find a job elsewhere, as indeed several other members of staff have ended up doing.

That is the end of Part 4.

Speaking Part 1

Training

Exercise 2

Question 1, Speaker A

Interlocutor: What do you enjoy most about studying English?

Speaker A: I like the way that it makes it possible for me to communicate with people all over the world.

Question 1, Speaker B

Interlocutor: What do you enjoy most about studying English?

Speaker B: I like the way that it makes it possible for me to communicate with people all over the world.

Question 2, Speaker A

Interlocutor: What's the most exciting thing that's ever happened to you?

Speaker A: Mm, that's a difficult question. But I think it might have been something that happened on my eleventh birthday. I was with my parents who were working on an archaeological dig on a northern island of Scotland when a schoolboy who'd just arrived to help on the site discovered treasure. It was a hoard of silver bowls and brooches. They're thought to have been there for nearly 1,200 years. That was certainly an extraordinarily exciting day.

Question 2, Speaker B

Interlocutor: What's the most exciting thing that's ever happened to you?

Speaker B: Um. Perhaps something that happened on my eleventh birthday. I was with my parents on an archaeological dig on a northern island of Scotland. A schoolboy arrived to help on the site for the first time. He discovered treasure. Er, it was a hoard of silver bowls and brooches. Um, they were probably there for nearly 1,200 years. Mm, that was certainly an extraordinarily exciting day.

Question 3, Speaker A

Interlocutor: What's your opinion of computer games?

Speaker A: I like computer games. I think most of them are very good, though some are not so good, of course. I play them a lot with my friends. My parents don't like computer games, but I think they're very fun.

Question 3, Speaker B

Interlocutor: What's your opinion of computer games?

Speaker B: Well, that depends. I like some computer games very much, particularly games based on sports like football or motor-racing or snowboarding. I'm not so keen on adventure games. I spend a lot of time playing computer games with my friends. My parents say I'm wasting my time, but I think it's a perfectly reasonable way to relax.

Question 4, Speaker A

Interlocutor: What kind of music do you enjoy listening to?

Speaker A: Er ... um ... I like ... er ... pop music. Um, I listen to it, um ... er, every day. Er ... um ... I listen to it, um ... on my iPod®. Er ... on my way to college.

Question 4, Speaker B

Interlocutor: What kind of music do you enjoy listening to?

Speaker B: Er, well, let me think. I like pop music. Yes, that's what I listen to most. I always have my iPod® with me and I listen to it on my way to and from college.

Question 5, Speaker A

Interlocutor: Who was your best friend when you were at school?

Speaker A: Sorry, do you mean when I was at primary school or at secondary school?

Interlocutor: As you like. Primary school, perhaps.

Speaker A: OK. Then … it was a girl who lived next door to me. Her name was, er, Tessa …

Question 5, Speaker B

Interlocutor: Who was your best friend when you were at school?

Speaker B: I think friends are very important when you are at school.

Exercise 4

1 How did you spend your last holiday?
2 What do you do to relax?
3 What are your plans for your career?
4 What have you achieved that you feel particularly proud of?
5 What new law would you like to be introduced?
6 Do you think the place where you are currently living is a good place for young people to grow up in?

Speaking Part 2

Training

Exercise 1

Interlocutor: How do you think the people in this picture are feeling?

Man: Well, the people here are at an airport, and they look as if they're waiting for their flight departure to be called. They may have been waiting for quite a while, because the woman on the left has fallen asleep on her husband's shoulder. He's reading a newspaper and is looking quite serious, so perhaps he's feeling a little anxious. The couple on the right seem to be work colleagues, and they could be discussing an issue relating to their work. But they seem to be feeling quite relaxed in each other's company. The woman in the middle is focusing on some papers. She looks as if she's totally concentrated on what she's reading. On the whole, no one seems to be feeling particularly stressed – they're probably all very used to waiting at airports.

Speaking Part 3

Training

Exercise 1

Man: So would you ever buy an electric car?

Woman: Well, let me think, that's quite a difficult one. On the one hand, they're obviously better for the environment in that they don't use petrol or diesel. But on the other hand, they'd need to be a bit more convenient to use before I'd seriously consider buying one. Um, how can I explain what I mean? I think it's not yet straightforward enough to recharge electric cars. It'll need to be quicker and easier to do that, I think, before large numbers of people start using them. How about you? What do you think?

Man: Well, I must admit I haven't really thought about it much before. But I certainly think that they sound as if they're a good idea. A friend of mine has actually just got one. What's it called? Um, wait a moment. It's on the tip of my tongue. Oh, anyway, he's only been using it for a couple of days, but he seems to quite like it. He did tell me, though, that you have to be extra careful driving it. It's so quiet that, er, you know, pedestrians don't hear you coming and, if they're not paying attention, they can step out into the street in front of you.

Test 2 Key

Reading and Use of English Part 1

Training

Review

1 You should first read the title and then read all through the text. This will help you understand the text, which will make the task easier for you.

2 Often the right answer is the only option that collocates with what is written either before or after the gap.

3 Often the presence (or absence) of a preposition before or after the gap means that only one option is possible.

4 It's always worth having a guess. You don't lose marks for a wrong answer. So eliminate any option you feel sure is incorrect and choose from the rest.

Useful language: checking for correct collocations

1 **1** drawn **2** attend **3** taking **4** know **5** sit **6** achieving **7** getting **8** have

2 **1** make **2** go/enjoy **3** have/throw/hold **4** take **5** meet/suit **6** make **7** shows **8** find **9** range/choice **10** area/field

Useful language: thinking about prepositions

1 **1** knowledge **2** visit **3** participate **4** get **5** thank **6** talks **7** reasons **8** advertisement

2 **1** I don't have much information about local history.
2 My stay at my grandparents' was a great success.
3 The new student didn't contribute to the discussion.
4 When does your plane arrive in/at Rio?
5 Polly wrote to congratulate the professor on his inspiring lecture.
6 My grandfather never discusses his life as a coal miner. (No preposition is needed after *discuss*.)
7 The article considers the consequences of the workers' strike.
8 I saw an article about/on a language course in the paper.

Exam practice

1 **D** The verb 'trigger' means 'to cause an automatic response'. A and B: Both verbs tend to be used about people – to 'provoke' or 'impel' someone to do something. C: 'Originate' looks back to where something came from, e.g. 'The idea originated from China', rather than forward to what will happen as a future consequence.

2 **A** You can rule out the other words both through their meaning and the grammar. B: 'Involve' would often be followed by an action of some kind, and is typically followed by a gerund, e.g. 'Doing a degree in a foreign language often involves spending a year in a country where the language is spoken.' C: 'Consists' is almost always followed by 'of'. D: 'Occupy' collocates most strongly with a place or position of some kind.

3 **B** Working out how the device is working will help you get to the correct answer. A compression system in the vest inflates and deflates airbags in order to create a sensation of tightness or loosening for the wearer. A: As well as its more frequent meaning of 'understand', 'realise' can mean 'make something real' – to realise a dream, for example – but that meaning does not fit here either. C: 'Pass' would be used about something less abstract – the compression system passes air through tubes perhaps. D: 'Construct' is usually used about something physical, typically a building of some kind. It does also collocate with some abstract nouns, e.g. 'theory' or 'plan', but not with something as vague as 'tightness'.

4 **A** This is the word that is used to describe the place and time where a novel or play is set. B: 'Position' is usually used to refer to a fixed place held by someone in, e.g. society or a team. C: 'Environment' is mainly used when talking about nature or about the place that people or animals inhabit. D: 'Part' might be used about a book, but it would mean a section of that book and so does not make sense here.

5 **B** The meaning here is that they used this particular book as an example to show how the device might work in practice. A: 'Enabling' requires a different structure, e.g. 'Using this novel enabled the scientists to test out their device.' C: 'Affecting' means influencing or impacting on and so does not make sense in this context. D: It is clear from the context that they were creating rather than just imagining how the vest might work with the book.

6 **C** 'Picked' here is a synonym for 'chose'. A, B, D: None of the distracting words can be used to give the idea of 'chose' or 'selected' and they do not make sense in this context.

7 **D** 'Range' collocates strongly with 'of emotions'. A and B: These nouns suggest size rather than variety and, although these words might work with 'locations', they do not work with 'emotions'. C: 'Amount' is used with uncountable nouns, e.g. 'an incredible amount of money/trouble/work' rather than with countable nouns such as 'locations' or 'emotions'.

8 **B** This is the only word which fits both in terms of grammar and meaning. A: 'Commented' would need to be followed by 'on'. C: 'Called' would require the 'as' which follows later in the sentence to be dropped. D: 'Remarkable' is a description rather than an explanation.

Reading and Use of English Part 2

Training

Review

1 No, it isn't. Understanding what the text is all about will help you find the right words for each gap.

2 No, not at all. It probably makes sense to do the ones you find easiest first.

3 You must write only ONE word in each gap.

4 You need to write a grammar word in each gap, e.g. preposition, pronoun, article, quantifier, auxiliary verb, etc.

5 No, you must choose one and write only that one down.

Considering meaning and grammar

1 1 **very:** 'Much' would need to be followed by a comparative adjective in a sentence like this, e.g. 'much fuller than I'd expected'.

2 **newly:** An adverb is needed to modify an adjective like 'refurbished'.

3 **healthily:** 'Healthy' is an adjective and would need to be followed by a noun, e.g. 'eat healthy food'.

4 **so:** 'Too' would be followed by a different pattern – 'too hot for us to eat outside …'.

5 **very:** 'Absolutely' does not collocate with gradable adjectives like 'disappointing' – it is used with non-gradable adjectives such as 'wonderful' or 'unique'. A gradable adjective is one that can be 'slightly' or 'a little', e.g. you can say 'slightly disappointing' or 'a little disappointing' whereas you can't say 'slightly wonderful' or 'a little unique'. 'Disappointing' is gradable, whereas 'wonderful' and 'unique' are non-gradable.

6 **to:** 'In' does not collocate when you are talking about plans for making changes.

7 **no:** 'Not' would need the indefinite article – 'there wasn't a lift available'.

8 **anything:** 'Nothing' would make the phrase into a double negative, which isn't correct in standard English. Note that 'without anything' means the same as 'with nothing'.

2 **1** would **2** a **3** missing **4** by **5** which **6** for **7** why **8** wants/decides (Note that the verb after 'everyone' must be singular.)

Useful language: focusing on phrasal verbs

1 take **2** bringing **3** got **4** put **5** make **6** go **7** do **8** made/took **9** get **10** bring

Exam practice

9 **When/If:** If you read to the end of the sentence, it becomes clear that a conjunction is needed for the sentence to hang together. It also becomes clear that a conjunction that gives a conditional idea is required.

10 **how:** 'How' is one word which can give the idea of 'the way in which'.

11 **with:** You have 'ties/links/connections' with someone or something.

12 **whatever:** 'Whatever' can give the idea of 'it does not matter what' in one word.

13 **to:** Although you might ask someone for their thoughts about something, 'give [careful] thought' needs to be followed by 'to'.

14 **Despite:** 'Despite the fact that' is a phrase often used to convey the same idea as 'although'.

15 **of:** This is the only preposition that can fit in the phrase 'workings of your business', which means 'how your business works'.

16 **whose:** The possessive relative pronoun is required to make the sentence hang together. It is a more concise way of saying 'someone who has qualities that match ...'.

Reading and Use of English Part 3

Training

Review

1 Reading the text all the way through will give you an idea of the general meaning of the text and this will help you find the right words.

2 Yes. You must spell the word correctly to get the mark.

3 You usually have to add a prefix and/or a suffix.

4 You might have to decide between a person noun or an abstract noun, for example 'developer' or 'development', or you might have to decide between a singular or a plural noun.

Useful language: spelling correctly

1 **1** accommodation **2** committee **3** negotiate **4** beginning **5** professional **6** appropriate **7** interesting **8** pronunciation **9** necessary **10** receive

2 **1** characteristic **2** normally **3** disappointed **4** changeable **5** marvellously/marvelously (US spelling) **6** business **7** shameful **8** embarrassment

Useful language: noting words from the same root

1 developments **2** developer **3** undeveloped/underdeveloped
4 misinterpreted **5** interpretation **6** interpreters
7 applicable (*applied* is also possible) **8** (re)applied **9** applications

Exam practice

17 **basis:** Although 'base' can also itself be a noun, it is used in more concrete contexts to mean 'the bottom part of an object'. 'Basis' is needed here to mean 'the most important ideas or facts on which something is based'.

18 **apprehensive:** Note how 'd' at the end of the verb changes to 's' to form this adjective meaning 'anxious about something in the future'.

19 **diversion:** Again, the last consonant of the verb changes when a suffix is added.

20 **mastery:** This is the abstract noun from the verb 'to master'.

21 **significant:** This is a useful synonym for 'important'.

22 **undeniably:** The grammar of the sentence makes it clear that you need an adverb to modify 'it is true that …' and the meaning of the sentence makes it clear that you need a negative prefix, as the writer is saying 'It can't be denied …'.

23 **vigorous:** Note that the 'u' in the noun is not used in the adjective form in UK as well as US spelling (in US spelling, the noun is 'vigor').

24 **depression:** This is the noun which can be used to mean 'a state of being very unhappy and feeling hopeless about the future'.

Reading and Use of English Part 4

Training

Review

1 Six (and the minimum is three)

2 Two

3 No, you must use it in exactly the same form.

4 Two. This means that it is always worth writing something. You may get at least one of the two marks.

Useful language: choosing the right expression

1 **1** **turned out:** 'Resulted in' here would need to be followed by a noun, e.g. 'resulted in disappointment'.

2 **a letter of apology:** This is a fixed collocation – we talk about a 'love letter' but not an 'apology letter'.

3 **the opportunity:** Margot might have the 'possibility *of* doing' something, but not the 'possibility *to* do' it.

4 **finding:** You have 'difficulty *(in)* doing something'; it is 'difficult *to* do something', but the noun 'difficulty' is not followed by an infinitive.

5 **leave:** It would also be possible to say 'I'll let you *have* details', but 'let' alone is not enough.

6 **going:** 'Recommend' cannot be followed by the infinitive with 'to' – you can say either 'I recommend going' or 'I recommend *you* go' but NOT '~~I recommend to go~~' or '~~I recommend you to go~~'.

7 **cleaning and decorating:** Both verbs must be in the same form – both verbs follow the preposition 'in' and so they must both be in the *-ing* form.

8 **where he found:** In indirect or reported questions, the auxiliary is not used: 'Where did he go?' – 'I don't know where he went' / 'She asked where he went', etc.

2 **1** not to LEAVE your projects in/at

2 TURNED out to be unexpectedly

3 had no DIFFICULTY (in) getting

4 to KNOW where Lisa went

5 would/'d RECOMMEND having a meal / eating

6 a letter of / an APOLOGY for making

7 not have the OPPORTUNITY to go / of going

Exam practice

The vertical line | shows where the answer is split into two parts for marking purposes.

25 **takes it | for GRANTED** 'Take it for granted' is a fixed expression meaning 'assume', i.e. 'accept something is true without even thinking about it'.

26 **is no college | I'd/would RATHER** 'I'd /I would rather' means 'I'd prefer'. Note that we say 'I'd rather study' but 'I'd prefer to study'.

27 **COME to | a decision** This phrase means 'decide', as does 'make up your mind'.

28 **had MISSED her flight | she would/'d** 'Given that' means 'since'. The same idea as the prompt sentence is given by a sentence using the pattern of a third conditional, i.e. *If* + past perfect + *would have* + past participle in the main clause ('to miss' = not to catch).

29 **me to | BRUSH up my French** The structure with 'encourage' is 'encourage someone to do something'. The phrasal verb 'brush up' means to 'improve something already learnt but partly forgotten'.

30 **for keeping/putting | her in the PICTURE** 'To keep/put someone in the picture' is an idiom meaning 'to inform or keep someone informed about a situation'.

Reading and Use of English Part 5

Exam practice

Review

All the pieces of advice in this exercise should be ticked.

Exam task

31 B 'With a free thumb, we have the ability to fashion tools easily. It is believed that we have been making tools for more than 2.5 million years. Yet that does not define us.' A: Although the writer does say that our free thumb makes it possible for us to make tools, that is not the point that he wishes to make. C: The writer mentions other creatures such as sea otters that also make tools. D: This may be true, but it is not a point that is made in the text.

32 D 'Just last year I watched hawks in Australia pick up burning sticks from a bushfire and drop them to spread the fire, flushing out or scorching potential prey.' A: That might be true in that they managed to pick up burning sticks, but that is not what impressed him. B: They are using the fire not to cook their prey but to make it come out of its hiding places in the bush. C: They were not starting fires but spreading fires that had already started.

33 B 'In the world of archaeology, the earliest sign of human control of fire is a hotly debated topic.' A: According to the text, the evidence 'appears to show' fire hearths from a million years ago – this is a much more tentative statement than A is. C: This is assumed rather than there being evidence to show it was the case. D: Although this may well be true, it is not a point that the writer makes.

34 A '[T]he fire became a focus for life, around which our forebears could gather in good cheer. (That sight is still played out nightly in the villages of the San Bushmen of the Kalahari.)' B: This may happen, but it is not what it says in the text. C: The text only talks about one aspect of the Bushmen's lives. In other ways, their way of life may perhaps be quite different from that of their ancestors. D: Harmful elements in food have been destroyed by cooking ever since people began to cook their food.

35 C 'We don't have to have been there to realise that the question of how to make fire from scratch would have occupied the minds gathered at the campfire. If I could travel back in time, I would hope to witness the first of our ancestors achieving this remarkable skill.' A: The writer mentions the telling of stories round a fire in the evenings but does not mention a particular desire to share this experience. B: It is experiencing the moment of it happening rather than learning how it actually happened that the writer says he would like to have seen. D: The writer makes the point that life was transformed by fire but does not express a desire to have witnessed that process in action.

36 D 'Our ancestors were able to spread out, exploring their landscape in smaller foraging parties with fire for safety and with smoke to locate each other again.' A: We are not told that people were afraid of the cold, simply that fire allowed them to move into lands where temperatures were colder. B and C: Although in a sense these statements are true, they are not the explanation provided as to why the discovery of how to create fire brought confidence.

Reading and Use of English Part 6

Exam practice

Review

1 They all give opinions relating to the same topic.

2 No, it is more likely that there will be two answers for one of the letters and so none for another.

3 No. All the questions will involve reading across the texts and understanding the relationships between them.

4 It will almost certainly be helpful to read the questions quickly first so that you have them in mind as you read the texts.

Exam task

37 C B says that literature 'teaches us about ourselves and other people and why we behave as we do', while expert C similarly points to the value of literature in teaching empathy.

38 B A, C and D all in some way relate a study of literature to employment prospects, whereas the focus of B is on the value of literature study for creating a well-rounded person.

39 D Expert A says that lecturers should make students aware that the writing skills they are gaining will help their employment prospects. Expert D mentions the desirability of students thinking about the skills they will gain when choosing what to study for a joint degree. Neither B nor C deals with this aspect of the topic.

40 B Expert C says that literature graduates will have good critical-thinking skills, and B conveys the same idea by saying that studying literature helps people question things. Neither A nor D specifically mentions the value of literature study in promoting thinking skills.

Reading and Use of English Part 7

Exam practice

Review

1 **1** C **2** E **3** A **4** F **5** B **6** D

2 *You could underline a great many words and phrases, as the paragraphs of the text connect in many different ways. However, the most direct connections are suggested by these phrases.*

After gap 41: The minerals rush … Dawson's …
After gap 42: It's … that investment in technology and people.
After gap 43: In his small office …
After gap 44: Trish Hume, for example, …
After gap 45: … the territory …
After gap 46: … such a remarkable environment …

A It is even larger …
B At his expanding compound …
C Today, the couple …
D In contrast, …
E Such creatures …
F … has brought to the fore a growing tension …
G But in other ways, …

Exam task

41 C The idea of paying for and heating living accommodation in the first paragraph of the text is taken up by the first sentence in C.

42 G The first sentence of G makes it clear that the preceding paragraph must have referred to a way in which the town had changed – as is the case with the paragraph before gap 42. The reference to 'that investment' just after gap 42 shows that the missing paragraph must end by mentioning investment of some kind in the mining industry, and it is there in G with 'mechanized army of bulldozers, drilling rigs, and flown-in workers'.

43 B The mention of Ryan at the end of the paragraph before gap 43 combined with the reference to 'his small office' at the beginning of the paragraph after the gap suggests that Ryan was the focus of the missing paragraph.

44 F The first sentence in the paragraph after gap 44 gives a clear indication that the missing paragraph must have made some reference to people being concerned about the natural environment of the Yukon. That is to be found in F in the discussion of the 'growing tension' before environmentalists and developers.

45 A The paragraphs before and after the gap suggest that the content of the missing paragraph will be focused on a description of the area. Paragraph A takes up the idea of 'enormous area' at the end of the paragraph before the gap and so clearly fits well here.

46 E Animals are mentioned at the end of the paragraph preceding the gap and these are referred to by 'Such creatures' at the beginning of E. Although paragraph D also refers to animals, it does not relate in any other logical way to the paragraphs before and after the gap and is ruled out by the introductory 'In contrast'.

Reading and Use of English Part 8

Exam practice

Review

Suggested answers

1 This is generally considered the best way to approach this task – that is why the questions come first on the question paper. Then you know what you are looking for in the texts.

2 It certainly wouldn't be sensible to read the texts thoroughly before looking at the items. You might perhaps want to skim them just to get a quick impression, but generally it's better to read the items first.

3 A lot of people recommend doing this. It's not essential, but it can be a very efficient way of approaching the task.

4 This is a very good idea. The questions in the Advice box relating to the exam practice task give you some guided practice in doing this.

5 This is often a very useful approach.

Exam task

47 B 'The club definitely helped. It's more fun and it isn't as easy to give up. I also picked up some useful tips.'

48 D 'My solution to this problem was to set myself a goal' – the problem was the difficulty of motivating herself, referred to at the end of the previous paragraph.

49 C 'I made sure I ate well that day, avoiding anything too heavy and drinking plenty of water, with a flapjack two hours beforehand to keep me going.'

50 A 'I'm self-employed with unpredictable working hours, so running seemed a good option. It's free and easy to fit into your life, as you can do it any time, and pretty much anywhere.'

51 B 'I learnt to focus on pushing out my breath when I felt tired, to help me run more efficiently and in a more relaxed way.'

52 A 'I … turned up for my first session feeling apprehensive that I wouldn't be able to keep up. But we took it slowly, jogging or walking until we were able to build up to running for 15 minutes.'

53 B 'I also picked up some useful tips.'

54 A 'I'd been doing yoga, but it wasn't giving me a cardiovascular workout, and as a sports journalist, I know how important aerobic activity is for heart health.'

55 D 'On race day, I began to feel nervous as, to my alarm, it turned out to be a proper event, with lots of people from running clubs coming with the intention of getting good times.'

56 B 'I knew I'd begun to overcome my boredom barrier when I spent 20 minutes jogging in the park on a beautiful summer evening without thinking about when I could stop.'

Writing Part 1

Training

Review

1 In Part 1, you have no choice of task.

2 You always have to write an essay.

3 You have to write 220–260 words.

4 You must choose two of the three listed points to discuss.

5 You should try to put things in your own words – but of course, if you use a word from the task, it would be very foolish to misspell it!

Reading the question

1 The aim of the essay is to discuss how students can best be prepared for their future working lives.

2–4 The answers to these questions will depend on your own opinions (or on what you feel you can present most effectively in English).

Useful language: showing a range of vocabulary

1 *Possible answers*

1 sewing, carpentry or woodwork, childcare, housework

2 tell students about work opportunities, provide careers advice, explain what jobs are available

3 working as an office junior, doing a Saturday job in a shop or café, doing voluntary work at a hospital

4 students, teenagers, youngsters, youth

5 jobs, employment, careers, trades and professions

2 This is an excellent answer to the task. It fulfils all the requirements of the task, so the answer to questions 1–6 and 8 is Yes.

7 Examples illustrating a good range of vocabulary could include 'ensure', 'arguably', 'knit', 'sew', 'essential, 'restrict themselves to', 'preferable', etc.

Examples illustrating a good range of structures could include any of the sentences in the task, as each one is well-constructed using a different structure.

9 This answer deserves top marks.

Exam practice

1 1 The issue is how to help people live healthier lives.

2 Education could relate to the topic either by teaching children at school about living healthily or by education aimed at all groups through the media. Legislation could relate to the topic by making unhealthy habits illegal and by using the legal system in various ways to enforce healthy habits. Facilities could relate to the topic in the sense that providing easy and cheap access to sports facilities could help to promote a healthy lifestyle.

3–6 The answers to these questions will depend on your own opinions (or on the ideas that you feel you can most effectively express in English).

2 **Essay**

Model answer

This model has been prepared as an example of a very good answer. However, please note that this is just one example out of several possible approaches.

> It goes without saying that good health is of benefit both to individuals and to the society in which they live. It is easier for healthy people to be happy, and they are also usually able to contribute more to the life of their community.
>
> But what can be done to encourage people to live healthy lifestyles? Clearly education has a very important role to play. This starts at primary school when the young child can learn about the value of exercise and a healthy diet. However, education should not only be aimed at schoolchildren. Adults, too, need to continue to be reminded about the importance of being active and eating nutritious food, through, for example, TV documentaries and newspaper or magazine articles.
>
> Education alone, however, is not enough. People need to have easy access to facilities which will enable them to exercise in an enjoyable way. There should be a nationwide network of sports centres, offering a range of classes and activities to suit all tastes and abilities. If attractive opportunities are not available, people are all too likely to slip into bad habits.
>
> Of the two measures outlined above, education is the more effective one. It is more far-reaching in that it relates to all aspects of living healthily. Moreover, it is, after all, through education that a person will learn why it is better to go to an exercise class than to lie on a couch in front of the television.

Notes

- *Appropriate introduction to the topic in the first paragraph*
- *Each of the next two paragraphs deals with one of the measures listed*
- *The final paragraph explains why one of these two measures is more important*
- *The essay is written in clear paragraphs*
- *The writer demonstrates a good range of structures and vocabulary*
- *The essay is in an appropriately neutral style*
- *The essay is the correct length (244 words)*
- *There are no language errors*

Writing Part 2

Training

Review

1 220–260

2 four or five

3 report, proposal, review, letter/email

Organising your writing

1 **1** Topic of each paragraph

1 Introduction – naming best and worst music videos seen

2 Outline of best video and why particularly good

3 Outline of worst video and why particularly bad

4 Explanation of importance of music videos for fans

5 Conclusion – own personal attitude to music videos in general

2 Topic sentences are:

1 The best and worst music videos I have ever seen were curiously by the same band.

2 The video for 'Dream Song' looked as good as the song sounded.

3 The video for 'Night Rider' began effectively but soon deteriorated.

4 Music videos are popular with fans because they help them to understand the meaning of the songs they accompany.

5 Although music videos like 'Dream Song' can be dramatic and original films, I generally prefer to listen to my music without an accompanying video.

3 The topic sentence is the first sentence in the five paragraphs. However, it can work successfully as the last sentence too.

2 *Sample answers (alternatives are possible)*

A Introduction – outline of situation

How teenagers see adults

How adults see teenagers

What teenagers and adults disagree about

Conclusion – how to improve the situation

B Introduction – overview of topic

Class's sporting interests as participants

Class's sporting interests as spectators

Recommendation – what college could do to encourage student involvement in sport

3 *Sample answers (alternatives are, of course, possible)*

A The relationship between teenagers and adults in my country sadly seems to be deteriorating.

Teenagers see adults as boring and out-of-date.

Adults tend to object to both the behaviour and the attitudes of teenagers.

Teenagers and adults disagree most typically about clothes, music and politics.

I believe there are a number of simple ways in which the situation could be improved.

B As class representative of the 30 first-year Linguistics students at Downton College, I have conducted a survey into my classmates' involvement in sport, and report on my findings below.

Three-quarters of the students in my class participate actively in some kind of sport at least once a month.

As far as being a spectator is concerned, only two students in the class expressed a total lack of interest in watching any kind of sport.

The main way in which the college could encourage greater participation in sport would be to extend the range of exercise and other classes offered at the college Sports Centre.

Useful language: good beginnings

1 1b is better because it shows a better lexical and structural range. 'Good' and 'bad' are rather inexpressive adjectives to be using at this level – especially in an opening sentence.

2 2a is better because it goes straight to the point. It is also engaging in that the writer comments that the questions were interesting – this suggests that he or she may have something interesting to say about them. 2b wastes too many words on irrelevant points when there is a word limit on the answer.

3 3b is better because it provides a clear introduction to the topic of the report. 3a is written in too colloquial a style and is too much of an opinion to be appropriate for the introduction to a report.

Writing Part 2

Exam practice

1 Personal preference

2 The sorts of factors you need to consider are:

- Do you understand the question fully?
- Could you deal with all the aspects of the question?
- Do you have the vocabulary you would need to write a good answer?
- Do you know how to write the type of text required?

The above questions are much more important than whether you find the question interesting or not.

Model answers

These models have been prepared as examples of very good answers. However, please note that these are just one example out of several possible approaches.

2 Email

Hi Anna,

Thank you for your email. I'm so looking forward to your visit to St Petersburg in July and I think it's a great idea to learn some Russian before you come.

I think the best advice about learning a language is to try to do a little every day – that's much more effective, in my opinion, than doing a lot once a week or once a fortnight. It'd be sensible to have some lessons but you'd have to do a lot of work on your own in between the lessons if you want to make good progress.

English-speaking people often think Russian's difficult to learn because we use a different alphabet, but in practice almost everyone manages to master Cyrillic letters very quickly. What is much harder is the grammar, as nouns and adjectives decline so each of them has about ten different forms, depending on what case it's in and whether it's singular or plural. I think you might find the vocabulary hard at first too, as most everyday words bear no similarity at all to English words.

Although vocabulary is difficult at first, I think that's what you should concentrate on. Don't worry too much about all those case endings – just focus on learning words. That way you'll be able to communicate, even if you make lots of grammar mistakes. I'll send you some lists of words and expressions that I think you'll find most useful – language that you might need in a museum or restaurant, for example.

All best wishes,

Natasha

Notes

- *The email opens and closes in an appropriate and friendly way*
- *The writer answers all the questions in the input email*
- *The answer demonstrates a good range of vocabulary related to language learning*
- *The answer uses appropriately informal language, e.g. contractions*
- *Correct length (256 words)*
- *No language errors*

3 Proposal

Proposal for subscriptions

I should like to recommend that the college subscribe to the following periodicals.

The Guardian

The first publication I should like to recommend is the UK daily newspaper, the *Guardian*. All the students at this college do at least one English course as part of their degree, and there are few better ways of keeping up and extending one's knowledge of a language than reading a newspaper. Of all the quality British papers, the *Guardian* is the one I recommend we subscribe to because it has a good coverage of international as well as UK news. In addition, it has many feature articles which do not date in the way that news stories may and so are worth keeping hold of for future study purposes.

The New Musical Express

The second periodical I would recommend is the *New Musical Express*. Most students here are very interested in pop and rock music and enjoy the articles in this weekly publication whenever they have the chance. I am sure that a subscription to the *NME* would be very widely read. Although students would imagine they are reading simply for pleasure rather than study purposes, they would probably be acquiring as much language as they would from reading a textbook.

If there is only enough funding to subscribe to one of these publications, then I would opt for the *Guardian*, simply because it has a broader range of articles, dealing with the arts, fashion, sport and science, as well as political news, thus helping the maximum number of students with their language studies.

Notes

- *The writer deals with all the points required by the task*
- *The proposal is clearly organised into paragraphs*
- *The first paragraph clearly states the reason for writing*
- *The writer uses a variety of sentence lengths and structures*
- *The register is appropriately formal – it avoids, for example, the use of contractions*
- *Correct length (259 words)*
- *No language errors*

4 Review

> Can you imagine Mr Bean as a teacher of English as a Foreign Language? Well, last night for me, that's what he was; I watched Rowan Atkinson play the lead role in *Quartermaine's Terms*, a play set in a Cambridge language school in the 1960s.
>
> It was an excellent play, a powerful mix of the comic and the tragic. The scenes all take place in the staffroom of the school, and through the conversations that happen there, the audience gradually becomes aware of the sadness that each of the teachers at the school has in his or her own personal life. Despite the loneliness or discontent at the heart of every one of their lives, the dialogue is witty, and the audience is truly often laughing through its tears.
>
> If the play has a weakness it is that it is perhaps a little slow to get moving. The second half is much more engaging than the first. But that, for me, was my only slight niggle. The acting from all the members of the cast was utterly convincing, the set was simple but effective, and the costumes were just right.
>
> The theatre where it took place was a lovely traditional theatre, rather old-fashioned, but in a way that suited the spirit of the play itself. The seating, however, was very cramped, making it hard for the long-legged to find a comfortable enough position for the two-hour performance.

Notes

- *The introductory question serves to engage the reader in a way suitable for any review (or indeed any magazine article)*
- *The answer deals with all the points required by the task*
- *Basic factual information is provided, but more space is devoted to the writer's opinion, as should be the case in any review*
- *The writer demonstrates a good use of vocabulary connected with the theatre – cast, costumes, set, etc.*
- *The answer is organised into well-defined paragraphs*
- *Correct length (237 words)*
- *No language errors*

Listening Part 1

Training

Review

1 You should use this time to read the questions and think about them. This is useful because (a) it will give you an idea of what the recording is going to be about, and (b) it will tell you what kind of information you need to listen out for particularly.

2 You should use this time to look again at any questions you did not get the answer to on the first listening. Then if you have any more time left, check through the questions you did answer.

Reading the questions

1 Extract 1

1 The question asks about agreement, so it requires you to think about the opinion of both speakers.

2 Fact – the three options all relate to specific things that someone might plan to do.

3 The woman's

Extract 2

1 A project they are working on together

2 They are all negative feelings, but A and C are focusing on the tutor's reaction to their work – A on his not noticing any improvement and C on his criticism of inaccuracy, while B is focusing more on the tutor's support in general.

3 No, it's about something that he promises he will do.

Extract 3

1 The man

2 The woman's

3 Possible changes in their company's performance and profile

2 The options are all possible.

Exam practice

1 **C** A: They say it is a topic they have already discussed many times. B: The woman liked one of the presenter's ideas, but the man says it was not new to him.

2 **B** A: The woman doesn't express any intention to change her habits, even though she has been recommended to do so. C: The woman says she has been given some advice rather than her planning to ask for some.

3 **B** A: She is pleased about the positive comments that the tutor makes and agrees that his suggestions will improve their work. C: She does not express any annoyance at this.

4 **A** B: They have already done their experiments. C: The woman promises to do this.

5 **A** B: The man says he probably will not want the woman to revise the task she has recently completed (the sales and profits targets). C: The woman is going to change arrangements for a meeting with a colleague, but doesn't mention the need to change their point of view.

6 **C** A and B: They are both mentioned, but the woman does not express any surprise in relation to them.

Listening Part 2

Training

Review

1 What kind of word is suggested by the prompt sentence – the name of a country or a type of job, for example

2 Yes, it is necessary to spell the words correctly.

3 No, you will not need to make any changes to the words you hear.

4 Between one and three

Answering accurately

1 1 quite beautiful

2 the environment

3 the whole truth

4 because of the weather

5 through the forest

6 he would always believe her

7 the parcel which I received

8 an interesting programme/program

9 a really quiet holiday

10 convenient and healthy food

2 *These are possible answers – you may have found other good ways of replacing the words in italics.*

1 Claire Davis was working as a *mechanical* ***engineer*** before she lost her job.

2 On returning to work after suffering from ***breaking a leg / a broken leg***, Claire learnt she had lost her job.

3 Claire almost immediately decided to visit ***America***.

4 Claire decided to spend time improving her ***swimming*** when she returned from her trip.

5 Claire loved seeing ***France*** when she was working as a holiday representative. (NB The names of most countries do not need the definite article, apart from *the USA*, *the UK*, *the Philippines*, etc.)

6 Claire now realises that her life in the past was very ***unsatisfactory***.

7 Claire would advise other people who lose their jobs not to ***worry***.

8 Claire has no feelings of ***anger*** towards the people who made her redundant.

3 1 **Australia** / Canada / the USA: The speaker lives in Canada now and spent his childhood after the age of one in the USA.

2 **remarkable** / normal: The speaker thought his childhood was normal at the time, though he now realises it was remarkable.

3 **geography** / international affairs: The speaker's sisters studied international affairs while he studied geography.

4 **waiter** / journalist: The speaker wanted to get a job as a journalist but had to work as a waiter until he was able to do so.

Exam practice

7 **(TV) presenter:** 'Who I particularly liked' is a paraphrase of 'favourite'.

8 **snow shoes:** She would go on a bike on a later trip, and her hopes of going further by sled on her first trip were disappointed. 'Bike' and 'sled' are also not possible in the given sentence because they would need 'a' before them.

9 **brightness:** 'Snow' or 'daylight' alone are not possible because it is the combination of snow and constant daylight that creates the brightness which struck Sally.

10 **mechanic:** 'Doctor' would make sense in the gap, but Sally says she postponed her plans to become a doctor.

11 **second:** 'Most enjoyable' is the paraphrase used here for 'favourite'.

12 **wind:** The phrase 'even worse' makes it clear that this was the hardest thing for Sally.

13 **blog:** The idea of 'kept in touch' is conveyed by 'knew how I was getting on and were able to add messages of encouragement to it'.

14 **(hot) bath:** The phrase 'the first thing I wanted to have when I got home' makes it clear that this is what Sally missed most.

Listening Part 3

Training

Review

1 Because it will give you a lot of information about the content and structure of what you are going to hear.

2 Because the right answer will usually use synonyms rather than the actual words in the question.

3 Yes, always

4 It's better to guess. You will get zero, not a penalty point, for choosing the wrong answer.

Useful language: topic vocabulary

1 take on

2 entrepreneur

3 undercharge

4 diversify

5 skill

6 mentor

7 erratic

8 external

9 recruitment

10 start-up

11 challenging

12 in-house

Using the preparation time

1 They make it clear that you are going to hear a man called Paul talk about his life as an entrepreneur who started an IT consultancy business.

2 The questions make it clear that you will hear about all the listed points except for 4, 7 and 8.

Exam practice

15 B A: He was working at the university where he had studied, but in IT support rather than a teaching post. C: He was doing the same things over and over again. D: Colleagues moved away because the job had become less enjoyable.

16 C A: His friends helped him after he'd made his decision. B: He says he has not found any book particularly helpful. D: He says he wasn't confident at first that he would be able to do it, just that he felt it would be interesting to try.

17 D Paul mentions all the other types of client, but it is clear that they are not his favourites.

18 A B: Although Paul found setting fees hard to start with, he took advice and this is no longer a problem. C: Paul's concern is with helping the team rather than with the impression he gives them. D: Paul seems pleased with the advice he mentions receiving.

19 D A: Paul says he doesn't know how other people use mentors. B: The mentor has just finished an MBA and so is presumably up-to-date with business theories, but Paul doesn't specify that he finds this useful. C: It is Paul who is coming up with the ideas and the mentor who is reacting to them.

20 B A: Paul is considering taking on new staff, but this is not definite. C: Paul has already moved to a new office. D: Paul will be using skills he hasn't used for some time rather than learning new skills.

Listening Part 4

Training

Review

1 Five

2 They are all separate individuals speaking on the same theme.

3 Two

4 No – some will and some won't.

5 Read the introduction and the statements for both of the tasks.

6 There are eight statements for each of the two tasks.

7 By using words that are similar to other questions but do not match in terms of what the speaker means.

8 It is up to you how you approach the task. You might like to try doing different tests in this book in different ways to see which you find best for you.

Reading the questions

1 1 in a small house in the suburbs

2 in a top-floor city flat

3 above a shop in a town

4 in a houseboat
5 on a farm
6 in a converted railway station
7 in a room in a relative's house
8 in a cottage in a village

2 *Possible answers*

A cottage in a village – small rooms with low ceilings, picturesque garden, peaceful, infrequent bus service to the town

B above shop in a town – our door is at the side of a butcher's, you go upstairs to our apartment

C converted railway station – the line has been taken up, some of the old signs remain

D top-floor city flat – great views, difficult when the lift breaks down, quite central

E room in a relative's house – it's pleasant sharing with family, grandma cooks for me

F small house in suburbs – poky, compact, tiny garden, easy reach of shops and schools

G farm – quite a long way from the nearest village, mainly arable with a few chickens

H houseboat – it can be chilly on the water in winter, it's surprisingly roomy on board

3 *Possible answers*

1 The neighbours play very loud music late at night.
2 You can never find anywhere to leave your car.
3 dear, costly, costs a fortune, pricey, exorbitant
4 have a lengthy commute, takes an hour or more to get to the office
5 There's nowhere to put anything.
6 The area has a good/bad name. The area is known for …
7 It looks over a rather dull landscape.
8 run-down, shabby, in need of a lick of paint, dilapidated

Exam practice

TASK ONE

21 F 'On the edge of town' is a synonym for 'suburbs'.

22 B The shop in question is a chemist's, and it's clear from the way the speaker describes the view 'over an urban sprawl' that the flat is in a town.

23 H The reference to the sound of water makes it clear that the speaker is talking about living on a boat.

24 E The relative in question is the speaker's grandmother.

25 G Early in the text it becomes clear that the speaker is living in the countryside, and the reference to cows makes it clear that she is talking about a farm.

TASK TWO

26 E 'Declutter' means 'get rid of things you no longer need'.

27 C 'Not cheap' conveys the same idea as 'expensive'.

28 A The noise is caused by people singing and laughing on the towpath late at night.

29 H The house being old, damp and draughty makes it clear that it is in need of some repair.

30 F 'Is generally thought of' is a way of introducing a description of something or someone's reputation.

Speaking Part 1

Training

Review

The main aims are 1 and 5.

Useful language: talking about yourself

2 *Possible answers*

1 People

What is your best friend like?

Who are you most like in your family?

What person do you most admire?

What qualities do you look for in a friend?

How would you describe your own character?

2 Work and study

What would be your ideal job in the future?

Which subjects did you enjoy and which did you not enjoy at school?

Can you tell me about your most memorable teacher?

Do you think you learn more by reading or by doing?

What kind of work experience have you already had?

3 Leisure

Which do you prefer and why – watching a sports event on TV or attending it in person?

What new leisure activity would you like to try?

What did you think of the last film you saw?

Would you recommend the last book you read?

What sorts of things do you collect – or can you imagine yourself collecting one day?

4 Travel

What's the most memorable journey you've ever made?

What, for you, is the most enjoyable means of transport, and why?

What would be your ideal car?

What was your journey here today like?

How do you prefer to spend your holidays?

5 Where you live

What do you like and what do you not like about the town where you live?

What would your ideal home be like?

If you could change one thing about your room, what would it be?

How would you describe the place where you live to a new e-pal or penfriend?

If you could live anywhere in the world, where would you choose to live, and why?

6 Learning English

What do you most enjoy about learning English?

What do you find hardest about learning English?

How do you see yourself using English in the future?

What experience have you had of using English in an English-speaking environment?

Do you think grammar or vocabulary is more important when you're learning English?

3 a This response is too short and doesn't give any information at all. It would be better to say something like:
'I don't know. I haven't decided yet. But I'm thinking I might perhaps do a teacher-training course and then try to get a job abroad.'

Remember it's better to say something that isn't true than to give a very short answer.

b This response is very inaccurate. This is a correct version:

'It depends on my exam results. I am interested in a lot of things. I hope I am going to get a job next year after I finish my degree at university. I am studying information technology so I think I should easily get a good job.'

It is particularly important to know the correct words for things like the subject you are studying or the job you have.

c This response is too abstract and doesn't answer the question. The point is to give personal information about yourself. There are, of course, many ways to improve this answer. One possibility would be:

'It's hard to know for sure. Sometimes I think I'd like to travel. At other times, I feel the most important thing is to get a good job. I've still got time to decide, though, because I won't graduate for another couple of years.'

Speaking Part 2

Training

Review

The statements are all false and need correcting.

1 In Part 2, you have to speak for one minute.

2 You have to comment on two out of three pictures.

3 The interlocutor will ask you two questions relating to the pictures and the same questions will be written above the pictures.

4 You will be asked to speculate about the pictures rather than describe them in detail.

5 Your partner will have to speak for a minute on a different set of pictures from yours.

6 You should not say anything until the interlocutor asks you a question.

7 The interlocutor will give you only 30 seconds to reply to the question which is asked after your partner has spoken.

Useful language: a sample response

1 **1** shows **2** getting **3** both **4** have **5** on **6** well **7** to **8** making ('taking' would also be possible here) **9** what **10** their **11** on **12** might ('may' is also possible here)

Speaking Parts 3 and 4

Training

Part 3

Review

1 The prompts in Part 3 are not on the same theme as the pictures in Part 2.

2 Part 3 is more like a conversation than Part 2.

3 It is not important that you come to a decision in Part 3.

4 You should not invite the interlocutor to give their opinion in Part 3.

5 It is not important that you and your partner should agree in Part 3.

6 It is not essential to discuss all the prompts you are given in Part 3.

Part 4

Review

1 discussion **2** topic **3** interlocutor **4** develop
5 opinion **6** explain **7** way

Useful language: choosing the right words

2 A: Shall I start? I think they all contribute to society but in very different ways. For example, medicine is probably the most important because it makes it possible for people to live longer and healthier lives and so contribute more to society. Do you agree?

B: Well, up to a point. I agree that medicine is very important, but so are other fields like sport.

A: Well, yes, that goes without saying, but surely it's the case that you can't fully enjoy sport unless you're in good health.

B: OK, fair enough. So what do you think about the arts? I can't help wondering whether they really contribute all that much to society.

A: But surely they make a huge contribution. They enrich people's lives enormously, for a start.

5 • Do you think people's salaries should depend on the contribution they make to society?

• What kinds of job do you think might actually have a negative impact on society?

• What factors would you take into account when considering how big a contribution a particular job makes to society?

Test 2 Transcript

Listening Part 1

Exam practice

You will hear three different extracts. For questions 1 to 6, choose the answer (A, B or C) which fits best according to what you hear. There are two questions for each extract.

Extract 1

You hear two business people discussing a workshop they have just attended. Now look at questions 1 and 2.

Man: I quite enjoyed that workshop, didn't you? I'd expected it to be a waste of time.

Woman: Me too! And that would've been ironic for a session focusing on time management! It's not exactly something we haven't discussed endlessly before.

Man: Well, that doesn't mean we know all there is to be known. I thought some very useful points came up.

Woman: Yes, I liked the presenter's comment that you should get someone else to take all the relatively unimportant decisions so you can give all your attention to the big ones.

Man: You mean like getting your PA to choose your lunch for you. It's a good idea, but I'd heard it before. I read about a US president who only bought grey suits so he didn't waste time deciding what to wear in the mornings. Actually, I thought it was the other people there who came up with ideas that I hadn't thought of before.

Woman: You've got a point. I liked that man's argument that daydreaming is actually a constructive activity rather than a waste of time. I'm going to get hold of the article he recommended about that.

Man: And then make more time for daydreaming?

Woman: I'm afraid I do quite enough of that already. I've often been advised to work on my concentration skills!

Extract 2

You hear two students talking about a project they are working on. Now look at questions 3 and 4.

Woman: Now we've had the tutor's comments back on the first draft of our psychology project, I suppose we'd better start thinking about where to take things from here.

Man: I've got time now if you have?

Woman: That's fine with me. So, it's good we've had some positive comments on what we've done so far. It's just a pity he now says we've got to include more concrete examples.

Man: Hm?

Woman: The ways in which advertisers make use of insights gained from the psychology of perception.

Man: Well, I can see how it'll improve our work.

Woman: Absolutely. But it's just a bit annoying he didn't mention it two weeks ago. We could have been looking out for examples as we were doing our background reading.

Man: Oh well, it can't be helped. If you like, I'll copy some illustrations from that book he recommended. My flatmate's just borrowed it from the university library. I think that's all we'll need to add really.

Woman: That'd be great. I'll make sure our figures are accurate. I mean the ones the tutor questioned.

Man: OK. I'm sure they're right, though. I wrote them down very carefully when we were doing our various little experiments.

Woman: I'm sure you did, but it won't hurt to check.

Extract 3

You hear two colleagues discussing an issue at work. Now look at questions 5 and 6.

Man: Gemma, do you think I could have a quick word?

Woman: No problem. Did you want to discuss the sales and profits targets that I've drafted for next year?

Man: That's right. Do you really think it's feasible that we'll be able to meet them?

Woman: Well, if we can create as much interest as we hope for in North America, then we should get there. And it's all looking quite promising, despite some fluctuations earlier in the year. You don't want me to revise the targets, do you?

Man: Probably not. But I've got a conference call with our New York office at three this afternoon and it'd be good if you could be there, so we can talk them through together. Is that all right with you?

Woman: Well, I'd arranged to meet someone from HR then, but I can tell them I'll be a bit late.

Man: Thanks. I'm really keen that we don't set ourselves unrealistic aims – though a bit of a challenge is always a good thing, of course.

Woman: Sure. And don't forget that we're spending less on the manufacturing process now. I was astonished to learn just how much less wastage there is now with our new machines. That'll help the bottom line.

Man: Absolutely.

That is the end of Part 1.

Listening Part 2

Training

1 14 Exercise 1

1. quite beautiful
2. the environment
3. the whole truth
4. because of the weather
5. through the forest
6. he would always believe her
7. the parcel which I received
8. an interesting programme
9. a really quiet holiday
10. convenient and healthy food

1 15 Exercise 3

Man: My name's George Fairham and I live in Canada now. However, I wasn't born there. I spent the first year of my life in Australia. My parents moved from there to the USA in the mid-50s. They never stayed more than a couple of years in the same place. When I was a child, I thought that was normal, of course, but now I realise that the childhood that my sisters and I had was remarkable. We saw a great deal of the world, and that's the best form of education anyone can have, in my opinion. It might be why I went on to major in geography at university. Or why my sisters both studied international affairs. After graduating, I wanted to find work in New York as a journalist. No newspaper there would take me on at that point, but I stayed in the city until they agreed. Until that happened, I earned my living as a waiter. That was an interesting experience …

Exam practice

1 16

You will hear a woman called Sally Batting talking about her experiences in the Antarctic. For questions 7 to 14, complete the sentences with a word or short phrase.

You now have 45 seconds to look at Part 2. You will need to play the recording twice.

Sally: Hello, my name is Sally Batting and I'm here today to talk to you about cycling in the Antarctic. You might well wonder what on earth made me decide to do something so crazy. Most people usually imagine that I went there because of my uncle who made a name for himself many years ago as an Arctic explorer, but in fact, if anything, he put me off with his stories of frostbite and other uncomfortable experiences. It was only when I was about 12 and saw a film of a TV presenter who I particularly liked crossing the Antarctic that I began to want to go there myself one day. Little did I imagine then that I'd actually have been there twice before I was 25.

I've always loved cycling, and my dream was to be the first person to make it to the South Pole on a bike. I did eventually get there on two wheels, though I didn't end up being the first person to do so. Anyway, the first time I made it to Antarctica, I didn't get as far as the Pole. I covered about 150 kilometres on snow shoes. That was an amazing experience. I was hoping to go further by sled, but the weather conditions were against us, and we had to return to our camp on the coast.

Despite those problems with the weather, I fell in love with the Antarctic on that first trip. You'd imagine that it would be the extreme cold that strikes you when you first arrive there, but in fact you're so well wrapped up in all the appropriate clothing that you hardly notice that. I certainly didn't find it a problem. What impressed me most was actually the brightness, resulting from snow all around, combined with 24-hour daylight – I was there in the Antarctic summer, of course.

So, as I said, I didn't make it to the Pole on that first trip, but I went home determined to get back there as soon as I could. I'd been intending to become a doctor, but decided to postpone my studies and earn some money to finance my next trip. I've always been quite good with engines and I found a job as a mechanic. I did lots of overtime and after two years, I'd made enough to head back to Antarctica with all the gear I needed to make a bid for the Pole.

The route to the Pole from the coast is in three sections which are usually referred to as 'legs'. The first is basically a steep climb inland and upwards from the coast to the Patriot Hills. The second is flatter and generally less hard going. I must admit I found that the most enjoyable stretch. Then there's the third leg and that's undoubtedly the most demanding. This is the long hard climb to the Pole, which lies about 2,800 metres above sea level.

It was all rather harder than I'd anticipated. I managed to cope with the physical exertion, as I'd been doing a lot of very demanding training before I set out. It was still exhausting, though. And the isolation was desperately hard to deal with. And even worse was the wind. That was so strong at times that I simply had to pitch camp and wait till it eased off.

Of course, I felt very lonely out there at times, but I was able to stay in touch with family and friends. Modern methods of communication have certainly transformed life for explorers and everyone else adventuring far from civilisation. I kept a blog and so my family knew exactly how I was getting on, and they were able to add messages of encouragement to it, which did a great deal to keep me going.

People often ask what I missed most on the trip and that's a hard one to answer. I really wished I could be lying in my own comfy bed at times, but was usually too tired to think about it too much. I did long for a hot bath, though – that was the first thing I wanted to have when I got home. I didn't really miss any kind of food or anything, though I must admit I've never enjoyed a cup of coffee more than the delicious cappuccino I had on the flight home.

That is the end of Part 2.

Listening Part 3

Exam practice

You will hear an interview with an IT consultant called Paul about how he started his own business. For questions 15 to 20, choose the answer (A, B, C or D) which fits best according to what you hear.

You now have 70 seconds to look at Part 3. You will need to play the recording twice.

Interviewer: So, Paul, you run your own IT consultancy business now. How did your career start?

Paul: Well, after graduating in computer science, I got a job in the technical support team of the university where I'd studied. I really enjoyed both the company of my colleagues and the technically challenging and interesting tasks I had to deal with, but after a few years, I began to see the same issues coming up again and again. Several members of the team left, as it was all getting much less stimulating.

Interviewer: So what made you actually decide to set up your own consultancy?

Paul: Well, it seemed to me that there was going to be a trend among many organisations towards taking on short-term external consultants for IT rather than employing a permanent in-house team. And I thought that would be an interesting way for me to go. I'm friends with a couple of guys who have a small start-up and they'd been operating for a few years. I wasn't sure I could do it, but they helped me get started. They gave me much more sensible advice than I've ever seen in any book or article for would-be entrepreneurs.

Interviewer: How do you get new clients?

Paul: Well, work is certainly erratic. For months I might only have recurring clients, and then suddenly could get four new ones in the same week. There's no one reliable source of work, so I diversify. I get a fair amount of work from recruitment agents, but some of the jobs they provide are not terribly challenging. And I get some work from people I was at uni with. I suppose about half of my work is repeat business from people I've helped before, and I like that. You start out from a position of knowing and trusting each other. Also, I go to conferences to meet people and to promote myself and my business. I've been told that there's at least a two- to three-year lag between presenting at conferences and getting work from them, so I'm not yet sure how much business is going to come to me that way.

Interviewer: What is the hardest part of running your business?

Paul: At first, I found it extremely difficult to know what to charge clients. I ended up drastically undercharging on a number of occasions before I realised I needed to get some financial advice from an expert. That helped me enormously. It's often said that the first week in business is the hardest. In my case, as I'm always moving on to provide support in a different company, nearly every week is in a sense the first week. I often have just that week to make a difference to that team, and that's a challenge but, fortunately, I like challenges!

Interviewer: Would you say you have a business mentor?

Paul: Sure. My business mentor is an old friend of mine. He recently finished a Master's in Business Administration and we talk every week about how I might develop my company. I wouldn't say I have a clear idea about how other people use a business mentor – and it's quite possible they do things very differently – but I have found our conversations very useful. It's great to have someone experienced to sound ideas off. I have great faith in his instincts.

Interviewer: What are your plans for this year?

Paul: Well, we've just moved to a great new office in the centre of town, so we'll enjoy being based there. I'm considering taking on a couple of new staff to keep things ticking over there while I deal with clients. I've got some very different new projects lined up over the next 12 months, so am looking forward to getting my teeth into those. I'm looking forward to having the chance to use some technical skills that I haven't had to call on for a while, in fact, so that'll be good.

Interviewer: Well, I wish you all the very best with that.

That is the end of Part 3.

Listening Part 4

Exam practice

Part 4 consists of two tasks. You will hear five short extracts in which people are talking about where they live. Look at Task 1. For questions 21 to 25, choose from the list A to H where each speaker currently lives. Now look at Task 2. For questions 26 to 30, choose from the list A to H what each speaker finds difficult about the place where they live. While you listen you must complete both tasks.

You now have 45 seconds to look at Part 4. You will need to play the recording twice.

Speaker 1

I used to rent a great penthouse flat on the twelfth floor of a tower block with amazing views over the city, but now I've managed to buy my own home. I couldn't afford anything too central, but I've got this nice place on the edge of town. It's not very big so I'm going to have to make myself declutter a bit. That's not going to be easy for me, as I'm a terrible hoarder, I'm afraid. It's reasonably easy to get into work every morning and it's fantastic to be able to park outside my own front door. Some of the rooms need quite a lot of work doing to them, so I'm going to have to spend all my coming weekends painting and decorating them. But I'll enjoy that, I know.

Speaker 2

I've recently moved to this area. I came here because it meant I'd have an easier journey to work. The daily commute by train took me over an hour from my old flat. It's not cheap to live here, unfortunately, but I've got loads of space, and the landlord's kept the place in not bad repair. The flat's over a chemist, so I can play my music as loud as I like in the evenings without disturbing anyone below me. From my windows, I can see the hills on the other side of the rather ugly urban sprawl, and I relish the feeling that the countryside where I grew up is still more or less within reach. I hope I'll be able to live on a farm again one day.

Speaker 3

I'm really lucky to live in a part of town that's not far from my work. I can cycle there in five minutes. I just love going to sleep with the sound of water lapping on the bows – very romantic somehow. The only problem is that it can be quite chilly sometimes in winter. Oh, and what's even more annoying is that I often get woken up by people singing and laughing as they walk along the towpath late at night. I can't stay here for ever – it belongs to my aunt who's got a job abroad for a year. There's not enough room for us both, so I'll have to move out when she gets back. But it's been fantastic to have the chance to live here. Especially as normally it'd be too expensive for me to afford.

Speaker 4

I just love trains, and my dream is to live in an old railway station, you know, one of those that's no longer in use and has been transformed into a living space. I've got my eye on one of those in a village near the city where I work. It's become a lovely – but expensive – little cottage. At the moment, I'm saving money by living at my grandmother's. I pay her a bit of rent, of course, but nothing like as much as I'd have to pay anyone else, especially if I wanted a room in such a nice area as this. I have a bedsit on the second floor. It's quite small, but there's enough room for everything I need. The house is old and damp, and the windows are draughty, so I hope they'll be fixed soon. But I can park in the drive and that's a big plus for me.

Speaker 5

I certainly can't complain about the views from my window. When it's a clear day, I can see snow-covered mountains in the distance. People think I'm mad living out here when I work in the city centre. That's a bit annoying, as they're reluctant to come and visit me, even though the station's only ten minutes away. I can get to work in 45 minutes, which is really not too bad at all. And I just love living here. In the evenings and at weekends, I help with the cows and find that enormously relaxing. This part of the country is generally thought of as being rather a dull place to live, but it suits me much better than living in some swanky flat in a modern block. If I can ever afford it, I'd like to buy a little old cottage in the neighbouring village.

That is the end of Part 4.

Speaking Part 2

Training

 Exercise 2

Speaker: The first picture I'd like to discuss shows two people getting married. This is obviously a very important ceremony for both of them. It would have involved a lot of preparations on the part of the bride and the groom and their families as well. They'd have had to do all sorts of things like making decisions about venues, choosing what to wear, getting their hair done and so on. They might well have had to organise a honeymoon too …

 Exercise 5

Interlocutor: Which of these ceremonies do you think would be most significant for the people?

Speaker: I think the wedding ceremony would be the most significant one for the people involved. Of course, graduating and winning sports prizes are also important and exciting, but they don't have such a huge impact on the rest of your life as marriage does.

Speaking Parts 3 and 4

Training

 Exercise 2

A: Shall I start? I think they all contribute to society but in very different ways. For example, medicine is probably the most important because it makes it possible for people to live longer and healthier lives and so contribute more to society. Do you agree?

B: Well, up to a point. I agree that medicine is very important, but so are other fields like sport.

A: Well, yes, that goes without saying, but surely it's the case that you can't fully enjoy sport unless you're in good health.

B: OK, fair enough. So what do you think about the arts? I can't help wondering whether they really contribute all that much to society.

A: But surely they make a huge contribution. They enrich people's lives enormously, for a start.

 Exercise 5

- Do you think people's salaries should depend on the contribution they make to society?
- What kinds of job do you think might actually have a negative impact on society?
- What factors would you take into account when considering how big a contribution a particular job makes to society?

Test 3 Key

Reading and Use of English Part 1

1 A Gas is used instead of the liquid. 'Substituting X for Y' means 'using X instead of Y'. B: 'To be replaced' requires 'by' after the verb. C: 'To be changed' requires 'into'. D: 'To be relieved' requires 'by' and refers to the ending of an unpleasant or painful situation.

2 D 'Properties' are the qualities of a substance, particularly ones that can be used in some way. A and B: These are things that are owned, usually by a person or people. C: These are the things contained within something, e.g. the contents of a cupboard or a book.

3 B 'To the full' is a fixed phrase – aerogels are not yet used as much as they can be. A, C and D: Although they have fairly similar meanings to B, they can't be used in this phrase with the required meaning.

4 B This is a phrasal verb giving the amount of something, i.e. 99.8% of the material is air. The amount describes the subject of the clause (air). A, C and D: These phrasal verbs are transitive, so in each case the subject and object refer to different things.

5 A This means that the heat doesn't change the flower in any way. B and D: The subject is normally human. C: This tends to be used of a person's opinion or behaviour, or to refer to a specific action.

6 C This means that aerogels are suitable for the specified purpose, even though they may not have been used in this way yet. A: This fits the structure 'There is a possibility that aerogels will be used ...'. B: This is normally used of people and is followed by an infinitive. D: This usually refers to a total amount, e.g. the seating capacity of a theatre.

7 C This is a type of economic activity in a country, e.g. the financial sector. A, B and D don't have this particular meaning. A: This is used when dividing into groups, e.g. grouping people according to their income. B: This can be part of a large company, e.g. the sales division. D: This is normally used of a geographical area.

8 A This means 'particularly dangerous' and can also have the sense of being very exciting, as in 'extreme sports'. B, C and D: These don't collocate with 'environments'. B is often used to describe a feeling. C means 'too much', e.g. 'excessive waste'. D means 'more than usual or reasonable', e.g. 'immoderate drinking'.

Reading and Use of English Part 2

9 after: 'After all' introduces additional information to support what has preceded it: 'work is likely to play a significant role in your life for many years' explains why 'Getting a job is too important to leave to chance.'

10 what: 'What' acts as the object of 'think about' and the subject of 'would really suit you'; it can often be replaced by the informal 'the thing that/which'.

11 which: 'Which' is a relative pronoun, and can follow prepositions. Placing the preposition in front of 'which' is more formal than ending a clause with the preposition, e.g. 'jobs which/that you have an aptitude for'.

12 it: 'It' is a 'dummy subject', standing at the beginning of a sentence instead of the true subject, 'to have your application turned down'.

13 but: 'Not only ... but also' is used to show that two related statements are true.

14 to: You can apply to an organisation, and apply for a job.

15 so: 'So ... that' links the degree to which something is true with a consequence: here, some companies are very obsessed with results and profits, and as a result, employees are under stress all the time.

16 whether: 'Whether ... or not' introduces alternative possibilities – you could or you couldn't work in an environment like that.

Reading and Use of English Part 3

17 conquest(s): 'by' shows that the meaning is passive; 'as a result of being conquered' has the same meaning.

18 civilisations / civilizations: 'a number of' introduces a plural noun. The spelling with 's' is usual in British English, and with 'z' in American English.

19 unknown: An adjective is required to describe the subject of the sentence, 'The Olmecs'. 'Virtually' means 'almost', so 'known' would not make sense. 'But' also suggests a contrast between their success for over a millennium and being unknown now.

20 instructive: Only a gradable adjective can fit into the structure 'a very ... guide'. Another adjective from the same root, 'instructional', is an ungradable adjective meaning 'containing instructions', e.g. 'an instructional leaflet'. Only gradable adjectives can follow 'very'.

21 inhabitants: Only a plural noun can follow 'these early ...'.

22 discoveries: Only a plural noun can follow 'numerous recent ...'. 'Discoverers' would also fit, but it refers to people who have discovered something, and 'draw on' means 'to use your knowledge of something to help you do something', so only 'discoveries' fits the meaning.

23 (up)risings: A noun is required, to match 'beginnings'. 'Uprising' and 'rising' are countable, so as there is no article before the gap, it must be plural.

24 implications: 'The' needs to be followed by a noun, and 'are' shows that it is plural.

Reading and Use of English Part 4

The vertical line | shows where the answer is split into two parts for marking purposes.

25 CAN'T have been | pleased to 'Can't have been' expresses a logical deduction or near certainty about the past, expressing the same idea as 'I'm sure Ben wasn't'. 'Pleased' is often followed by an infinitive, e.g. 'Pleased to meet you.'

26 hardly EVER | does what 'Hardly ever' means the same as 'very rarely'. Here, 'what' means 'the things that'.

27 TURNED out | to be The meaning of 'to turn out' here is 'to be discovered finally and surprisingly'. It is followed by an infinitive.

28 had I been | in such A When a sentence begins with 'Never', there is inversion of the subject ('I') and the first auxiliary verb ('had') or a form of 'do'. The negative 'Never' with 'such' means the same as 'the most (dangerous)'.

29 to FILL the vacancy/post | caused/created/left 'To fill a vacancy' means 'to appoint somebody to a job that nobody is doing, and so is available for someone new'. 'To cause, create or leave a vacancy' gives the reason why the job has become available.

30 in ACCORDANCE with | his 'In accordance with' means 'obeying or following a rule or wish'. The preposition 'with' is followed by a noun, so 'wishes' here is a noun, not a verb. It is therefore preceded by 'his', not 'he'.

Reading and Use of English Part 5

31 B The reviewer says that in *Birdlife*, Hurst has chosen to repeat *Gold's* 'winning formula', which he goes on to criticise. A: He mentions the different aspects of gold, without emphasising that it is a wide range. C: He expects *Birdlife* to repeat the success of *Gold*, but his criticisms make it clear that he doesn't feel it deserves that success. D: He applies his criticisms to both books (this is made clear by 'repeat a winning formula').

32 A Truman says that Hurst doesn't help readers to interpret information or identify similarities, and that there is 'not enough synthesis'. B: He doesn't claim that she misunderstands the significance of any myths, only that she includes too much detail. C: He makes it clear that Hurst doesn't interpret the myths; it is left to readers to do so if they wish. D: He is not concerned with the number of cultures, but with the amount of detail and lack of analysis.

33 A This refers to the last part of the third paragraph, about birds and people communicating to the advantage of both parties. B: There is no suggestion that the honeyguide has been trained to behave in the way it does. It might be spontaneous behaviour. C: The reviewer doesn't mention the possibility of greater exploitation of birds. D: On the contrary, the honeyguide is presented as being useful to human beings, by leading them to honeycombs.

34 D '[O]n this scale' refers to a large amount, i.e. the length of the journey. '[R]ecord', too, refers to the tern's journey as being the longest undertaken by any bird. A, B and C are all aspects of Arctic terns' lives, but the text doesn't contain any measurements connected with them that would make sense of 'record' and 'scale'.

35 C Truman describes Hurst's wish to revert to the farming methods of the past as 'a forlorn hope', i.e. something that is very unlikely to be achieved; and 'she can hardly expect' also implies that although she wants this to happen, it is very unlikely. A: The reviewer doesn't dispute Hurst's claim that 'their habitat is damaged or even destroyed'. B: There is no suggestion that Hurst misunderstands certain subjects; it is her opinion regarding the relative importance of birds and agriculture that the reviewer disagrees with. D: There is no indication that reading *Birdlife* has made him change his opinion – whatever that was before he read it.

36 B He finds the book 'interesting' and says he 'enjoyed' at least part of it, but suggests there are no new insights in it: the chapter on mythology is largely factual, and he ends by saying the book 'has little to say to serious ornithologists'. A: The book doesn't seem to mention anything still to be learnt about birds. The final paragraph suggests it would be a good introduction to the subject for people who know little or nothing about them, which implies it contains only information already familiar to ornithologists. C: Like *Gold*, the book deals with a number of facets of the subject, but there is no suggestion that it provides a clear overview: describing *Gold* as being like 'a series of magazine articles' suggests it is bitty, with no attempt at an overview. D: Although the book has chapters on different aspects of the subject, there is no indication that the reviewer thinks this is unusual.

Reading and Use of English Part 6

37 A Neither artist C nor artist A is concerned about whether people share their interpretation. Artist C says, 'But if in the end people can't see it as I do, so be it,' and according to artist A, 'I want people to look at the finished painting and make some sense of it, regardless of what that is.' Artist B says, 'People have the habit of reading an image', and artist D says they want 'to make people observe'; but neither of them expresses an opinion about other people's interpretations.

38 B Neither artist D nor artist B believes their choice of subject matter is significant. Artist D says, 'Why I happened to paint this place rather than that has no significance', and artist B says about what they draw, 'They're all chosen pretty arbitrarily.' Artist A says they 'look at something and consider using it in a painting', implying that they only choose subjects that they can make 'function within the painting'. Artist C paints 'an object or shape that has to mean something to me', so their choice is significant.

39 D Artist C describes the act of painting as being 'in the hands of the painting, almost its slave, having to do whatever it requires, however unreasonable it seems at the time.' Artist D, on the other hand contrasts the struggle that artistic creation may be for some people with their own experience: 'for me it's almost the reverse, almost a relaxation'. Artist A's and B's opinions are similar to Artist C's: Artist A is under a great deal of pressure while painting, and artist B feels tense and takes days to recover.

40 A Artist A plans the painting process: first making sure the geometry will work, 'Then I work out how to get from that starting point to the finished painting.' The other three artists don't plan their work. Artist B says, 'I really let the painting evolve in its own way, until I realise that it's complete.' According to artist C, 'After making that initial choice, I let the painting itself take over – it's a very spontaneous process,' and for artist D, 'I'm usually surprised by how my paintings turn out, because I don't feel I exert control over what happens.'

Reading and Use of English Part 7

41 G 'This groundbreaking idea' refers to the influential experiment of setting up 'the world's first factory', which workers went to instead of working at home ('a cottage industry'). This idea is picked up in describing modern offices as 'places where you go'.

42 E 'Above all' introduces the best of the 'good reasons why the model has flourished' in the previous paragraph, and 'popular' expresses a similar idea to 'has flourished'. The following paragraph introduces changes that might mean 'employment as we have known it' may be ending.

43 A The previous paragraph introduced 'technology and demographic shifts' as forces that are changing work, and expanded on the effects of technology. In A, the writer explains the demographic shifts – 'we are all living longer and working for longer'.

44 D 'This is true up to a point' relates to what is claimed, according to the previous paragraph. The following paragraph enlarges on 'the erosion of the boundary between work and other parts of life'.

45 B 'They save money on expensive office space' relates to desks in the previous paragraph: workers 'no longer expecting to be chained to a desk' implies that fewer desks, and therefore less office space, are needed.

46 F '[T]he fact is' introduces the 'reality' mentioned in the previous paragraph, which means that what people are tempted to think may be wrong. The 'continuities with the past' and idea that 'that unstructured form of work' may not come into being are picked up in the following paragraph, which gives a reason 'why tomorrow might turn out to be not so different from today'.

Reading and Use of English Part 8

47 D 'Ensure your CV is up-to-date and accessible on your computer, because you'll need to produce it every time you go after a position.' Jobs are also mentioned by advisers B, C and E, but not preparation for making applications.

48 A 'Although that tends to be the stereotype that everyone knows, most students are level-headed, and don't merit the bad reputation that they suffer from as a group.'

49 E 'Whether you're living in a university hall of residence or sharing a flat, you should make your space truly yours', and the careers adviser later refers to having 'a comfortable base'. Adviser A says that at university, you might be living in 'a room that is far less comfortable than you are accustomed to', but doesn't suggest doing anything to feel at ease in it.

50 B 'However, there's the danger of falling behind with your studies, or not having enough time to sleep. And let's face it, if your friends are planning a fun evening and you have to go to work instead of joining in, it could be very frustrating!' Adviser C says that getting a job 'may not always be advisable', without specifying any disadvantages. Advisers D and E also mention jobs, without referring to any disadvantages.

51 C '[Y]ou might try to keep up with them, and find yourself heavily in debt.' All the other advisers mention finance, but say nothing about borrowing money.

52 B 'It's useful to draw up a budget, listing your likely outgoings during the term ... and how much you'll have available.' All the other advisers mention money, but not making a financial plan.

53 D With reference to 'freshers' week', adviser D says, 'you should see this as a good chance to try something new, or something you'd never imagined doing before.'

54 A 'Your experience until now has probably been that homework was pretty much regulated, with repercussions if you didn't do it; a degree course requires far more independent work.' Advisers C and E mention school, without making a contrast between school and university studies.

55 C '[D]on't let yourself get caught up in a group that is more affluent than you are.' Advisers A, B and D also mention socialising, but don't say anything about caution.

56 E '[Y]our going to university may be a big change for your family.' Advisers A and B also mention family, but not the effect on them of your being away.

Writing Part 1

1 Essay

Model answer

This model has been prepared as an example of a very good answer. However, please note that this is just one example out of several possible approaches.

When people spend time abroad, it is clearly an enriching experience for them as individuals, but the fact that they have gained this experience also brings benefits to the society in which they live.

Firstly, there are advantages for business. If people have spent time living in another country, they will have acquired some knowledge of the language of that country. They may not have become fluent, but they will almost certainly be able to communicate in that language. They will also have learnt about the mentality and customs of the society in question and this, along with their language skills, will stand them in very good stead when it comes to doing business with that country.

Secondly, there are cultural advantages. People who have lived abroad will have experienced the cultural life of a country different from their own. They will have listened to new kinds of music and seen fresh approaches to painting and other visual arts. If they are artistic themselves, this will have a very positive impact on their own creativity, which in turn will bring benefits to their own society as well as to them as individuals.

Of the two benefits to society of foreign travel which have been discussed above, the more significant is, in my opinion, the business one. Successful business between countries has all sorts of positive consequences, from increased employment opportunities to better working conditions for staff. The travel experience of employees is only one small factor contributing to business success, but it certainly plays a not insignificant part in this.

Notes

- *Opening paragraph introduces the topic*
- *Two of the points are addressed and developed*
- *One of the benefits is chosen as more significant and an explanation is provided as to why this one was chosen*
- *The essay has a clear structure*
- *Appropriate register – not too informal*
- *Good use of collocations, e.g. 'an enriching experience', 'acquire knowledge', 'do business with', 'play a part'*
- *Good variety of structures used, e.g. 'people who have lived abroad will have experienced', 'successful business between countries has all sorts of positive consequences, from ... to ...'*
- *No language errors*
- *Correct length (260 words)*

Writing Part 2

2 Email

Style

Neutral to formal

Your email should use language that is appropriate for a piece of writing to a business.

Content

Your email should express clearly what your company does, what its IT training needs are, and why the needs are urgent. The company receiving the email should know exactly what is hoped for.

Organisation

Write in clearly defined paragraphs.

Use appropriate opening and closing formulae for an email to a business.

3 **Report**

Model answer

This model has been prepared as an example of a very good answer. However, please note that this is just one example out of several possible approaches.

> **Modern English Literature Course**
> This term I completed the new Modern English Literature course. On the whole, I found it an extremely valuable addition to the other courses offered by the Language Department in this college.
>
> Strengths
>
> What I appreciated most about this course was its breadth. It dealt not only with the novel but also with poetry and drama, and it covered writers from a wide range of countries in the English-speaking world. The lecturer provided us with a lengthy bibliography, which is particularly useful in that it includes brief notes on each of the titles listed. In all, the course gave us an excellent introduction to the topic, as well as offering many suggestions as to how best to follow up the issues we had been discussing.
>
> Weaknesses
>
> In my opinion, the course had only two weaknesses. Firstly, the lecture theatre where it was held was not big enough for such a popular course and, secondly, the instructions for the coursework assignment which the lecturer set us were not as clear as they might have been.
>
> Suggested improvements
>
> It goes without saying that I would recommend that the course take place in the college's largest lecture hall in future and that the assignment be reworded to avoid ambiguity. However, I would also recommend that the course tutors make better use of the department website. For example, forums could be set up for further discussion of some of the issues raised by the lectures.

Notes

- *Use of an appropriate title*
- *Opening paragraph sets the context*
- *All the points from the question are dealt with in the answer*
- *Clearly organised in paragraphs*
- *Appropriate use of headings*
- *Good range of vocabulary, e.g. 'on the whole', 'a valuable addition', 'it goes without saying'*
- *Shows ability to handle a range of structures, e.g. 'What I appreciated most about the course was …' and 'It dealt not only with … but also …'*
- *Variety of sentence length*
- *Appropriate register – neither very formal nor very informal*
- *No language errors*
- *Correct length (245 words)*

4 **Proposal**

Style

Neutral to formal

Your proposal should use language that is appropriate for a piece of formal writing.

Content

Your proposal should make recommendations about both green spaces and street art in your town. It should explain how what you propose would improve the quality of life of the people who live there. You should try to express your ideas clearly and persuasively.

Organisation

Write in clearly defined paragraphs.

Include a title and sub-headings.

Listening Part 1

1 B A: The woman hasn't made a mistake. C: She says, 'the manager allocates work to everyone, and that's all we have the chance to do,' but doesn't say she has too much work.

2 C A: She says, 'you can start and finish late, if you want to, though I don't'. B: She says that unlike most of her colleagues, she works on Friday afternoons.

3 C A: The woman thought the production was very interesting. B: She says turning the play into farce didn't really work for her.

4 A B: The man loved the soundtrack, but the woman found a lot of it quite distracting. C: They agree that the scenery was poor.

5 B A: The man says Isabel has let him down 'again', so he is not surprised. C: He believes she must have known about driving her children to school when she agreed to pick him up, so that can't be unexpected.

6 C A: He doesn't know anyone else who's going who could pick him up. B: Although he considers not going, the woman persuades him it's better to arrive late than not at all.

Listening Part 2

7 **coach:** Because few people owned cars, Bennett bought a coach to use for trips to the Lakes. The coach left Manchester in the morning and returned late that night, and the all-in price included meals.

8 **Africa:** The largest number of trips are to South America, and Africa is the second biggest category. The company offers only a few European destinations, and it is considering Central America for the future.

9 **thrilling:** '[H]er opinion' reflects 'I'd call it' in the transcript.

10 **balloon:** The other option, a helicopter ride, is in the morning.

11 **architecture:** 'Susan is particularly impressed' reflects 'can compare with any in the world, in my opinion' in the transcript.

12 **glaciers:** '[M]ountains' refers to the 'granite peaks' in the transcript.

13 **whale(s):** In listing the wildlife off the coast, only whales are mentioned twice – killer whales and humpback whales.

14 **viaduct:** Susan talks about a train trip that leaves in the morning, climbs the mountains as far as a viaduct, then returns to Salta.

Listening Part 3

15 D A: The connection with the town's 300th anniversary was made after the council had decided to hold the festival. B: Angela hopes this will be a side effect of holding the festival. C: The interviewer says that some festivals are intended to raise money for charity, but neither speaker says this is true of the Marston festival.

16 B A: She had been involved in festivals, but in a more junior role. C: She had contacts with various artists and performers, but doesn't say that was a reason for her appointment. D: She says she isn't an arts expert.

17 C A: Angela mentions spending time organising the work, because there are so many volunteers. B: She mentions how expensive it would be to pay everyone, but doesn't say anything about raising funding. D: She mentions various areas of expertise, such as sound and lighting, but implies there were volunteers for those activities as well as non-specialised ones.

18 D A: She says she doesn't blame other people when things go wrong, but this is 'by temperament' – not something she is learning from organising the festival. B: She says she sometimes reacts to the stress by wanting to resign, but she doesn't comment on whether that is a bad response. C: She seems able to cope with stress quite well, but she already knew she could, as it is part of her temperament.

19 C A: They agree that wouldn't be very original, and Angela says she wanted something different. B: The connections are between events and aspects of the town, not between events. D: Angela mentions clubs following up the events when the festival has finished.

20 A B: Angela says she is most interested in the arts, implying that she would rather organise an arts festival than one in another field. C: She says she wouldn't be a performer in a festival. D: She mentions her current assistant, but doesn't say she needs more help.

Listening Part 4

TASK ONE

21 C Having found what he thought was the same laptop online at a much lower price, he saw the manager to ask for a discount. The store had ordered a particular laptop, but that was before the speaker spoke to the manager.

22 G She bought a pair of shoes as a present for her niece, who wasn't keen on them, so she wanted to get her money back. The shoes weren't faulty.

23 E He wanted to buy a dishwasher, but the shop assistant seemed ignorant about them, so he asked to see the manager. He feels he had poor service, but doesn't complain to the manager about it.

24 F She wanted to report the behaviour of the shop assistant, who had tried to charge a lot for delivery, and had then been rude to her. She didn't want to cancel a delivery.

25 A The mirror he had bought was scratched, and he wanted to exchange it for one in perfect condition. The price of the mirror had been reduced, so that wasn't why the speaker talked to the manager.

TASK TWO

26 E The speaker felt a fool for confusing the two laptop models. He accepted the manager's offer of a free carrying case.

27 D The manager sent out mixed messages about doing what the speaker asked. She seemed 'almost hostile' towards her, but apparently believed what she said.

28 H He thought the manager was rude to break off their conversation several times to talk to various assistants. He doesn't say that he is a loyal customer.

29 C She says she was thankful that the manager understood why she was annoyed. She considered never shopping there again, despite having been a loyal customer, but didn't decide that.

30 A The speaker expected anyone working in retail to assume the customer is always right, but found he couldn't convince the manager. It is likely that he was annoyed, but he doesn't say so.

Test 3 Transcript

Listening

This is Advanced Trainer *Test 3, Listening Part 1.*

I'm going to give you the instructions for this test. I will introduce each part of the test and give you time to look at the questions. At the start of each piece, you will hear this sound:[tone]

You will hear each piece twice.

Remember, while you're listening, write your answers on the question paper. You will have five minutes at the end of the test to copy your answers onto the separate answer sheet.

There will now be a pause. Please ask any questions now, because you must not speak during the test.

Now open your question paper and look at Part 1.

PART 1

You will hear three different extracts. For questions 1 to 6, choose the answer (A, B or C) which fits best according to what you hear. There are two questions for each extract.

Extract 1

You hear two friends discussing the woman's new job.

Now look at questions 1 and 2.

Man: How's your new job going, Annie? It's with a software company, isn't it?

Woman: Yes. Well, I have to say I'm not enjoying it as much as I'd hoped. I thought I'd have plenty of freedom to develop new games, but it's all very structured: the manager allocates work to everyone, and that's all we have the chance to do.

Man: Mm, that's a shame.

Woman: Still, it'll give me useful experience to put on my CV for when I apply for a more senior position, so I'm glad I took this job rather than the other one I was offered – it's a means to an end, really.

Man: What are the hours like?

Woman: Oh, we have flexible hours, which I like. You have to work 37 hours a week, but you can start and finish late if you want to, though I don't. Most of my colleagues work four long days and finish at lunchtime on Fridays, so after that I often have the office to myself. It's a good opportunity to concentrate without the usual interruptions.

Man: I wish I could have Friday afternoon off! It'd be great to have a longer weekend.

Woman: I don't mind. I don't go away at the weekend as often as you do.

Man: That's true.

Extract 2

You hear two friends discussing a play they have both seen.

Now look at questions 3 and 4.

Man: What did you think of the production, Amanda? I really enjoyed it.

Woman: Me too. I thought it was very interesting. I know the director emphasised the comic aspects of the play – well, it was turned into a farce really, wasn't it? And although that didn't really work for me, it made me realise that I'd been misinterpreting the play ever since I first saw it. I'd always thought it was very serious, because of the awful things that happen to the hero, but that's not the only way of looking at it.

Man: I see what you mean. Actually, I loved the music, or rather the soundtrack.

Woman: Mm. All those strange sounds, you mean, like the heartbeat and the white noise?

Man: Yes. It was really atmospheric.

Woman: I found a lot of it quite distracting – I couldn't always concentrate on what was happening on stage because I was wondering how they'd created the sounds. The lighting was quite different, though, particularly the way they used spotlights to show the hero's isolation from everyone else on stage.

Man: Mm. That worked really well, didn't it? But as for the scenery ...!

Woman: I bet I could design better scenery, even though I've never done it before!

Man: I'm sure you could.

Extract 3

You hear a man telling a friend about a phone call he has just had.

Now look at questions 5 and 6.

Man: I've just had a call from Isabel. Would you believe she's let me down again?

Woman: No!

Man: All I wanted was a lift to the conference on Wednesday. I mean, she'll practically be going past my door, so it wouldn't have been any trouble to her.

Woman: So why won't she?

Man: Oh, there's a good reason – there always is with her. Something to do with driving her children to school. Well, she must have known about that when she agreed to pick me up in the first place. Goodness knows what time she'll turn up at the conference.

Woman: How will you get there?

Man: To be honest, I'm tempted not to go at all. I know there are no buses from here early enough – that's why I needed a lift. And I don't know anyone else who's going who could pick me up.

Woman: How much of it would you miss if you went by bus?

Man: The whole of the first session, I think. Maybe more.

Woman: Well, surely that's better than not going at all? After all, you've been looking forward to it, and you said it would be useful.

Man: Mm, I suppose you're right. OK, I'll do that.

That is the end of Part 1.

Now turn to Part 2.

PART 2

You will hear a woman called Susan Foster talking about holidays organised by the company that she works for. For questions 7 to 14, complete the sentences with a word or short phrase.

You now have 45 seconds to look at Part 2. You will need to play the recording twice.

Woman: Good evening. My name's Susan Foster, and I hope to interest you in the tours that we offer at Bennett's Holidays.

First, some background. The company was founded in the early twentieth century by a businessman, John Bennett. He lived in Manchester, in the north of England, which isn't too far from the Lake District. The Lakes were a popular destination, and as very few people owned cars in those days, Bennett bought a coach to provide transport. He offered excursions at an all-in price that included meals, leaving in the early morning and returning to Manchester late that same day. This continued until the 1950s, though by then the company also offered seven-day holidays.

During the next few decades, overseas package holidays were introduced – initially only to European destinations, but since 2005, the largest proportion of our trips are to South America. Although we still offer a few holidays in Europe, our strategy of advertising tours in Africa has really paid off – it's now our second biggest category. And we're currently looking into possibilities in Central America, too.

Argentina is one of our most popular destinations, and it's an enormously varied country. Several of our tours start in the capital, Buenos Aires, a city that's noted for its elegant boulevards, but there's a great deal more to see. I expected it to be quite interesting, but now I've been there, I'd call it one of the most thrilling cities I've ever been to, offering everything from tango in the streets to fascinating museums.

On our Buenos Aires holidays, you can see the city and its surroundings from the air, by taking a helicopter ride in the morning, or a balloon trip as the sun goes down.

You can also book a two-centre holiday, combining Buenos Aires with Montevideo, the capital of Uruguay. Montevideo has a rich cultural heritage, and it's very cosmopolitan. While many people are knocked out by the sandy beaches – and they're certainly very attractive – its architecture can compare with any in the world, in my opinion.

Another holiday that starts in Buenos Aires includes flying south to spend three days among the glaciers that slowly flow between granite peaks. This is a simply spectacular area, and I guarantee the memories will stay with you for ever.

Several of our holidays bring you face-to-face with nature. For instance, you can combine a stay in Buenos Aires with three days on the Valdes Peninsula to see the wildlife off the coast – elephant seals, sea lions, dolphins and, depending on the season, killer whales, humpback whales and penguins.

Another fascinating add-on to a stay in Buenos Aires is to fly to Salta, in north-west Argentina. From there, you can travel more than 400 kilometres on a train, which leaves around seven in the morning, climbs up the mountains as far as a viaduct that's over 4,000 metres above sea level, and arrives back in Salta at midnight. The views of the landscape are just breathtaking.

Now I'd like to talk a little bit further ...

That is the end of Part 2.

Now turn to Part 3.

PART 3

You will hear a conversation on a local radio station between a presenter and Angela Staveley, the director of an arts festival in the town of Marston. For questions 15 to 20, choose the answer (A, B, C or D) which fits best according to what you hear.

You now have 70 seconds to look at Part 3. You will need to play the recording twice.

Man: Marston town council is planning a major arts festival for later this year, and today we're going to have a look behind the scenes and learn something about how such a big event is organised. In the studio with me is Angela Staveley, the festival director. Welcome, Angela.

Woman: Thank you.

Man: Now, lots of towns hold festivals of one sort or another, sometimes to raise funds for local charities, but I believe this is the first one in Marston. This year marks 300 years since the town is thought to have been founded. Is that the reason for the festival?

Woman: Actually, that connection was only made after the council had reached a decision. But there's a certain amount of prestige attached to holding an arts festival – at least, if it's successful.

Man: Yes, a lot of towns and cities are known for theirs.

Woman: And attract loads of visitors. Marston is aiming to be in the same league.

Man: And when a festival works really well, it brings people together in a way that doesn't happen every day.

Woman: Exactly. If we achieve that, it would be a bonus – the icing on the cake.

Man: You were appointed festival director. You've been involved in festivals before, haven't you?

Woman: Yes, though in a more junior role. Not that I'm an arts expert, by any means, but through that work, I got to know several of the artists and performers who are going to appear here in Marston.

Man: I understand your last full-time job was with a transport company, where you were in charge of several big projects.

Woman: That's right. They gave me a good reference, and that helped me to get the job with the council.

Man: I'm sure it hasn't all been plain sailing. What's the biggest challenge you've faced?

Woman: Organising a festival like this means getting all sorts of people involved, to do everything from publicity to cleaning the venues, and some of it's highly specialised, like sound and lighting. Paying everyone for their work would be prohibitively expensive, so the festival largely depends on volunteers. I've been amazed by how many we have – far more than we need, to be honest, so I've spent a long time making sure there's something for everyone to do. Not a problem I'd had before!

Man: Can I ask how having such a responsible job affects you personally? It must be time-consuming and probably very stressful at times.

Woman: All the time, to be honest. And occasionally I find myself on the point of wanting to resign when something really frustrating happens.

Man: But you haven't given up so far.

Woman: Not yet! It helps that by temperament I've always been able to look for solutions rather than blaming other people when things go wrong. One thing I've noticed, though, is that this job is part of a pattern in my life, where I'm frantically busy while the particular activity is underway, then collapse in a heap when it's finished. I need to do something about that – though probably not just yet!

Man: Now, what about the programme of events? You were largely responsible for that, I presume.

Woman: Not entirely. I came up with the big picture, the underlying principle that I wanted the festival to reflect.

Man: Which was?

Woman: Well, if you think about many arts festivals, their objective is to have a wide range of activities, so there's something for everyone. Now that's very good, of course …

Man: But not terribly original.

Woman: Exactly. I wanted something a little different, to give people a reason for attending an event even if they weren't particularly interested in that particular art form. So, many of the events, such as an exhibition of photos of residents, highlight a particular facet of Marston. Another example is a performance of old songs about working in a factory, to reflect our industrial past.

Man: I like it!

Woman: Thanks. I'm hoping it'll inspire local clubs to follow up some of the events when the festival has finished.

Man: Will you direct more arts festivals?

Woman: Quite possibly. As an amateur painter and singer myself, it's certainly the field I'm most interested in, though not as a performer. But I'd make sure I'm involved from the outset. In this case, the town council had drawn up outline plans before I was appointed, and that hasn't always proved helpful. Luckily, my assistant was put in place before I was, so he's been able to fill me in on what happened before I came along.

Man: Angela, many thanks.

Woman: Thank you.

That is the end of Part 3.

Now turn to Part 4.

PART 4

Part 4 consists of two tasks. You will hear five short extracts in which people are talking about speaking to the store manager in a shop. Look at Task 1. For questions 21 to 25, choose from the list (A–H) the reason each speaker gives for speaking to the store manager. Now look at Task 2. For questions 26 to 30, choose from the list (A–H) how each speaker felt after speaking to the store manager. While you listen you must complete both tasks.

You now have 45 seconds to look at Part 4. You will need to play the recording twice.

Speaker 1

What happened was that the store ordered a particular laptop for me, and they just asked me for a small deposit. Meanwhile, I had a look online and found the same laptop for a fraction of the price, though the delivery charge was on top of that. So I went back and asked the manager for a discount. Well, when we went into details, it turned out the two computers were different models, which I hadn't realised. He said it was easy to confuse them, but I felt such a fool! Anyway, he offered me a free carrying case, which he didn't need to in the circumstances, so I accepted gratefully. And I'm sure I'll shop there again.

Speaker 2

I never like asking to see a shop manager. The last one I saw seemed almost hostile at first. She said what I wanted was against company policy, but she could understand how I felt, so she'd make an exception. She really sent out mixed messages. What had happened was that I'd bought this really expensive pair of shoes for my niece. I'd spent ages choosing them, with a lot of help from the shop assistant. But as soon as my niece opened the package, it was obvious she wasn't keen. So I said I'd get my money back, and give her something else instead. That's why I wanted to see the manager. But I almost wish I hadn't bothered.

Speaker 3

You'd hope that people working in retail at least know *something* about what they're selling. But I wanted to buy a dishwasher, and the assistant serving me seemed completely ignorant about the various models. I mean, he didn't even seem to understand about the different energy ratings! So I asked to see the manager, in the hope that she'd be more knowledgeable than the assistant. Well, she was quite helpful, but what I couldn't forgive was that she kept breaking off in the middle of our conversation to talk to various assistants who walked past us – nothing to do with what we were discussing. I thought it was so rude. That's not the way to encourage customers to be loyal.

Speaker 4

I went to buy a bike for my brother, and wanted it delivered. Well, you'd think I was asking for the moon! I was prepared to pay extra, but the assistant wanted to charge me a fortune.
I refused, and said I wouldn't buy the bike, and then she was quite impertinent. I insisted on seeing the manager, to report her behaviour – though I assumed the manager would side with his staff. I was on the point of saying I'd never shop there again, despite having been a good customer over the years, but to give him his due, he understood why I felt as I did, which I was thankful for. I still didn't buy the bike, though.

Speaker 5

I once had occasion to speak to a shop manager who was fiercely loyal to her staff and suspicious of mere customers. I explained what had happened, but it was impossible to convince her – it was the assistant's word against mine, and the assistant won hands down. I thought that in retail 'the customer is always right', but obviously not. You see, I'd bought a large mirror on special offer, but when I got home I found it was scratched. I went back to get one in perfect condition, because it was meant to be a wedding present. But the assistant said there'd been a sign saying that was why the price was reduced. There certainly wasn't.

That is the end of Part 4.

There will now be a pause of five minutes for you to copy your answers onto the separate answer sheet. Be sure to follow the numbering of all the questions. I will remind you when there is one minute left, so that you're sure to finish in time.

You have one more minute left.

That is the end of the test. Please stop now. Your supervisor will now collect all the question papers and answer sheets.

Test 4 Key

Reading and Use of English Part 1

1 **B** A: 'Search' without 'for', is followed by a place, e.g. 'to search a house for stolen goods'. C: A direct object following 'seek' refers to what is being looked for, e.g. 'to seek a solution to a problem'. D: 'Enquire' is intransitive.

2 **D** Only D can refer to a particular type of something, e.g. technology.

3 **A** This use of 'feel' means that somebody watching the interviews nowadays gets the impression that they are over-rehearsed. None of the other options can be 'over-rehearsed'.

4 **C** This is the only option that collocates with 'team' to refer to the position of its leader.

5 **A** Only A can be used with 'technological' to refer to what couldn't be done.

6 **C** A and B: 'Archaic' and 'bygone' are not used to refer to somebody's job in the past. D: 'Outgoing' refers to people as they leave their job and are replaced, e.g. 'The outgoing president had a long conversation with her successor.'

7 **B** Only B can be used with 'changes' to mean 'caused the changes to happen'.

8 **B** This means 'creating something again that has been destroyed'. A and D are normally used of objects, e.g. 'I lost the application form, so I asked for a duplicate', 'a replica of an old ship', and C is used of paintings or images of people.

Reading and Use of English Part 2

9 **Unlike:** This is a preposition. It makes a contrast between Neanderthals (who developed in Europe and Asia) and Homo sapiens (who developed in Africa).

10 **long:** It often collocates with 'ago' to refer to a period of time.

11 **from:** 'Far from' means 'not at all'.

12 **any:** This often follows 'hardly' to mean 'a very small amount'.

13 **least:** 'At least' is used here to reduce the effect of a statement, i.e. possibly not Denisovans but only their DNA.

14 **with:** This normally follows 'to interbreed'.

15 **Whatever:** This means 'it doesn't matter what the precise connection was'.

16 **it:** 'Were it not for' is a fixed phrase. The sentence means that we only know something about the relationship because of advances in DNA retrieval and sequencing.

Reading and Use of English Part 3

17 **global:** An adjective is required to classify the noun 'community'.

18 **primarily:** An adverb is needed to modify the verb 'do'.

19 **marginalised / marginalized / marginal:** An adjective is required to classify the noun 'communities'. Here, it refers to communities that are not powerful.

20 **compliance:** The preceding adjective ('strict') and following preposition ('with') show that a noun is required.

21 **consultancy:** 'A' needs to be followed by a singular noun; 'consultant' can only refer to one person, but 'the Collective' is a group of people. A 'consultation' is a process or activity, and so can't refer to the people.

22 **expertise:** 'The ... of' requires a noun, which must refer to something that staff, etc. have, i.e. expert knowledge and skill.

23 collaborative: An adjective is required to classify the type of work.

24 empower: 'Will' needs to be followed by the infinitive of a verb.

Reading and Use of English Part 4

The vertical line | shows where the answer is split into two parts for marking purposes.

25 SUCH a confusing film, | I had 'So' can precede an adjective (here 'confusing') or adverb; 'such' has the same meaning but precedes a noun ('film').

26 director's resignation | RESULTED from '[R]esulted' needs a noun ('resignation') as its subject, and is normally followed by 'from'. The sentence shows that the resignation came after the cause (the disagreement).

27 most considerate person | I (have) EVER 'I have yet to meet' means 'I have never met' (in the whole of my life up to the present). The superlative ('most considerate') is often used with a perfect tense and 'ever', although the past simple is also used in American English.

28 come to TERMS | with 'To come to terms with' is a phrase that means 'to gradually accept a sad or difficult situation'.

29 been for Miranda, | I'd/I would STILL 'If it hadn't been for' is a standard phrase that means 'without'.

30 made it difficult/hard | to PIECE together 'To piece together' means 'to create something (here, an explanation of what had happened) by joining several things together (here, the witness statements)'.

Reading and Use of English Part 5

31 C 'There is a widely held belief that change must mean deterioration and decay.' This idea is reinforced in 'standards have fallen markedly' and 'blame'. A: Older people are said to be aware of the differences, but there is no indication of whether or not younger people are aware of them. B: Reference is made to changes in language education in schools, but there is no mention of whether or not this raises awareness of language change. D: There is no suggestion that public understanding of language development is increasing.

32 A These are described as controversies gaining 'current attention' and also referred to in the 18th and 19th centuries. B: Alford's contemporaries thought 'the language was rapidly decaying', but the writer doesn't comment on the speed of change, either now or in the past. C: The writer makes the point that the 'list of unacceptable changes' tends to be the same in every generation – 'many of the usage issues recur', and most of Alford's usage issues 'are still with us'. D: The two examples suggest that they are not undergoing linguistic change – the two phrases were used both in 1863 and in the present.

33 B The writer contrasts the changes in the languages and communication problems of Papua New Guinea with the fact that 'as a rule', change is minimal. A: The writer implies that the prevailing view of linguistic change is that it occurs on a large scale, as in Papua New Guinea, so the example itself supports that view – which is challenged in the sentence beginning 'But as a rule'. C: The writer suggests that generalisations about linguistic change are wrong ('But as a rule … '), but not that they are dangerous. D: There is no discussion of the potential effects of linguistic change.

34 D '[I]t is because change is so infrequent that it is so distinctive and noticeable.' A: The writer suggests that 'precise and efficient communication' is important, and notes that the public notice change and are often pessimistic about it, but there is no reference to inconsistency in the value they place on accurate communication. B: There is no reference to reversing language changes. C: There is no mention of measuring language change.

35 A '[T]hose who try to plan a language's future waste their time ... – time which would be better spent in devising fresh ways of enabling society to cope with the new linguistic forms that accompany each generation'. B: The writer mentions teaching 'a common standard', without making the point that this is necessary to make communication possible – his emphasis is on 'recognizing the existence and value of linguistic diversity'. C: 'The need to develop a greater linguistic awareness and tolerance of change, especially in a multi-ethnic society' suggests that language change does not tend to be tolerated in multi-ethnic societies. D: Communication difficulties may or may not arise, but they are not mentioned in the paragraph.

36 B The writer says 'there is no evidence' for the view that languages become increasingly complex, or progress to a higher 'level of excellence'. A: The writer supports this idea – 'Nor, when languages change, do they move in a predetermined direction.' C: He mentions languages dying out, but doesn't express an opinion on whether or not this should be prevented. D: The evolution of languages is discussed, but there is no reference to categorising them accordingly.

Reading and Use of English Part 6

37 D Only reviewer D is unconvinced by Miller's view of the future, so A and C agree with reviewer B, but D doesn't.

38 A Reviewers A and C both think Miller is suitably qualified to write the book, but reviewers B and D do not.

39 B Reviewer B believes Miller is too limited to earlier studies of documentaries, while the other three reviewers consider that she uses them as a foundation and builds on them.

40 D Reviewers A and D agree with Miller's criticism of television companies for not making more use of documentaries, while reviewers B and C disagree with her.

Reading and Use of English Part 7

41 D 'Here' refers to 'the eastern side of the tourist town of Zermatt', and the two glaciers that are mentioned are part of the 'glacier system'.

42 B 'We' refers to the 'British team', and we are told it is 'late in the evening'. The following paragraph continues the time sequence with 'overnight' and 'the next day'. The small group 'who had already left to set up camp on the edge of the glacier' are 'the advance party' mentioned in the following paragraph.

43 A The fact that the railway was closed (in the previous paragraph) explains 'a day later than planned'; 'station' shows that they travelled on the mountain railway, 'the first stage in our journey up to the glacier' (previous paragraph); 'the three kilometres we still needed to travel' refers to the next stage of the journey, from the station to the advance party's camp by the glacier.

44 F '[E]xploring' refers to 'the work we had come to do' in the previous paragraph (this is made clear in the paragraph after 41). '[T]he team split into two' looks ahead to 'both parties' in the following paragraph.

45 C 'All these fascinating sights' refers back to the description of the surroundings in the previous paragraph, and 'my photography' refers to 'capture as many images … as possible'. '[M]eltwater' is referred to again in the following paragraph.

46 G 'This was one reason why it was so important to identify what exactly was happening' refers to the shrinkage of the glacier, in particular the reduction by 'a staggering 290 metres over the summer of 2007'. The 'water' that is mentioned recurs in the following paragraph.

Reading and Use of English Part 8

47 D 'What we knew about running a company you could write on the back of an envelope.'

48 C '[A] tutor on the course put me in touch with a fashion business she knew. ... Her recommendation must have swung them in my favour, because they took me on.'

49 B 'I eventually left to start my own fashion design business. Since then, we've branched out into household goods like tablecloths and bedding.'

50 A The designer's college tutors were very positive and he/she won a couple of awards. However, getting a job afterwards was very difficult.

51 C The job 'wasn't ideal', and the designer says that 'In retrospect, I think I'd have been better off setting up on my own.'

52 A The designer was offered a job because 'my saving grace was that I was so keen to learn more about fashion.'

53 D The designer was given 'some invaluable advice' by 'a couple of established designers,' and says 'it was remarkably generous of them'.

54 B As a child, the designer 'loved the glamour of the world of fashion,' but later found it was 'sheer hard work, long hours and a lot of stress', with just 'a touch of glamour occasionally'.

55 C The designer realised they 'needed to learn CAD', because the lack of that skill affected the chances of getting a job.

56 B '[T]he boss seemed happy to teach me all about the business side of things. That really stood me in good stead when I eventually left to start my own fashion design business.'

Writing Part 1

1 Essay

Model answer

This model has been prepared as an example of a very good answer. However, please note that this is just one example out of several possible approaches.

It is generally accepted that it is a good thing for people to keep themselves informed about what is happening in the world, to be up-to-date with current events and trends. But which aspects of life is it most important to know about?

Firstly, people need to know about the news. They need to know about the main social and political issues facing not only their own country but also others. It is part of a person's important general knowledge to have an understanding of the situation in different places around the world. This will mean reading more than one newspaper on a regular basis, as well as watching the news and documentaries about social issues on television.

Secondly, it is important to keep up-to-date with the arts. We should all know what is going on in the worlds of music, theatre, books and art. I do not mean that this should include only highbrow culture. I believe that we should all also know about popular singers and writers. Our aim should be to become fully rounded and well-informed citizens.

Of the two aspects of life discussed above, the more important one is, in my opinion, that of current affairs. Both aspects of life are undoubtedly important, but ultimately social and political issues are likely to have a more far-reaching impact on our lives than the arts, and so it is vital that we keep up-to-date with the news.

Notes

- *Opening paragraph introduces the topic*
- *Two of the points are addressed and developed*
- *One of the aspects is chosen as more significant and an explanation is provided as to why this one was chosen*
- *The essay has a clear structure*
- *Appropriate register – not too informal*
- *Good range of vocabulary relating to the theme, e.g. 'highbrow culture', 'fully rounded', 'well informed'*
- *Variety of sentence length and structure*
- *No language errors*
- *Correct length (239 words)*

Writing Part 2

2 Review

Style

Any style as long as it is consistent

Content

Your review should consider two videos you have seen online made by ordinary people. They should contrast in that you enjoyed one but not the other. Your review should make it clear why you felt as you did about each of them.

Organisation

Write in clearly defined paragraphs.

3 Letter

Model answer

This model has been prepared as an example of a very good answer. However, please note that this is just one example out of several possible approaches.

Dear James,

We are all very much looking forward to meeting you when you come to spend some time working with us soon. We all hope that you will enjoy your time here and will find it productive.

In many ways, you will probably find our branch rather different from yours. We are a slightly smaller branch, and our premises are considerably older than I believe yours are in Australia. More significant is the fact that the company's research and development is based here, and so we are very much focused on how the company might diversify in future. I imagine that you might find this aspect of our work stimulating. We are a small, relatively young team, here. Many of us are fairly recent graduates in either engineering or business.

Life for you here will, of course, not only be about work. I'm sure you'll want to do some travelling around the country while you're with us. Do let us know where you'd particularly like to go and we'll make some arrangements for you. There are a couple of excellent theatres in this town. Have a look at their programmes on the web and drop us a line to say what you'd like us to book you tickets for. Tickets often sell out quickly, and it makes sense for us to get hold of them before you get here.

Do please let me know if there's anything else you'd like to know before you arrive.

All best wishes,

Simon

Notes

- *Uses appropriate opening and closing formulae*
- *Tone is friendly but still businesslike*
- *All the points from the question are dealt with in the answer and are developed appropriately*
- *Clearly organised in paragraphs*
- *Good range of vocabulary relating to the workplace and leisure activities*

- *Variety of sentence length*
- *Appropriate register – informal and friendly*
- *No language errors*
- *Correct length (249 words)*

4 **Report**

Style

Neutral to formal

Content

Your report should briefly describe the traffic situation in your town. It should then go into more detail about the extent to which it meets the population's needs and should give an explanation of the town's most serious traffic problem. You should try to express your ideas as clearly as possible.

Organisation

Write in clearly defined paragraphs.

Include a title and sub-headings.

Listening Part 1

1 **C** The paintings were hard to see. A: The advance publicity referred to 'a range of artists', without indicating the number – it was the woman who 'imagined there'd be hundreds of works'. B: There was one painting by 'an artist I really love'.

2 **B** The man is put off by the people who attend exhibitions. A: He knows he isn't an art expert, but doesn't suggest he discovered this at exhibitions. C: He is in favour of talking about paintings 'in a way that can be understood' and 'without going on' about them.

3 **A** Tony says his colleague seems resentful that he has more money than she has. B: Marion asks Tony if the bad treatment is 'because you're new', but he doesn't accept that explanation. C: Tony says he doesn't think his colleague being much older than him is the reason for the way she treats him.

4 **B** Tony reluctantly agrees with Marion about talking to his line manager. A: Marion says that Tony should only look for a new job 'as a last resort', and he doesn't pursue the idea. C: Tony says he isn't brave enough to talk to his colleague about the issue.

5 **A** Ross says the publisher has changed the brief without discussing it with him. B: Although the deadline is just after his holiday, he doesn't say he will have to cancel the holiday. C: He says he will receive ten per cent of the price of each book sold, so being paid for the extra work 'doesn't apply'.

6 **A** Erica thinks her cousin was silly to get worked up: she would have done better to accept the changes. B: She doesn't say anything about her cousin's or Ross's motives for writing. C: Her cousin tried to persuade the publisher to rethink the changes, but without success.

Listening Part 2

7 **shopping experience:** Jack contrasts the importance of profit and range of products with the customers' shopping experience.

8 **stressed:** Jack talks about treating all customers in a friendly way; but says it is very important to make someone who is stressed relax a little.

9 **shopwalkers:** Several members of staff, including managers, take on the role of shopwalkers, and offer to help anyone who seems to need assistance.

10 **suggestion scheme:** Jack says the suggestion scheme makes it easy for anyone to put forward ideas for improvements.

11 **talent day:** Employees who are interested in promotion can talk to him about it when the store holds a 'talent day'.

12 **stock:** The stock arrives at night, and some staff start work at 6 am to put it on the shelves before the store opens at 7.

13 **manual:** Unlike most supermarkets, the store uses a manual system.

14 **weather:** Every day, when the managers of each department order stock, they consider the effect of the weather on sales.

Listening Part 3

15 **C** They don't think A or B were disappointing, and only Jason was disappointed with the support from tutors – Cathy was satisfied with it.

16 **D** Jason doesn't usually get distracted – it is Cathy who has become more focused; and Jason generally trusts his judgement.

17 **C** Cathy thinks the topic is OK, but she isn't sure what exactly to do, so can't yet do her best. They agree that they 'don't need to come up with anything really original'.

18 **D** They agree that the timing of the field trip has made it hard to keep up-to-date with assignments. Cathy says the field trip stopped her feeling that the subject was dry, and Jason wanted the trip to last longer.

19 **B** Jason says, 'the trip's confirmed that I can't see myself doing it for the rest of my life', so these are not 'fresh' doubts.

20 **A** Cathy says she feels she could contribute to research into alternative energy sources. Although she'd like to encourage the public to use less energy, she thinks it may not be the best use of what she's learning.

Listening Part 4

TASK ONE

21 **E** The speaker's father thought she was too impatient, and she decided to prove him wrong. Her parents used to go ballroom dancing, but made her give up the idea of going too.

22 **F** The speaker says he went to the gymnastics club at school because most people did. The club was intended to be a way of getting fit, but that wasn't why the speaker went.

23 **G** When the speaker saw ice skating on TV, she decided to make a living as an ice skater. A schoolfriend was taken ice skating, but didn't recommend it to her.

24 **C** The speaker wanted to do something that would engage his brain. Making friends in the school bridge club was a by-product of joining, not his purpose.

25 **B** The speaker's parents suggested taking up a hobby to meet other children. Tennis was her own choice – she wasn't introduced to it by either of her parents.

TASK TWO

26 **H** The speaker is surprised how few people make models. She mentions having to be careful and accurate, but doesn't say anything about the standard she has reached.

27 **C** The speaker may give up gymnastics now, because he is demoralised by the ease with which younger people do it. He is aware of his relatively limited ability without needing to reassess it. He could carry on if he wanted to.

28 **D** The speaker wanted to win a national competition, and did so the second time she entered. She has become quite well known, but she isn't pleased about that – she is concerned that people have high expectations of her.

29 **A** The speaker has realised that although he was one of the better players at school, experts are at a very much higher level; his standard is lower than he used to think.

30 **B** The speaker is surprised to have reached a high level. She doesn't say that winning regional tournaments was a target.

Test 4 Transcript

Listening

This is Advanced Trainer *Test 4, Listening Part 1.*

I'm going to give you the instructions for this test. I will introduce each part of the test and give you time to look at the questions. At the start of each piece, you will hear this sound: [tone]

You will hear each piece twice.

Remember, while you're listening, write your answers on the question paper. You will have five minutes at the end of the test to copy your answers onto the separate answer sheet.

There will now be a pause. Please ask any questions now, because you must not speak during the test.

Now open your question paper and look at Part 1.

PART 1

You will hear three different extracts. For questions 1 to 6, choose the answer (A, B or C) which fits best according to what you hear. There are two questions for each extract.

Extract 1

You hear two friends discussing an art exhibition.

Now look at questions 1 and 2.

Man: How was that art exhibition you said you were going to, Hazel?

Woman: It wasn't bad, I suppose, but I have to admit I didn't enjoy it all that much.

Man: Why was that?

Woman: Well, I heard on the radio that it was going to have paintings produced in the last hundred years by a range of artists. And I somehow imagined there'd be hundreds of works, but there can't have been more than 80 or so. The trouble was, only a small part of the gallery was used for the exhibition, so the paintings were crowded together, with some so high up the wall that you couldn't see them properly. And the one painting they had by an artist I really love was one of those.

Man: What a shame! Actually, I've stopped going to art exhibitions altogether. There's something about the crowd that goes to every exhibition that really puts me off. They're probably perfectly nice really, but I've overheard so many conversations that seem terribly pretentious. I know I'm not an art expert, but at least I can talk about paintings in a way that can be understood. And after all, you can appreciate a painting without going on about it, can't you?

Woman: I know exactly what you mean!

Extract 2

You hear two friends, Tony and Marion, discussing a problem at Tony's workplace.

Now look at questions 3 and 4.

Woman: How's your new job, Tony?

Man: The job itself is fine, but there's a woman in the department who treats me as though I shouldn't be there at all. She's really unpleasant to me.

Woman: Is that because you're new, so you're the underdog until the next person is appointed?

Man: Judging by some of the things she says to me, she seems to resent the fact that I'm not struggling financially, while she is. And she's really sarcastic about the fact that I can afford to do things like going away for the weekend.

Woman: Is she much older than you?

Man: Yes, though I don't think that's the reason. What do you think I should do, Marion?

Woman: What about having a quiet conversation with her, to explain how she makes you feel?

Man: Hmm. That's probably a good idea in theory, but I don't think I'm brave enough. In fact, I'm even thinking of leaving and looking for another job.

Woman: You should only do that as a last resort, Tony. Your line manager is responsible for what goes on in the department. That's the person who should sort it out.

Man: She seems very stressed, so I didn't want to bother her.

Woman: I really think you should.

Man: Mm. I suppose you're right. OK, I will.

Extract 3

You hear a writer called Ross telling a friend called Erica about a problem he has with his publisher.

Now look at questions 5 and 6.

Man: Erica, you know that school textbook I'm writing?

Woman: Yes.

Man: Well, the publishers have just changed their minds about what they want. It'll take weeks to rewrite what I've already done, and the deadline is just after the holiday I'm planning.

Woman: Surely they'll extend the deadline?

Man: Apparently not.

Woman: Will they at least pay you for the extra work?

Man: I'll be getting ten per cent of the price of each book sold, so it doesn't apply. And admittedly the changes are quite sensible, so it'll probably boost sales in the long run. But still, I don't like the way they've unilaterally changed the brief without even asking me for my opinion.

Woman: Mm. Something very similar happened to my cousin. She was very unhappy about it, and put a lot of time and energy into trying to get the publisher to rethink the changes. In the end, she refused to go on with the book, and criticises the publisher whenever she has a chance. But it's silly, really, because she got so worked up she made herself ill. If she'd accepted the changes with good grace, she'd have written a good book and probably made some money from it.

That is the end of Part 1.

Now turn to Part 2.

PART 2

You will hear Jack Charlesworth, the manager of a UK supermarket, talking to a group of business students about his work. For questions 7 to 14, complete the sentences with a word or short phrase.

You now have 45 seconds to look at Part 2. You will need to play the recording twice.

Man: Good morning. My name's Jack Charlesworth, and I'm the manager of a large supermarket in London. As you're studying business, I'm here to tell you about my work.

You might think the most important thing for a supermarket in a big chain like ours is the profit we contribute to the company's bottom line, or the range of products we offer customers. But to me, it's what I would term their shopping experience. I want customers to feel that they're treated as individuals. We have thousands of customers a week, so obviously we can't recognise *all* our regulars, but we do our best to treat everyone – whether they're old customers or new – in a friendly way. If someone's stressed when they come in, it may only take a smile from an employee to make them relax a little, and that's something we take very seriously.

In many stores, one of the sales assistants offers to help you as soon as you go in the door. That always makes me feel uncomfortable, so we do it differently. We have several members of staff, including managers, mingling with customers and acting as shopwalkers – a rather old-fashioned term, but we still use it. They don't bother people who know what they're doing, but if anyone seems to be in need of assistance, one of our team will offer to help them.

That personal contact goes right through the store. For example, I make a point of chatting to all the staff – nearly 400 of them. We have a weekly managers' meeting, which staff representatives attend, and a suggestion scheme, to make it easy for anyone to put forward ideas for improvements. We've implemented a lot of those, over the years. And we want employees who are interested in promotion to have the chance to discuss that, so from time to time we hold what we've named a 'talent day'. Anyone can come and talk to me then, and usually we plan a training programme to help them work towards a new job.

It can be hard, working in a supermarket. We open at seven six days a week – later on Sundays. The stock is delivered overnight and needs to be put on the shelves before the doors open, so some people start work at six to do that. The cleaning company we use come in then, as well.

We order daily from the company's distribution centre, for delivery that night. Most supermarkets use an automated computer system – sales are automatically recorded, and when numbers go below a certain level, the system places an order. However, we have a manual one. The managers of each department decide what to order, because they know what they've sold and what they're likely to sell the next day. They take into account factors like the weather, which has the biggest effect on retail sales after the general state of the economy, and so of course has to be considered every day.

Now let me move on ...

That is the end of Part 2.

Now turn to Part 3.

PART 3

You will hear a geology professor asking two students, Cathy and Jason, about a field trip they have just returned from. For questions 15 to 20, choose the answer (A, B, C or D) which fits best according to what you hear.

You now have 70 seconds to look at Part 3. You will need to play the recording twice.

Professor: Now, before you write your reports on the field trip you've just done, I'd like to hear what you thought – what was good, anything you found disappointing ... Jason.

Jason: Well, I've got fairly mixed feelings about it. I was relieved there weren't more people – with it only being four days, there was time to get to know everyone, and that wouldn't have been possible if there'd been many more. Would you agree, Cathy?

Cathy: Yes, definitely.

Jason: I wish we'd stayed in a youth hostel, though. Camping's all very well when it's warm, but last week's weather certainly wasn't ideal.

Cathy: No, I was shivering even when I was in my sleeping bag. What was good, however, was that the tutors could spend a fair amount of time with each of us, to advise us on our projects.

Jason: Mm, I could've done with some more help. I only managed to have one in-depth discussion with my tutor.

Cathy: Oh, I talked to mine whenever I got stuck.

Jason: Lucky you!

Professor: OK. What would you say you got out of the trip?

Cathy: The main thing was that I'm pretty impetuous by nature, and I tend to act before I think. My tutor encouraged me to take the time to think things through before doing anything, and I forced myself to do that during the trip.

Jason: I did the same thing – it was something I realised I needed to work on. I don't think my judgement's generally wrong, but I'm sure I could often make better decisions, with a bit more thought. Actually, the feedback I get from tutors is generally pretty positive, particularly on things like planning assignments.

Cathy: I found the trip helped me to be more focused. I hope I can keep that up, now we're back at uni.

Jason: That isn't usually a problem for me.

Professor: Mm. How far did you each get with your projects?

Cathy: Well, I'm struggling a bit. I think the topic's OK ...

Jason: You're researching some fossils, aren't you? That's pretty standard stuff.

Cathy: Yes, but my tutor said I'm trying to cover too much: I need to go into depth about one aspect.

Jason: But at this level, we don't need to come up with anything really original, do we?

Cathy: No, I suppose not. But until I've sorted out exactly what to do, I won't really be able to do my best.

Professor: And what about you, Jason?

Jason: I'm getting on OK, thanks.

Professor: Right. Now, how do you think the field trip fits in with the course as a whole?

Jason: Well, I could happily have gone on for another few days, but coming at this stage in the term makes it quite hard to keep up-to-date with assignments. I've got two due in next week, and I won't be able to finish them in time.

Cathy: Mm, I'm with you. I've just had to ignore everything else until I've got this project out of the way – and even packing and getting ready for the trip seemed to take forever.

Jason: Mm.

Cathy: Mind you, I think what I've learnt on the trip will be useful for much more than just this project. All the books and lectures were beginning to seem quite dry and academic, and the trip's made me realise they're actually about something interesting.

Professor: OK. Would you say the trip has affected how you feel about the course? Jason?

Jason: Well, I was really keen on geology when we started the course last year, but I wasn't sure whether I wanted to go on with it after uni.

Professor: Why not?

Jason: It's all the statistical analysis. I didn't think I'd like it, and, in a way, the trip's confirmed that I can't see myself doing it for the rest of my life. It's not that it's all that hard, but I find it quite tedious.

Cathy: So do I!

Professor: And what about you, Cathy? Have you got plans for when you graduate?

Cathy: I'm not sure. I'd like to do something to make the general public see the need to use less energy, but that may not be the best use of what I'm learning on the course.

Jason: There's a lot of interesting research going on in the whole area of renewable energy, isn't there?

Cathy: Yes, things like harnessing the power of tidal rivers to generate electricity, and of course, wind power. They can help us reduce our dependence on fossil fuels like oil and coal, and they're far less damaging to the environment, too. I feel I could make a contribution there, so I'll probably go into something like that.

Professor: And finally, what did you think ...

That is the end of Part 3.

Now turn to Part 4.

PART 4

Part 4 consists of two tasks. You will hear five short extracts in which people are talking about their leisure activities. Look at Task 1. For questions 21 to 25, choose from the list (A–H) the original reason each speaker gives for choosing their leisure activity. Now look at Task 2. For questions 26 to 30, choose from the list (A–H) how each speaker feels about their leisure activity now. While you listen you must complete both tasks.

You now have 45 seconds to look at Part 4. You will need to play the recording twice.

Speaker 1

When I was a child, my parents used to go ballroom dancing. I wanted to go too, but they said having two dancers in the family was quite enough, so I gave up that idea, but I was quite annoyed. So when I thought of making model aeroplanes, and my father said I was too impatient, I was determined to prove him wrong, so that's what I started doing. I think I made the right choice, and I still make models when I have the time. It surprises me how few people seem to do it, because you learn about aviation and history, and you have to be very careful and accurate. It's very satisfying when you finish a model.

Speaker 2

I've been keen on gymnastics since I was a teenager. It started when a new teacher at school set up a weekly gymnastics club, to encourage us to get fit, I suppose. It really caught on, and for a while practically everyone went, which to be honest was the only reason I did. Then people began to get bored, and moved on to something else. But I found I was quite enjoying it, so I carried on. Then, when I got my first job, I joined a gymnastics club in my home town. It was fun for a few years, but I may give it up now – it's quite demoralising seeing younger people doing things effortlessly that I struggle to do!

Speaker 3

One of my schoolfriends was taken ice skating by her parents. She wasn't particularly enthusiastic about it, but I was dying to go – I'd seen it on TV and thought it was brilliant, and had even decided to make a living as an ice skater! So they started taking me with them, and I was completely hooked. I made good progress, and soon set my sights on winning a national competition. I knew it would be hard work, but I won the second time I entered. I was absolutely thrilled! It made me quite well known in the ice-skating world, but that's not so good, because people have such high expectations of me.

Speaker 4

I've been playing bridge since I was at school. There, I was one of the better players, but the more I play, the more I realise there's a world of difference between that level and playing with experts. I'm so envious of their ability. I took up bridge because when I was a child, my parents used to watch TV for hours – the more mindless, the better. But I wanted something that would engage my brain. Then, when I was 11, I changed schools, and the new one ran a weekly bridge club. It was exactly what I needed. I loved trying to work out the best strategy for winning, and I made friends with several of the other children.

Speaker 5

My family moved abroad when I was 12. I wasn't very happy at my new school, so my parents suggested I took up a hobby where I could meet other children with a similar interest. I chose tennis, mainly because there was a club near our home that accepted children. It really paid off, because I became really close to some of the children I met there, and we still see a lot of each other 20 years later. I didn't think I'd be much good at tennis, but I really took to it. I've now won a couple of regional tournaments, which is way above what I expected. In fact, it's hard to believe I've got to that level.

That is the end of Part 4.

There will now be a pause of five minutes for you to copy your answers onto the separate answer sheet. Be sure to follow the numbering of all the questions. I will remind you when there is one minute left, so that you're sure to finish in time.

You have one more minute left.

That is the end of the test. Please stop now. Your supervisor will now collect all the question papers and answer sheets.

Test 5 Key

Reading and Use of English Part 1

1 B This is the only option that means 'I can't understand why people pay to be scared'. A: 'Daze' means to stun or disorientate someone, physically or psychologically. C: 'Elude' means to avoid being caught or achieved. D: 'Defy' means to refuse to obey someone.

2 D The adverbial phrase 'to be honest' is used to draw attention to the truth of what is said or written. A: 'Direct' has a similar meaning but isn't normally used in that structure. B: 'Clear' is more often used in the phrase 'let me make it clear'. C: 'Distinct' can refer to speaking in a way that can easily be heard.

3 A It means 'to want something very much', and takes a direct object; the other three options are followed by 'for'.

4 C Used of the heart, it means to beat strongly and fast. The other options are rarely used of the heart.

5 D This is the only option that is followed by the preposition 'to'; the others are followed by the direct object.

6 A Here, 'to score' means 'to achieve a mark'. B and C: 'Mark' and 'grade' both mean 'to give points to a piece of work'. D: As a verb, 'point' has meanings such as 'to draw someone's attention to something', while somebody can win points (the noun) in a game.

7 C This is the only option that collocates with 'experiences'. A: 'Severe' is often used to describe something that causes hardship or pain, e.g. 'a severe difficulty'. B: Meaning 'strong', 'burning' collocates with 'desire', 'ambition' and some other nouns. D: 'Fierce' collocates with 'competition', 'opposition', etc.

8 A Memories and strong feelings are often said to 'fade with age'; the other options are not used in this context.

Reading and Use of English Part 2

9 which: This is a relative pronoun referring to the clause 'your school needs photographs of the pupils'.

10 ourselves: 'To pride oneself on (something)' is a reflexive phrasal verb.

11 instead: 'Instead of', like 'rather than', introduces something that is to be replaced by what is in the main clause ('read this letter').

12 why: 'Why not' is a common way of making a suggestion.

13 as: 'To regard the photos as perfect mementos' means the children will consider the photos to be perfect mementos. Note that both plural forms 'mementos' and 'mementoes' are standard.

14 Although/Though/While/Whilst: Any of these words can introduce a contrast between the expectation that is created by the clause, and what actually happened; here, the writer expected that the complications that arose would make the photographer feel anxious or upset, but that didn't happen.

15 how: 'How well' can mean 'very well', as it does here, i.e. Jane interacted very well with the children. It can also mean the degree to which something is the case, e.g. 'I wonder how well she is getting on with the children' leaves it open as to whether she is getting on well or badly, or to any degree in between.

16 be/get: 'To be/get in touch (with someone)' means to contact them.

Reading and Use of English Part 3

17 exceptions: 'Few' shows that a plural noun is required.

18 curiosity: '[T]heir own' needs a noun to follow it. Note that the 'u' of 'curious' is omitted in 'curiosity'. Similarly, the adjective from 'humour' is 'humorous', without the second 'u'.

19 discoveries: '[T]heir' is followed by a noun; it is plural, as the discoveries relate to more than one scientist ('others') – even if each one has only made one discovery, there is more than one in total.

20 recognition: A noun is needed to follow 'the'.

21 biographical: An adjective is required to fit 'a ... approach'; 'biographical' classifies the type of approach, meaning it focuses on people's lives.

22 revelations: '[O]ne or two' and the adjective 'surprising' need to be followed by a noun, and 'one or two' requires the noun to be plural. Note that the 'a' of 'reveal' is omitted in 'revelation'.

23 historians: '[T]oday's' requires a noun, and 'who' shows that it refers to a person or people; 'they' in the following sentence makes it clear that the noun must be plural.

24 unacceptable: This is an adjective to describe 'approach'; 'even if' shows that there is going to be a contrast, so the negative 'unacceptable' is necessary, to contrast with the positive idea of 'give my comments a fair hearing'.

Reading and Use of English Part 4

The vertical line | shows where the answer is split into two parts for marking purposes.

25 CALL off the meeting / CALL the meeting off | unless When the second word in a transitive phrasal verb is an adverb (like 'off') rather than a preposition, it can go before or after a noun or noun phrase; however, if the object is a pronoun, the adverb must go after it ('call it off'). 'If' plus a negative ('if we can't') is equivalent to 'unless' plus a positive ('unless we can'), and vice versa ('if we can' = 'unless we can't').

26 turns/shows UP at parties | at every The phrasal verbs 'to turn/show up' can both mean 'to arrive or attend', usually to join a group of people. They are often applied to something unexpected. 'At every opportunity' is a fixed phrase meaning 'whenever it is possible'.

27 to POPULAR belief/opinion (,) | not 'Contrary' is followed by the preposition 'to'. 'Popular' refers to people in general, as opposed to the sense of being liked by many people. So 'popular belief' and 'popular opinion' mean something that most people believe.

28 is DUE to | (her/a) lack 'To be due to' introduces the cause (lack of money) of a state of affairs ('the shabbiness of Karen's clothes'); 'which is why' introduces the result. The noun 'lack' can be used with or without an article, possessive pronoun, etc.

29 until Sarah left | that the EXTENT 'Not until', like 'only when', implies surprise that the action didn't happen earlier. 'The extent of' expresses degree, and is equivalent to 'how much'.

30 it HARD | to get to 'It' is a dummy object, used to avoid the alternative structure, 'Jeremy found getting to grips with the sheer scale of the challenge he faced hard.'

Reading and Use of English Part 5

31 C The writer refers to several 'spooky theories', and contrasts them with the 'more plausible explanation' given by neuroscientists. A: Neuroscientists have pieced together an explanation, which shows they believe that people really have the experience. B: The writer claims that '[m]ost people' have had the experience, but there is no suggestion that scientists believe it is less common. D: The writer mentions all sorts of theories about 'non-scientific cause[s]', but does not comment on whether or not they can be disproved.

32 A The writer compares constructing a conscious experience out of components with manufacturing a car, and goes on to explain the complexity of an experience, pointing out that 'there is actually much more to it' than we are aware of. B and C: The writer argues that experiences are made up of many components, with no suggestion that B or C is the case. D: Other people play a part in bumping into someone, which is an example of an experience – there is no suggestion that other people always have a role.

33 D According to the writer, a feeling of recognition (familiarity) is usually attached to experiences that match memories, but is sometimes mistakenly attached to a new experience. A, B and C: These focus on emotions, but although the explanation involves the part of the brain that creates emotions, *déjà vu* is explained in terms of recognition, not emotion.

34 C The attribute is being quick to recognise things, which is useful because it may be a factor in intelligence. A: Although the brain being quick to recognise things is mentioned, there is no suggestion that this is related to a lack of patience. B: Level of education and *déjà vu* may both be caused to some extent by intelligence – the former doesn't cause the latter. D: *Déjà vu* is linked with the brain, not a person's environment.

35 B Moulin mentions a man as someone to whom *déjà vu* is a constant companion – a number of actual and potential experiences are mentioned that seem to him to repeat earlier ones. A: There is no indication of whether or not *déjà vu* can be treated. C: Watching TV is given as an example of the man's experience of *déjà vu*, but there is no suggestion that TV affects his condition. D: The man's attitude towards the condition is not specified, but the implication is that he found it disturbing, not comforting: he is mentioned as an example of 'an unfortunate few', with *déjà vu* as 'a serious blight', and in the next paragraph it is described as 'tedious'.

36 D 'And make sure that you don't sign on the dotted line until the moment has passed.' A: Both the writer and Moulin focus on dealing with situations of *déjà vu*, but don't suggest the experience is more likely to occur in specific situations which can be avoided. B: Moulin warns about the risk of trusting strangers and being exploited, but neither he nor the writer mentions evidence that they will not be exploited. C: Moulin advises sufferers to 'constantly remind themselves that the sensation is false', but doesn't mention checking with other people.

Reading and Use of English Part 6

37 C Reviewer B says the production tells us nothing about today's world, and according to reviewer C, it didn't make the setting modern. Reviewer A has a different opinion – 'Perhaps Barlow's intention was to hold up a mirror to the fragmentary nature of today's world, and if so, she could be said to have succeeded', and reviewer D believes the production shows 'the universality of the play's themes'.

38 C Reviewer C believes Mason gives insight into the character: 'His quirks and eccentricities convey the depth of Hamlet's despair, and his need to present a mask to the world.' The other three reviewers don't agree: reviewer A ends by saying 'As the final curtain fell, I realised I knew the character of Hamlet no better than I did at the beginning'; reviewer B says Mason's performance 'tells us nothing about Hamlet himself', and reviewer D implies something similar: 'he made it impossible for the audience to sympathise, let alone identify, with him.'

39 A Reviewer C ended up feeling positively towards Mason's delivery – 'By the end, I could have gone on listening to him for hours' and reviewer A believes Mason 'delivers his lines thrillingly'; in contrast, reviewer B doesn't warm to Mason's 'vocal tricks', and reviewer D calls his delivery 'a parody'.

40 D Reviewer A believes Barlow's 'great number of ingenious devices' don't fit together to make a coherent whole, but reviewer D has a positive view – Barlow comes close to confusing us 'but just stops short', and the reviewer describes the director's ideas as 'mind-boggling and exhilarating'. The other two reviewers agree with reviewer A: reviewer B calls the ideas 'a mishmash', and reviewer C finds her ideas 'highly distracting'.

Reading and Use of English Part 7

41 G 'By then' refers to when Mockridge died, and summarises his achievements, which are referred to in the following paragraph – 'this degree of success'.

42 B 'This impression of weakness' refers to Mockridge's shyness and difficulty with handling 'roughness'.

43 E 'Any laughter' is part of the officials' wonder and disbelief when they met Mockridge. 'Alex McPherson, who was timing the cyclists for the club' is mentioned again in the following paragraph ('The official').

44 C 'The next week, and the next, Mockridge again won' gives more detail about 'this was just the start of Mockridge's run of victories' in the previous paragraph.

45 F The phrase 'trailed well in the rear' means the same as 'lagged behind' in the previous paragraph, and 'get back to the matter in hand' refers to him starting to pedal again.

46 A '[T]he pair' refers to Mockridge and Goodwin.

Reading and Use of English Part 8

47 D The 'unexpected information' is about the flautist working 'rather incongruously' as a butler; although C refers to 'some surprising detail', it relates to 'several famous musicians', not just one.

48 B This section describes the procedure of Rowe's initial experiment, in which participants listen to a piece of music and then answer some questions, and of his follow-up experiment; 'data' refers to the findings of the experiments.

49 A '[T]he expectation that more scholars will be encouraged to investigate this fascinating resource.'

50 C One section of Saunderson's book will be devoted to extracts from the letters, 'presented on a month-by-month basis'.

51 D One of Hutchinson's aims is 'to share tips and resources, in order to help [musicians] to maximise their professional opportunities'.

52 C Saunderson is drawing on 'a recently discovered archive of unpublished letters'.

53 A The business context of opera houses in the first half of the 18th century includes 'their management, contracts with singers, musicians and composers, their working conditions and performance fees'.

54 C This section mentions the fact that 'musicians, painters, sculptors, intellectuals and many others contributed to a ferment of creativity that left its mark on all concerned'.

55 B Rowe's findings are related to 'current theories in psychology about the perception of time'.

56 A '[T]he materials are familiar to legal researchers.'

Writing Part 1

1 **Essay**

Model answer

This model has been prepared as an example of a very good answer. However, please note that this is just one example out of several possible approaches.

It seems that increasing numbers of people are choosing these days to leave their regular salaried job in order to become self-employed. But why do people choose to do so? What are the advantages of this way of life?

Firstly, perhaps the main attraction of being self-employed is that it leaves you in control of your own schedule. If you prefer to work late at night so that you can take the following day off to go to a concert at your child's school, then you can do so. You don't have to ask anyone's permission to leave the office whenever you wish.

A second major advantage of working for yourself is that you are in charge of all decisions connected with your business. When you're employed by someone else, you have to do what they wish, regardless of whether you feel it is the best course of action or not. To be in control of how you work is something that makes the self-employed lifestyle very attractive for many people.

Of the two advantages of being self-employed discussed above, the more significant one is the fact that you are in charge of your own timetable. To be able to spend time with friends and family when you wish to is worth sacrificing the regular monthly pay cheque for. As long as you can earn enough for your requirements, then you can enjoy the extra flexibility that self-employment allows far more than you would a bit of extra money in the bank.

Notes

- *Opening paragraph introduces the topic*
- *Two of the points are addressed and developed*
- *One of the advantages is chosen as more significant and an explanation is provided as to why this one was chosen*
- *The essay has a clear structure*
- *Appropriate register – not too informal*
- *Good use of collocation, e.g. 'major advantage', 'course of action', 'be worth sacrificing'*
- *Variety of sentence length and structure*
- *No language errors*
- *Correct length (252 words)*

Writing Part 2

2 **Proposal**

Model answer

This model has been prepared as an example of a very good answer. However, please note that this is just one example out of several possible approaches.

Research Proposal

This proposal is for a research project to be funded by one of the travel grants that you are currently offering students.

Nature of research

I am a doctoral student at the University of London and am preparing a thesis on the otter. My work is focusing on the extent to which humans have encroached on their habitat, and the impact that this has had on their population.

The project I should like to propose is for a study into the otter population in Sweden. It would involve travelling to Sweden in order to speak with the zoologists who specialise in working on otters there.

Sweden is a particularly interesting example in that the country has managed to halt the decline in its otter populations. Finding out exactly how this was brought about would have important implications for otter conservation in other areas too.

Benefits of the project

Carrying out the project outlined above would clearly be of benefit to my own personal research. However, that is not the reason why I am requesting a travel grant from you. I believe that if we can learn from the Swedish experience, then we will be more successful in conserving otters in this country, and so future generations will also have the opportunity to see this lovely creature.

I also believe that my contact with Swedish ecologists may turn out to be useful in terms of gaining knowledge about preserving other animals as well as the otter, and the more plants and animals we can prevent from becoming extinct the better.

Notes

- *Use of an appropriate title*
- *Opening paragraph sets the context*
- *All the points from the question are dealt with in the answer and are developed appropriately*
- *Clearly organised into paragraphs*
- *Demonstrates an ability to use more complex vocabulary, e.g. 'encroach', 'habitat', 'preserve', 'extinct'*
- *Variety of sentence length*
- *Appropriate register – no colloquialisms or other inappropriately informal language*
- *No language errors*
- *Correct length (259 words)*

3 **Letter**

Style

Neutral to formal

Your letter should use language that is appropriate for a letter to a magazine.

Content

Your letter should describe a national celebration held in your country. Your letter should explain why the celebration is enjoyable for the public and also why it has a socially useful purpose. You should try to make your points in a clear but persuasive way.

Organisation

Write in clearly defined paragraphs.

Include appropriate opening and closing formulae.

4 **Review**

Style

Neutral

Content

Your review should focus on a tourist destination that is familiar to you. This could be either a resort or a specific attraction such as a castle or a theme park. Your review must mention both positive and negative aspects of the destination and must suggest at least one way in which it could be made more appealing to tourists.

Organisation

Write in clearly defined paragraphs.

Listening Part 1

1 **C** The woman is worried that the choir's normal audience may not want to hear the music they've chosen to perform. She is not concerned about the choir or rehearsals.

2 **B** He should be designing the poster, but is finding it difficult, so he suggests that he does the programme instead.

3 **B** The man says northerners are friendlier than southerners in terms of starting a conversation with strangers, for example at a bus stop. However, he distinguishes this from long-term friendships.

4 **A** The woman thought going to a dance class would be a good way of making friends, but at first she was disappointed.

5 **B** The man thought he knew about the subject, but the programme included some information he wasn't aware of.

6 **C** The man thought the presenter spoke too slowly, but the woman thought he spoke at the right speed.

Listening Part 2

7 **pollution:** Caroline says rivers were turned into drains to carry away pollution caused by industry. Sewage had always been discharged into rivers, without the rivers being put in pipes.

8 **diseases:** This was a side effect, because it wasn't known at the time that putting rivers in pipes limited the spread of certain diseases.

9 **habitats:** Habitats for plants and fish require sunlight, which doesn't reach rivers in pipes.

10 **level:** Sections of pipes that don't meet accurately could cause problems for fish.

11 **blockage:** A blockage in a pipe could cause the water to collect behind it, potentially increasing the risk of flooding.

12 **block of flats:** A river underneath a block of flats washed away its foundations.

13 **documents:** Caroline says she is consulting old maps and documents that mention rivers.

14 **valleys:** Caroline says that by using software to show the contours of the land, along with old maps, she can find valleys that might contain a river.

Listening Part 3

15 **D** Giles originally intended to spend a year abroad, but realised while he was in Belgium that he needed to stay longer, in order to learn more about the people and what it's like to live in the country. He found work so as to support himself – it wasn't his purpose in going abroad.

16 **A** Penny discovered during the trip that she knows much less about the world than she thought, and Giles says he learnt more than he expected. Although they mention food, languages and talking to other people, there is nothing about them that they both found unexpected.

17 **A** Penny thinks it's sad when tourists aren't interested in the place where they're staying. On the whole, she believes that the effects of tourism on traditional crafts, infrastructure and a region's economy are positive.

18 **C** Giles turned down an invitation to go to Indonesia because of his sense of responsibility towards the owner of the café where he was working.

19 **C** He is applying to do a Master's degree in politics, which will help him to work in political journalism. He mentions working abroad as a possibility, not as something he has decided to do.

20 **B** Penny says that travelling gave her a new perspective, so she experienced culture shock when she returned home. She mentions being disappointed with other countries and having nothing left to look forward to as possible experiences which she didn't have. She mentions seeing old friends and doing what she used to do without saying whether or not it was a relief.

Listening Part 4

TASK ONE

21 **E** The man hardly listened to what the manager instructed him to do, because she didn't ask him politely. As a result, he did the wrong thing.

22 **H** She agreed to a customer's unreasonable demand, and left it to her line manager to deal with the problem.

23 **B** He says he once got it wrong when updating records.

24 **F** She didn't tell her boss that a colleague was using the internet for her own purposes, which was against company rules.

25 **A** He didn't realise who 'Jack' was when the latter called him.

TASK TWO

26 **H** The man enjoys going to customers to repair equipment, because in some cases he gets on well with their staff.

27 **E** The company uses the in-house newsletter to praise staff for particularly good work.

28 **B** The staff suffer from the same problems, so they cooperate and often get together in their free time.

29 **G** The office closes at lunchtime on Fridays. It is possible to work in the afternoon, although without being paid overtime.

30 **D** The man is satisfied when his clients value his advice.

Test 5 Transcript

Listening

This is Advanced Trainer *Test 5, Listening Part 1.*

I'm going to give you the instructions for this test. I will introduce each part of the test and give you time to look at the questions. At the start of each piece you will hear this sound:[tone]

You will hear each piece twice.

Remember, while you're listening, write your answers on the question paper. You will have five minutes at the end of the test to copy your answers onto the separate answer sheet.

There will now be a pause. Please ask any questions now, because you must not speak during the test.

Now open your question paper and look at Part 1.

PART 1

You will hear three different extracts. For questions 1 to 6, choose the answer (A, B or C) which fits best according to what you hear. There are two questions for each extract.

Extract 1

You hear two members of an amateur choir discussing a forthcoming concert.

Now look at questions 1 and 2.

Man: How do you think rehearsals are going for the choir's next concert?

Woman: Well, we're doing some really demanding pieces ...

Man: We certainly are!

Woman: ... and I have to wonder whether they might not be too challenging for our normal audience – ticket sales haven't picked up yet, and it isn't all that long till the performance. But as far as the choir's concerned, we're doing some thorough, detailed work in the rehearsals, and really getting to grips with the music, so we should master it all. It's a shame some people have had to miss rehearsals, though the extra one next weekend should make up for it.

Man: Right.

Woman: How are you getting on with designing the poster?

Man: Not too well, I'm afraid. I've been so busy I just haven't been able to make time for it. I started thinking about it this morning, and to be honest, I can't come up with an attention-grabbing image. Time's running short, so I was wondering if you could take care of it for me. Then I could concentrate on finishing off the programme instead – it doesn't need to go to the printer's for another couple of weeks, but the poster's getting urgent. What do you think?

Extract 2

You hear two people talking about making new friends.

Now look at questions 3 and 4.

Man: Hi, Claire. I haven't seen you for a long time.

Woman: Ah, that's because my company sent me to a branch in the north for six months.

Man: Oh! How was your social life while you were there? People are much friendlier in that part of the country than us southerners, aren't they? At least, whenever I've been there – if I've been waiting for a bus, say – someone will probably strike up a conversation, though that's as far as it went. Admittedly I've never been there for long enough to want to make friends for life, and that's a different thing altogether.

Woman: I tried to meet people. You know I used to go to a weekly tango class?

Man: Mm?

Woman: I found a class while I was there – bound to be a good way of meeting people with similar interests, I thought. At first, most people acknowledged my presence in the class, but whenever I suggested to anyone that we had a cup of tea afterwards, they muttered some excuse about not having time. It was very disappointing. But after a while they seemed to thaw, and it turned out all right in the end. In fact, I was quite sorry to leave.

Extract 3

You hear two friends discussing a television programme about genetics.

Now look at questions 5 and 6.

Woman: Did you see that TV programme yesterday about genetics?

Man: Yes, I did.

Woman: I found it fascinating. What did you make of it? As it's your field, you must already have known all about it.

Man: I wouldn't say that. In fact, I was impressed: some of the interviews with scientists were about research I wasn't aware of, and I'd thought I was keeping up with developments! Virtually everyone watching should have learnt something from it. And it was good how it managed to make some very complicated subject matter clear, so even people without any prior knowledge could understand.

Woman: Absolutely. I thought the way they demonstrated scientific principles using balloons, coloured water and so on was brilliant. It certainly helped me to understand.

Man: My only reservation was the presenter. He spoke so slowly I felt like shaking him!

Woman: Really? I was relieved! He gave me time to take in what he was saying, and think about it. Any faster, and I'd have been lost. I was glad the programme was just an hour long, though – I couldn't have concentrated for much longer.

Man: Well, I didn't have any problem concentrating, but an hour is quite long enough. And of course there's another part next week.

That is the end of Part 1.

Now turn to Part 2.

PART 2

You will hear a student called Caroline talking about her research project into rivers that have been made to flow underground. For questions 7 to 14, complete the sentences with a word or short phrase.

You now have 45 seconds to look at Part 2. You will need to play the recording twice.

Woman: Good morning. My name's Caroline MacArthur and I'd like to tell you a little about my research project into rivers that have been turned into underground streams. Of course, some rivers flow underground naturally, but I'm interested in the ones that have been put into pipes deliberately.

In Britain, a number of rivers were buried underground in large pipes during the Industrial Revolution of the 18th and 19th centuries. Rivers had always been used for sewage, but in this period, industry created pollution that affected lots of rivers, either deliberately or by accident. The aim was that it should be carried away by turning the river into a drain. One benefit, although this wasn't known at the time, was that covering rivers limited the spread of water-borne diseases. This led to significant improvements in the quality of people's lives.

Because underground rivers have no sunlight, plants can't photosynthesise, and so existing habitats were effectively destroyed, and there was no chance of new ones developing. In other words, the river ended up with no plants and no fish.

Another reason for the lack of wildlife was that when rivers were put into pipes, sections of pipe that were supposed to meet precisely didn't necessarily, and the difference in level could be great enough to prevent fish from passing along the stream.

Nowadays, we know covering rivers over isn't a particularly effective way of dealing with flooding. In fact, it can make the risk worse: one reason being that pipes may suffer a blockage, causing the water to back up. Similarly, if the pipe is under pressure from large amounts of flood water, it may collapse. In either case, serious damage is a potential outcome.

Let me give you an example. A few years ago, a block of flats had to be evacuated. What nobody knew was that a river flowed underneath it in a pipe. So, when a serious storm caused the pipe to collapse, the river spread out and washed away the foundations of the building, putting it at serious risk of falling down. It cost millions of pounds to demolish the building and construct a new one. Rather short-sightedly, perhaps, the river remained underneath the building, in a new pipe.

It's remarkable how few underground rivers are known, and identifying the unknown ones can be very difficult. I'm consulting old maps, of course, and I'm also looking at documents that mention rivers which aren't visible these days. Apart from that, I'm using software that shows the contours of the land, and maps where water would run if it flowed naturally through the landscape. Comparing the results of this with old maps predicts fairly accurately where there are valleys – often ones that aren't at all visible on the ground. And these often contain an underground river.

That is the end of Part 2.

Now turn to Part 3.

PART 3

You will hear an interview for a student magazine with Penny and Giles, who have both just returned to Britain after travelling around the world. For questions 15 to 20, choose the answer (A, B, C or D) which fits best according to what you hear.

You now have 70 seconds to look at Part 3. You will need to play the recording twice.

Interviewer: Penny, Giles, thank you both for coming. As I explained in my email, I'm planning to write an article for the university magazine about former students who've travelled round the world. Giles, lots of British people spend a year abroad, don't they, as Penny did.

Giles: Yes, that was my original plan, too, when I graduated, but it turned into five years. I first went to Belgium, intending to stay for a week then move on, but it soon dawned on me that all I'd get out of it would be a tourist's view. I'd know virtually nothing about the people, or what it's like to live in the country. So I got a temporary job as a waiter and decided to spend a few months in every country I visited. It would also give me the chance to develop my writing skills. You see, my ambition is to become a journalist, so I set a goal of producing three articles a week about the places I visited, and keeping them to see how my writing was improving.

Interviewer: Penny, did you have many surprises during your trip?

Penny: Oh yes! I've always been interested in the rest of the world, and thought I was reasonably well-informed. But the trip proved to me that actually I'm pretty ignorant. Food, for instance – I was amazed at the sheer variety in different places. I ate lots of delicious dishes.

Giles: I did too, though I've never been very adventurous when it comes to food. But I learnt so much more on the trip than I'd anticipated – about all sorts of things. I even managed to pick up a smattering of several languages. I really made an effort, because of course lots of people don't speak English.

Penny: Yes. I wouldn't have coped without all those people who listened patiently while I struggled to speak their language!

Interviewer: Did you meet many tourists on your travels?

Penny: I visited several tourist areas and was really struck by the impact that tourism has. All the new hotels, roads and other infrastructure. I suppose that benefits the local economy, as it creates jobs. And tourism even gives an impetus to traditional crafts to some extent, because visitors buy locally produced items as mementos. I don't have a problem with tourism if people are interested in the local culture and want to learn about the place, but so often they're only interested in sunbathing or playing golf, say, without any curiosity about the place or the residents. That's really sad.

Interviewer: Giles, are there incidents you could tell me about, that I could put in the article?

Giles: Well, I spent three months in Thailand, again working in a café, and met a group of young Australians who were also travelling, and we had a good time together. The day before they left for Indonesia, one of them said, 'Why not come with us?' Well, it was really tempting, because I love doing things without having to plan ahead. But that was the one occasion when I felt I had to say no, because I didn't want to let the café owner down at such short notice. It was a shame, but it was the right decision.

Interviewer: And do you now intend to try and break into journalism? You mentioned that was your plan.

Giles: That's right. But I've still got itchy feet, so I may go abroad to work on an English-language newspaper or magazine. Writing about travel seems the obvious thing to do, but I'm finding it repetitive. Actually, I developed an interest in politics during my trip, and I'd like to develop that further, so I'm applying to do a Master's degree, which I hope will be useful if I want to go into political journalism afterwards.

Interviewer: Penny, how did you feel when you finished your trip?

Penny: Travel has been my dream since I was a child, so it was great to spend a year abroad. But I knew that turning a dream into reality is risky. Foreign countries that seem exotic from a distance can be quite mundane when you're there, or you may feel you've achieved your dream too early in life, and there's nothing left to look forward to. Luckily, it wasn't like that for me. But I certainly experienced culture shock when I came home – going abroad had given me a totally new perspective. So I'm enjoying seeing old friends and doing the things I used to do – but I'm looking forward to going abroad again.

Interviewer: Giles, what did you find …

That is the end of Part 3.

Now turn to Part 4.

PART 4

Part 4 consists of two tasks. You will hear five short extracts in which people are talking about their jobs. Look at Task 1. For questions 21 to 25, choose from the list (A–H) the mistake that each speaker made in their job. Now look at Task 2. For questions 26 to 30, choose from the list (A–H) what each speaker particularly likes about their job. While you listen you must complete both tasks.

You now have 45 seconds to look at Part 4. You will need to play the recording twice.

Speaker 1

There are some people at work who seem to delight in making you feel small, and some, if they want you to do something, who wouldn't ask politely if their lives depended on it. That really makes me mad, and I can't listen to them. That was my downfall once, when a manager gave me a job to do, and I scarcely heard what she said. And of course, I got it wrong. On the other hand, there *are* advantages to working here. At least I get out of the office to repair equipment that other companies have bought from us. There are some firms where I get on well with their people, and we have a good laugh.

Speaker 2

The best thing about the company I work for is that they know they depend on the staff, so they do things like using the in-house newsletter to praise people who've done particularly well in the past month. We manufacture office equipment and sell it to other businesses. I'm in sales, and I strongly believe it's important to keep customers happy. So once, when the purchasing manager of a major client asked me for an impossibly big discount, instead of refusing, as I should have done, I chickened out and agreed. I thought I'd make him happy, and leave it to my line manager to deal with the fallout. I have to admit she was furious with me, and I can't blame her.

Speaker 3

We're chronically understaffed at work, and there are constant deadlines, so we're always under pressure, and the scope for making mistakes is enormous. My job is keeping records up-to-date, and practically the worst thing you can do is get it wrong. Well, that's only happened once, but boy, did my boss make me feel small. So now I work late several times a week, to keep on top of things. All the office staff at my level are in the same boat, of course, so we all pull together. We often get together outside work, too, mainly to celebrate birthdays. It's just as well our boss doesn't hear what we say about him, though!

Speaker 4

There are five of us in the office – we're practically in each other's pockets, and we all feel responsible for everything that happens. So when I realised a colleague was spending hours doing personal stuff on the internet, which we've been specifically banned from doing, I couldn't bring myself to do anything about it. When our boss discovered what was happening, and that I hadn't said anything, he was pretty annoyed, understandably. One nice thing is the office closes at lunchtime on Fridays. Customers are sometimes frustrated that we won't arrange meetings for that afternoon, but it's great to have the time off. People occasionally work into the afternoon, to catch up, but we aren't paid any extra for that.

Speaker 5

As a freelance business consultant, I work on my own. I'd quite like to have colleagues, but it's no big deal. I measure my success by whether my clients value my advice and turn to me next time they need help. And luckily most do. I'm always on the lookout for potential clients, and pride myself on making whoever I'm talking to feel they're the most important person in the world. It's good for business! Recently someone called me who I'd met a month previously, and just introduced himself as 'Jack' – not even his surname. He assumed I'd know at once who he was, but I didn't. He seemed very disappointed, and I may have lost him as a client.

That is the end of Part 4.

There will now be a pause of five minutes for you to copy your answers onto the separate answer sheet. Be sure to follow the numbering of all the questions. I will remind you when there's one minute left, so that you're sure to finish in time.

You have one more minute left.

That is the end of the test. Please stop now. Your supervisor will now collect all the question papers and answer sheets.

Test 6 Key

Reading and Use of English Part 1

1 B This means they exist everywhere, which fits with 'regardless of a person's country'. A: 'Thorough' describes something, such as a search, as being very detailed and careful. C: 'Sweeping' describes something that has an effect on many people, such as changes, generalisations, etc. – here, the writer doesn't say the association has an effect. D: 'Expansive' means 'covering a large area'.

2 D 'Country of origin' and 'place of origin' are fixed phrases. Although the other words also refer to the start of something, they are used in different contexts.

3 A 'To conduct' and 'to carry out' collocate with 'an experiment'.

4 A It means 'to cause something to happen', which fits the meaning of the sentence.

5 C It means 'to represent in the form of a map'; so the volunteers were asked to show on a 'map' of the body the places where they felt any stimulus.

6 B It means that the results were always, or almost always, the same, which fits the meaning of the sentence.

7 D It means 'improved'. The other options don't collocate with 'sensations'.

8 C It means 'physical or mental illnesses', which fits the meaning of the sentence and of the examples, depression and anxiety.

Reading and Use of English Part 2

9 on: This normally follows 'impact' to indicate what is affected by the impact.

10 which: This refers back to 'process'.

11 as: '[U]ndertaken as part of' shows that Scholes carried out this study in relation to his role in Berminton's project.

12 like: Here, 'like' introduces an example, and means 'such as'.

13 take: 'To take place' is a fixed phrase meaning 'to happen', 'to be held'.

14 may/might/could: One of these modal verbs followed by 'well' means 'it is very likely' – much more likely than with the modal verb alone.

15 Should: The inversion of the subject and modal verb ('Should this prove') is more formal than using 'if' and 'should' ('If this should prove'), and much more formal than 'if' without 'should' ('If this proves').

16 nothing/little: This means that Scholes believes awareness will be raised, even if little or nothing else is gained.

Reading and Use of English Part 3

17 unexpectedly: An adverb is required, to modify the verb 'has arisen'; 'unexpectedly' is the only adverb related to 'expect', and it is often used in relation to jobs becoming available.

18 technician/technologist: 'He or she' makes it explicit that the word refers to a person, and that it should be in the singular ('a' also indicates this). Usually, in this context, 'technician' is used to refer to someone with special skills, particularly in science or engineering.

19 installation/installing: '[T]he ... of' shows that a noun is required; 'installation' is more common in this structure than the gerund 'installing'. Although 'instal(l)ment' appears to come from the same root (historically this is not the case), it refers to payment of part of a debt, or sections of a story, neither of which fits the meaning of the sentence.

20 maintenance: Note the change of spelling in the root from 'tain' to 'ten'. This also applies to 'retain/retention' and 'detain/detention'.

21 desirable: An adjective is needed to describe '[f]ormal IT qualifications', in parallel with the adjective 'essential'. 'Desired' tends to be limited to fixed phrases, such as 'to have the desired effect'.

22 willingness: 'A' shows that a noun is needed. It means 'being happy to do something is necessary'. The noun 'will' can mean determination or mental power (as in 'the will to live', 'to have a strong will'), but doesn't quite fit this context.

23 excellence: A noun is needed as the direct object of 'to achieve' and it is modified by 'in every aspect of its activities'. Note the double 'l' in 'excellence' and 'excellent'.

24 employees: '[I]ts' needs a noun, and there are several that come from 'employ', including 'employer' and 'employment'. '[T]o be committed' suggests that its subject is likely to be a person or people. 'Employers' would refer to the company itself, so does not fit the sentence. '[A]ll' shows that if the noun is countable, it must be in the plural.

Reading and Use of English Part 4

The vertical line | shows where the answer is split into two parts for marking purposes.

25 was taken | ABACK at/by This is a phrasal verb meaning 'to greatly surprise someone'. In the passive, it can be followed by 'at' or 'by'.

26 empty/unoccupied | at the TIME of '[A]t the time of' is followed by a noun or *-ing* form, e.g. 'at the time of writing'.

27 DESPITE the company('s) | offering 'Despite' is a preposition, so it must be followed by a noun phrase or a structure using a present participle ('offering'). The subject of the present participle is 'the company'. In more formal use, the possessive 'company's' is possible.

28 give her a LIFT, | she would / she'd 'To give someone a lift' means to allow them to ride in your vehicle (usually a car), without charge; the sentence is in the form of a third conditional.

29 take any/much / a lot of | NOTICE of 'To take notice of' something means 'to pay attention to' it. 'Didn't take any notice' means 'paid no attention', so doesn't exactly match the first sentence, but 'paid little attention' is sometimes used to mean 'none, or almost none'.

30 opposition to the proposal | DATES back The possessive form of ('residents') shows that a noun is required; 'opposition' is usually followed by 'to' something; 'to date back to' is a phrasal verb, and refers to when something started (an alternative is 'to date from').

Reading and Use of English Part 5

31 D It would be 'humiliating' to come to the party (which here means 'produce a book to join existing ones') 'empty-handed', i.e. without contributing anything. A: She doesn't mention the difficulty of the task. B: She doesn't say she relied on other books when writing her own. C: She mentions the possibility that very few copies of her own book will be sold, but doesn't say that applies to all books on drama.

32 A Thornton hopes that her fascination and enthusiasm are 'catching', like an illness; in other words, that readers will start to feel the same way about drama as she does. B: She says that her book is unlikely to become a bestseller. C: She hopes people will buy the book 'whether or not they are persuaded by my opinions', so she seems content for some readers to disagree with her. D: She only refers to one emotional response to drama.

33 B She was 'infuriated' by Hyde's book because of his 'very circumscribed view'. A: There is no mention of any personal contact with Hyde. C: There is no suggestion that Hyde's book opened her eyes to anything. D: Hyde distinguished between good and bad drama, but based on criteria that Thornton disagrees with.

34 A Thornton spent five years researching and writing the book, because of the 'serious gaps' in her knowledge. B: She doesn't mention any difficulties in carrying out her research. C: Ancient Greek and Roman drama is her 'particular field', but the book has a much greater scope – hence the need for a lot of research. D: She mentions how she felt the morning after deciding to write the book, but not how she feels now.

35 C She tried to make her work 'recognised and appreciated by many' – that was 'the road [she] went down'. A: An academic book 'would attract a tiny readership', but she wants more readers than that. B: Detailed information about sources would be part of an academic book, but that was not what she decided to write. D: She mentions promotion in relation to writing an academic book, but that was not what she decided to write.

36 D The questions that she has tried to answer relate the plays to their audiences. A: She mentions tracing the development of each genre over the centuries, but abandons that approach in favour of what she 'finally opted for'. B: She decided against doing this because 'so many of [the playwrights] are anonymous'. C: This 'had a certain appeal', but she finally opted for a different approach.

Reading and Use of English Part 6

37 B Larry Jones claims that if a new airport is constructed, 'the current airports wouldn't then require new runways', while Karen Macmillan disagrees: 'it will only be a matter of time before expansion of the existing airports will become inevitable'. Neither Bernie Dodd nor Isabel Smith expresses an opinion on the matter.

38 C Both Isabel Smith and Bernie Dodd oppose the destruction of wildlife habitats. Larry Jones argues that the destruction is necessary, and Karen Macmillan implies that it is necessary, but hopes the the harm caused can be limited ('mitigated').

39 A Isabel Smith and Larry Jones believe larger planes will become available, limiting any increase in the number of flights. Karen Macmillan and Bernie Dodd strongly suggest that the number of flights will continue to grow.

40 C Bernie Dodd dismisses the claim that a new airport would reduce noise and improve air quality in London. The other three experts believe a new airport would save Londoners from extra pollution.

Reading and Use of English Part 7

41 E 'One of these ... a leading mathematician' can only refer to one of a number of people, that is, Ada's 'succession of tutors'. '[T]he leading scientists of the day' is picked up by 'Among their number' and the introduction of Babbage in the following paragraph.

42 G 'This mechanical calculator' in G and '[t]he device' in the following paragraph both refer to the Difference Engine. As this is 'Babbage's first invention', the calculator can't be the later and more advanced Analytical Engine.

43 A '[T]his prototype' refers to Babbage's first invention, the Difference Engine, and the scientific conference in Italy is picked up by 'this event' in the next paragraph.

44 D '[T]hem' refers to the notes which Lovelace wrote. '[T]his insight' relates to her suggestion that the device should be able to compose music.

45 C 'Unlike him' contrasts what 'Lovelace realised' – what 'she saw' in the previous paragraph – with Babbage's more limited insight. '[T]he document' is her translation of the memoir, mentioned earlier and also in the next paragraph.

46 F The explanation of '[t]his realisation' adds to the statement in the previous paragraph concerning software. This idea is new and strange 'for the time', that is, 'for such an early stage in the history of the computer.'

Reading and Use of English Part 8

47 C The writer points out both that the customer's family and friends are more likely to hear about poor service than the managers or owner of a store; and writing 'without inhibition' in product reviews implies that customers are more inhibited if they are speaking to staff.

48 A If customers feel that staff ignore them, or treat them as an inconvenience, the feeling makes them unwilling to buy.

49 D The writer says that discussing alternatives ('different options') leads to a win-win situation ('a positive outcome for both sides').

50 B The writer says that 'going the extra mile' (i.e. doing more than the minimum) can make customers loyal to the company, meaning that they will shop there a number of times in the future.

51 D The writer advises staff to listen to a customer who is dissatisfied, and to discuss different options for dealing with the situation.

52 C The writer says that bad experiences are not easy to forget.

53 A The writer mentions face-to-face, phone and email contact with customers.

54 B According to the writer, if the employee is polite in their initial greeting on the phone, the client will usually be more agreeable.

55 D The writer points out that in some cases a customer who is complaining is frustrated by something unconnected with the store.

56 A The writer mentions satisfied customers 'creating new customers' and acting as 'an effective referral system for future customers'. They are described as essential to the business – its 'life blood'.

Writing Part 1

1 Essay

Model answer

This model has been prepared as an example of a very good answer. However, please note that this is just one example out of several possible approaches.

Natural resources are, on the whole, finite, and it is important to make sure that we do not waste them. For the sake of future generations, we must use them wisely. But how can we ensure that we do this?

Unfortunately perhaps, the most successful method is undoubtedly to make the wasteful use of resources a criminal offence. Some countries already fine citizens who put recyclable waste into bins intended for landfill sites, and such legislation should be used more widely. Companies, in particular, should be prosecuted if they do not have a responsible attitude towards scarce resources.

Secondly, the media should take a much more active role in encouraging people to use resources well. Resources are often wasted because the public do not appreciate how scarce they are or how serious the implications of their overuse are for our descendants. So there need to be regular stories in the papers or documentaries on television presenting not only information about how wastefulness is endangering the future but also examples of good practice. In this way, people will be given the information that they need in order to make a difference themselves.

Of the two ways of encouraging appropriate resource use discussed above, the more effective is, in my opinion, the legislative approach. Media campaigns have a very important role to play but, human nature being what it is, making wasteful use of scarce resources illegal is more likely to have an effect than simply educating the public through the media.

Notes

- *Opening paragraph introduces the topic*
- *Two of the points are addressed and developed*
- *One of the benefits is chosen as more significant, and an explanation is provided as to why this one was chosen*
- *The essay has a clear structure*
- *Appropriate register – not too informal*
- *Good range of vocabulary, e.g. 'recyclable waste', 'endangering', 'should be prosecuted', 'how serious the implications ... are for ...'*
- *Variety of sentence length and structure*
- *No language errors*
- *Correct length (250 words)*

Writing Part 2

2 Proposal

Style

Neutral to formal

Your proposal should use language that is appropriate for a piece of writing in a work context.

Content

Your proposal should state clearly what people do at your workplace, providing an explanation as to why this might interest TV viewers. It should also make some specific suggestions as to the approach the programme might take, e.g. you might suggest interviews with key people or focusing on one particular department in the workplace.

Organisation

Write in clearly defined paragraphs.

Include a title and headings.

3 **Review**

Model answer

This model has been prepared as an example of a very good answer. However, please note that this is just one example out of several possible approaches.

> **Have Fun at Panton Pool**
>
> Panton Swimming Pool is an excellent swimming pool. The main pool is Olympic-sized and there is also a smaller pool for young children. The facilities therefore are suitable both for the serious swimmer preparing for competitions and for families just wanting to have fun. The best thing about the pool is the fact that its walls are almost entirely glass. The building is set in a park surrounded by trees and so, as you swim, you have wonderful views and can almost imagine you are swimming out of doors.
>
> It is conveniently located near the town centre, and I use it regularly before work. I swim for pleasure and to keep fit. After my swim, I often enjoy a cup of coffee in a pleasant little café there. The café serves delicious soup and sandwiches and, even when I'm not planning to go in the water, I sometimes meet a friend there for a snack and a chat. The facilities there also include a small shop where you can buy costumes, swimming caps and goggles, as well as a few other items, such as sports bags and towels, that might be of interest to users of the pool.
>
> The one aspect of the pool I should like to see improved is the changing area. The cubicles are cramped, and there are not enough lockers, particularly as several of them always seem to be out of use with broken locks or hinges.
>
> But once in the water, you should certainly have a thoroughly enjoyable time at the Panton Swimming Pool.

Notes

- *Use of an appropriate title*
- *Opening paragraph sets the context*
- *All the points from the question are dealt with in the answer and are developed appropriately*
- *Clearly organised in paragraphs*
- *Good range of vocabulary relating to swimming*
- *Shows ability to construct more complex sentences, e.g. 'The best thing about the pool is the fact that its walls are almost entirely glass' and 'The one aspect of the pool I should like to see improved is the changing area'*
- *Variety of sentence length*
- *Appropriate register – neither very formal nor very informal*
- *No language errors*
- *Correct length (260 words)*

4 **Report**

Style

Neutral to formal

Content

Your report should be about an electronic gadget. The specific gadget should be named at the beginning of the report. The report must explain what the gadget can do, as well as how you yourself use it. It should also include an explanation of the extent to which it meets your needs. You should try to express your ideas clearly and constructively. It does not matter whether you describe a gadget that basically suits all your needs or one that is unsatisfactory in some way.

Organisation

Write in clearly defined paragraphs.

Include a title and sub-headings.

Listening Part 1

1 A B: The man says he will be going to somewhere fairly near the town where he grew up. He doesn't say that is his reason for applying for the job. C: He isn't sure he wants the extra responsibility.

2 C A: His house is in an area where a lot of people want to live. B: He says the house has a garden and garage, which people seem to expect.

3 A B: He thought the novel ended at a logical point in the story. C: He had difficulty with the style at first, but gradually started enjoying it very much.

4 C A: The book has been shortlisted for a prize for fiction – it hasn't won it. B: One of the other people in her book club recommended it.

5 B A: The woman is prepared to keep the dishwasher. C: She implies that they wouldn't be justified in asking for a refund because the shop hadn't *promised* to deliver the dishwasher in the morning.

6 C A: The woman mentions the complicated controls, but the man thinks they would get used to them. B: The man is concerned about having enough space in the kitchen, but the woman suggests moving a cupboard to make room for the cooker.

Listening Part 2

7 **security:** Gavin talks about the lack of job security that affects most football managers.

8 **name(-)plate:** Only the word 'Manager', without his name, is on the nameplate on his office door.

9 **rented accommodation:** He says many managers rent somewhere to live, but his home is close enough for him to live there and commute to work.

10 **resources:** Apart from some of the best-known clubs, most have very few resources, such as money, staff and equipment.

11 **dressing rooms:** He painted all the dressing rooms last summer, while his wife painted some of the offices.

12 **recruitment:** He says recruitment, particularly of players, is the most important part of his job.

13 **reporters / the press:** Gavin says he enjoys the conversations with reporters at the regular press conferences.

14 **ball control:** Yesterday's training session concentrated on ball control; practice for the goalkeepers was included, without being the main focus of the session.

Listening Part 3

15 D A: Jane refers to new shops in Buckworth East, but doesn't mention more customers using the existing ones in the village. B: The development only provides the new housing required for Buckworth, so it won't reduce the amount of new housing that the council wants in other villages. C: She mentions new shops and other facilities in Buckworth East, but doesn't say it will be a self-supporting community.

16 **A** B: Jane says many new residents will be able to walk to work. C: She says that jobs will be created on the site, but not that there will be too few. D: She says parking has been dealt with by providing a high ratio of garages to homes.

17 **D** A: He says he doesn't think concerns about the protection of animals and trees are justified. B: A bus company is planning a service to Buckworth East. C: He says the number of new homes has been reduced, but doesn't comment on the new number.

18 **A** B: Jane says objections have to be considered, and some projects have to go ahead despite the objections, but doesn't say it is necessary to explain why. C and D: She says most objectors are reasonable people, holding sincere views, but doesn't comment on the accuracy of their information or on a need to evaluate their motives.

19 **C** A: She mentions a proposed community centre, but it can't be built. B: She talks about the possibility of new residents joining existing clubs, without commenting on their level of interest. D: She says she expects new clubs to be started in Buckworth East, but that existing clubs will continue.

20 **B** A: The interviewer says some people think their objections have been overruled, but contrasts these with 'the vast majority'. C: He says there is little awareness of the opportunities. D: Some people believe village life will be damaged, but the interviewer contrasts these with 'the vast majority'.

Listening Part 4

TASK ONE

21 **D** The man says that the firm he worked for had a foreign owner (parent company). He moved to the parent company's head office in the foreign country, to join a team consisting of staff from around the world.

22 **B** A university in another country offered the woman a position.

23 **F** He thought that if he went abroad, he might find more job opportunities than at home.

24 **H** The university where the man worked invited him to teach on its new overseas campus.

25 **A** The woman thought the research position would look good on her CV – that is, it would make her an attractive candidate when she applied for jobs later on.

TASK TWO

26 **H** He says that not having much money made him realise a lot of the things he used to spend money on were unnecessary.

27 **C** The woman discovered that she wasn't as open to new experiences or as flexible as she had thought.

28 **A** The man realised that he had been wrong to think his job such an important part of his life. He was pleased that his job abroad gave him time to develop his interest in painting.

29 **G** Living abroad made him realise what came easily to him and what didn't.

30 **F** She says that she and her old friends were living different sorts of lives and had less and less in common.

Test 6 Transcript

Listening

This is Advanced Trainer *Test 6, Listening Part 1.*

I'm going to give you the instructions for this test. I will introduce each part of the test and give you time to look at the questions. At the start of each piece you will hear this sound:[tone]

You will hear each piece twice.

Remember, while you're listening, write your answers on the question paper. You will have five minutes at the end of the test to copy your answers onto the separate answer sheet.

There will now be a pause. Please ask any questions now, because you must not speak during the test.

Now open your question paper and look at Part 1.

PART 1

You will hear three different extracts. For questions 1 to 6, choose the answer (A, B or C) which fits best according to what you hear. There are two questions for each extract.

Extract 1

You hear two friends discussing a new job that the man is about to start.

Now look at questions 1 and 2.

Woman: I hear you've got a new job, Donald. Congratulations!

Man: Thanks, Liz.

Woman: But I gather it'll mean moving.

Man: Yes, back to Scotland, which is where I grew up. Fairly near the same town. I'll be able to go mountaineering as often as I like – it's only a short drive to my favourite area. That's the main reason I applied.

Woman: And is it a better job than you've got now?

Man: Well, it's higher up the ladder, and the pay's better, but I'm not totally convinced I'm ready for the extra responsibility.

Woman: I'm sure you'll manage! So I suppose you'll be selling your house.

Man: Yes, in fact, I've had it on the market for a few weeks now. It's quite a difficult property to sell, despite being in a sought-after area, because in terms of size and price it's suitable for first-time buyers – young married couples, in particular – but it's quite quirky. It's easier to sell a standard, small three-bedroom house, and in mine the rooms are irregular shapes, and the bathroom's downstairs, rather than in the usual place.

Woman: But you've got a garden and a garage, haven't you?

Man: Oh yes, which is just as well, because people seem to expect them, these days.

Extract 2

You hear two friends discussing a novel.

Now look at questions 3 and 4.

Woman: I've just bought this novel, Harry. Do you know it?

Man: Yes. In fact, I've just finished reading it.

Woman: Oh, do tell me what you thought of it.

Man: Well, it's written in a pretty idiosyncratic style. It took me several chapters to see what the author was doing, and why, but then I was hooked. In fact, I enjoyed the book so much that when I came to the end, I wanted to find out more – what happened to the characters in the rest of their lives! Even though it ended at a logical point in the story.

Woman: I've heard the hero is very complex.

Man: Yes. I could see a lot of myself in him, which was one reason I enjoyed it. I wouldn't have thought it's your sort of novel, though.

Woman: Perhaps it isn't, but one of the people at my book club mentioned it and praised it to the skies, and I really like other books by the same novelist, so even though this is supposed to be very different from what she's done before, I must read it. And it's been shortlisted for a fiction prize, so obviously a lot of people think it's good.

Extract 3

You hear a husband and wife discussing new appliances for their home.

Now look at questions 5 and 6.

Man: I think we should ring the shop about the dishwasher. After all, we paid extra for delivery, and it was very inconvenient having to wait all day. They ought to refund the money.

Woman: To be fair, they only said they'd try to come in the morning, but they couldn't promise. What annoys me is that the leaflet they gave me was very inaccurate. They really should revise it so other people don't get misled. I can understand them not having every model in stock, but it meant I could only go by what the leaflet said. I really think I should give them a call about it tomorrow.

Man: Why? Would you have chosen a different model?

Woman: Probably, but I suppose I can live with this one. Now what about the cooker I want? Have you looked it up online?

Man: Yes. It's much bigger than our present one.

Woman: I'm sure we could move a cupboard to create more space. My only reservation is that it looks quite daunting – all those controls!

Man: We'd get used to them. But do you think it's worth spending so much on it? We're away a lot, and often have cold food at home – isn't the old cooker good enough?

Woman: Hmm, you've got a point. OK, let's forget that idea.

That is the end of Part 1.

Now turn to Part 2.

PART 2

You will hear Gavin McFarland, the manager of a football club, talking to some students about his work. For questions 7 to 14, complete the sentences with a word or short phrase.

You now have 45 seconds to look at Part 2. You will need to play the recording twice.

Man: Hello. I'm Gavin McFarland, and I gather you're interested in hearing about the life of a football manager. Well, I manage a not-very-successful team, and if I don't put you off it as a career, nothing will!

Let me start with the worst thing about the work, and it affects most managers. My job security is extremely limited. I'm the club's eighth manager in ten years, and I'll almost certainly get fired if the team continues to do badly. If I'm lucky, and they begin to show signs of life, I might be told I can stay till the end of the season – with no guarantees beyond that. In fact, on my office door, there's a nameplate that simply says 'Manager': no name permitted, no need to replace it for the next manager.

For that reason, many managers live apart from their families, in rented accommodation – there's no point in going through the upheaval of moving to another town if you'll probably have to move again months later. I'm lucky – my home is a half-hour drive away, so I can live there.

Then if your club isn't very well off, with hardly any staff or equipment – and very few have the resources of some of the best-known clubs – you'll find yourself doing all sorts of things, simply because there's nobody else, and you can't afford to bring someone in. Last summer, my wife painted some of the offices – and let me assure you, she wasn't paid for that – while it fell to me to paint the dressing rooms – the whole lot. Not a bad job, but not what I was expecting when I became a football manager!

Right, I'd better go on to the nitty gritty of the job. At the heart of it is recruitment – particularly of players, of course. I knew I'd be judged on the basis of the first player I brought in – I simply had to get it right, or I'd soon be out on my ear. Night after night I went to watch matches around the country, to look for talent and, hopefully, persuade a player I could see had potential to join us. The first player I signed up has been very good for us. Since then, I've brought in two more guys, and they're doing well. Long may it continue!

Another interesting part of the job is the regular press conferences. We time them so they don't coincide with the ones held by bigger clubs in the region – otherwise we wouldn't manage to attract any reporters at all. As it is, we're lucky to get more than half a dozen. I enjoy the conversation – some of them really want to catch you out, and making sure you don't say anything you shouldn't is quite a challenge!

I'm normally involved in training sessions, along with the coach. Two days ago, we worked the players into the ground, so yesterday we gave them a fun session, concentrating on ball control, and ending up with some practice for the goalkeepers.

OK, now it's time to...

That is the end of Part 2.

Now turn to Part 3.

PART 3

You will hear an interview on local radio with Jane Robinson, the Public Relations Officer of a company developing a former air base. For questions 15 to 20, choose the answer (A, B, C or D) which fits best according to what you hear.

You now have 70 seconds to look at Part 3. You will need to play the recording twice.

Man: Next on the programme, we discuss the proposed Buckworth East development. As we all know, the air force has vacated its base in the village of Buckworth, and the site is about to be developed under the name Buckworth East. The plan is for 250 new houses and premises for small businesses. With me now is Jane Robinson, PR Officer for the development company. OK, Jane, what's so good about this development?

Woman: Quite a lot, actually. The council wants 5,000 new homes to be built in the whole area over the next ten years. That'll mean new housing estates in lots of local villages, which will have a major impact on existing facilities, like schools; not to mention the quality of life of the residents of the villages. The old airforce site is large enough to provide all the new housing that the council wants in Buckworth. Villagers will benefit, too, as the new shops, etcetera, in Buckworth East will provide extra facilities for residents.

Man: Mm, but isn't it true that a lot of people are against this development?

Woman: Yes, but they're overlooking the positive aspects. The new residents will probably have cars, and yes, they'll add to traffic flows, but the creation of jobs on the site will mean many residents will be able to walk to work, so they won't add to rush-hour travel. And there'll be a high ratio of garages to housing units, so parking has been dealt with. Then a third of the new homes will be sold at little more than cost price. Unfortunately, that's still beyond many potential purchasers' means, but that's a national problem rather than one specific to Buckworth.

Man: But local people are unhappy with quite a lot of aspects of the plan, aren't they? I know the initial proposal of 500 new homes has been scaled down, but surely there's a need for suitable premises for a playgroup and nursery: the ones in the village are far too small. It's been pointed out that public transport to the site is very limited, though I understand a bus company has announced it will modify existing services to call at Buckworth East. Something else that's been raised, though I don't feel this is justified, is that insufficient attention is being paid to protecting animals and trees on the site.

Woman: Let's face it, there are always people who'll object, because there's a downside to everything. I'm sure most of them are perfectly reasonable people, with sincerely held views, but if every project was cancelled because somebody objected, nothing would ever be done, and we wouldn't have enough homes or jobs. And they're surely fundamental entitlements for everyone. Of course, we have to consider all objections carefully, but there's a limit to how far they can be met.

Man: OK. How do you envisage relations between the residents of Buckworth East and of the village, Jane?

Woman: It's perhaps unfortunate that the site is physically slightly separated from the village, er, with what will be a public park between them, so there's a built-in division. But it certainly isn't inconceivable that they'll become a single unit in due course, given goodwill on both sides. To a certain extent, it's up to the current villagers. They should actively encourage new residents to get involved by joining existing clubs, like the historical association and the gardening club. We *had* hoped that the new community centre which we proposed for land between the two areas would have helped to solve potential problems, but the council refused planning permission, so that won't happen. It remains to be seen, when the new residents move in, how soon a sense of community develops, but my guess is that new clubs will spring up on the site, perhaps in competition with existing ones. Don't forget, Buckworth East will have a larger population than the existing village.

Man: The council has just published the results of a survey of Buckworth villagers. Have you had a chance to look at them?

Woman: No, I haven't.

Man: There seems to be little awareness of the benefits the development will bring them, like additional jobs and shops. Some people claim that the council has simply ignored their objections, and perhaps it's the same people who see it as the destruction of village life. The vast majority, though, are fatalistic: they know there's a need for additional housing in the area, and wish none of it was going to be in Buckworth, but recognise that the air base is a more suitable site than covering the countryside with new houses. So it's a necessary evil.

That is the end of Part 3.

Now turn to Part 4.

PART 4

Part 4 consists of two tasks. You will hear five short extracts in which people are talking about living in a foreign country. Look at Task 1. For questions 21 to 25, choose from the list (A–H) the reason why each speaker moved abroad. Now look at Task 2. For questions 26 to 30, choose from the list (A–H) what each speaker mentions about their experience of living abroad. While you listen you must complete both tasks.

You now have 45 seconds to look at Part 4. You will need to play the recording twice.

Speaker 1

Ever since university, I'd been a software engineer for the same firm, which had a foreign owner. Then the parent company offered staff in its subsidiaries around the world the opportunity to join a new team, based in their head office. I liked the idea, and my wife was keen, too, so I applied, and was given a six-month contract. The company only offered a limited relocation package, so we didn't take much with us. On top of that, the pay wasn't brilliant. It was hard to cope at first, but eventually it dawned on me that I didn't really need half the things I used to spend my money on.

Speaker 2

I've just come back from five years abroad – and not a moment too soon. I'd always boasted I was open to new experiences and pretty flexible, but boy, was I wrong! Almost everything was different from home, and I really missed the security of knowing what to do in most situations, without needing to think about it. I was really enthusiastic at first, though in retrospect I suppose I felt flattered that I'd been headhunted. Without wanting to sound arrogant, I had quite a good reputation in my field – I'm a geologist – so when a university in another country offered me a position, I was interested. My husband was happy about it, too, so we went.

Speaker 3

When I graduated, I couldn't get a job that fitted my career plans, and ended up as a paper pusher. It was humdrum work, with no prospects, and I felt trapped. Then a friend suggested going abroad. I had nothing to lose and thought there might be openings that didn't exist at home. My partner liked the idea, and we headed off, and both got jobs that covered the rent, but not much more. It was wonderful, and I realised my priorities had been wrong. OK, so my job was fairly tedious, but I had time for other things. I'd always dabbled in painting, and now I started taking it seriously. That more than makes up for an unfulfilling job.

Speaker 4

Living abroad taught me a lot. I've never described myself as introspective, but I spent a lot of time on my own while I was there, as I didn't have any family, and I don't make friends easily. And all the demands of living in a different environment highlighted what came easily to me, and of course what didn't. It was rather an eye-opener, to be honest. The reason I'd gone was that the university where I had a research position opened a campus overseas, and I was one of the people they approached about teaching there. Well, I was keen on the idea, the pay was good, so I said yes, and I'm glad I went.

Speaker 5

I'd finished studying, and my job applications were getting nowhere. Then I saw a research position abroad that would look really good on my CV, so I went all out to get it. A couple of eminent academics in my field agreed to be my referees, and I was offered the post on a three-year contract. It wasn't at all the type of environment I was used to. Some things were better than at home, others worse, but on balance the positives outweighed the negatives. But because I was living a very different sort of life from my friends at home, we seemed to have less and less in common. In some cases, we completely drifted apart.

That is the end of Part 4.

There will now be a pause of five minutes for you to copy your answers onto the separate answer sheet. Be sure to follow the numbering of all the questions. I will remind you when there is one minute left, so that you're sure to finish in time.

You have one more minute left.

That is the end of the test. Please stop now. Your supervisor will now collect all the question papers and answer sheets.

Sample answer sheet: Reading and Use of English

53114

OFFICE USE ONLY - DO NOT WRITE OR MAKE ANY MARK ABOVE THIS LINE

Cambridge Assessment English

Candidate Name		Candidate Number	
Centre Name		Centre Number	
Examination Title		Examination Details	
Candidate Signature		Assessment Date	

Supervisor: If the candidate is ABSENT or has WITHDRAWN shade here O

Advanced Reading and Use of English Candidate Answer

Part 1

1	A O	B O	C O	D O
2	A O	B O	C O	D O
3	A O	B O	C O	D O
4	A O	B O	C O	D O
5	A O	B O	C O	D O
6	A O	B O	C O	D O
7	A O	B O	C O	D O
8	A O	B O	C O	D O

Instructions

Use a PENCIL (B or HB).

Rub out any answer you want to change using an eraser.

Parts 1, 5, 6, 7 and 8:

Mark ONE letter for each question.

For example, if you think A is the right answer to the question, mark your answer sheet like this:

0 A B C

Parts 2, 3 and 4: Write your answer clearly in CAPITAL LETTERS.

For parts 2 and 3, write one letter in each box

0 EXAMPLE

Part 2

		Do not write below here
9		9 1 O 0 O
10		10 1 O 0 O
11		11 1 O 0 O
12		12 1 O 0 O
13		13 1 O 0 O
14		14 1 O 0 O
15		15 1 O 0 O
16		16 1 O 0 O

Continues over →

OFFICE USE ONLY - DO NOT WRITE OR MAKE ANY MARK BELOW THIS LINE

Page 1 of 2

53114

Sample answer sheet: Reading and Use of English

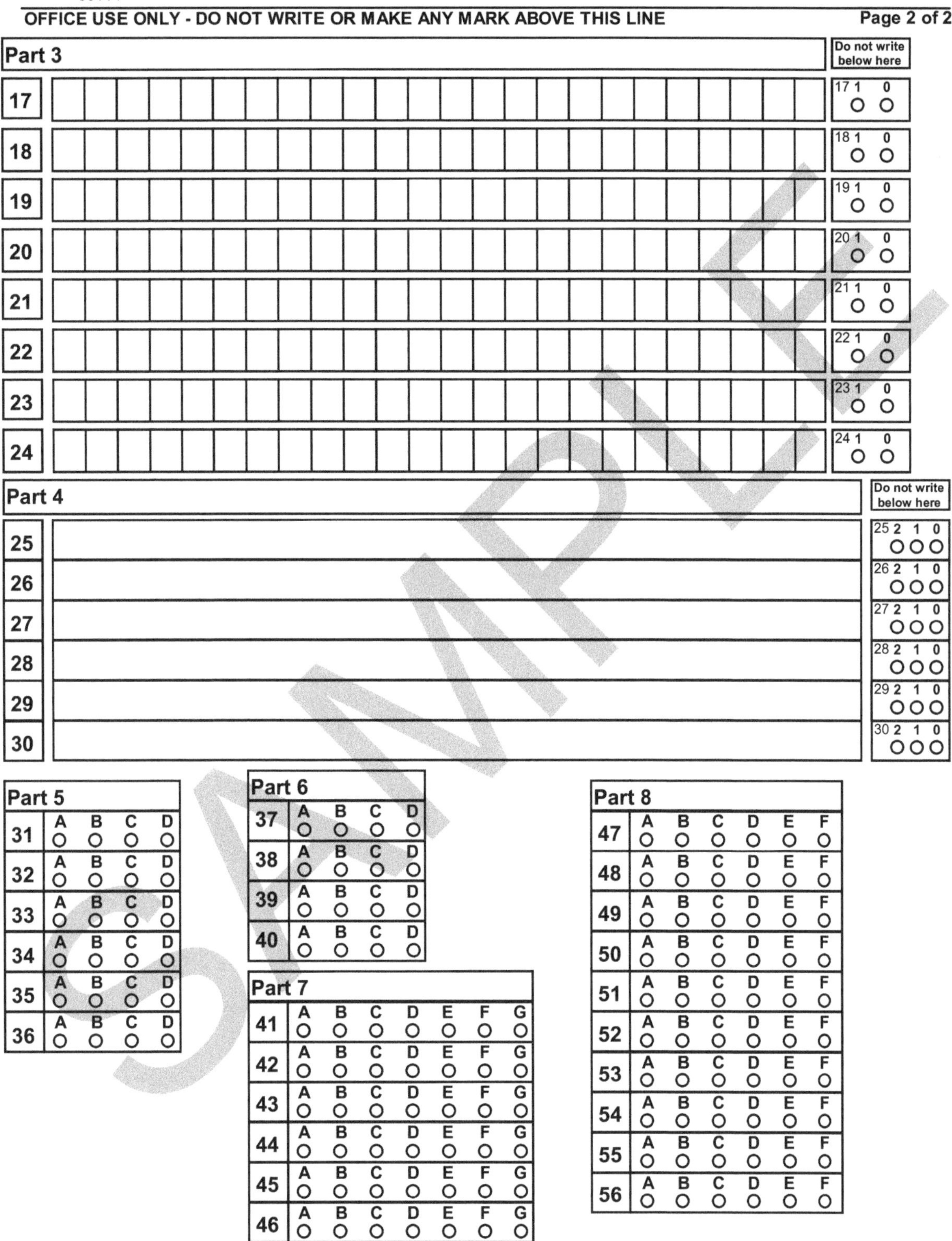
53114

OFFICE USE ONLY - DO NOT WRITE OR MAKE ANY MARK ABOVE THIS LINE

Page 2 of 2

Part 3 — Do not write below here: 17–24 (1 / 0)

Part 4 — Do not write below here: 25–30 (2 / 1 / 0)

Part 5: 31–36 (A B C D)

Part 6: 37–40 (A B C D)

Part 7: 41–46 (A B C D E F G)

Part 8: 47–56 (A B C D E F)

OFFICE USE ONLY - DO NOT WRITE OR MAKE ANY MARK BELOW THIS LINE

Page 2 of 2

53114

Sample answer sheet: Listening

1036

OFFICE USE ONLY - DO NOT WRITE OR MAKE ANY MARK ABOVE THIS LINE

Cambridge Assessment English

Candidate Name		Candidate Number	
Centre Name		Centre Number	
Examination Title		Examination Details	
Candidate Signature		Assessment Date	

Supervisor: If the candidate is ABSENT or has WITHDRAWN shade here O

Advanced Listening Candidate Answer Sheet

Instructions

Use a PENCIL (B or HB).

Rub out any answer you want to change using an eraser.

Parts 1, 3 and 4:

Mark ONE letter for each question.

For example, if you think **A** is the right answer to the question, mark your answer sheet like this:

0 A B C

Part 2:

Write your answer clearly in CAPITAL LETTERS.

Write one letter or number in each box.

If the answer has more than one word, leave one box empty between words.

For example:

0 NUMBER 12

Turn this sheet over to start

OFFICE USE ONLY - DO NOT WRITE OR MAKE ANY MARK BELOW THIS LINE

Page 1 of 2

1036

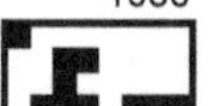

Sample answer sheet: Listening

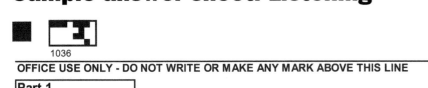

1036

OFFICE USE ONLY - DO NOT WRITE OR MAKE ANY MARK ABOVE THIS LINE

Part 1

1	A O	B O	C O
2	A O	B O	C O
3	A O	B O	C O
4	A O	B O	C O
5	A O	B O	C O
6	A O	B O	C O

Part 2 (Remember to write in CAPITAL LETTERS or numbers)

		Do not write below here
7		7 1 O 0 O
8		8 1 O 0 O
9		9 1 O 0 O
10		10 1 O 0 O
11		11 1 O 0 O
12		12 1 O 0 O
13		13 1 O 0 O
14		14 1 O 0 O

Part 3

15	A O	B O	C O	D O
16	A O	B O	C O	D O
17	A O	B O	C O	D O
18	A O	B O	C O	D O
19	A O	B O	C O	D O
20	A O	B O	C O	D O

Part 4

21	A O	B O	C O	D O	E O	F O	G O	H O
22	A O	B O	C O	D O	E O	F O	G O	H O
23	A O	B O	C O	D O	E O	F O	G O	H O
24	A O	B O	C O	D O	E O	F O	G O	H O
25	A O	B O	C O	D O	E O	F O	G O	H O
26	A O	B O	C O	D O	E O	F O	G O	H O
27	A O	B O	C O	D O	E O	F O	G O	H O
28	A O	B O	C O	D O	E O	F O	G O	H O
29	A O	B O	C O	D O	E O	F O	G O	H O
30	A O	B O	C O	D O	E O	F O	G O	H O

OFFICE USE ONLY - DO NOT WRITE OR MAKE ANY MARK BELOW THIS LINE

Page 2 of 2

1036

Sample answer sheet: Writing

Answer Sheet Page 1

Part One Answer You must write within the grey lines.

Test 1 Training Speaking Part 2 (see page 63)

Useful language: hypothesising

Exercise 1

- How do you think the people in this picture are feeling?

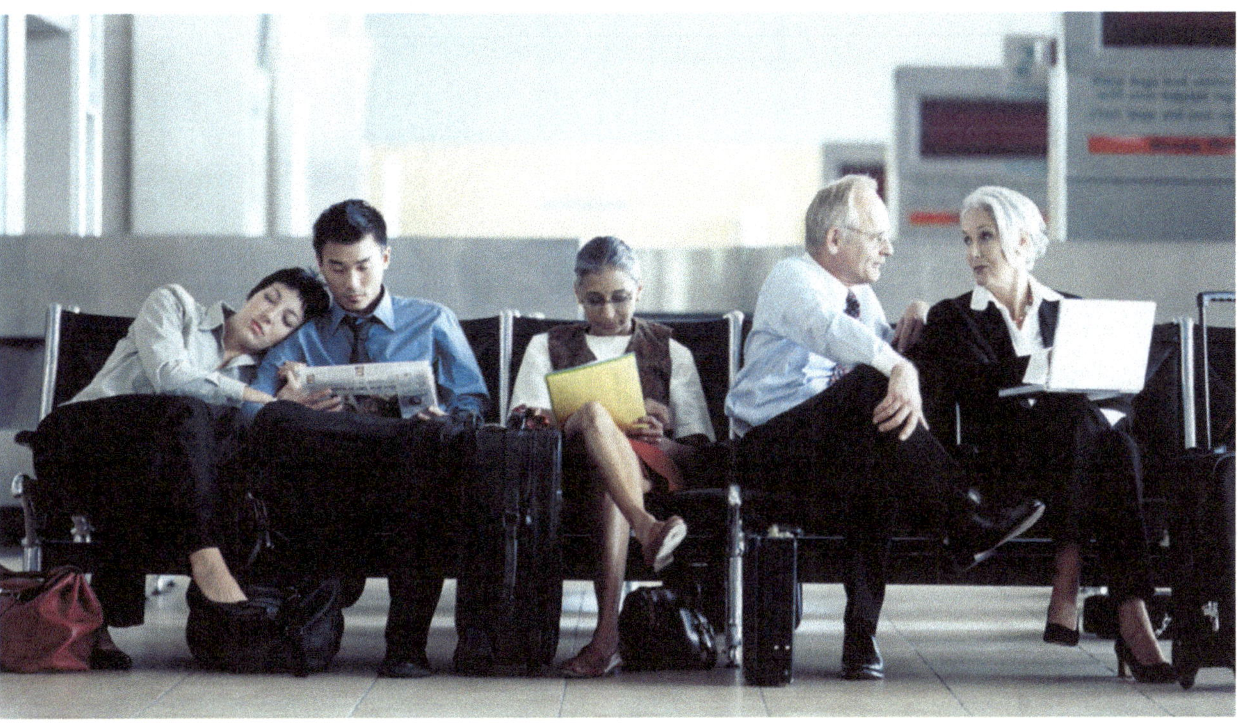

Exercise 2

- What do you think the people in this picture are talking about?

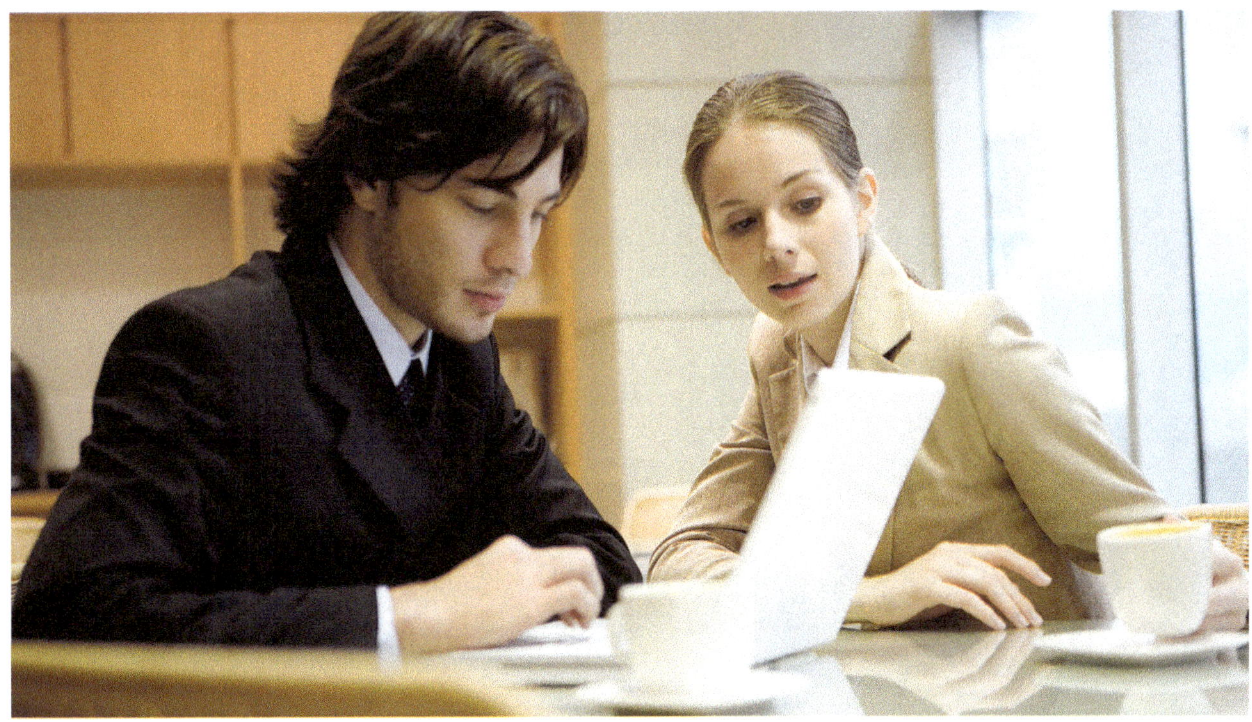

Test 1 Training Speaking Part 2 (see page 63)

Useful language: comparing and contrasting

Exercise 2

- What different aspects of college life do the pictures show?
- How might these students benefit from learning in these ways?

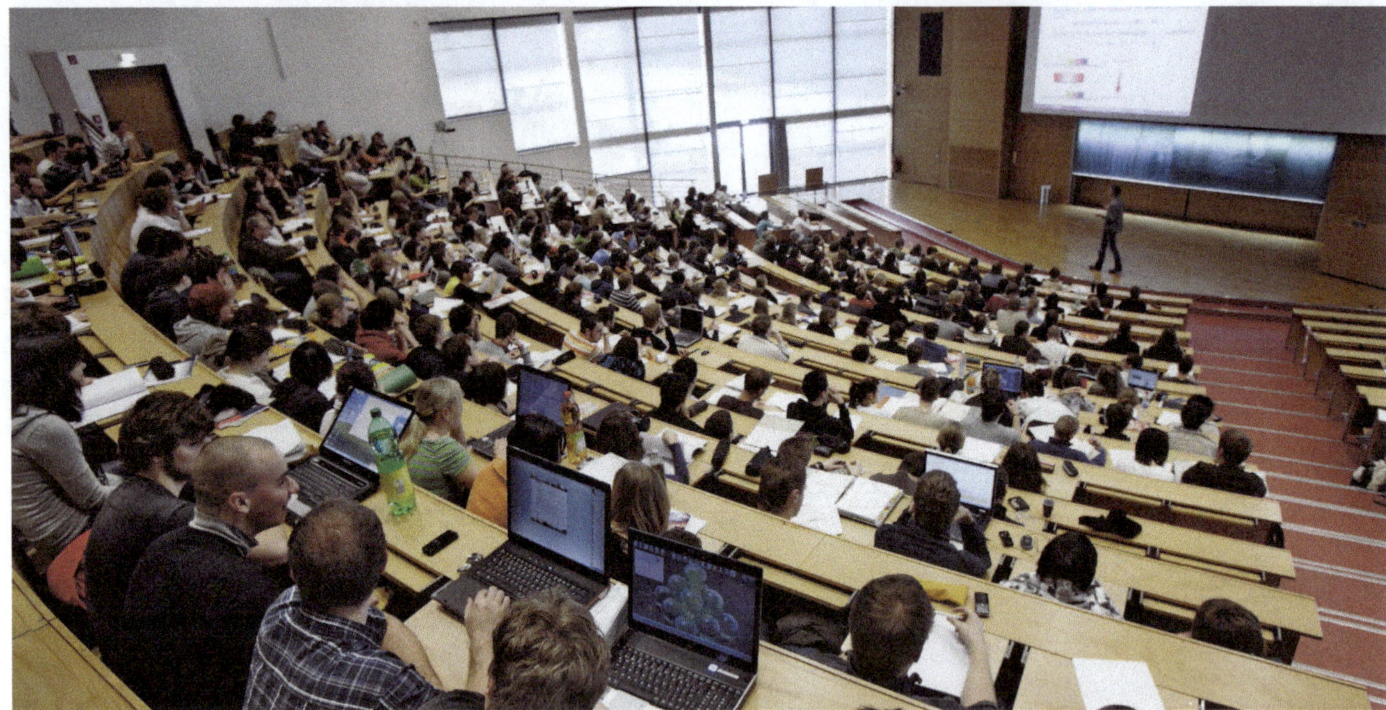

Test 1 Exam practice Speaking Part 2 (see page 64)

Candidate A

- What do you think the people are reading about?
- How important might reading be to the people in these situations?

Test 1 Exam practice Speaking Part 2 (see page 64)

Candidate B

- Why do you think the people are making their journey?
- What difficulties might the people face in making their journeys?

Test 1 Exam practice Speaking Part 3 (see page 66)

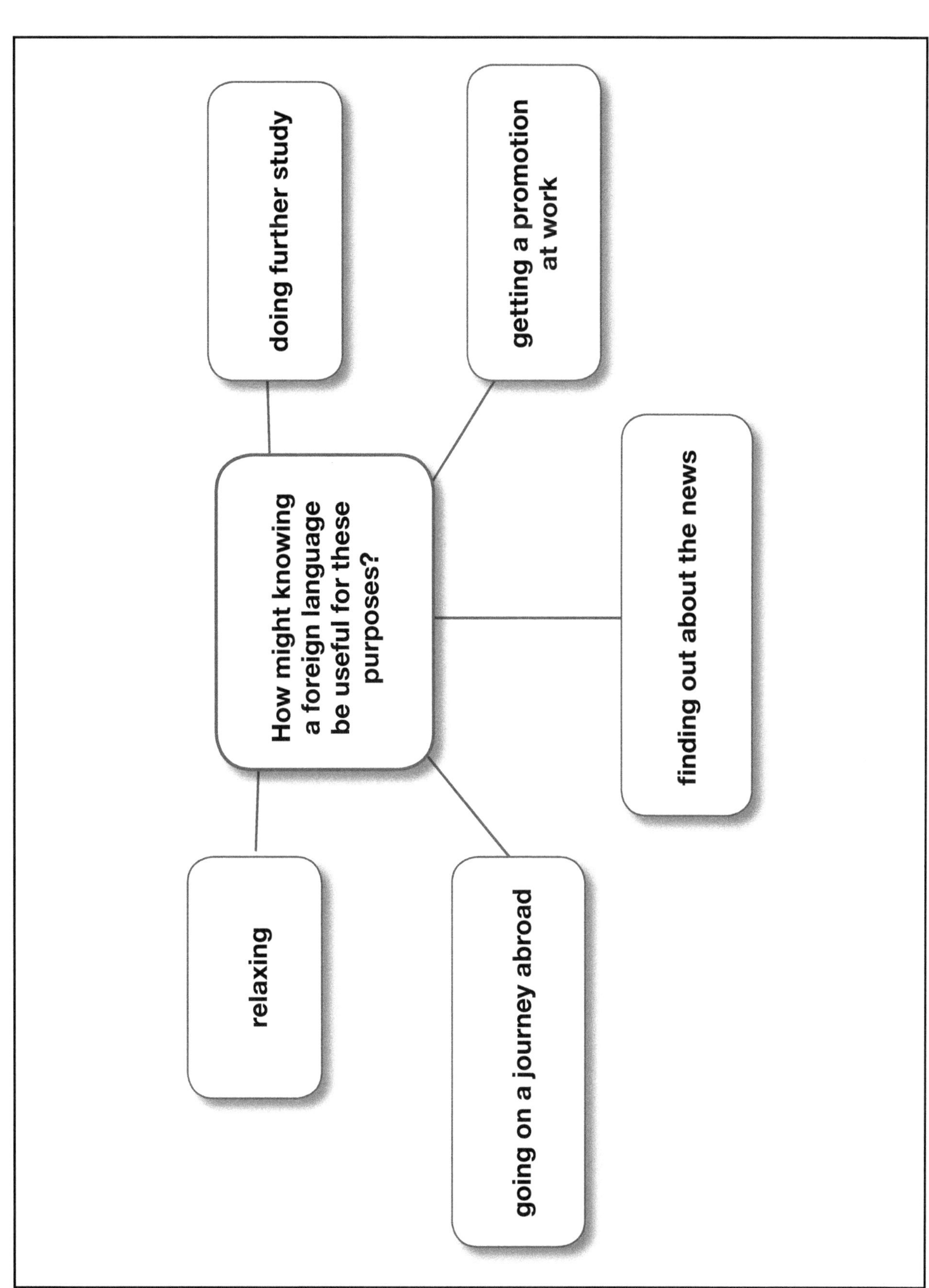
How might knowing a foreign language be useful for these purposes?
doing further study
getting a promotion at work
finding out about the news
going on a journey abroad
relaxing

Test 2 Training Speaking Part 2 (see page 102)

- How difficult might it have been for the people to reach these important ceremonies?
- How will the ceremonies change the lives of the people involved?

Test 2 Exam practice Speaking Part 2 (see page 103)

Candidate A

- What sort of help do you think the people need?
- How might the people be feeling?

Test 2 Exam practice Speaking Part 2 (see page 103)

Candidate B

- What kind of music do you think the people are listening to?
- How might the music affect the way the people feel?

Test 2 Exam practice Speaking Part 3 (see page 106)

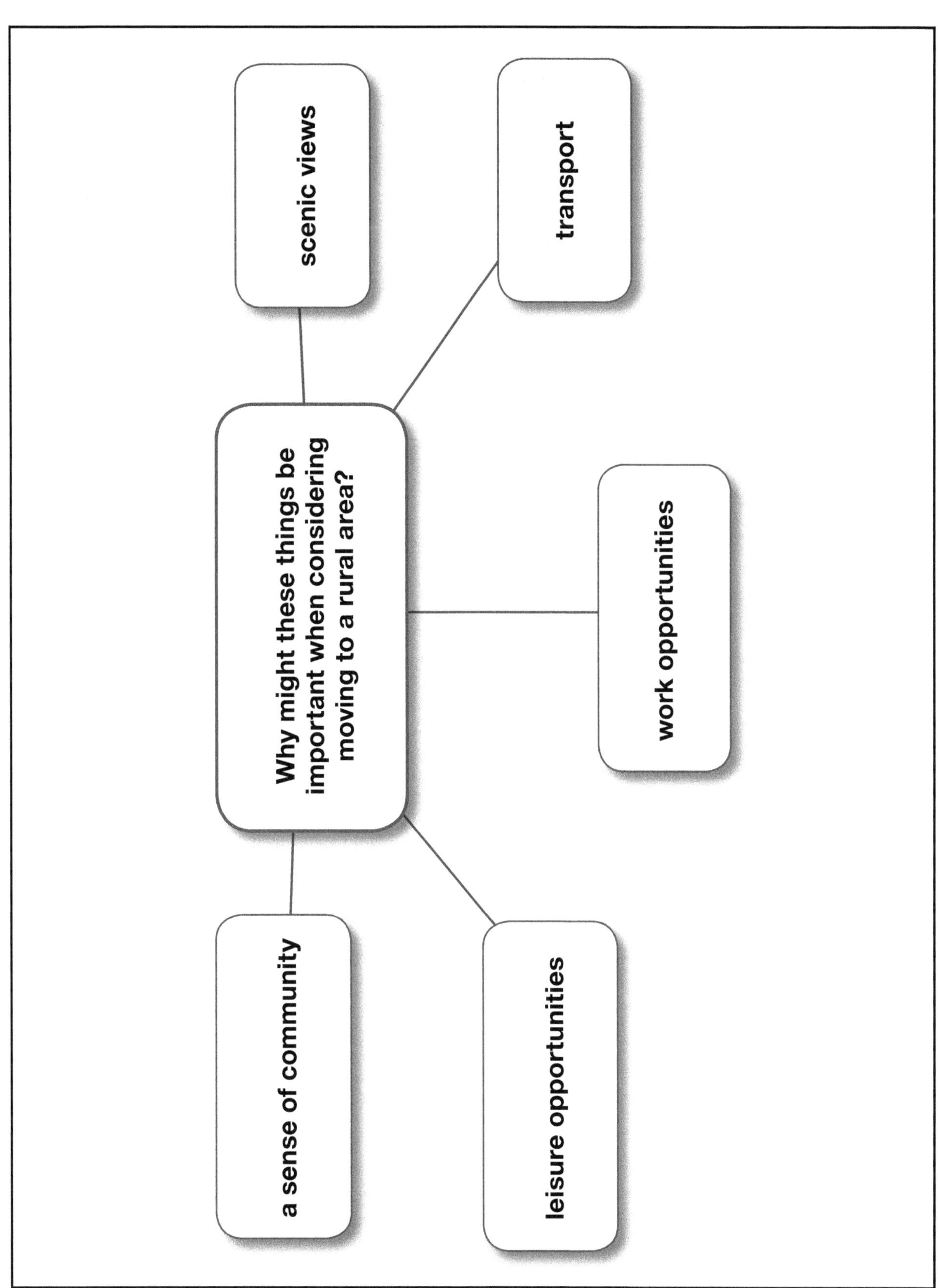

Why might these things be important when considering moving to a rural area?
scenic views
transport
work opportunities
a sense of community
leisure opportunities

Test 3 Speaking Part 2 (see page 128)

Candidate A

- What do you think the relationships between the people are?
- Why are the people laughing?

Test 3 Speaking Part 2 (see page 128)

Candidate B

- Why do you think people want to learn skills like these?
- How difficult might these skills be to learn?

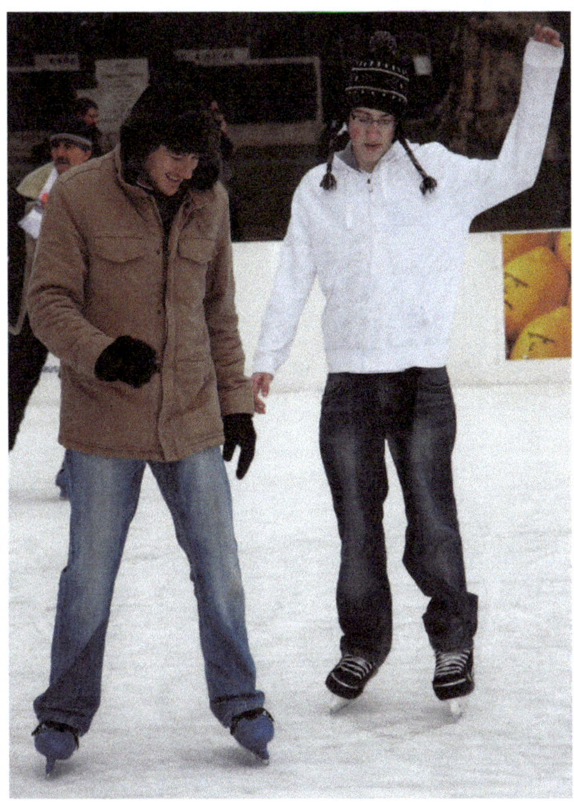

Test 3 Speaking Part 3 (see page 129)

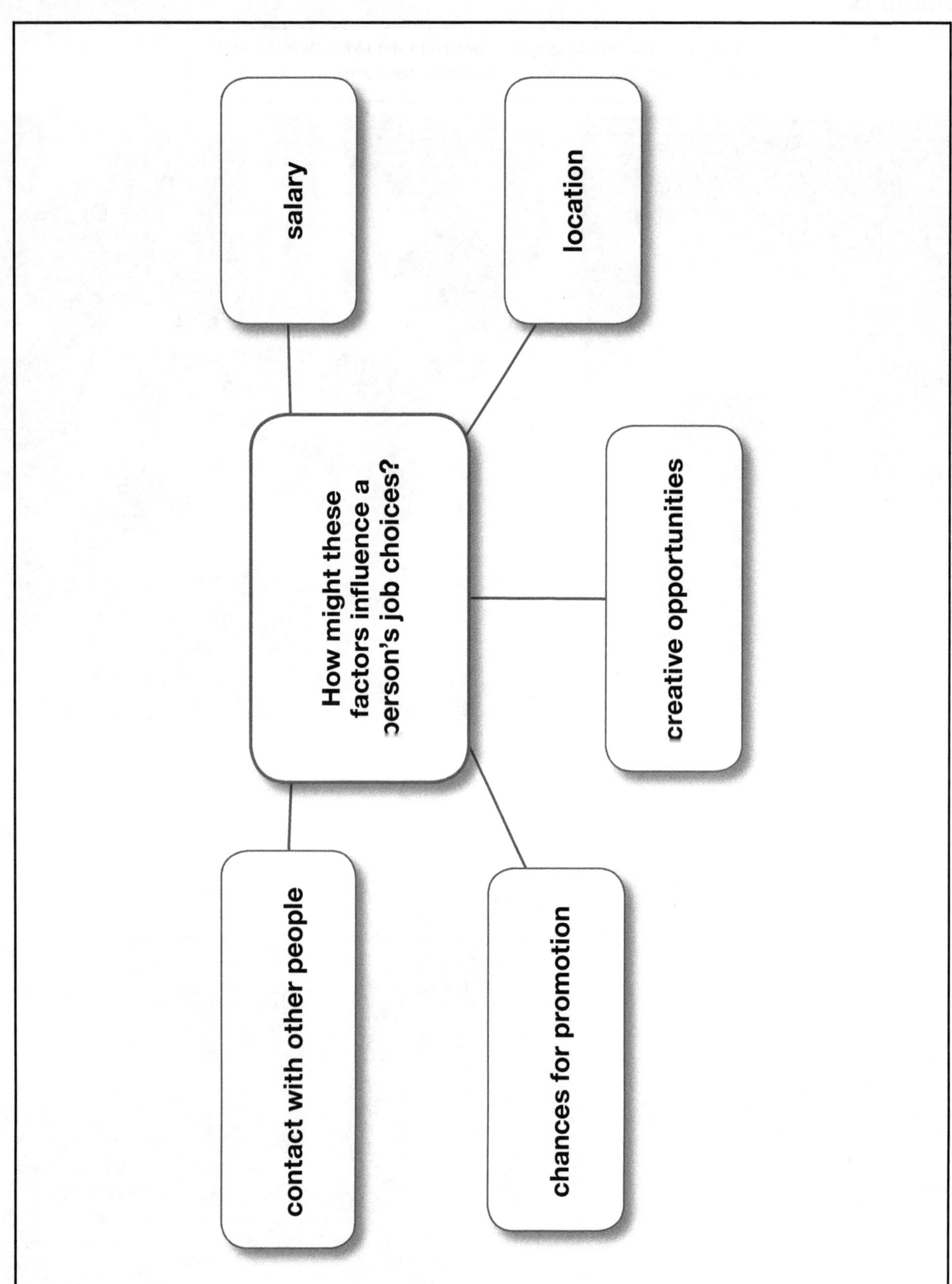
How might these factors influence a person's job choices?
salary
location
creative opportunities
chances for promotion
contact with other people

Test 4 Speaking Part 2 (see page 150)

Candidate A

- What difficulties might the people have performing in these different situations?
- How memorable do you think the performances might be for the audience?

Test 4 Speaking Part 2 (see page 150)

Candidate B

- Why do you think these people are dancing in these different situations?
- How do you think the people might be feeling?

Test 4 Speaking Part 3 (see page 151)

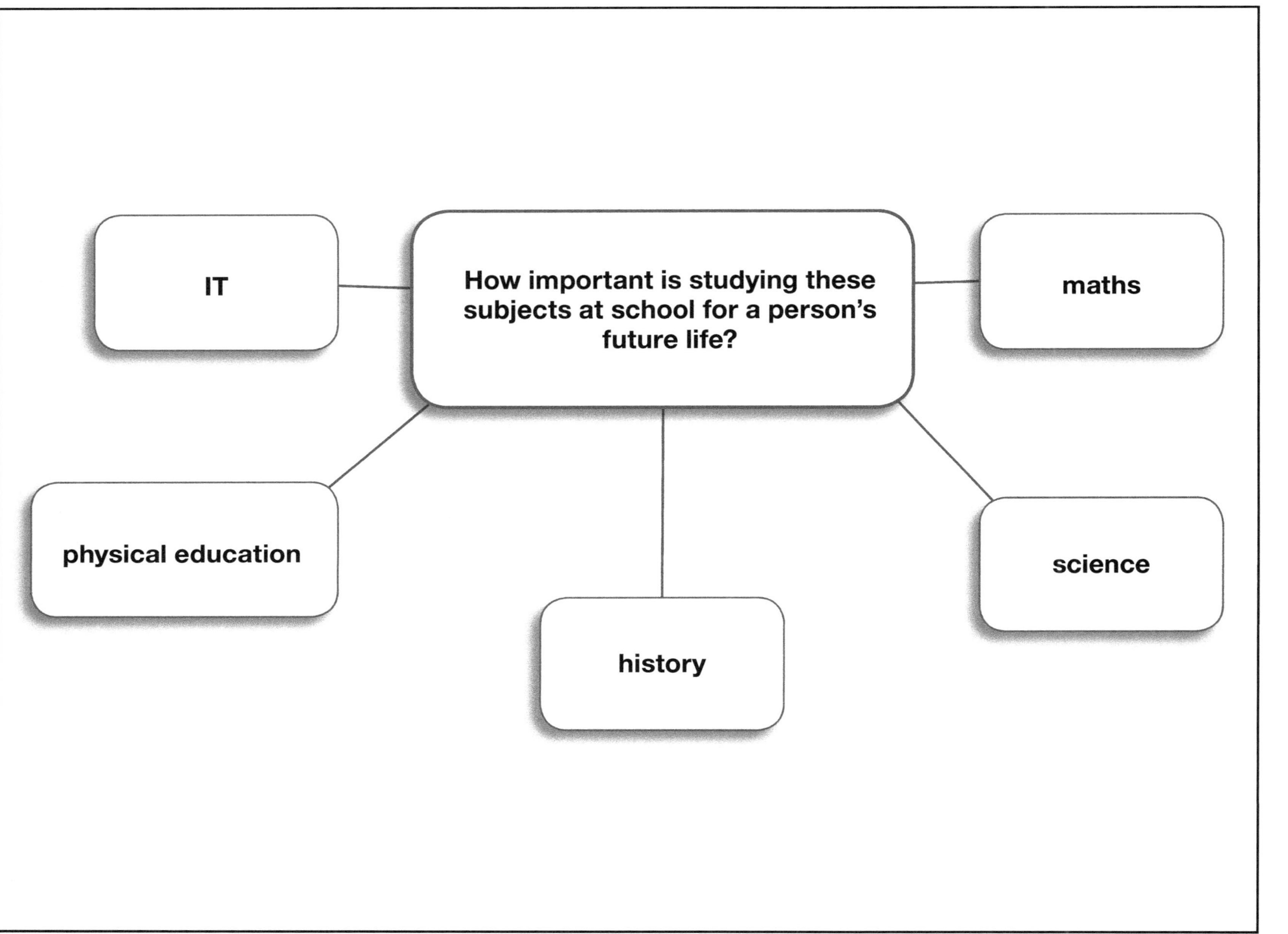
How important is studying these subjects at school for a person's future life?
IT
maths
physical education
history
science

Test 5 Speaking Part 2 (see page 172)

Candidate A

- Why might the people have chosen to do these activities?
- How beneficial might doing these activities be for the people?

Test 5 Speaking Part 2 (see page 172)

Candidate B

- Why might the people be dressed in these ways?
- How important do you think the clothes are to the people?

Test 5 Speaking Part 3 (see page 173)

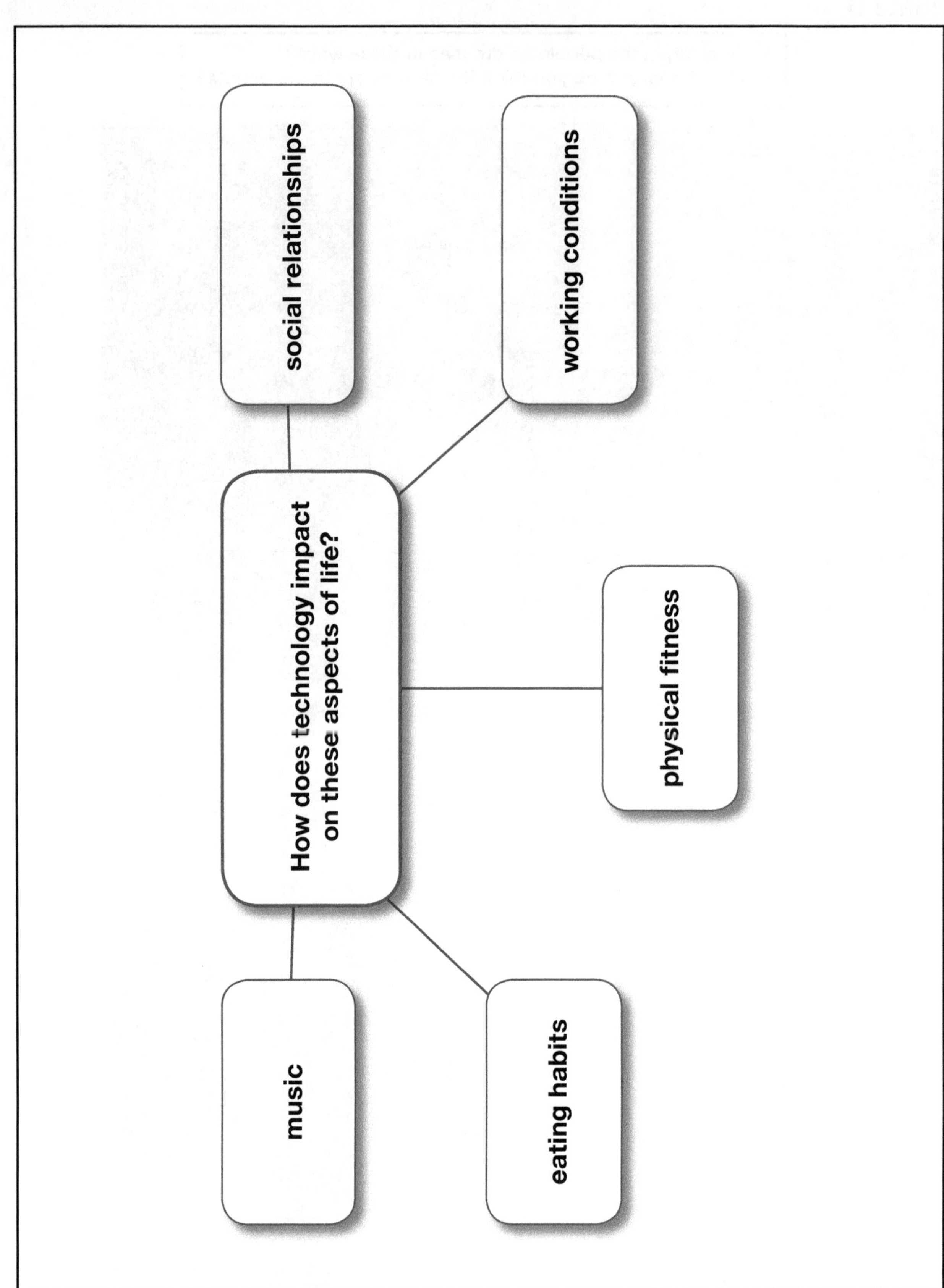
How does technology impact on these aspects of life?
social relationships
working conditions
physical fitness
eating habits
music

Test 6

Speaking Part 2 (see page 194)

Candidate A

- Why might the people have chosen to eat together in these places?
- What do you think the people might be talking about?

Test 6 Speaking Part 2 (see page 194)

Candidate B

- **What skills might these people need to do their jobs well?**
- **What disadvantages might these jobs have?**

Speaking Part 3 (see page 195)

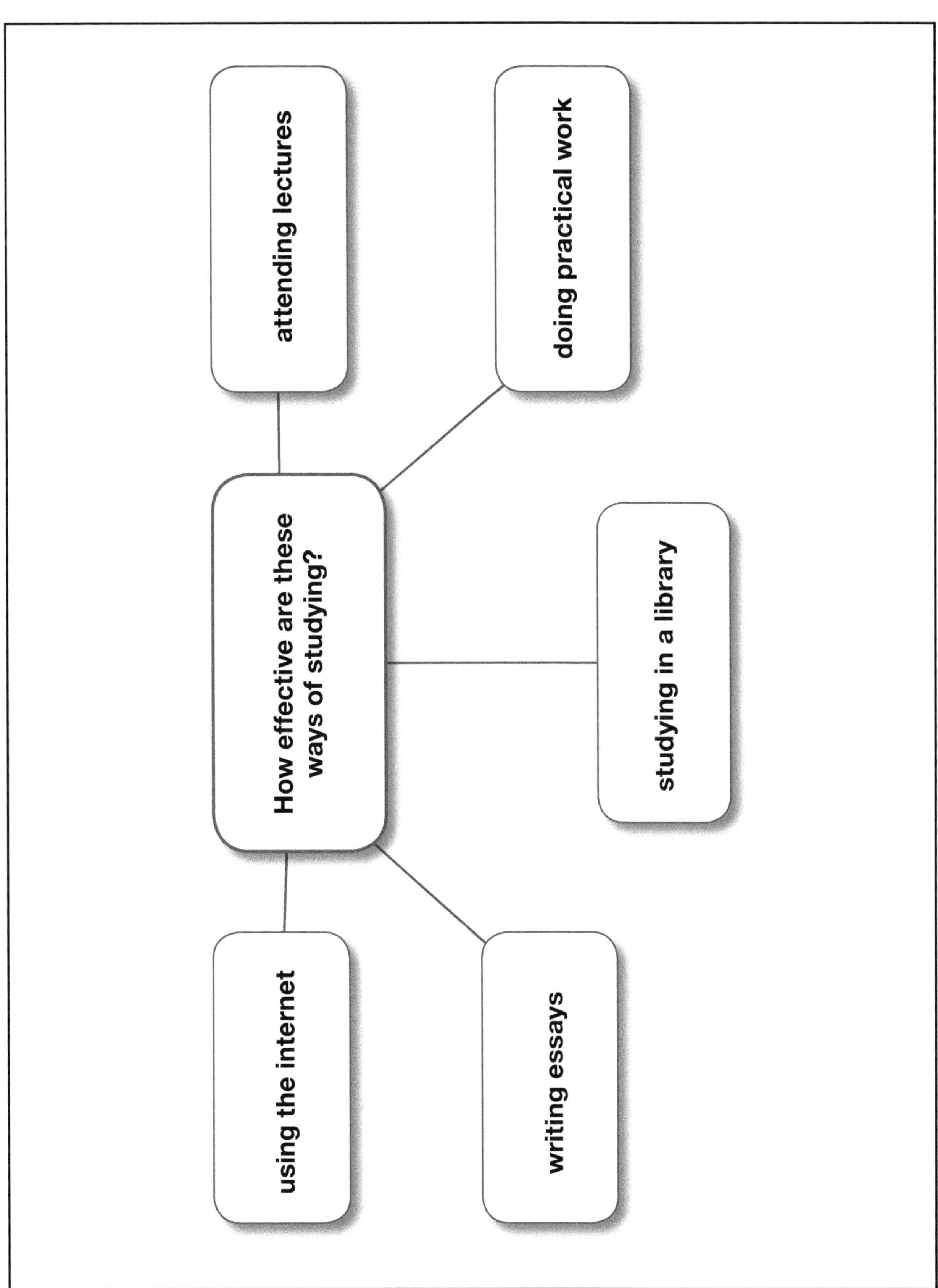
How effective are these ways of studying?
attending lectures
doing practical work
studying in a library
writing essays
using the internet